Does the popular notion of a "broken h
ing in reality? Can grief affect the body
medical care and may even be life-threa
Health constitutes a comprehensive review of what is known
about the impact of bereavement on surviving partners. Drawing
on the work of psychologists, sociologists, epidemiologists, and
psychiatrists, Wolfgang and Margaret Stroebe offer a theoretically
coherent perspective focused on conjugal loss.

After a thorough discussion of stress and depression models of
bereavement, the authors present their own theoretical approach,
emphasizing social contacts and the interpersonal nature of grief.
They then examine the psychological and medical consequences
of bereavement: Are the bereaved at higher risk than those who
have not lost a partner? What has research revealed about the
causes, symptoms, and outcomes of grief? Key questions about
recovery from grief are also addressed: Is the health risk of
bereavement severe enough to have lasting or even fatal consequences? Is it possible to identify those bereaved who are at high
risk before their health suffers? What are the strategies that are
most likely to lead to effective coping? Can attempts at intervention be effective? In evaluating the relevant findings, the Stroebes
consider important methodological issues that have often been
neglected in research on bereavement.

The Stroebes' combination of theoretical integration and
methodological rigor will make *Bereavement and Health* a standard text for years to come. A wide range of researchers and students in the behavioral, social, and medical sciences will find it a
useful resource, as will mental health professionals in such allied
fields as social work and nursing.

Bereavement and health

Bereavement and health

The psychological and physical consequences of partner loss

WOLFGANG STROEBE
and
MARGARET S. STROEBE

University of Tübingen

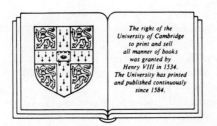

The right of the
University of Cambridge
to print and sell
all manner of books
was granted by
Henry VIII in 1534.
The University has printed
and published continuously
since 1584.

CAMBRIDGE UNIVERSITY PRESS

Cambridge
New York   New Rochelle   Melbourne   Sydney

Published by the Press Syndicate of the University of Cambridge
The Pitt Building, Trumpington Street, Cambridge CB2 1RP
32 East 57th Street, New York, NY 10022, USA
10 Stamford Road, Oakleigh, Melbourne 3166, Australia

First published 1987

Printed in Canada

Library of Congress Cataloging-in-Publication Data
Stroebe, Wolfgang.
Bereavement and health.
Bibliography: p.
Includes index.
1. Bereavement – Physiological aspects.   2. Loss
(Psychology)   3. Grief – Physiological aspects.
4. Stress (Psychology)   5. Diseases – Psychological
aspects.   I. Stroebe, Margaret S.   II. Title.
BF575.G7S77   1987   155.9′37   87–11627
ISBN 0 521 24470 6 hard covers
ISBN 0 521 28710 3 (paperback)

British Library Cataloguing-in-Publication applied for.

Copyrights for Figures and Tables. Acknowledgment is made to the following
publishers, authors and journals for permission to reproduce materials:

The American Sociological Association. Gove, W. R. Sex, marital status and
suicide. *Journal of Health and Social Behavior,* 1972, 13, 204–13. Table 1
(widowed to married ratios).

Pergamon Journals Ltd. Holmes, T. H., & Rahe, R. H. The social readjustment
rating scale. *Journal of Psychosomatic Research,* 1967, 11, 213–18. Table 3:
Social Readjustment Rating Scale.

Maddison, D. C., & Viola, A. The health of widows in the year following
bereavement. *Journal of Psychosomatic Research,* 1968, 12, 297–306. Table 5
(data for total samples).

British Medical Journal. Parkes, C. M., Benjamin, B., & Fitzgerald, R. G.
Broken heart: a statistical study of increased mortality among widowers. *British
Medical Journal,* 1969, 1, 740–3. Figure 1.

Baywood Publishing Company Inc. Stroebe, M. S., Stroebe, W., Gergen, K., &
Gergen, M. The broken heart: reality or myth? *Omega,* 1981, 12, 87–106.
Table 1.

John Wiley & Sons Ltd. Stroebe, W., Stroebe, M. S., Gergen, K., & Gergen, M.
The effects of bereavement on mortality: a social psychological analysis. Table
22.2. In J. R. Eiser (Ed.), *Social Psychology and Behavioral Medicine,* 1982.

Office of Population Censuses and Surveys: "Crown Copyright." Series DS no.
1: *Occupational Mortality: 1970–1972.* Figure 3.4 (married and widowed data).

For
MARY HARROLD

In memory of
MERVYN HARROLD
HILDE STROEBE
ERNST STROEBE

Contents

vii

Contents

Preface

Like most human behavior, the writing of this book was motivated by a multiplicity of goals. First, we wished to stress the interpersonal nature of bereavement and the coping process. In the past, coping with bereavement has been considered an intrapersonal phenomenon, yet interpersonal relationships are likely to be critical, not only as determinants of the intensity of symptoms and duration of grief, but also of the ultimate outcome of bereavement. Second, our aim is to provide a theoretical perspective for bereavement research. Since much research has been generated by clinicians with a concern for alleviating problems and symptoms, emphasis has been on issues rather than theory. We therefore review theories of relevance to bereavement, and develop our own, the deficit model, in the following pages. A third objective is to provide a comprehensive review of empirical research on bereavement. Bereavement is a topic to which contributions have been made from diverse disciplines, including public health, epidemiology, sociology, and psychiatry. We have attempted to integrate this research from different areas in the present volume. Fourth, a basic concern is to provide methodological guidelines for bereavement research. Over the past two decades, a vast amount of research on bereavement has appeared in the journals and in books. There has been very little written, however, on basic principles of research design for the area of bereavement. Thus, detailed discussion is given to methodological issues, and empirical studies are carefully examined with regard to the validity of their inferences.

It is unlikely that we would ever have embarked on the study of bereavement, a topic unrelated to the research interests of either of us at the time, had it not been for many stimulating discussions held with Ken and Mary Gergen, out of which grew a number of joint research projects. We also gratefully acknowledge the support and encouragement of the late Henri Tajfel, mentor to both of us, and one of the most significant persons in our academic and personal lives. Mention must also be made of the many people who tolerated our absorption in the writing of this book. Foremost among these is our daughter Katherine, for whom it was often hard to take the abstraction of not only one, but both parents, but who always remained cheerfully distractive.

We are also grateful to the following colleagues who have read previous versions of chapters of the book and who provided insightful comments: James Averill, Andrew Cairns, Ken Gergen, Howard Giles, Robert Hansson, Mary Harrold, Arié Kruglanski, Jürgen Margraf, Reinhard Pietrowsky, and Paul Rosenblatt. Others who have been indispensable for a variety of reasons include Hannelore Omasta and Günther Domittner.

The Tübingen Longitudinal Study of Bereavement, referred to frequently in the following pages, was funded by a grant to W. Stroebe from the Deutsche Forschungsgemeinschaft. We gratefully acknowledge their support.

Wolfgang and Margaret Stroebe

1 Introduction

1.1 The broken heart: fact or folklore?

Most people can think of instances from their own experience, or from sources such as literature, drama, or folklore, of people suffering from "a broken heart" or from "a lack of the will to live" following the death of a loved person. The epitaph by Sir Henry Wootton succinctly expresses this sentiment:

> He first deceased; she for a little tried
> To live without him; liked it not, and died.

Thus, the notion of the broken heart seems to be more than a metaphor. Clearly, the view is held that grief can affect physical health and that death may occur during bereavement as a direct result of the sadness and anguish over the loss of a person whom one loved and to whom one was close.

Over the centuries, allusions to grief as a causal factor in disease and death have been frequent and have come from very diverse sources. As early as the eighth century B.C., in the writings of the legendary epic poet Homer, we find reference to the notion that grief alone can kill. Homer described the visit of the wandering Odysseus to the Kingdom of the Dead and the brief reunion with his deceased mother, who related to him the following account of her own death:

It was not that the keen-eyed Archeress sought me out in our home and killed me with her gentle darts. Nor was I attacked by any of the malignant diseases that so often make the body waste away and die. No, it was my heartache for you, my glorious Odysseus, and for your wise and gentle ways that brought my life and all its sweetness to an end. (*The Odyssey*, Book XI, "The Book of the Dead")

The belief that grief can kill was not only widely held by poets but was shared by scientists as well. Thus, Robert Burton, an English clergyman of the seventeenth century, author of a widely read and highly influential book, *The Anatomy of Melancholy* (1977), presented a wide range of examples to support his conclusion that grief can have negative effects on

1

those smitten with it. He used the suicide of Aegeus, who drowned himself, "impatient of sorrow for his son's death" (1977, p. 360) as an example of a most extreme reaction to loss. But he also drew on the writings of the early physicians to demonstrate lesser health consequences of bereavement, such as depressive reactions and suicidal tendencies:

Montanus, counsil. 242, had a patient troubled with this infirmity, by reason of her husband's death, many years together. Trincavellius, lib. 1, cap. 14, hath such another, almost in despair, after his mother's departure, *ut se ferme praecipitem daret,* and ready through distraction to make away himself; and, in his fifteenth counsel, tells a story of one fifty years of age, "that grew desparate upon his mother's death"; and, cured by Fallopsius, fell many years after into a relapse, by the sudden death of a daughter which he had, and could never be recovered. (1977, p. 360)

Burton further argued that grief was not only felt for the loss of personal friends and close relatives but also when national heroes died. He used an example from England to demonstrate his view that "the fury of this passion is so violent, sometimes, that it daunts whole kingdoms and cities" (1977, p. 360): "How we were affected here in England for our Titus, ... Prince Henry's immature death, as if all our dearest friends' lives had exhaled with his" (p. 361). Burton was even aware of cross-cultural differences in the extremity of grief responses. He noted the customs of "pagan Indians," whose wives and servants died with them voluntarily.

Burton's views on the deleterious consequences of bereavement were widely shared by the medical profession. Grief was even listed as a cause of death in some early mortality statistics. Thus, in Dr. Heberden's Bill (cited in Parkes, 1986), which classified the causes of death in London for the year of 1657, "griefe" was made responsible for ten deaths. Benjamin Rush (1835), an American physician, even gave a detailed description of the organ malfunctions which he assumed to be responsible for death from grief. According to Rush, autopsies of bereaved individuals typically show "congestion in, and inflammation of the heart, with rupture of its auricles and ventricles" (Parkes, 1986).

With this rich fund of observations in support, it is difficult to deny credence to the view that bereavement can be responsible for the negative health consequences attributed to it, including the ultimate consequence, death. Nevertheless, according to present-day scientific standards, none of these anecdotes can be considered evidence for the alleged increase in health risk following bereavement. Even the observation that somebody died from heart disease shortly after the loss of his or her spouse does not prove that grief was itself the cause of death. With such individual case histories we can never rule out the possibility that a person would have died from the same cause at the same time even without the loss experience. Heart diseases are after all the most frequent cause of death. As the loss of a loved person through death is also a not-too-infrequent occurrence in any given population, it can be expected that some of these heart deaths occur in more or less close temporal proximity to the loss experience. From what we know about "illusory correlations" (Chapman, 1967; Hamilton & Gifford, 1976) it is further to be expected that the co-occurrence of two such distinctive events is likely to be overestimated. Since the similarity in the two events should further contribute to the perception of a causal link between them, the development of the myth that bereavement is associated with ill health or death could be explained by psychological principles of information processing.

And yet, as we know today, this belief is more than a myth. Although the impact of grief on health cannot be demonstrated in the individual case, the hypothesis that recent bereavement is associated with greater health risks can be examined by comparing the health status of large numbers of bereaved individuals to that of a nonbereaved comparison group. Probably the first analysis of this kind which is still acceptable by present-day scientific standards was conducted in 1858 by Farr (1975), who drew attention to the differential mortality rates across marital status groups for the population of France. On the basis of his analysis of mortality rates for the unmarried, married, and widowed, Farr concluded that being married was much healthier than being unmarried. "Marriage is a healthy estate. The single individual is more likely to be wrecked on his voyage than the lives joined together in matrimony." But, he went on, if "unmarried people suffer from disease in undue proportion the have been married suffer still more" (p. 440).

Farr's analysis of the relationship between bereavement and mortality marks the beginning of a systematic empirical investigation in this area that has now, in the twentieth century, grown into a fairly substantial body of evidence. The pattern of marital status differences in mortality that Farr found over a century ago has been repeatedly confirmed despite dramatic changes in major causes of death.

Four decades after Farr's publication, at the turn of the century, the French sociologist Durkheim wrote his classic analysis of suicide patterns, in which he pointed out that the widowed succumb to this particular form of violent death with remarkable frequency. Durkheim (1951) demonstrated that the suicide risk of the widowed is considerably higher than that of comparable married individuals, a difference that is still apparent in more recent suicide statistics.

Just as the bereavement–mortality relationship has become the subject of scientific investigation, so has that of bereavement with mental and physical illness. Impetus for this work can most clearly be traced to Freud's well-known paper of 1917, "Mourning and Melancholia," which provided much in terms of a theoretical–conceptual perspective on grief, and to Lindemann's (1944) article entitled "Symptomatology and Management of Acute Grief," which was the first detailed study of bereavement reactions. In his 1944 paper and in an interview study of patients suffering from ulcerative colitis published in 1950, Lindemann also provided the first systematic evidence suggesting an increase in the risk of physical and mental illness following bereavement. Although, like much pioneering work, Lindemann's (1944, 1950) studies would not satisfy the methodological standards of today, most of the conclusions he derived from his investigations have stood up well in later, more rigorous empirical research.

1.2   Scope and objectives of the book

The objective of this book is to examine, from a social psychological perspective, the effects of loss of a loved one on the persons who survive the death. The focus is on death of a spouse, for the effects are extreme following conjugal bereavement, and most research has concentrated on partner loss. The first task addressed in Chapter 2 is to consider the nature of grief as the emotional reaction to loss and to describe its symptomatology. The second half of the chapter focuses on the course that grief normally runs, and on the distinction between normal or uncomplicated grief and abnormal or pathological symptoms and sequences. At the heart of this discussion is the question of how to define what is normal versus abnormal grief in the first place.

The examination of grief reactions in different cultures undertaken in Chapter 3 highlights this issue. Outcomes of grief vary from ritual suicide (to which Burton, in our previous example, drew attention) to compulsory remarriage. Symptoms vary from wailing at prescribed times to stoic suppression of tears. Anthropologists have been aware of the differences in mourning customs between cultures for a long time, but very little attention has been paid to cultural differences in the emotional response to bereavement. It appears that the symptoms and stages of grief differ remarkably between cultures. What is considered normal or natural in one culture would be classified as pathological in another. Infliction of self-injury following bereavement, which occurs in some non-Western cultures, is one example. And yet, there is also a great deal of similarity in the basic symptoms of grief. The evidence reviewed in this chapter suggests that individuals from very diverse societies do experience feelings of sadness and despondency on the loss of a person to whom they were close.

Theories of grief should help one to understand the symptomatology of grief as well as the health deterioration some individuals experience after the loss of a partner. Most importantly, however, a theory of grief should further the development of therapies to ameliorate or prevent pathological grief reactions. We distinguish two types of grief theories, namely, depression models and stress models. Depression models, which will be presented in Chapter 4, analyze grief as an emotional reaction to loss and help one to understand many of the emotional symptoms of the grief reaction. Stress models view bereavement as a stressful life event and offer an explanation for the health consequences resulting from bereavement. These models are discussed in Chapter 5.

Stressful life events like the death of a spouse do not operate in the same manner on one's bodily system as the entry of some alien bacteria. And yet, these life crises have been shown to be associated with health deterioration. The conception of partner loss as a stressful life event integrates the study of bereavement into a body of research which has linked psychosocial stress to a number of health consequences and has isolated some of the behavioral and physiological processes assumed to mediate these relationships. Research on these processes is discussed in Chapter 6.

While for most of the widowed grief runs a normal, if harrowing, course, for others the effects can indeed be devastating. In the next part of the book (Chapter 7) we examine how the health consequences of bereavement range from distress and depression to mental and physical illness and premature death. Research from epidemiology, sociology, and other related disciplines shows that the probability of succumbing to specific psychological and physical ailments increases considerably on bereavement.

Why does grief have such differential effects on its sufferers? We address this question in Chapter 8 by looking at the characteristics that distinguish those who suffer a severe loss effect, as we term it, from others who emerge from the experience of grief with relatively mild effects. For example, predisposition to mental and physical ailments may be a major intervening variable. Further, the type of death of the spouse (for example, if the death was of a young partner, and was very sudden and unexpected) is predictive of outcome. In this discussion of risk one must include those factors present prior to bereavement, those directly concurrent with the death, and subsequent factors (for example, secondary stresses such as financial problems, social isolation, etc.), which could all contribute to bereavement outcome.

The identification of risk factors is only useful if we are able to help those bereaved who are at risk to cope better with their loss. Thus, in the last chapter (Chapter 9) we discuss whether there are effective ways of reducing the risk of poor bereavement outcome. In this, we not only consider self-help groups and counseling programs but also the many ways in which relatives and friends can help the bereaved to cope with their loss.

2 The symptomatology of grief

2.1 Grief, mourning, and bereavement: a conceptual clarification

The terms grief, mourning, and bereavement are often used interchangeably in everyday language. For example, someone who has suffered the death of a family member or close friend may either be said to be "mourning the loss," "grieving," or "grief-stricken," or may perhaps be described as "bereft" at the loss. These statements may elicit slightly different ideas about the response of the person to death, but the overlap in meaning is considerable. It is reflected, too, in dictionary usage. Webster's dictionary defines *to mourn* as "to feel or show grief or sorrow; especially to grieve over someone's death," and *to grieve* as "to cause grief or sorrow to; cause to suffer; distress."

Following conceptual distinctions which have been made in bereavement (e.g., Gorer, 1965; Parkes, 1986) and emotion research (e.g., Averill, 1968, 1979), the terms will be differentiated here in the following way: *Bereavement* refers to the objective situation of an individual who has recently experienced the loss of someone significant through that person's death. Bereavement is the cause of both grief and mourning. *Grief* is the emotional (affective) response to loss, which includes a number of psychological and somatic reactions. It has been defined as an emotional syndrome (Averill, 1979; Lindemann, 1944), that is, a set of responses covarying in a systematic way. While some responses may be more symptomatic of grief than others, no single response is essential to the syndrome. *Mourning* refers to the acts expressive of grief. These acts are shaped by the mourning practices of a given society or cultural group, which serve as guidelines for how bereaved persons are expected to behave. As Durkheim stated succinctly:

Mourning is not a natural movement of private feelings wounded by a cruel loss; it is a duty imposed by the group. One weeps, not simply because he is sad, but because he is forced to weep. It is a ritual attitude which he is forced to adopt out of respect for custom, but which is, in large measure, independent of his affective state. (1976, p. 443)

7

Examination of such public rituals or mourning customs has long been a major topic for investigation among anthropologists and sociologists (e.g., Durkheim, 1976; Huntington & Metcalfe, 1979; Radcliffe-Brown, 1964).

It is perhaps worth noting that the psychoanalytic school, and those influenced by it, use the term mourning synonymously with the way grief has been defined by us. This usage goes back to the English translation (Freud, 1959) of Freud's (1917) seminal contribution to the field, "Trauer und Melancholie" as "Mourning and Melancholia." The German word *Trauer* refers to both the experience as well as the expression of grief. It is therefore quite possible that in discussing *Trauer* Freud was referring to grief rather than mourning.

2.2   Normal and pathological grief

Grief is a normal affective response to the loss of a loved person which, if it runs an uncomplicated course, does not require therapeutic intervention. The pattern of normal grief responses has been extensively studied (e.g., Clayton, Desmarais, & Winokur, 1968; Gorer, 1965; Lindemann, 1944; Parkes, 1965) and this section will begin with a description of the findings of this research.

2.2.1   *The course of normal grief*

The most surprising feature of the phenomenology of normal grief is the opposing nature of some of the symptoms. We find anger and apathy, weight loss and weight gain, preoccupation with or suppression of memories of the deceased, and removal versus treasuring their possessions. There is, however, a certain uniformity shown by bereaved persons, which led Lindemann (1944), in his classic paper, to call grief a "definite syndrome with psychological and somatic symptomatology." Lindemann, a psychiatrist, was deeply concerned with understanding the emotional disturbances following bereavement and in trying to make mental health professionals aware of the contribution they could make in helping the bereaved adjust to their loss and resolve their grief. His first aim was therefore to describe the grief syndrome in some detail, outlining its normal course.

Lindemann's observations were based on a varied sample of people, who had also undergone very different types of loss through death (though neither individual differences nor type of death were examined as variables contributing to the grief syndrome). Included were psychoneurotic patients who became bereaved while under treatment, relatives of patients at the hospital, relatives of members of the armed forces, and finally, the group for whom the study is best known, bereaved victims of the Coconut Grove fire disaster and their close relatives. The latter group thus included individuals who had themselves been in the fire, some suffering from severe burns, and who therefore had the double ordeal of their own injuries and a frightening experience, and that of losing someone in the same tragedy.

Despite the somewhat unusual composition of his sample, Lindemann was able to identify most of the features of the grief response typically observed with recently bereaved individuals. The most striking features common to people suffering from "acute grief" were somatic distress, (experienced as waves of discomfort including sighing respiration, lack of strength, and digestive symptoms), preoccupation with the image of the deceased, guilt feelings (self-accusations of negligence, exaggeration of small omissions), hostile reactions to others, and loss of patterns of activity (e.g., overtalkativeness, restlessness, lack of zest, problems in social interaction).

Subsequent accounts of the symptomatology of grief (e.g., Bowlby, 1981; Clayton et al., 1968; Glick, Weiss, & Parkes, 1974; Gorer, 1965; Marris, 1958; Parkes, 1965; Wretmark, 1959) as well as psychometric instruments for the assessment of the psychological impact of bereavement (Faschingbauer, DeVaul, & Zisook, 1977; Horowitz, Wilner, & Alvarez, 1979; Sanders, Mauger, & Strong, 1979; Jacobs, Kosten, Kasl, et al., 1986; Zisook, DeVaul, & Click, 1982) have generally confirmed Lindemann's extrapolation of these factors as distinctive of grief, but they have also added a number of further symptoms. On the basis of these and other accounts a more complete list of grief symptoms has been compiled (Table 2.1). It should be emphasized, however, that not all of these symptoms appear in every bereaved person, nor at any one time in the duration of bereavement.

The observation that some of these grief symptoms seem to be particularly characteristic of certain time periods during bereavement has led some authors (e.g., Bowlby, 1981; Brown & Stoudemire, 1983; Clayton et al., 1968; Parkes, 1965) to concentrate on relating the occurrence of particular symptoms to the duration of bereavement; thus, shock and disbelief are more typically found among the recently bereaved, whereas symptoms of depression extend over a longer period, recur frequently, and only gradually abate during a period of months or even years.

Although there are differences of opinion about how many phases a bereaved person traverses, some describing three, others four or as many

Table 2.1. *List of grief symptoms*

Symptom	Description
A. Affective	
Depression	Feelings of sadness, mournfulness, and dysphoria, accompanied by intense subjective distress and "mental pain." Episodes (waves) of depression may be severe and are sometimes (but not always) precipitated by external events (locale, receiving sympathy, reminders of shared activities, anniversaries, meetings, etc.). Feelings of despair, lamentation, sorrow, and dejection predominate
Anxiety	Fears, dreads, and forebodings such as fear of breaking down, of losing one's mind or going mad, of dying, fear of being unable to cope without spouse, separation anxiety, fear about living alone, financial worries, and worries about other matters previously dealt with by spouse
Guilt	Self-blame and self-accusation about events in the past, notably about events leading up to death (feeling that more could have been done to prevent death). Guilt feelings about behavior toward partner (should have treated differently, made different decisions)
Anger and hostility	Irritability toward family, in child rearing, with friends (feeling they lacked understanding for and appreciation of the deceased, and about the bereaved's grief). Anger about fate, that death has occurred, anger toward the deceased spouse (e.g., about being left alone, not provided for), toward the doctors, nurses of spouse
Anhedonia	Loss of enjoyment of food, hobbies, social and family events, and other activities which had previously been pleasurable even if the spouse were not actually present. Feeling that nothing can be pleasurable without spouse
Loneliness	Feeling alone even in the presence of others, and periodic bouts of intense loneliness, notably at the times when spouse would have been present (evenings, weekends) and during special events that they would have shared
B. Behavioral manifestations	
Agitation	Tenseness, restlessness (atypical), jitteryness, overactivity often without completing tasks (doing things for the sake of the activity), searching behavior (looking for spouse, even though they "know" this is useless)

Table 2.1. *(cont.)*

Symptom	Description
Fatigue	Reduction in general activity level (sometimes interrupted by bouts of agitation mentioned above); retardation of speech and thought (slowed speech, long latencies); general lassitude
Crying	Tears and/or watery eyes, general expression one of sadness (drooping of sides of mouth, sad gaze)

C. Attitudes toward self, the deceased, and environment

Symptom	Description
Self-reproach	See A: Guilt
Low self-esteem	Feelings of inadequacy, failure, and incompetence on one's own, without spouse; worthlessness
Helplessness, hopelessness	Pessimism about present circumstances and future, loss of purpose in life, thoughts of death and suicide (desire not to go on living without spouse)
Sense of unreality	Feeling of "not being there," of "watching from outside," that events in the present are happening to someone else
Suspiciousness	Doubting the motives of those who offer help or advice
Interpersonal problems	Difficulty in maintaining social relationships, rejection of friendship, withdrawal from social functions
Attitudes toward the deceased	*Yearning* for deceased, waves of longing, calling out for him/her, intense pining *Imitation* of deceased's behavior (e.g., manner of speaking, walking), following deceased's interests, pursuits *Idealization* of deceased: the tendency to ignore any faults, exaggerate positive characteristics of spouse *Ambivalence:* alternation of feelings about deceased *Images* of deceased, often very vivid, almost hallucinatory: firm conviction of having seen/heard spouse *Preoccupation* with the memory of the deceased (both with sad and happy memories) and need to talk, sometimes incessantly, about deceased, to the exclusion of interest in any other topic

D. Cognitive impairment

Symptom	Description
Retardation of thought and concentration	Slowed thinking and poor memory; see also B: Fatigue

E. Physiological changes and bodily complaints

Symptom	Description
Loss of appetite	(Occasionally, overeating) accompanied by changes in body weight; sometimes, a considerable loss of weight

Table 2.1. *(cont.)*

Symptom	Description
Sleep disturbances	Mostly insomnia, occasionally oversleeping; disturbances of day/night rhythm
Energy loss	See B: Fatigue
Bodily complaints	These include headaches, neckache, back pain, muscle cramp, nausea, vomiting, lump in throat, sour taste in mouth, dry mouth, constipation, heartburn, indigestion, flatulence, blurred vision, pain on urination, tightness in throat, choking with shortness of breath, need for sighing, empty feeling in abdomen, lack of muscular power, palpitations, tremors, hair loss
Physical complaints of deceased	Appearance of symptoms similar to those of the deceased, particularly of those symptoms of the terminal illness (e.g., heart fluttering if loss were from heart attack); the bereaved may be convinced of having the same illness that afflicted the deceased
Changes in drug taking	Increase in the use of psychotropic medicines (tranquilizers, etc.) in alcohol intake, in smoking
Susceptibility to illness and disease	Particularly infections (lowering of immunity), also those relating to lack of health care (cancer, tuberculosis, etc.), and stress-related diseases (e.g., heart conditions)

as five stages, accounts of the duration and succession of phases through which bereaved persons pass are generally, with a few exceptions (notably Clayton et al., 1968, who conclude that recovery is rapid; and Barrett & Schneweis, 1980, who argue that grief persists for many years), fairly consistent (Bowlby, 1981; Gorer, 1965; Parkes, 1986). Nevertheless, it can be very misleading to make definitive statements about the time of onset or duration of phases of grief, or about the presence of specific symptoms occurring at a particular time or stage of bereavement, for there are considerable individual differences with regard to each of these aspects. Individuals vary greatly in their responses to loss not only in their general ability to cope, but also in mode of expression. For example, even in the initial period, when most feel stunned and unable to accept the fact of death, individual reactions vary from calm withdrawal to seeking the company of others. Further, phasal sequences which have been taken as useful descriptions of how the bereaved respond have been shown to overlap to a large extent in time, with individuals oscillating back and forth between them. Parkes (1986) described this tendency as follows: "Grief is not a set of symptoms which start after a loss and then gradually fade away. It involves a succession of clinical pictures which blend into and replace one another" (p. 27).

Nevertheless, it is extremely helpful for the purpose of diagnosing pathological grief to view grief as running a phasic course, for it is otherwise difficult to determine whether a bereaved person is suffering from delayed, or absent, grief. Given the above cautions, the following regularities have been noted as reflecting the course that uncomplicated grief usually takes:

Numbness. Like the first reaction to any catastrophe, the initial response to loss through death is often one of shock, numbness, and disbelief. This may last only for a few hours, or may extend over a period of several days. It may be interrupted at times by outbursts of anger or of deep despair. The recently bereaved person frequently feels dazed, stunned, helpless, immobilized, and lost or disorganized. Somatic symptoms may already be evident, such as sighing respiration, throat tightness, and a sensation of emptiness in the abdomen. The loss may be denied initially, which many regard as a protective reaction to an event that is too shocking to accept. The function of denial among terminal patients has been systematically explored (see, e.g., Beilin, 1981). There are similarities between the two types of loss, and denial in bereavement is likely to serve similar functions.

Characteristic of this phase, too, is an automatic continuation of life as before. But periods of calm may be punctuated by sudden outbursts of anger or of anguish, and even in the quiet interim periods, the bereaved person is often restless, tense, and apprehensive.

Yearning and protest. The initial numbness gives way to a period of strong emotions, with extreme psychological distress and physiological arousal, as awareness of the loss develops. This is accompanied by intense yearning for the lost person, with pangs of deep pining, and spasms of uncontrollable sobbing. At this stage there is often an overriding urge to search for the deceased, even to call out for him or her. Despite a growing awareness of the irreversibility of loss, the desire to try to recover the person is sometimes impossible to overcome. This is a time, then, of intense preoccupation with the deceased (there may even be occasions when a vivid sense of the presence of the deceased is felt).

The bereaved moves restlessly around the environment, searching, and is intensely, almost obsessively, preoccupied with memories, thoughts, and possessions of the deceased. Anything unrelated to the deceased has little or no purpose or significance; the bereaved person appears withdrawn and introverted.

In addition to the tendency to search for the deceased, which is one of the most distinctive features of this stage, anger is also particularly common. This is sometimes self-directed, taking the form of self-reproach with feelings of guilt about minor omissions concerning the deceased (particularly during the terminal illness), but, overwhelmingly, anger is directed toward others who proffer consolation or aid. Sometimes anger is expressed toward the deceased person, for having left the spouse. Anger is particularly frequent among younger bereaved who have lost someone through an unexpected, untimely death. It is important to note how common this symptom is, particularly as it seems somewhat anomalous to the emotion of grief and to remember that, at this stage of bereavement, unless it is extremely intense and unrelenting, it is not indicative of pathological grief.

Already, during these relatively early days of bereavement, there is evidence of a remarkable range of incompatible or contrary feelings. We find restless searching coupled with the realization that this is useless, intermittent hope with repeated disappointment, extreme agitation and periods of calm or even lethargy, and loss of awareness of other loved persons countered by accusations and anger toward them. Paralleling this complex array of psychological symptoms are the physical ones, which persist long after the loss. Frequent among these are loss of weight, sleep disturbances, somatic pain symptoms, and a general feeling of discomfort, all of which may be apparent at this stage.

Despair. Eventually, as the first year draws on, searching for the lost person is abandoned and the permanence and irrevocability of loss is recognized. But, rather than feeling on the road to recovery, for many widowed this stage is more devastating than any earlier one. It is at this time that one so often hears the bereaved say of their grief that, "It seems to get worse rather than better." At this time too, which may extend for months or even a year or two, the bereaved person despairs that anything worthwhile in life can be salvaged, and apathy and depression set in. The process of overcoming these reactions is slow and painful. Withdrawal from people and activities is typical, and lack of interest or involvement are hard to overcome. Inability to concentrate on routine tasks or to initiate any new activity is very common. Somatic symptoms also persist, including sleeplessness, loss of appetite and weight, and gastrointestinal disorders.

Recovery and restitution. Fortunately, for most people, the severe and grueling bouts of depression and the sense of hopelessness that accompany them begin to be interspersed, with increasing frequency, by more positive and less devastating feelings. The bereaved person starts to accept the changes in him- or herself and in the situation, and to deal with these with increased effectiveness. This means coming to terms with the new identity, as widow(er). It implies the relinquishing of all hope that the lost spouse can be recovered. It also means filling the roles and acquiring the skills previously undertaken by the spouse (or finding others to help in these respects) and resuming social life.

At this time, independence and initiative return and it is not uncommon for the bereaved to suddenly break off a supportive relationship on which he or she had relied. Such attempts on the part of the bereaved to stand on their own feet and reject support should be regarded as part of the recovery process. Too often they are taken personally and the relationship is upset for a long time. Such reactions by the bereaved's relatives and friends can be detrimental to the ultimate recovery of the bereaved, for social support, even if temporarily rejected, is critical to their health and welfare. Despite the instability of social relationships, during this period the bereaved person does move toward establishing new friendships and contacting old friends, and away from a total preoccupation with memories of the deceased, from whom an increasing degree of detachment is achieved.

The difficulty of this process of recovery and restitution is easy to underestimate. In fact, the effort to regain identity and purpose in life, to adopt new roles and skills, is a constant strain in itself, and leads to intense loneliness. Not least is the problem of "recurrences" of symptoms that had subsided. Very often this happens on dates of particular significance, such as the anniversary of the death, the deceased's birthday, the wedding date or holidays, and the phenomenon has come to be known, although not without criticism (see, e.g., Baltes, 1977; Birtchnell, 1981) as *anniversary reactions* (Hilgard, 1953; for a review, see Fox, 1985). Although for most bereaved life becomes tolerable and enjoyable again after a year or two, the view that "You never get over it, you just get used to it," as Silverman (1976) poignantly put it, seems to be true of the feelings of a substantial proportion of the widowed.

Conclusions. The course that grief takes in the months and years following bereavement has been outlined because this is necessary for the theoretical interpretation of the grief response. For practical purposes too it is helpful to know what the usual or typical reactions are. Many bereaved people suffer additional, unnecessary anxiety about the symptoms that they have, particularly if they find themselves prone to spells of dizziness and sickness, hair loss, and other such symptoms that they do not connect directly with grief. To know that these are commonly experienced and are not indicative of incipient illness or "going out of one's mind" is reassuring and therapeutic. Knowing, too, that the course of grief is much longer than the recovery period of a few weeks that is often expected, and that the bereaved need support and understanding for a much longer time, is equally important.

Nevertheless, while this outline may serve as a rough guide to what the bereaved have to endure, there is some danger that the phases become interpreted as normative prescriptions for how the bereaved *should* respond. In actual fact, there is not one simple process of recovery through which bereaved persons pass, with a pattern of symptoms that is invariant and that apply, in a fixed sequence, to all sufferers. As we cautioned before, bereaved people vary as much in their expressions of grief as they do in any other emotional response.

We have also drawn attention to the constant interplay between feelings: disbelief, hope, and despair; the coming and going of anguish and rage; acceptance and yearning; intense distress and apparent adjustment. Rather than a clear transition through progressive phases, there is a constant alternation of affective responses, even between those features (such as numbness, despair, and anger) which distinguish the phases. Thus, simple analyses by stages alone, without reference to this complexity, cannot be made.

Not only is there considerable overlap between the phases, but certain stages may be abbreviated or may be absent completely. The sequence of phases may even be reversed. It is, for example, not uncommon for anger and protest to precede numbness in cases where the deceased had undergone an unsuccessful operation. The target of anger is then frequently the medical doctor who had performed the operation. In addition to the fact that grief responses vary because individuals grieve in personal ways, there are many other sources of variability, which we look at in greater detail later (see Chapter 8). It seems likely that future research efforts will be directed toward the identification of differential patterns of grief (cf. Parkes & Weiss, 1983) following different types of loss (e.g., the termination of ambivalent or dependent relationships, or following sudden loss).

2.2.2 *Pathological grief*

Much has been written during the past couple of decades on the distinctions between normal and pathological grief (see, e.g., Brown & Stoudemire, 1983; Pedder, 1982; Volkan, 1970; Wahl, 1970). While it is not easy to draw the line between these categories, it is useful to keep in mind the distinction between pathological grief and clinical depression (which we consider in the next section). As a general guideline, one may say that pathological grief occurs when the grief reaction has itself "gone wrong" for some reason, in some way. Clinical depression may, in certain instances, be considered one type of pathological grief reaction, since a full-blown depressive episode may come about as a result of bereavement. Obviously, there are also cases of clinical depression which have not been brought about by the loss through death of a loved person and which therefore have nothing to do with grief. Obviously too, depression often occurs in bereavement without reaching the criterion of "clinical" depression.

Thus, the term morbid or pathological grief is used to refer to grief reactions which show a marked deviation from the normal pattern and are associated with maladjustment and psychiatric problems. Grief reactions of psychiatric patients whose illness came on subsequent to the loss of a loved person frequently seem to follow such atypical patterns (see, e.g., Parkes, 1965). Since there is no clinical diagnosis called *pathological grief,* those suffering from morbid grief reactions and entering medical or psychiatric care may be treated for "reactive depression" or some similar condition.

Undoubtedly, the papers of Freud (1917) and Klein (1934, 1940) were seminal in the theoretical analysis of pathological grief. However, the first systematic, empirical study of morbid grief reactions in a sample of the recently bereaved was conducted by Lindemann (1944). He argued that the delay in onset of grief, the apparently cheerful and griefless acceptance of the loss of a loved person, was the most striking and frequent form of morbid grief. During the period of delay, the bereaved may either behave normally or show alternations in their behavior which, according to Lindemann, represent "distorted pictures" of one special aspect of the grief syndrome. Examples of such distortions are overactivity without a sense of loss, the acquisition of symptoms belonging to the last illness of the deceased, hostility against doctors and friends, and alterations in relationships with relatives and friends. "These alterations may be considered as the surface manifestations of an unresolved grief reaction, which may respond to fairly simple and quick psychiatric management if recognized" (Lindemann, 1944, p. 144). Thus, for Lindemann the concept of morbid grief was closely linked to the notion of *grief work* as a natural and necessary process in the recovery from loss. It is the failure to successfully "work through" grief which is at the root of the morbid grief reaction.

Unfortunately Lindemann's (1944) distinction between normal and morbid grief reactions lacks empirical substantiation. As Parkes (1965) criticized, Lindemann failed to give a clear account of normal grief or state his criteria of normality. He presented the results of his interviews with bereaved patients in an anecdotal fashion without data on the frequency of the symptoms observed. Finally, his subjects, who included psychoneurotic patients from his own psychiatric practice (who had lost relatives during the course of treatment), can hardly be considered a representative sample of the population.

Parkes (1965), among the earliest of his important contributions to the bereavement area, conducted a more systematic study in which he compared the symptomatology of psychiatric patients (whose psychiatric problem had begun during the terminal illness or within six months after the death of a parent, spouse, sibling, or child) with that of a sample of randomly selected London widows, who had been interviewed by Marris (1958). Using the figures given by Marris for the frequency of symptoms as typical for normal grief reactions, Parkes (1965) concluded that only one out of his twenty-one patients had reactions which fell within the limits of normal grief. "In all the rest the typical reaction was in some way distorted or exaggerated and it was this distortion or exaggeration which caused the patient to be regarded as mentally ill" (p. 4).

Drawing on the data from this study as well as on earlier work by Anderson (1949) and Deutsch (1937), Parkes (1965), in a paper which has been very influential in the area, developed a classification of morbid grief reactions which extended the conceptualization suggested by Lindemann (1944). In addition to the variety of nonspecific reactions such as psychosomatic and psychoneurotic disorders, Parkes (1965) identified three forms of pathological reaction to grief: *chronic, delayed,* and *inhibited.* More recently, this categorization has been revised (see Parkes & Weiss, 1983), and we will discuss these important changes shortly.

Chronic grief refers to the indefinite prolongation of grief. This is a "morbid illness in which anxiety, tension, restlessness, and insomnia predominate, and self-reproachful ideas and angry outbursts are common" (Parkes & Weiss, 1983, p. 14). Often "identification symptoms," those resembling the symptoms of the terminally ill spouse, occur. Chronic grief is usually very intense, symptoms being highly exaggerated compared with normal reactions. Exemplary of the chronic grief reaction is the English monarch Queen Victoria who mourned the loss of Prince Albert for the rest of her very long life. She had been very dependently attached to him during their marriage and could not tolerate any separation from him. After his death she idealized him completely: "To have conceived of him as anything short of perfect – perfect in virtue, in wisdom, in beauty, in all the glories and graces of man – would have been an unthinkable blasphemy" (Strachey, 1971, p. 187). She developed a grudge against her subjects, whom she regarded as failing to rate her husband at his true worth. She grieved intensely, wore black permanently, and retained his possessions just as they were. Right into her old age, "every bed in which Victoria slept had attached to it, at the back, on the right hand side, above the pillow, a photograph of the head and shoulders of Albert as he lay dead, surmounted by a wreath of immortelles" (Strachey, 1971, p. 234). While during her lifetime Queen Victoria came to be considered the model of widowed virtue, whose example was to be copied, to us today she presents a paradigm of the chronically, abnormally, grief-stricken.

Delayed grief, which was already described by Lindemann (1944), takes place when a normal or chronic grief reaction occurs only after an extensive delay, during which the expression of grief is inhibited. In the interim period the bereaved person may behave quite normally or may show some symptoms of "distorted" grief. The latter range from compulsive overactivity, to acquisition of symptoms of the deceased's last illness, medical illnesses, alienation and isolation, or severe depression without a sense of loss.

Inhibited grief. In this type of grief most of the normal grief symptoms are absent. Psychoanalysts believe, however, that the unresolved grief is given expression in some form and that the affective disturbance of grief is channeled into somatic symptoms (e.g., Deutsch, 1937; Stern, Williams, & Prados, 1951). Parkes (1965) did not observe any cases of inhibited grief reactions among his psychiatric patients and there are few descriptions of such syndromes in the literature. Parkes (1965) suggested that there may be no absolute difference between inhibited and delayed grief and that the two types of grief simply represent different degrees of "successful" defense.

It should be noted that the finding that psychiatric patients whose illnesses seem to have been triggered by a loss experience also exhibit morbid grief reactions (Parkes, 1965) does not imply that all bereaved individuals who show some form of atypical grief are in need of psychiatric treatment. For example, although chronic grief is typically associated with depressed mood states, it need not impair an individual's functioning in everyday life. Thus, Queen Victoria seemed to be perfectly able to cope with the demands of high position, despite her chronic grief.

Even in cases of delayed or inhibited grief, therapeutic interventions may not always be helpful. Lindemann's recommendation that delayed reactions should be transformed into normal grief by a therapy which encourages the full expression of grief is based on the assumption that the delay is due to a maladaptive repression of healthy affect and that grieving will follow the normal course once the defenses against grief have been removed. That this may not always be the case is suggested by Parkes's (1965) findings that each of his cases of delayed grief later developed chronic grief reactions.

These early descriptions of pathological grief, useful as they are in categorizing responses, do not go very far in identifying factors that predict which of the bereaved will be vulnerable to the different types of pathological grief. More recently, Bowlby (1979, 1981) and Parkes and Weiss (1983) addressed this issue in a systematic way, and related syndromes of pathological grief to such antecedent factors as the expectedness of the loss or the relationship to the deceased. Since the theory of Bowlby will be discussed extensively in Chapter 4, we will focus here on the classification of grief symptoms developed by Parkes and Weiss (1983).

Basing their interpretation largely on their empirical findings from the Harvard Bereavement Study, Parkes and Weiss (1983) identified three major causes of pathological grief and described different patterns of grieving related to each of these. The first of these is the *unexpected-grief syndrome*. This, clearly enough, relates to the occurrence of sudden or untimely losses. Such losses typically give rise to defensive reactions of shock or disbelief, although high anxiety may be present despite this. Complications of this pattern take the form of a persisting sense of the presence of the deceased, self-reproach, and feelings of continued obligation to the deceased. The second pattern is the *ambivalent-grief syndrome*. This syndrome occurs subsequent to a relationship that had been ambivalent, or filled with arguments or disagreements. Parkes and Weiss describe the initial reaction to such a loss as one of relief, with little need felt to grieve, and little anxiety. Later, this phase is succeeded by one of pining and despair. The bereaved's grief may extend beyond that for the lost person to a loss of hope in marriage or relationships in general. Self-punitive feelings may persist, and a desire to make amends for past failures or wrongs. Parkes and Weiss regard these two types of bereavement, that following a sudden death and that following an ambivalent relationship, as the causes for most delayed grief syndromes which are in need of psychiatric care. A third type of loss, that following the termination of a relationship that had been characterized as highly dependent or clinging, is described as causing the *chronic-grief syndrome.* Grief over a loss is expressed without a delay, and continues for an abnormally long period of time. Helplessness is particularly characteristic of this syndrome. Parkes and Weiss (1983) emphasize that it is not always the survivor who was the more dependent member, indicating that the pattern of dependency within the relationship may have been more complex than it appears at first sight.

The delineation of these pathological reactions is an important contribution because it enables one to identify patterns of grief with distinctive etiologies and clinical symptoms. It follows that the different patterns of grief will require different kinds of supportive intervention (which the authors also elaborate). Thus, while one must await further empirical findings to establish the applicability of Parkes and Weiss's analysis to samples other than the small one that they investigated, this differentiated approach has important implications not only for the understanding of the grief process and its pathological variants, but also for therapy.

2.3 Grief and clinical depression

Sadness and despair are so much part of normal grief that, at least in Western cultures, it is considered pathological if a person who has recently lost his or her spouse does not show signs of depression. What then distinguishes these normal grief responses from clinical forms of depression? Can the "normally" grief-stricken individual be considered clinically depressed? Since affective disorders such as clinical depression involve an accentuation in the intensity or duration of otherwise normal emotions, the borderline between the normal and the pathological is always difficult to draw and this difficulty is even greater in the presence of bereavement. Before discussing the distinction between normal grief and depression, we will therefore describe the symptomatology of clinical depression.

2.3.1 The symptomatology of clinical depression

The most common and central symptom of depression is that of depressive mood and pervasive feelings of sadness (Klerman, 1978). Patients describe themselves as "sad," "blue," "despondent," "gloomy," or "down in the dumps." Another mood that is frequent in depressed individuals is that of anxiety. A sense of fear and intense worry is frequently reported.

A second set of characteristic signs of depression are severe deficits in motivation. Severely depressed patients typically report that previous sources of gratification (e.g., hobbies, social events, time spent with family or friends) no longer provide them with any pleasure (Klerman, 1978). The general loss of gratification is also reflected in a loss of interest in food and a decline in sexual drive.

Depressed patients also show characteristic biases in their interpretation of reality, which Beck (1967) has termed the cognitive triad: The individual has a negative self-concept, a negative view of the world, and a negative appraisal of his future. Loss of self-esteem is indeed typical for individuals suffering from depression, who seem to be convinced of their own worthlessness and inadequacy. Since they are prone to attribute unpleasant occurrences to themselves, they respond with intense feelings of guilt and self-reproach. They believe themselves to be no longer able to cope with their daily routine and are overwhelmed by intense feelings of helplessness. The future appears grim and hopeless. Life seems no longer worth living, and in severe cases, depressed individuals often entertain thoughts of ending their lives. In fact, the risk of suicide is quite elevated during episodes of acute depression. Further, patients frequently become so preoccupied with their obsessional ruminations of self-doubts, self-reproach, and worries over their future, that they are distracted from concentrating on environmental demands. As a consequence, they often complain about difficulties in concentrating, slowed thinking, poor memory, and similar problems.

Depression is also characterized by a number of physical manifestations. Sleep disturbances are one of the most characteristic signs of depression. Patients experience difficulties in falling asleep, excessive restlessness during the night, frequent nightmares, and early morning awakening. A small minority of depressed patients suffer from hypersomnia, the desire to sleep a great deal of the time. Patients also experience changes in their activity level, becoming either agitated or lethargic (psychomotor retardation). While the two states usually do not coincide, patients may exhibit both patterns at different times throughout a depressive episode. Finally, the loss of appetite typically results in drastic weight loss in the majority of depressed individuals.

2.3.2 Criteria for the diagnosis of clinical depression

In an attempt to provide reliable criteria for the diagnosis of all forms of clinical depression, Feighner, Robins, Guze, et al. (1972) assembled a list of symptoms which corresponds to our description of depressive symptomatology. These authors require that patients exhibit a severely depressed mood state for a period of one month or more, and at least five or more of the following symptoms, to be diagnosed as "definite depression":

(1) Poor appetite or weight loss (positive if 2 lb a week or 10 lb or more a year when not dieting). (2) Sleep difficulty (include insomnia or hypersomnia). (3) Loss of energy, e.g. fatigability, tiredness. (4) Loss of interest in usual activities, or decrease in sexual drive. (5) Feelings of self-reproach or guilt (either may be delusional). (7) Complaints of or actually diminished ability to think or concentrate, such as slow thinking or mixed-up thoughts. (8) Recurrent thoughts of death or suicide, including thoughts of wishing to be dead. (Feighner et al., 1972, p. 58)

2.3.3 The distinction between grief and clinical depression

In his classic analysis of grief and clinical depression, Freud (1917) suggested a number of differences between the two states. Normal grief was characterized by profoundly painful dejection, a loss of interest, and an inhibition of activities. *Melancholia* or clinical depression, on the other hand, which Freud attributed to the existence of ambivalence toward the lost person, were characterized by feelings of guilt, self-reproach, and a lowering of self-esteem. Some support for this hypothesis comes from Parkes (1986) who in a comparison of results from his studies of widows with psychiatric problems (Parkes, 1965) and of normal widows (Parkes, 1971b) found a higher incidence of reported feelings of guilt and self-reproach among the widows who had developed psychiatric problems. However, in view of the small size of Parkes's sample of bereaved psychiatric patients ($n = 14$) and since feelings of self-reproach and guilt are also very much part of the normal grief response, the presence of such feelings can hardly be considered a reliable criterion to distinguish normal grief from clinical depression. Nevertheless, one critical difference may lie in the type of guilt that is manifested: Worden (1982) suggests that guilt in the bereaved is usually connected with some specific aspect of the loss, whereas guilt in clinical depression is associated with a general sense of culpability. It is easy to imagine, for example, that a bereaved person might feel intensely guilty about having been absent at the time of the death of a loved one, but that no feelings of self-blame would pertain with respect to events in general. It would be useful to explore this claim further, with the help of empirical data (for a recent review of guilt and its origins in relation to bereavement, see Warner, 1985).

Since Freud (1917), it has often been argued that grief and clinical depression differ in that the former is either not (or at most briefly) accompanied by the loss of self-esteem commonly found in most clinical depressions. This criterion is not unproblematic either. In a study of recently bereaved individuals conducted in Tübingen (for a description, see Chapter 7.2.1) young widowers and widows who were not clinically depressed nevertheless suffered a lowering of self-esteem when compared to matched married controls. However, in their study of elderly widows Breckenridge, Gallagher, Thompson, and Peterson (1986) did not replicate this finding.

In our view, grief becomes clinically relevant when the depressive reactions are excessively intense and when the process of grieving is unduly prolonged. A diagnosis of clinical depression may be based on the criteria of both intensification and of prolongation. Thus, if a widow (or widower) shows signs of extreme sadness, derives no gratification from previously pleasurable activities, has lost her (his) appetite and complains about restlessness, insomnia, and loss of concentration, these symptoms will be considered quite normal if they occur within months after the bereavement. If, on the other hand, they are still present after a couple of years, then clinical depression is likely to be diagnosed and some sort of psychotherapy or medication recommended. The risk of psychiatric problems seems to be particularly high after a delay or inhibition of the initial grief response (e.g., Lindemann, 1944).

While it is not easy to differentiate between normal, appropriate grief and pathological or disproportionate grief, an attempt by Wahl (1970) to identify general characteristics of both normal and, in his terms, "neurotic" grief work provides useful guidelines for such a differentiation. He identified and compared a small sample of bereaved with normal ($n = 9$) and neurotic ($n = 19$) grief reactions. Characteristics of neurotic grief reactions, in contrast to normal ones, were listed as follows: (1) excessive, disproportionate, and protracted grief; (2) profound feelings of irrational despair and helplessness (plus loss of personal identity); (3) feelings of personal vulnerability and thanatophobia (death fear); (4) inability to cope with ambivalence toward the deceased; (5) personification of effect (deceased died as personal rejection of them); impaired self-esteem; (6) personification of causation (i.e., persistent irrational belief that death was their fault); (7) needs, dependency, and affect bound to the deceased; (8) similar symptoms (in some cases) as those of the deceased; (9) protracted apathy, heightened irritability, aimless hyperactivity without appropriate affect. Clearly, however, any of these characteristics show up, perhaps with lesser intensity, in normal grief (cf. Table 2.1).

Finally, it must be emphasized that the absence of a clear boundary separating normal grief from clinical depression should not be mistaken to imply that grief and depression are one and the same syndrome. This is not the case, as a comparison of our descriptions of grief and depression will show. First, there are a number of symptoms which are characteristic of grief but not depression (e.g., yearning for the deceased, imitation of his or her behavior, preoccupation with memories of the deceased, feeling of "not being there," "watching from outside"). Second, grief is not a set of symptoms which start after the loss and then gradually fade away, but involves a succession of stages which blend into each other (Parkes, 1986). Thus, initial numbness is soon replaced by pining and yearning, which many believe to reflect separation anxiety (Bowlby, 1971; Parkes, 1986). Only after that does depression become the most salient characteristic of the grief response. Third, while clinical depression is certainly one form of pathological grief response, there are other forms of pathological grief (e.g., inhibited grief), which are not characterized by depression. Thus, although depressive symptoms represent a "final common path"(Akiskal & McKinney, 1973) between grief and depression, it should be remembered that, despite the overlap, grief and depression form two distinctive and distinguishable syndromes.

3 Is grief universal? Cultural variations in the emotional reactions to loss

3.1 Introduction

Following the description of the symptomatology of grief in the last chapter, this chapter explores the relationship between culture and grief, investigates whether the core of grief symptoms common to Western cultures can be demonstrated interculturally, and discusses the implications of cultural patterning of grief for the theoretical analysis of this emotion. Since psychologists typically lack the inclination or skills to conduct observational studies in a great variety of different cultures, we have to base our analysis of cultural variations in grief reactions on ethnographic data collected by anthropologists. This is problematic because emotional components of responses to death, of central interest to psychologists, are not directly the subject matter of anthropologists, who focus on public rituals or mourning customs (e.g., Durkheim, 1976; Huntington & Metcalfe, 1979; Radcliffe-Brown, 1964).

Can we draw any inferences about private grief experiences from such public display of mourning behavior? The answer to that question depends to some extent on the theory of emotion on which one's understanding of grief is based. If we conceive of emotional experience as the subjective reflection of a bodily state, then grief as the physiologically driven emotional response to loss can be clearly distinguished from the norm-governed public display of emotions involved in mourning. If, on the other hand, one accepts that the emotional experience is itself shaped by social norms, that both grief and mourning are socially constituted response patterns (Averill, 1982), then the study of mourning rituals may well provide valuable information on the nature of the grief experience in a given culture. To clarify this issue and to further our understanding of the nature of emotional responses, we begin our discussion of the cultural relativity of grief with a brief review of some of the basic assumptions of emotion theory.

26

3.2 The role of cultural factors in emotion

There are two potential avenues by which cultural factors may shape emotional experience, namely through *appraisal processes* and through *feeling rules*. Ekman (1971) argued that the emotional reactions to most events are learned, and learned in such a fashion that the elicitors will often vary with culture. For example, the appraisal of a given situation as joyful or embarrassing is largely determined by cultural factors. Cultural factors may be less important, however, in linking grief to loss experiences. There is evidence from primate research (Mineka & Suomi, 1978; Reite, Short, Seiler, et al., 1981) and observational studies of children (Bowlby, 1979) to suggest that grief is a characteristic response of many species to the loss of an attachment figure and may thus be fairly independent of learning processes. The biological basis of grief has been convincingly argued by Averill (1968, 1979) and by Bowlby (1960, 1961, 1971). Human beings, like many other primates, are group-living and require a social form of existence for survival (Averill, 1968). If separation from the group cannot be avoided (as in cases of death of a partner) the relevant reactions for returning to it may nevertheless run their course, even if this causes acute psychological and physiological distress (Averill, 1979).

This would limit the cultural influence on the emotional reaction to loss to one avenue, namely to the shaping of the emotional experience itself. There is a great deal of disagreement among emotion theorists, however, as to whether the emotional experience resulting from the appraisal is merely a reflection of cultural norms or "feeling rules" (Hochschild, 1979) or patterned by the bodily reactions elicited by the emotional event. Theories of emotion can be placed on a continuum according to the degree to which they conceive of emotions as physiologically driven or shaped by culture. At one extreme we have the proprioceptive-feedback theories of James (1950), Lange (1922), Izard (1971, 1977), and Tomkins (1962, 1963), who understand emotions as determined by bodily states. The other extreme is represented by the social constructivist approaches of Averill (1982) and Hochschild (1979), for whom emotions are culturally constituted.

3.2.1 *The proprioceptive-feedback theory of James and Lange*

The best-known version of a proprioceptive-feedback theory is that of James (1950), which is considered so similar to Lange's (1922) approach that the two are usually referred to as the James–Lange theory. The basic tenet of this theory has been aptly formulated by James (1950) in his widely quoted statement:

... bodily changes follow directly the perception of the exciting fact, and that our feelings of the same changes as they occur is the emotion. Common sense says we lose our fortune, are sorry, and weep; we meet a bear, are frightened, and run; we are insulted by a rival, are angry, and strike. The hypothesis here to be defended says that this order of sequence is incorrect, that the one mental state is not immediately induced by the other and that the bodily manifestations must first be interposed between. The more rational statement is that we feel sorry because we cry, angry, because we strike, afraid because we tremble, and not that we cry, strike, or tremble, because we are sorry, angry or fearful, as the case may be. (1950, pp. 449–50)

Thus, James argued that our subjective emotional experience is patterned by the feedback from the activity of our bodily organs. The two sources of bodily information he considered are expressive behavior and autonomic or visceral action.

According to this theory, the quality of the experience of grief is determined by the feedback from the physiological changes which take place in grieving. Grief is the subjective reflection of the feedback from changes in the state of various bodily systems such as the facial muscles, "the weeping, with its profuse secretion of tears, its swollen reddened face, red eyes, and augmented secretion from the nasal mucous membrane," the "weakness of the entire voluntary motor apparatus," the contraction of the "vaso-motor apparatus," the contraction of the smaller vessels of the lung (which Lange made responsible for the breathlessness typical in grief) and many other changes "which are so indefinitely numerous and subtle that the entire organism may be called a sounding board" (James, 1950, p. 450).

Although James (1950) explicitly considered expressive behavior as one of the sources of bodily information, most textbook descriptions of the James–Lange theory misrepresent it as a theory which construes emotion solely in terms of feedback from viscera and the autonomous nervous system. Expressive behavior is not even mentioned as a source of bodily information in some of the most widely read accounts (e.g., Schachter, 1964). Since cultural factors have little effect on autonomic and visceral action, there is no place in such a theory for cultural influences on emotional experience. Thus, little variability should be expected across cultures in the symptomatology of emotions.

If one consults James (1950) directly, it becomes obvious, however, that cultural factors could influence emotional experience in his version of the proprioceptive-feedback theory. James not only assumed that facial feedback was one of the sources of bodily information which patterned our emotional experience, but he also suggested that one could block feelings by enacting expressive patterns which were in conflict with the emotions one was experiencing at the moment:

... if we wish to conquer undesirable emotional tendencies in ourselves, we must assiduously, and in the first instance coldbloodedly, go through the outward movements of those contrary dispositions which we prefer to cultivate. The reward of persistency will infallibly come, in the fading out of the sullenness or depression, and the advent of real cheerfulness and kindliness in their stead. (1950, p. 463)

Since facial and other outward expressions of emotions are frequently affected by social norms, the assumption that voluntary control of facial expressions can shape the emotional experience suggests one mechanism by which cultural norms can influence emotional experience.

Most of the critics of the proprioceptive-feedback theory completely disregarded James's discussion of the role of facial expression in emotion. Thus, Cannon's (1929) devastating attack on the James–Lange theory is exclusively aimed at disproving the role of feedback from viscera and the autonomous nervous system. Cannon (1929) argued that if the assumption that our emotions are merely the experiential reflection of certain physiological changes in viscera and the autonomous nervous system were correct, it would follow that different emotions should be associated with different patterns of physiological changes. Furthermore, it should be possible by inducing such reactions (e.g., with epinephrine injections) to create emotional experiences in the individual. Cannon (1929) and later Schachter (1964) discussed evidence which seemed to demonstrate that neither of these assumptions of the James–Lange theory could be maintained. It was neither possible to distinguish differential patterns of physiological changes associated with different emotions, nor did the induction of arousal through the injection of epinephrine cause emotional experiences (e.g., Cantril & Hunt, 1932; Landis & Hunt, 1932; Maranon, 1924). The majority of individuals who had been given epinephrine injections reported feelings of arousal but not emotion.

3.2.2   *The cognition–arousal theory*

To accommodate these findings, Schachter developed a *cognition–arousal theory* of emotion which conceives of emotions as patterned by cognitions rather than by bodily reactions. The bodily reactions, in this case general physiological arousal, merely constitute the clay from which the emotions are molded. According to this theory, an emotional state is the result of the interaction between two components: an unspecific physiological arousal and a cognition about the arousing situation. Since an emotion is only experienced if the arousal is labeled in terms of the emotionally relevant cognition, Schachter implicitly assumes a third component to be necessary for an emotional experience, that is, the attribution of the arousal as caused by the situation.

Schachter and Singer (1962) tested this theory in an ingenious experiment, which demonstrated that individuals who had unwittingly been aroused by the injection of what they believed to be a vitamin, but which was in fact epinephrine, experienced different emotions depending on situational cues manipulated by the experimenters. Thus, when subjects, during the onset of the arousal, were placed with a confederate who either behaved angrily or euphorically, they would themselves show signs of anger or euphoria. These signs were more marked than those of subjects who had been injected with a placebo solution. Although later attempts to replicate these findings have met with little success (Erdman & Janke, 1978; Maslach, 1978), Schachter's theory is still the dominant theory of emotion in social psychology as well as sociology.

According to this theory, the experience of grief would result whenever unspecific physiological arousal is attributed to a loss or some other grief-arousing event. By "interpreting" the arousal as *caused by* the loss, the individual feels grief. One limitation of Schachter's theory is that although it is left to the individual to shape his or her emotional experience, the processes by which individuals learn what they should experience in different situations are not spelled out. As we have demonstrated in our discussion of the symptomatology of grief, emotional syndromes consist of a differentiated set of responses and it is difficult to understand how different individuals with independent interpretations could consistently mold their arousal into the same complex pattern. One way this consensus could be accounted for in terms of a cognition–arousal theory is to assume that culture patterns emotional experiences by providing individuals with culture-specific *feeling rules,* that is, guidelines about how arousal should be interpreted in various situations. Thus, cultural norms would be the source of both grief and mourning.

3.2.3   *The social constructivist approach*

This solution has been adopted by the social constructivist approach (e.g., Averill, 1982; Hochschild, 1979). According to this perspective, the way that individuals interpret their arousal and what they feel is guided or even determined by cultural norms or feeling rules. These feeling rules are social norms which prescribe certain emotions as appropriate for a given social situation (Hochschild, 1979). Similarly, Averill (1982) defined emotions as transitory social roles and emphasized that in order to count as a social role, the emotional response must be meaningful in terms of social expectations and that the person must attempt to conform his or her behavior to those expectations. In terms of this approach, grief is a complex syndrome of emotional responses, which is constituted by social norms and rules and incorporates bodily reactions as well as expressive and instrumental actions. If it is accepted, however, that emotional experiences are culturally constituted, it must be assumed that different cultures impose different rules. According to this perspective, therefore, a great deal of variation across cultures has to be expected in the symptomatology of emotional syndromes such as grief.

3.2.4 The concept of "emotion work"

The assumption that emotional experiences are influenced or governed by social norms has implications which go beyond the attributional rules incorporated in Schachter's cognition–arousal theory. Since deviant behavior is negatively sanctioned by society, individuals must be able to control emotional experiences to avoid sanctions and to bring their emotions in line with societal expectations. Hochschild (1979) uses the concept of *emotion work* to refer to attempts by the individual to arouse the emotions they think they should feel in a given situation or to suppress emotions which they think are inappropriate. From her descriptions of various techniques of emotion work, it becomes evident that Hochschild (1979) considers bodily feedback part of the emotional experience and also accepts that there is some interplay between cognition and physiological reactions. She distinguished three techniques:

One is cognitive: the attempts to change images, ideas, or thoughts in the service of changing the feelings associated with them. A second is bodily: the attempt to change somatic or other physical symptoms of emotion (e.g., trying to breathe slower, trying not to shake). Third, there is expressive emotion work: trying to change expressive gestures in the service of changing inner feeling (e.g., trying to smile, or to cry). This differs from simple display in that it is directed toward change in feeling. (1979, p. 562)

By incorporating these assumptions into the social constructivist approach Hochschild seems to accept that emotions are to some extent patterned by bodily reactions (otherwise it would make little sense to work on them). She thus narrows the gap between her position and that of William James (1950) who, as we mentioned earlier, believed that emotions could be controlled through the control of one's facial expression.

3.2.5   *Conclusions and implications*

Despite significant discrepancies between the various theories of emotion discussed in this section, all except the simplified version of the proprioceptive-feedback theory allow for some influence of societal norms on the emotional experiences. Thus, only this oversimplified position, which seems to have mainly served the function of a target for social constructivist attacks, would maintain that mourning and grief are completely independent response systems. According to the theory actually espoused by James (1950) emotions are shaped by feedback from facial as well as visceral reactions to the emotion-arousing event. Thus, going through the full display of sadness and despair which is required during mourning is likely to evoke some form of emotional experience consistent with this expressive display.

Let us hasten to add, however, that the research on the influence of voluntary facial movements on emotions is less than conclusive. Thus, Tourangeau and Ellsworth (1979), who had subjects watch a film eliciting sadness or no emotion, while holding their facial muscles in the position characteristic of fear or sadness, or in an effortful but nonemotional grimace, did not find any effect of these voluntary facial expressions on emotional experience. However, the fact that the short-term role-playing engaged in by these subjects was insufficient to influence emotional experience does not rule out the possibility that the long-term display of emotions during mourning, which involves posture as well as facial expression, has some impact on altering the mourners' emotions. Furthermore, Laird (1984), a supporter of the facial feedback hypothesis, contrasted the results of ten studies which demonstrated that manipulated facial expression does produce corresponding emotional experience with "Tourangeau and Ellsworth's sole published failure to demonstrate this relation" (p. 909). He also argued that six other studies, using a different but theoretically consistent paradigm, also observed facial feedback effects. However, other researchers in the area of emotion (e.g., Leventhal, 1984; Winton, 1986) find this evidence less than conclusive.

To the social constructivist both mourning and grief are culturally constituted response patterns or transitory roles which mainly differ in the level of involvement. Thus, from a social constructivist perspective, the study of mourning rituals should provide valid information about the emotional experiences of the mourners. Although social constructivists are somewhat vague about the exact nature of the contribution of bodily reactions to the emotional experience, Hochschild's discussion of emotion work indicates that she accepts that emotional experiences are shaped by both distinct bodily reactions as well as social norms. This position, which avoids complete cultural relativity while allowing for some variation across cultures in emotional symptomatology, seems eminently plausible to us. It appears also to be consistent with the findings of cultural variation in grief symptoms as well as in the duration of grief, to be discussed in the remainder of this chapter.

3.3 Cross-cultural variations in symptomatology: the case of crying

In view of the limitations of ethnographic descriptions of grief reactions, it would make little sense to examine evidence of the presence of the whole syndrome of grief described in the previous chapter. Rather we will adopt the strategy of examining in detail one symptom, crying, which combines a number of characteristics to make it ideally suited for our purpose: (1) Crying out of sadness is a uniquely human experience: Though animals may shed tears because of irritants to the eyes, they never do from sorrow. (2) Crying is considered a normal symptom of grief in the West, provided that its expression is not too extreme or prolonged. (3) The fact that crying is the universal response of babies and small children to unpleasant or painful experiences tends to indicate that crying during bereavement expresses authentic feelings and/or attempts to socially communicate that such feelings are being experienced. (4) There is evidence to suggest that the link between facial expression of emotion and emotional experience is stable across cultures: Studies using facial photographs depicting various emotions have shown that emotional expressions can be correctly identified in all the cultures studied. Thus, Izard (1977) reported data from a study of twelve different nations or cultures, which indicated cross-cultural agreement in the categorization of pictures reflecting these basic emotions. Similar results were found by Ekman and Friesen (1971) in a study of children and adults in New Guinea, who did not speak English and lived far away from any white settlements. This evidence has been considered strong support for a genetic link between emotional experience and facial expression of emotions (e.g., Izard, 1977).

3.3.1 *The presence of crying in other cultures*

Rosenblatt, Walsh, and Jackson (1976) examined the occurrence of crying among bereaved persons in different cultures, as described in the ethnographic literature on seventy-eight societies. They found reports of crying after bereavement in all but one of the cultures that could be rated on crying after loss (seventy-three societies). In most of the cultures crying was judged to be a frequent response. Rosenblatt et al. (1976) regarded this as strong evidence that people from cultures very dissimilar to our own respond in a similar way emotionally to what we find here.

But does the fact that crying was absent in one culture imply that this emotional response does not occur universally? Rosenblatt et al. (1976) examined this particular culture (the Balinese) in somewhat more detail and at first hand. They argued that lack of crying when bereaved was in line with Balinese emotional responses in other situations: The investigators observed that sometimes, when recounting tragic events, relaters even laughed or smiled. They interpreted this in terms of an effort to control the emotional response and suggested that the Balinese were fearful that they would cry if they did not force the opposite expression. Rosenblatt related this to religious beliefs which encourage calmness, and to the belief that communication with the gods is impeded if such equanimity is not maintained (personal communication).

Along similar lines the Norwegian anthropologist Wikan (1986), who has done extensive field work in Bali, argued that the assumption that the Balinese do not cry is misleading and built "on the mistaken assumption that the public domain constitutes the whole of a people's culture" (p. 6). She argued that the pressure in Balinese culture against any expression of grief is partly due to the "belief that emotions exert a direct influence on health through their effect on spiritual and bodily resistance to illness and afflictions of every kind" (p. 9). To protect one's health and welfare one must cultivate "good" emotions and attitudes that will strengthen one's spirit and body.

Thus, even though the Balinese tend to suppress the overt expression of grief, there is some evidence that this is due, for cultural reasons, to a stoic suppression of this behavior, rather than to lack of emotional feeling. According to this interpretation, the presence of smiling and laughter during grief in the Balinese is not evidence for the absence of feelings of sorrow, but rather represents a desperate attempt to control them. A similar phenomenon, practiced for a different reason, has been observed among the Japanese, who may smile at strangers or acquaintances during bereavement, not to control their own emotion, but in order not to burden others with their grief (Izard, 1977).

Occasionally accounts can be found of an absence of crying, or indeed of any emotional expression of grief, following certain types of bereavement (though not of others), which would be the cause of acute grief in the West. For example, Johnson (1921, cited in Eisenbruch, 1984a) observed that the Yoruba of Nigeria apparently unfeelingly disposed of their dead babies by throwing them into the bush. However, this "barbaric" or "unthinkable" response to loss, in our terms, becomes very understandable when the significance of the death for these bereaved parents is known: Their dead baby, if buried, would be considered as deeply offending the earth shrines who bring fertility and ward off death (Eisenbruch, 1984a).

If these analyses are correct, then we have no instances so far of any peoples who respond to loss of a close person with emotional indifference. We return to the discussion of possible exceptions to the universality of grief in the general discussion later. So far we have found evidence to support the position that crying and emotional upset seem to be universal even though overt expression may be tailored to cultural norms and values.

3.3.2 Types and occasions of crying in other cultures

Rosenblatt et al.'s (1976) ingenious study was, by the constraints of the data, limited to a secondary analysis of only the occurrence and frequency of crying. If one looks more closely at the crying behavior, then a different impression about the universality of crying during bereavement emerges, for, just as there are individual differences in crying behavior within our own culture, so are there differences not only in the frequency but also in the type and timing of crying in and between other cultures.

To illustrate, reports of crying at funerals come in from all over the world: It seems to be a usual time for people to cry. But here the similarity between cultures ends. In the West crying from grief is typically spontaneous. Those close to the deceased person tend to be overcome with grief and to shed tears, sob, or even cry out loud. This is permissible behavior and evokes sympathy rather than censure from others. But it is not required by custom. In certain other societies, on the other hand, crying is not merely tolerated but required at certain moments. At other times it is strictly forbidden, when weeping and wailing and tears can be seen to stop as soon as they started. Such ceremonial or ritual crying has been the subject of much anthropological investigation. While psychologists, due to the absence of further evidence, might tend to discount such information as irrelevant to the emotion of grief, such analyses have been central to anthropology. For examples of such ceremonial weeping and interpretations regarding the emotion of grief one needs to look at anthropological or ethnographic accounts more closely.

A classic example is recorded in *The Andaman Islanders* by Radcliffe-Brown (1964), who analyzed ritual weeping and who based his whole theory of social integration on the ritual expression of sentiments, taking the Andaman Islanders as an example. Radcliffe-Brown recorded the occasions on which the Andamese "sits down and wails and howls and the tears stream down his or her face" (1964, p. 117). The occasions for such displays include specific times after death. For example, at the end of the period of mourning there is communal weeping, indulged in by friends of mourners who have not themselves mourned.

The pattern of ritualistic weeping among the Andamese contrasts with that among the Bara of Madagascar. Huntington and Metcalfe (1979) reported that the Bara wail ritually only at funerals, and at only two specific times during the ceremony: While the body is lying in the women's hut before burial, and just before the secondary burial of the exhumed bodies. During preparations for burial and exhumation weeping is strictly prohibited. Different again is the pattern among the Thonga of South Africa. Junod (1927; reported in Rosenblatt, 1981) described the funeral procedure after the burial and prayer as follows: "The wailing begins. The women get on their feet and shout loudly, throwing themselves on the ground. The wife of the deceased cries more than anyone else" (Rosenblatt, 1981, p. 143).

Mandelbaum (1959) gave a detailed account of funeral practices among the Kota people, who live in a remote part of India. As in the above examples, public weeping occurs at specific times. Mandelbaum describes how the Dry Funeral begins. This ceremony is a second funeral held once each year, or every two years, for all those who have died since the previous Dry Funeral. Mandelbaum (1959) gives a compelling account of weeping behavior at the commencement of this ceremony:

Bereaved women stop in their tracks. A rush of sorrow suffuses them; they sit down where they are, cover their heads with their shoulder cloths, and wail and sob through much of that day and the next. Men of a bereaved household have much to do in preparation for the ceremony and do not drop everything to mourn aloud as do the bereaved women. But even they stop from time to time to weep. Most grief-stricken of all are the widows and widowers. (p. 193)

A final example of ritualistic weeping comes from Papua New Guinea. Among the Huli people keening begins when someone dies. Scores of women gather, as the news spreads, to join in. They gather at the *duguanda,* which literally means "crying house," where the body lies, and weep freely, bewailing their loss. Frankel and Smith (1982) describe the crying as intense and continuous. It reaches a pitch of anguish at the interment the following day. After the funeral those women closest to the deceased may return to the duguanda, sometimes remaining there for weeks and crying intermittently. Only women are permitted to do this.

As Frankel and Smith (1982) note, "In contrast to this intimacy of shared grief available to women, a weeping man seems a comparatively solitary figure. His fellows will try to distract him, jollying him along, and seeming to suffer some discomfort at his display of grief" (p. 303).

3.3.3 *Sex differences in crying behavior in other cultures*

The above and other anthropological accounts show that, as in the West, it is more often the women than the men who cry following death. Rosenblatt et al.'s (1976) analysis of the ethnographic literature supports this; of sixty societies which could be rated for sex differences in crying during bereavement, thirty-two were judged to have similar crying frequencies for males and females. In all of the remaining twenty-eight, adult females had a greater crying frequency than men. It seems that there is a culturally determined inclination of men in certain societies to suppress tears. This does not necessarily mean either that men experience less emotion of grief or that the sex difference is completely culturally determined: Bindra (1972) reported that men experience watery eyes significantly more often than women, whereas women were significantly more prone to have flowing tears. Further, Bindra suggested that greater amounts of lacrimal fluid released by young women may make it more difficult for them to suppress the flow of tears.

3.3.4 *The interpretation of ritualistic crying*

The above examples clearly show that, even though crying may occur in practically all societies, very different patterns of weeping following a death can be found. How can this be interpreted? One central issue here is whether the ritualistic crying that has so frequently been documented by anthropologists is actually indicative of grief, that is, of an emotional reaction of sadness. The impression from these accounts is hardly one of the spontaneous expression of feeling that we expect in the West. In contrast to the uncontrollable overflowing of tears that bereaved people here are prone to, crying in these other cultures often appears mandatory, and the individual appears to be in complete control of the production of tears. Are they really sad or are they indifferent?

Anthropologists have offered several interpretations of ritualistic crying. Their accounts reflect implicit theories of emotions which could be placed somewhere between the positions of James and Hochschild.

They typically assume some kind of interaction between ritual crying and emotional experience. Thus, Durkheim (1976) concluded from his early study of funeral rites of Aboriginal Australians that ritualistic weeping is experienced by the mourners with an emotional reaction of sorrow. Emotional feelings of sadness were not, however, thought to lead to participation in the funeral rite in the first place. Durkheim (1976) believed that the emotional reaction of grief actually developed and was intensified by participation: "Sorrow, like joy, becomes exalted and amplified when leaping from mind to mind, and therefore expresses itself outwardly in the form of exuberant and violent movements" (1976, p. 400). Thus the obligatory display is thought to lead to an emotion of grief. And by sharing the sorrow of others, commitment to them and to the group as a whole is confirmed. Radcliffe-Brown (1964) argued in a similar way that the sentiment of sorrow was not the cause of ritualistic behavior such as communal weeping: Mourners came to feel emotion through participation. But there is an important difference between the two theories. Radcliffe-Brown did not interpret the emotional response as one of sorrow at this point, but as one of a feeling of attachment between persons. He argued that it was the purpose of the rite to affirm the existence of a social bond between two or more persons (Radcliffe-Brown, 1964).

Other accounts of ritualistic weeping are at odds with either of these two interpretations. Henry (1964) and Rosenblatt (1981), who reported the former study by Henry, have no trouble in accepting the notion that feelings of grief similar to those in the West are observed. Henry (1964) described the death of a baby among the Kaingang of South America:

I was awakened several hours before dawn by the frantic keening of Waikome. One by one, others joined her, and I knew then that the baby was dead. As I watched, the emotion gradually grew more intense. . . . There was no play-acting here, no singling out of those whom relationship obliged to weep from those who could just look on. Those who were not affected kept aloof and performed their daily tasks. (1964, p. 66)

So which, if any, of these interpretations is correct? As they are not really contradictory, they could all be valid, the differences being either due to the perspective taken or to differences in the cultures studied. Thus, Durkheim's suggestion that ritual crying will intensify existing emotions would be quite consistent with our theoretical perspective. Furthermore, as crying also signals to others that an individual experiences grief, it could increase the feeling of attachment within a cultural group. Finally, the mourning rituals of the Kaingang may differ from those of the cultures studied by Durkheim and Radcliffe-Brown. If there were no normative prescriptions regulating crying, it is quite possible that those

Kaingang who cried did so because they were overcome by feelings of grief.

Unfortunately, it is very difficult to evaluate the validity of these interpretations given only the data presented by these authors. For example, one has no way of knowing from the anthropological accounts whether the Andamese or Thonga either feel sorrow during ritual weeping, or whether their grief may have caused them to weep privately or at other times which were not the subject of observation. At the other extreme, the account by Henry (1964) of the Kaingang clearly attributes an emotional response of grief as occurring during ritual wailing. This may be a correct interpretation, but it is also possibly a purely subjective and unwarranted interpretation on the part of one observer.

Attribution theorists (e.g., Bem, 1972; Kelley, 1973) have made it clear that when there are strong norms to behave in a certain way, personal attributions cannot be made. Thus, when mourning customs are strongly prescribed, no one can tell whether the individuals are play acting or whether they are feeling grief. We would argue, however, that the existence of cultural norms which regulate crying during mourning can also be used as evidence for the universality of grief. Norms are not ends in themselves, but typically develop for some reason. If there never had been any crying during mourning in a given society, it would seem pointless for norms regulating crying to develop.

3.3.5 Conclusions

The evidence presented above does indicate that crying is a frequent response to loss through death by some people in both Western and non-Western cultures. We have no reports of an absence of crying through indifference to the death of a close relative or friend in other cultures. The examples given above show differences in the occasions after a death on which crying is appropriate, tolerated, or even required, and in the type of crying that is exhibited publicly. But it is also remarkable how consistently, despite cultural differences, crying behavior occurs among bereaved persons.

3.4 Symptoms of grief particular to non-Western cultures

In reading accounts of bereavement in other cultures, whether preliterate or literate, past or contemporary, one becomes aware, as evident in the preceding sections, not only of responses general to cultures and of responses which typify only Western cultures, but also of the possibility of finding symptoms with which we are unfamiliar in the West.

3.4.1 *Self-infliction of injury*

One of the most obvious of these is self-infliction of injury, documented so vividly by Durkheim (1976) for Australian tribal peoples. Durkheim cites an account made by an ethnographer called Stanbridge:

... everywhere ... we find this same frenzy for beating one's self, lacerating one's self and burning one's self. In central Victoria, when death visits a tribe there is great weeping and lamentation amongst the women, the elder portion of whom lacerate their temples with their nails. The parents of the deceased lacerate themselves fearfully, especially if it be an only son whose loss they deplore. The father beats and cuts his head with a tomahawk until he utters bitter groans, the mother sits by the fire and burns her breasts and abdomen with a small firestick. Sometimes the burns thus inflicted are so severe as to cause death. (1976, p. 392)

It is striking how widespread various practices of cutting or mutilation of the body are, or have been, during mourning, even though not apparent in Western cultures today: Self-infliction of injury is recorded in the Old Testament (Jeremiah, Amos, Isaiah, etc.) and in ancient Greece, Assyria, Armenia, and Rome. It has been described for Africans, Abyssinians, Liberians, Native North Americans, Turks, Polynesians, and Australian tribes, among others (see Frazer, 1911, 1914, 1923; and, for a summary, Pollock, 1972). Despite variations, the basic pattern is very similar across the different groups, the world over and throughout time.

The significance of self-mutilation has been a matter of much debate (e.g., Huntington & Metcalfe, 1979). Are these acts of anger and aggression turned inwards (just another way of blaming oneself and showing remorse), or are they to keep off the spirit of the dead and derive from fear and dread of vengeance from above? Do they relate to inner emotions at all? Durkheim's opinion was that such rituals have the function of strengthening social bonds and confirming group solidarity though, as Huntington and Metcalfe (1979) query: "How can he claim that the violent, destructive, unplanned-for and negative behavior surrounding a death fulfills this sociologically Pollyanna-like function?" (p. 31).

Cawte (1964) maintained not only that self-infliction of injury still occurred among Australian Aborigines but that this was motivated by fear of blame, which compounded "true" feelings of grief:

A variant of reactive depression is the common-place aboriginal grief. After misfortunes ranging from trivial injury to the death of a dog, a group of natives is seen sitting in a ring wailing and lamenting. After a serious loss or a death, self-infliction of injury is still routine, and bears little resemblance to the attempted suicide common in modern western culture. In all this formal expression of grief, the recognizable motivation is fear of blame. When society attributes misfortune to evil-wishing by some person, extreme scrupulosity in mourning is necessary to disavow personal blame. The motive of wishing to avoid being blamed for the incident compounds whatever true grief may be felt. (p. 470)

If the interpretation of self-infliction of injuries as aggression towards the self is correct, then parallels can certainly be found in Western cultures. In this case, the overt expression would be the cultural variant, whereas the underlying emotional feeling (self-blame, anger, remorse, etc.) would be similar across cultures. Again, the emotional concomitants of the observed behavior need further investigation before firm conclusions can be made.

3.4.2 Horror at the corpse and fear of the ghost

Two further symptoms of grief in non-Western cultures are readily found in the literature. Anthropologists have focused on horror at the corpse (accompanied at times by a feeling of contamination) and fear of the ghost as being the dominant feelings of survivors. They (notably Wilhelm Wundt) have been criticized by Malinowski (1982) for assuming this "half-truth," and the point is well taken:

The emotions are extremely complex and even contradictory; the dominant elements, love of the dead and loathing of the corpse, passionate attachment to the personality still lingering about the body and a shattering fear of the gruesome thing that has been left over, these two elements seem to mingle and play into each other. (1982, p. 48)

Nevertheless, these feelings seem to be specific to certain non-Western cultures, with many of the reports coming from earlier times. The Hopi, for example, are afraid of the dead (Mandelbaum, 1959) and, like the Kotas and many other peoples, believe that death brings pollution:

The sovereign desire is to dismiss the body and the event. The urge is to dispatch the spirit to another realm where it will not challenge the Hopi ideals of good, harmonious, happy existence in *this* world and where, as a being of another and well-known kind, it can be methodically controlled by the ritual apparatus of the Hopi culture. (Mandelbaum, 1959, p. 203)

Further accounts of fear of the ghost of a deceased person abound, for example, among the Native American Maya (Steele, 1977) and Navajo (Miller & Schoenfeld, 1973). These are in contrast with accounts from the West, where fear of the corpse or ghost are not acknowledged among symptoms of grief. They would, in fact, probably be considered pathological here if overt or verbalized. On the other hand, until recently death was a relatively taboo topic and dissociation from the corpse was almost complete: Few Westerners, in comparison with those from other cultures, have actually seen a corpse (cf. Mitford, 1963). Further, in the West, even if people typically show no fear of the ghost or spirit of the deceased, great respect is felt toward them; no evil should be spoken of the departed, they are memorialized and prayed for.

3.4.3   *Conclusions*

Certain symptoms of grief with which we are unfamiliar do appear in certain other cultures. It is interesting to note that those described above appear not idiosyncratically for just one single non-Western culture, but for a number of cultures, as if here, too, one is observing a "core" response to bereavement. It is also notable that the manifestations of these symptoms can often be tied closely to beliefs about death and the afterlife. Finally, while the expression of grief may vary across cultures (due, for example, to these different beliefs), similarities in core responses (e.g., self-injury, with aggression toward the self) can be drawn between the non-Western symptoms described above and those found in Western cultures.

3.5   Phases of grief in cross-cultural perspective

As described in the previous chapter, bereaved people in Western cultures move through a succession of reactions to loss over the course of the weeks and months following a death. The "typical" sequence of phases among the bereaved in Western cultures can be summarized as follows. The numbness and shock of the first few hours or days is replaced by yearning, pining, and searching for the deceased. When the futility of attempts to recover the beloved person is realized, and this may take many weeks, despair and depression set in. This is a time of great desolation and feelings of hopelessness, when life seems hardly worth living at times. It is only very gradually that the bereaved adjust to life without the loved person and restitution and recovery begin to take place. In fact, bereavement researchers (e.g., Parkes & Weiss, 1983; Rosenblatt, 1981) have come to realize that the whole process of adaptation to life without the deceased may take very much longer than the calendar year that is typically regarded as the acceptable time for "getting over" a loss. Further, although symptoms may recede and greater proportions of each day be spent in equilibrium and even enjoyment, at later periods, too, it is possible for bouts of utter despair or yearning to recur.

Information from other cultures provides fascinating contrasts with the pattern of recovery outlined above. In some, not only are mourning practices rigidly and stringently laid down but the timing for inherent feelings of grief of the bereaved are also prescribed. In the following sections examples of very short phases of grief as well as of extended phases will be discussed.

3.5.1 *Abbreviated phases of grief*

One of the most extreme examples of abbreviated responses to loss occurs among the Navajo, which clearly demonstrates the "interplay between various psychodynamic mechanisms and cultural influences," as Miller and Schoenfeld (1973, p. 187), who studied this tribe, phrased it. A traditional pattern of mourning is followed not only by those who adhere to traditional religious beliefs but also by many Native Americans who are members of the Christian churches which have been founded on this reservation. The accepted pattern of mourning among the Navajo is limited to a period of only four days. During this period, and this period alone, is expression of grief and discussion of the deceased condoned. Even then, an excessive show of emotion is frowned upon by the community. When the four days have passed, the bereaved are expected to return to normal everyday life, not to grieve, and neither to speak of the deceased nor discuss their loss. Underlying this is the fear of the power of the spirit of the dead person and the belief that this can do the living harm.

It certainly looks from this account as though the Navajo recover from loss without the long and harrowing months of grief that are to be endured elsewhere. For these people, normal functioning is resumed at a time when bereaved people in the West have hardly realized the impact of their loss and would scarcely be in a frame of mind to do routine chores, let alone take up a full working and social life as if nothing had happened. Miller and Schoenfeld (1973) are, however, of the opinion that there is a high price to pay for this apparently easy transition through bereavement, at least among the Navajo. They argue that there is a direct causal link between prohibition of mourning and grieving and the occurrence of pathological grief reactions (notably of depression) among these people.

The Navajo are not alone in the brevity of their reactions to loss. Similarly abbreviated responses have been recorded for a number of other cultures (see, e.g., Mandelbaum, 1959; Steele, 1977; Volkart & Michael, 1957). The pattern found among the Navajo is, for example, not unlike that of another Native American tribe, the Maya; for here, too, at least in ancient times, the period of mourning and apparent grieving lasted a matter of days rather than months. Steele (1977) reported that this was a time at which the community sanctioned the display of intense feelings of loss and despair during the first four days of bereavement, as exemplified in profuse crying. But social pressure was brought to bear on the bereaved to delimit the mourning period and curtail overt expressions of grief beyond this time. The bereaved were encouraged by others to turn their thoughts and activities away from the deceased. Again, mourning rituals served the important purpose of "providing a safe separation of the spirit from the earth and the speeding of it on its journey to the other world, where the soul or spirit would be of no danger to the living" (Steele, 1977, p. 1065). A widow would become "unclean" on the death of her husband, and remain so as long as the tie to the deceased remained. Pressure was therefore strong for the rituals to be completed and the widow's time of uncleanliness to be over.

A final example of abbreviated grief is worth considering because of the contrast with the above examples and with phases in the West. The Samoans, whose key value is reciprocity, were reported by Ablon (1971) to recover rapidly and comparatively painlessly from loss of loved ones, even when, as Ablon observed, this followed a sudden and disastrous fire. Some five years after this catastrophic event Ablon questioned the bereaved retrospectively on their grief experiences, using items derived from Lindemann's (1944) account of grief in the West. While, not surprisingly, little active grief was elicited, due to the time interval since the catastrophe, what was remarkable was the Samoans' reactions to Lindemann's items. Ablon was repeatedly told that Samoans "do not have these things" and that there was no widespread depression among bereaved persons. The implication of this is that Samoans, in contrast to the Navajo, do not suffer the risk of pathological grief due to the shortness of the grieving period.

3.5.2 *Protracted phases of grief*

Far more protracted are the phases of readjustment among the Kota of south India. These people still, to a large extent, follow the ancient forms of funeral rites of their culture, which required two funeral ceremonies, the so-called Green and Dry Funerals. Interestingly, the terms "green" and "dry" are analogous to a cut plant. The first funeral, held shortly after the death when the body is cremated, is called "green" because the loss is new in the minds of the bereaved and a fresh experience to them. The second ceremony usually takes place at annual intervals and is a large and extended ceremony (lasting eleven days) for all those who have died since the previous one. It is termed "dry" because by then the loss is dried up, withered, or sere. Thus, these terms seem analogous too to psychological reactions of severence from the deceased.

Certainly, the Dry Funeral marks the ending of the sanctioning of grief. The ceremony provides ample opportunity for the venting of sorrow, which, Mandelbaum (1959) suggests, may help the bereaved to overcome their grief. After a first phase in which the deceased are individually memorialized, and one during which a second cremation is enacted (when low voices and pervasive sadness characterize the atmosphere) there is an abrupt ending of the mood of somberness. When the morning star is sighted by those at the funeral place, dancing and feasting suddenly begin, and the widowed perform a number of rituals each of which bring them back more closely to normal social life. When night falls a pot is ceremoniously broken, the mourners return quickly to their village, and the widowed have sexual intercourse, preferably with a sibling of the dead spouse. This signifies a further normalization in social relationships of the widowed. Mandelbaum (1959), in detailing such roles and prescriptions for behavior among the Kota, emphasized how they served an important function in bringing the bereaved through their shock and sorrow and back to a normal status in the society. Although the bereaved are encouraged to let their grief have overt expression, the period for indulging this is limited far more specifically and stringently than is normal practice in the West.

That the Kota Indians grieve for their dead is evident to Mandelbaum (1959), who describes the widowed as shocked and disoriented by loss, as being bewildered and withdrawn from others. Personal sorrow is felt, though its expression is culturally stereotyped and clearly prescribed across time, as are the newly widowed role requirements. There are, then, both notable similarities and notable differences with Western cultures in the phases through which the grief-stricken Kota pass.

Like Mandelbaum (1959), Mathison (1970) also related favorable adjustment to loss of a loved one to the more structured ritualized role of the widowed in non-Western cultures. The role provided for widows in the Trobriand Islands, for example, was regarded as serving as an "effective emotional release." Mathison described the first phase of grief among these islanders as encompassing the several days of funeral rites, during which the widow is expected to howl loudly with grief and shave her head. Following this stage, she enters a cage built into her home, and

remains in the dark there for a period of six months to two years, in order
to avoid her husband's ghost from finding her. Maladaptive as this may
seem to us, she is never left alone, and at the end of the prescribed period
she can anticipate a ceremonial cleansing, being attired in a colorful grass
skirt, and being free again to remarry, which, we are told, very often happens. Mathison (1970) comments on this healthy situation as follows:

The widow has the comfort of a highly structured period of mourning in which
she knows exactly what response society expects of her. She is given a socially
accepted way to express grief openly. Though she has lost one role, she is supplied
with another very formal role to play out for a definite period of time. She can
then look forward to assuming the role of wife again with the approval of her
kinsmen and peers. (p. 209)

Among the most highly prescribed sequences of mourning rituals are
those of Orthodox Jews. The length of time traditionally permitted for
completion of mourning is a calendar year, after which the bereaved are
expected to return to a more normal social life. Jewish customs have been
described as highly supportive for the bereaved, as they detail in almost
every particular just how the bereaved person should behave. In line with
this clear prescription of behavior, Gorer (1965) found that the Orthodox
Jewish community in Britain stood alone as one which knew how to con-
sole a bereaved person on first contact after loss. The mourner is greeted
with a standard phrase expressing condolence and this demands no reply;
after it has been spoken the conversation proceeds normally.

Pollock (1972) goes so far as to suggest that each of the several stages
of mourning prescribed by the Jewish religion can be related to one of the
psychological phases through which healthy grieving progresses. It is certainly true to say that the bereaved are assisted both by the family and
the community to face loss. Strict laws and rituals exist not only for the
bereaved but also for their comforters, the latter role being frequently
praised in the Torah. Thus, for example, the seven days of mourning after
the burial, called the "Shiva," is a time when the family is united, the
mourners generally being gathered in one dwelling, namely, "The House
of Shiva." This is a period of lamentation and weeping, when friends
come to express concern, share their sorrow and give companionship.
The bereaved are encouraged to talk of their loss and are offered comfort.
This process of grieving is considered beneficial (Goldberg, 1981). The
following period, called the "Sheloshim," which covers the thirty days
after burial, provides a transition for mourners to return to more active
involvement in community affairs. The end of this period marks the end
of ritual mourning. Finally, the "Unveiling" at the end of thirty days is a
commemorative service and the formal dedication of the stone to the

deceased. This service indicates that the soul of the deceased has been redeemed and it signifies the official closure of the mourning period (Goldberg, 1981). However, this does not mean that the loved one will be forgotten. The expression of grief is encouraged on anniversaries and on certain holidays, and it is considered normal to dwell on and to relate memories of the departed at times of joy and sadness. The community continues to support the bereaved at these times, although excessive grief is frowned upon.

3.5.3 Conclusions

Given only these few examples, it is evident that there are substantial differences in the rules laid down by cultures as to how long the deceased should be grieved over and how long mourning should last. Grief is channeled in all cultures along specified lines. Anthropologists have frequently observed that among the few universal practices pertaining across all cultures are those which dispose of the deceased and prescribe mourning behavior for the survivors. But what is sanctioned or prohibited in one culture may differ diametrically from what is or is not permitted in another.

That the individual emotional response of grief to loss is influenced and also, to some extent, ritualized by mourning rites is generally accepted by the social anthropologists who have provided most of the information. We have no way of knowing, however, whether a Navajo or a Samoan widow who, after four days of mourning and grieving apparently puts her loss behind her and returns to normal daily routine life, actually succeeds in grieving no more. What one can say, quite unequivocally, is that the phases of mourning and the overt expression of grief across the duration of bereavement are not universal.

3.6 Cultural variables and differences in the duration of grief

It becomes evident from the preceding examples of differences in the duration of grief, that factors such as attitudes towards death, religious beliefs, or persisting ties or bonding with the deceased are generally employed in explanation of differences in the duration of grief. These variables all have to do with the meaning that the loss has for bereaved persons in a particular culture. However, as follows from some of the theoretical approaches described at the beginning of the chapter, others have focused on the possibility that the performance of prescribed bereavement rituals themselves have an impact on the duration and course that grief will take. A third group of variables reflects cultural difference in social support during bereavement. Clearly, these three types of explanation are neither mutually exclusive nor are they contradictory. Because researchers have tended to focus on the one or the other type of cultural variable, they are considered separately below.

3.6.1   *The personal meaning of loss*

In Western cultures the bond that is felt with the deceased person by their bereaved is not relinquished easily or quickly. Understanding the process through which it is considered necessary to go to sever this tie has been given a place of central importance by theorists in the field, notably, Freud (1917), Lindemann (1944), and Bowlby (1981). The period of searching for the deceased is understood in terms of attempts to recover the lost object and retain the tie; constant talking of the deceased, recalling joint experiences, hearing his or her voice or movements around the house, preparing things unwittingly (setting the table for two), treasuring possessions and photos, are all seen as indications of a fundamental desire not to relinquish the bond with the lost person.

Natural though this bonding seems to us, it is by no means universally found, and systematic differences in patterns of grief can be related to cultural differences in the personal meaning of loss. This is illustrated by contrasting two very different cultural groups, the Hopi and the Japanese. Among the Hopi of Arizona the funeral ceremony, in contrast with other ceremonies which are held with great elaboration, is a small and meager affair, conducted and forgotten as quickly as possible. The reason for this is that the Hopi dislike and are afraid of death and the dead. After the burial service the survivors try to forget the deceased and carry on life as usual. This too is in accordance with their general beliefs about the afterworld. Many rituals are performed for the express purpose of breaking off contact between mortals and spirits.

In this context their strong desire to forget the deceased as individuals becomes understandable. They in fact express no desire whatsoever to recall the memory of a deceased person for any reason at all. Certainly, no occasion is given for singing the praises or recounting the contribution of the deceased person to the society: "The sovereign desire is to dismiss the body and the event" (Mandelbaum, 1959, p. 203).

Quite different is the meaning of loss and its impact on personal adjustment of survivors that is found in Japan. Both in Shintoism, the indigenous religion of the country, and in Buddhism, which is also widely practiced, the deceased become ancestors. In the Shinto religion the deceased become *Kami-sama. Kami* means god, or divine. As Yamamoto (1970) explained, the significance for the bereaved of the belief that the deceased become ancestors is that they can maintain contact with the departed person: "The ancestor remains accessible, the mourner can talk to the ancestor, he can offer goodies such as food or even cigars, altogether the ancestor is revered, fed, watered, and remains with the bereaved" (p. 181). Contact with the deceased in this way is facilitated by the presence in practically all homes of an altar, where the ancestor is worshipped (or, more accurately, revered).

Yamamoto (1970) attributed the relatively easy acceptance of loss among the Japanese widows, as compared with those in Western cultures, to the belief in an afterlife for the deceased, and to the cultivation of the sense of their continued presence as ancestors.

These two examples illustrate that identification mechanisms are closely bound to a society's beliefs about the meaning of life and death, and the nature of the afterlife. But these are not the only mechanisms underlying cultural differences in the meaning of loss. For not only is the tie to the deceased closely related to these beliefs, but also to the extent of dependency on the deceased and the availability of others after death as replacements. Volkart and Michael (1957) cite an example of the Ifaluk, a Micronesian culture, among whom the immediate family is less central in the upbringing of children than is typically found elsewhere. Grief for family members is keenly felt, but of short duration, ending usually with the funeral. Likewise, in contrast to societies such as the traditional Japanese described above, where veneration of the deceased is expected of the widowed, are those which provide for an early replacement of loss and continuity of the role of wife. Among the Ubena tribes in Africa, where the widowed are provided with new mates on the death of their husbands, grief, though genuinely felt, is also short-lived (Culwick & Culwick, 1935, cited by Averill, 1968).

It is evident from research in the West that the trauma of loss or separation is greater, the more the attachment and/or dependency toward the lost person (Bowlby, 1971, 1975, 1981). What becomes evident from the cross-cultural variations described above is that cultural norms with regard to patterns of attachment strongly affect the emotional response following death.

3.6.2   *The impact of bereavement rituals*

Just as more attention has been paid to the description of mourning customs and funeral rites than to the cross-cultural patterning of the emotion of grief, so have theoretical analyses been directed toward explaining the social function of these customs rather than looking at their potential benefit for, or adverse effects on, the individual. Funeral rites have been interpreted as serving the social function of strengthening group solidarity (Mandelbaum, 1959), as reflecting and shaping social values (Geertz, 1973), as "rites of passage" by incorporating individuals into the group and its culturally defined roles and statuses (Van Gennep, 1977), as ensuring continued social cohesion (Malinowski, 1982), and as social bonding (Radcliffe-Brown, 1964).

In contrast, early interpretations of grief (Freud, 1917; Lindemann, 1944) disregarded completely the potential impact of mourning rites and other social influences on the course of grief. With his critique of this intrapersonal perspective and his analysis of the role that society plays in assisting the bereaved through their grief, Gorer (1965) was largely responsible for a shift in interest of researchers in the field to a more interpersonal approach. Since then, the role that rituals play in dealing with grief has been emphasized by a number of researchers in the area of bereavement (e.g., Marris 1958; Firth, 1961; Eisenbruch, 1984b; Mandelbaum, 1959; Volkart & Michael, 1957). Most of these accounts claim that adherence to rituals moderates the bereavement reaction in a positive way, and many take the example of the United States as a culture which has become deritualized and which leaves bereaved persons helpless as to what to do following loss. This was argued by Mandelbaum (1959) in his chapter "The Social Uses of Funeral Rites." It is supported, too, by the study by Aguilar and Wood (1976), who claimed that Mexican funeral rites lead to good bereavement outcomes, and who criticized the impact of North American culture on Mexican patterns.

Salzberger (1975) similarly criticized the ideological and ritual deficits in the West, and pointed to the negative consequences for bereaved persons. Gorer (1965) drew attention to the fact that the majority of bereaved persons in Britain suffered long-lasting grief and depression because of the lack of secular rituals to help them and reincorporate them into society.

Pollock (1972), as noted above, argued that Orthodox Jewish mourning rites follow the "natural" grief process, that "cultural mechanisms . . . were probably derived from the awareness of intrapsychic needs of the individuals, singly and collectively, and the necessity for achieved social–psychic equilibrium through institutional regulations" (p. 38). It would be useful to know whether Jewish persons who adhere to these traditional stages adjust better to bereavement than those who do not.

That extreme brevity of rituals could also have negative effects on coping with grief was suggested by Miller and Schoenfeld (1973). In their study of the mourning rites of the Navajo, which limit mourning to a period of four days only, Miller and Schoenfeld (1973) argue that there is a direct causal link between the prohibition of mourning and an increase in the incidence of postbereavement depression among these people. Unfortunately, the evidence presented to support this suggestion is rather inconclusive.

Finally, a recent proponent of the view that bereavement practices affect recovery from grief (Eisenbruch, 1984b) has made a comparative analysis of bereavement practices of diverse ethnic and cultural groups in the United States. Eisenbruch argued that, while adapting partly to Western patterns, at the same time these groups adhere to the bereavement procedures of their own culture and that such a "deep cultural code" has implications not only for the course of grief, but for diagnoses of pathological grief and health care of the bereaved from different cultural origins. Again, little empirical data is available to support these plausible arguments.

In summary, then, although there is little empirical evidence, there seems to be substantial agreement that following culturally prescribed rituals aids recovery from bereavement. The absence of rites and rituals has been causally linked by many observers to increased distress, depression, and to poor ultimate grief outcome.

3.6.3 *The role of social support*

Others have explained cultural differences in grief responses, in symptomatology and outcomes, in terms of cultural differences in support systems. Melanie Klein (1940) was the first to draw attention to the role played by family and friends in promoting recovery after loss, a theme which was taken up by Gorer (1965). Lopata (1979), in a more detailed analysis, later argued that grief is more rapidly resolved in those societies where there is family and community support (or both), taking historical changes within the United States as evidence, rather than present-day, cross-cultural comparisons. Ablon (1971) considered patterns of social support in Samoa, comparing them with those in the United States and also concluded that grief is more rapidly resolved in cultures where there is family or community support for the bereaved.

These writers see social support as a buffer to the stress of bereavement. More detailed indications about precisely how social support helps the bereaved have been given by a few. Ramsay (1979) pointed to the importance of reviewing of death events in a social setting and the grief-work facilitation available in some cultures. Similarly Parkes and Weiss (1983) emphasized that encouragement of the overt expression of grief, which varies between cultures, goes some way to counteract delayed or avoided grief responses.

However, some (e.g., Amir & Sharon, 1982; Lopata, 1975, 1979) have also emphasized the negative effect that intended social support can have on bereavement recovery. In some cultures role expectations, social control, or pressure from the support group toward normalcy may be a hindrance to the resolution of grief. This is a point which Lopata (1975, 1979) argued convincingly. Working with the widowed in Chicago, she reported how undue pressure is frequently put on the widowed by informal support groups to normalcy regarding the behavior and timing of emotions. This can lead to much distress on the part of widowed persons if, for example, they feel unable to initiate social contact, conform to expectations, or follow the proffered advice.

3.6.4 *Implications of cross-cultural differences*

What is the significance of these cross-cultural differences in bereavement patterns for the theoretical analysis of the health consequences of partner loss? One way of viewing bereavement customs and beliefs in different societies is that they represent different attempts at providing solutions to the putative problems (mental and physical health detriments) brought about by bereavement. We later analyze the range of these problems (see Chapter 5; also W. Stroebe, Stroebe, Gergen, et al., 1982), categorizing them as deficits in social, emotional, instrumental, and validational support. Loss of these different types of outcomes is alleviated in a variety of ways, with varying degrees of effectiveness (with respect to the health and well-being of survivors) in the different cultures. One would predict from this model, that those societies with clearly defined customs and/or clear-cut beliefs about particular deficits would evince lower symptomatology and fewer problems with regard to that specific aspect of loss.

Examples in support of this interpretation are not hard to find among the above descriptions (although, as we noted, the psychological implications are drawn inferentially). Thus, the Buddhist or Shinto custom of ancestor reverence alleviates loss of the companionship for the deceased by maintaining contact with the departed relative as an "ancestor." Survivors accordingly reported a continued sense of the presence of the deceased and comparatively few problems with longing and loneliness. Or, the loss of a sexual partner is substituted among Kota Indians, on return to normal social life, by sexual intercourse with the deceased spouse's sibling, a provision which would be expected to ameliorate this deficit. Further, the dry funeral of this culture could be interpreted as a way of providing "closure" to grieving, a permission to the bereaved to stop grieving, which is lacking in Western cultures and may be related to chronic grief among the latter.

On a general level, it can be surmised that order or structure in one's life is lost when someone around whom one's daily activities revolved is taken away and that the very existence of such cultural norms concerning behavior following bereavement provides new orienting structure and a substitute, at least temporarily, for previous patterns of activity which have been disrupted by the death event (for a conceptual framework that addresses the *process* of cognitive change in terms of "goal" and "means" shifts see Kruglanski & Jaffe, in press).

3.7 Instances of the apparent absence of grief: Do they weaken the case for universality?

While practically all scientific investigations that we have found support the position that grief over the loss of a close person is universally felt, a few isolated accounts of reactions in certain cultures seem to indicate an absence of grief through apparent indifference to a death. Very different types of examples come to mind. One thinks of reports of Iranian women, who are said in some cases to be happily proud when their children die "in the name of Allah." Different again is the behavior of the Irish at a wake, a "mourning" ceremony which is anything but a subdued, harrowing occasion and is little marked by displays of the emotion of grief. These examples do not seriously challenge the claim for the universality of grief in the form we have argued, since we have stressed the cultural patterning of the emotion. Thus, as Flesch (1969) describes it, the "traditional Irish wake and funeral required strict adherence to an established pattern, down to the actual words and wailing which followed the corpse to the grave" (p. 237). With regard to reports of Iranian women, it would be consistent with our earlier discussion if the fact that one's son is considered to have died a "heroic death" for a "worthwhile cause" should soften the blow of the loss and that at times pride might outweigh feelings of grief. However, the absence of expressions of grief could also be the result of social pressure against the public display of grief which might be believed to undermine the war effort.

There is one account in the literature, however, which is sufficiently detailed to challenge the claim for the universality of grief, the description of the Ik, given by Colin Turnbull (1972) in his monograph *The Mountain People*. According to Turnbull, the Ik simply abandon their dead by the roadside as if no affection had been felt and no grief experienced on their loss: "I had seen no evidence of family life. . . . I had seen no sign of love. . . . I had seen things that made me want to cry, though as yet I had not cried, but I had never seen an Ik anywhere near tears or sorrow" (pp. 129–30). However, there seems to be serious doubt among anthropologists about the validity of the description of the Ik given by Turnbull (1972). For example, Barth (1974) called Turnbull's account "poor anthropology in method, in data, and in reasoning . . . deeply misleading to the public it sets out to inform" (p. 100).

There are good reasons for arguing that grief is in a sense innate: As we noted at the beginning of this chapter, there are many species that show attachment behavior to other members of their species and considerable distress on death or separation. In certain cases cultural beliefs or norms "override" the natural grief reaction and dictate that a death is not responded to with grief. Thus we would argue that it is not indifference to the death which leads to an absence of overt grief but conformity to culturally determined patterns, whatever these in a particular culture might be.

3.8 General conclusions

The answer to the question we posed for this chapter, "Is grief universal?" cannot be a simple yes or no. On the one hand, we have argued that the available evidence supports the view that people in very diverse societies do experience feelings of sadness and despondency on the loss of a person to whom they were close. There are neither reports of indifference being the typical response to death of a friend or relative, nor ones of joy or happiness predominating. As far as can be said on the basis of nonexhaustive data, then, grief seems to be universally felt.

On the other hand, manifestations of grief in different cultures are extremely varied: Whereas in the West despair and depression and many other symptoms of grief last for months and even years, in certain parts of the world any overt sign of grief ceases after a matter of days and there is every indication that the trauma of loss is overcome in the space of a very short time. It appears that symptoms and phases of grief are modified very considerably by cultural factors, and, while no specific empirical examinations exist to test this more closely, systematic variations across cultural groups in social support and social norms, in funeral rites and in the meaning assigned to loss, can be linked with differences in the emotional reaction to loss. These cultural variants do, then, appear to have a moderating influence on the symptoms and phases of grief. We have suggested that these different cultural prescriptions may represent attempts of particular societies to come to terms with the deficits arising through a death of those persons who survive.

4   Depression models of grief

4.1 Introduction

That we should feel sad and depressed when we lose somebody we love is so self-evident that it does not seem in need of theoretical explanation. And yet, there are many aspects of grief which challenge our everyday understanding. It is difficult to comprehend, for example, that bereaved individuals are often so angry and aggressive that they alienate those who try to help them, or that some seem to search for the deceased, although they know that this is futile. A theory of grief should help one to understand these symptoms. It should also explain why the death of a loved person results in enduring physical and mental impairment for some people when the majority of bereaved individuals seem to be able to cope with the loss without such health deterioration. But, most importantly, a theory of grief should allow one to develop strategies of therapy to ameliorate or prevent pathological grief reactions.

There is no theory which fulfills all of these expectations. Traditionally, theories of grief have either focused on the emotional reaction to loss or on health consequences. Thus, grief theories can be divided into two groups according to their focus, namely *depression models* and *stress models*. Depression models, which will be described in this chapter, analyze grief as an emotional reaction to loss, although different approaches conceptualize the loss in different theoretical terms. Depression models help one to understand many of the emotional symptoms of the grief reaction. They also form the theoretical bases for therapeutic interventions. However, unlike the stress models which will be discussed in the next chapter, depression models contribute little to our understanding of the increased risk of physical illness following bereavement.

4.2 Grief and object loss: a psychoanalytic approach

4.2.1 *Mourning and melancholia*

The classic analysis of grief and mourning invariably referred to by any treatise on bereavement is Freud's (1917) paper "Mourning and Melan-

56

cholia." The ideas expressed in this monograph became not only the basis for the psychonalytic theory of depression, but also greatly influenced later conceptions of the emotion of grief. In view of the great impact of Freud's (1917) theory of grief on the field of bereavement, it is somewhat surprising to realize that grief as a psychological process in its own right was, in fact, never at the center of Freud's interest. In his paper Freud (1917) conducted a comparative analysis of mourning and melancholia (grief and clinical depression), to demonstrate that grief could serve as a model for clinical depression: Both are reactions to a loss, and both are characterized by depressed mood, loss of interest, and inhibition of activities. As indicated earlier (Chapter 2.3.3), Freud believed that the major difference between the two states was the absence in healthy grief of guilt, self-reproach, and of a lowering of self-esteem.

We know today that neither the evidence on clinical depression nor that on grief is fully supportive of this view: First, even Freud (1917) seemed to have encountered problems in identifying loss experiences in some of his own cases of depression and had to resolve this discrepancy by suggesting that the memory of the loss may sometimes be repressed. Second, as we pointed out earlier (Chapter 2.3.3), self-reproach and low self-esteem, thought somewhat more typical of pathological grief, are quite frequently encountered in healthy grieving.

4.2.2 *The psychological function of grief*

Why does the loss of a loved person lead to grief and sometimes to clinical depression? In psychoanalytic theory, as in behaviorism, individuals are assumed to develop attachment or love toward those persons who are important for the satisfaction of their needs. Love is conceptualized as the attachment (cathexis) of libidinal energy to the mental representation of the loved person (the object). The more important a person is, the greater the cathexis, or vice versa. When a loved person is lost through death, the survivor's libidinal energy remains attached to thoughts and memories of the deceased. Since the individual has only a limited pool of energy at his or her disposal, this cathexis to the lost object has to be abandoned in order to regain the energy resources bound by the lost object. To sever these ties to the lost object, the energy has to be detached by a process that Freud termed "hypercathexis" (Ueberbesetzung). Since the struggle to "decathect" the loved object requires the investment of additional free energy, it forces the grieving individual to turn his back on the real world.

Thus, Freud (1917) sees the psychological function of grief as freeing the individual of his or her ties to the deceased, achieving gradual detachment by means of reviewing the past and dwelling on memories of the deceased. The process of grief work is successfully concluded when most of the libido is withdrawn from the lost object and transferred to a new one. A persuasive description of the process of grief work has been given by the psychoanalyst Erich Lindemann:

> This grief work has to do with the effort of reliving and working through in small quantities events which involved the now-deceased person and the survivor: the things one did together, the roles one had vis-à-vis each other, which were complementary to each other and which one would pass through day by day in the day's routine. Each item of this shared role has to be thought through, *pained* through, if you want, and gradually the question is raised, How can I do that with somebody else? And gradually the collection of activities which were put together in this unit with the person who has died can be torn asunder to be put to other people. So it can be divided among other future role partners, who then become loved a little – not much, perhaps, at first – but become tolerable, with whom one can do things and have companionship. (1979, p. 234)

In other words, in this view grief work is essential to the resolution of grief: Going through this task cannot be circumvented if the survivor is to avoid a pathological development of grief. Further, it is noteworthy that grief work is seen very much as a task for the griever alone. There is little or no discussion of the role that others can play in helping the sufferer. In fact, since involvement with others could distract the griever, who should invest all his or her energy in the struggle to "decathect" the loved object, their influence might even be considered negative.

4.2.3 *Pathological grief*

Freud (1917) discussed clinical depression as the only form of pathological grief. The key to deciphering the processes leading to clinical depression can be found, according to Freud (1917), in what he believed to be the major difference in symptomatology between normal and pathological grief: the presence of guilt, self-reproach, and lowered self-esteem in clinical depression but not in normal grief. Freud (1917) argued that the real target of these self-accusations is not the self but the lost love object. The cause for this pathological development is the existence of ambivalence in the relationship with that person. Depression results from disappointment with a love object, withdrawal of libido from the object onto the ego, and identification of the ego with the object. Thus, Freud (1917) argued that the existence of ambivalence in the relationship with the lost object prevents the normal transference of the libido from that person to a new object. Instead, the libido is withdrawn into the ego: "the shadow of the object fell upon the ego." In other words, after the lost object is incorporated (introjected) into the ego by a process of identification, the hostile part of the ambivalence which had been felt toward the person manifests itself in the hatred and sadism which is discharged against the ego in self-reproach and self-accusations (Mendelson, 1982).

A few years later in *The Ego and the Id,* Freud (1923) abandoned the assumption that identification is only characteristic of pathological processes, in favor of the notion that any libidinal withdrawal from a lost object is accomplished by means of the ego identifying with the lost object. Thus identification with the lost object can now be assumed to be as typical for normal as for pathological mourning. This leaves us with ambivalence as the major cause of pathological developments. Although Parkes and Weiss (1983) present evidence suggesting an association between ambivalence in marriage and pathological grief processes, it seems unlikely that ambivalence will be the only cause of such pathological reactions.

4.2.4 *Conclusions*

Many of the assumptions on which Freud (1917) based his comparison of grief and clinical depression had to be revised by himself or others. Thus, the suggestion that guilt and self-reproach were symptomatic of clinical depression but not grief is inconsistent with empirical evidence (Parkes, 1986). The assumption that identification with the lost love object was exclusive to clinical depression had to be abandoned when, in the course of the development of his structural theory, Freud (1923) came to the conclusion that identification with a lost love object (the opposite-sex parent) played an important role in normal development. Finally, by addressing only one form of pathological grief, Freud offered a limited theory of pathological reactions to loss.

And yet, the paper on mourning and melancholia is a document to Freud's powers of observation. Although not exclusive to pathological grief, guilt and self-reproach are more frequent in pathological than normal grieving (Parkes, 1986). Furthermore, strong identification with the deceased can be considered an early indicator of a pathological development (Parkes & Brown, 1972). But even if these assumptions had been completely wrong, his daring proposal that a process as painful and aversive as grieving serves an important psychological function would justify the place of "Mourning and Melancholia" as a landmark in the development of the psychology of bereavement. The idea that "working through" grief is essential for a successful outcome to grief has had a persisting influence on subsequent theories and therapy programs, although, one must add, that this predominantly intrapersonal analysis biased subsequent analyses against examining the potential impact of *inter*personal processes on recovery from grief.

4.3   Grief and loss of attachment: an ethological approach

4.3.1   *Grief as a general response to separation*

The theory of attachment developed by John Bowlby (1960, 1961, 1971, 1975, 1979, 1981) integrates ideas from psychoanalysis and ethology. It offers a functional interpretation of grief but, unlike the psychoanalytic concept of grief work, it emphasizes the biological rather than the psychological function. Central to Bowlby's theory is the assumption that attachment behavior has survival value for many species and that grief as the negative aspect of attachment is a general response to separation. In his monumental trilogy *Attachment and Loss,* Bowlby (1971, 1975, 1981) presented evidence from his own studies with children (Bowlby, 1960; Robertson & Bowlby, 1952), as well as from the ethological literature, to support his thesis that the protest–despair sequence of phases observed in bereavement is a characteristic response of many species to the disruption of strong affectional bonds.

The first description of the biphasic response to separation came from observational studies of 2–3-year old healthy children, who had been separated from their mothers for a limited period of time to stay in a residential nursery or hospital ward (Robertson & Bowlby, 1952; Bowlby, 1960). These children reacted to the separation at first with tears and anger and with demands for the return of their mothers. This phase of protest, during which the children appeared to be still hopeful of a quick reunion, typically lasted for several days. Then the children became quiet. They gave the impression that they were still preoccupied with thoughts of their mothers and yearning for their return, but their hopes seemed to have faded. They were in a phase of despair. These two phases often alternated, with hope turning into despair and despair turning into hope. Finally a great change occurred. The memory of their mothers seemed to fade. Sometimes the children even failed to show signs of recognition when they became reunited with their mothers. If reunion occurred after they had been away and unvisited for weeks or even months, they were frequently unresponsive to their parents for hours or even days. When this unresponsiveness finally subsided, it was replaced by an intense show of emotion, of clinging, on the one hand, and rage and anxiety whenever the mother briefly left the child on the other hand.

For many parents, this pattern of behavior among toddlers will not seem unfamiliar. One vivid example was related to us by a friend, the mother of a 3-year old, who on returning from a journey was surprised to discover that her delight at the reunion with her young son appeared to be far from mutual. He ignored her completely. Hoping to break the ice, she gave him the small clockwork mouse (a much longed-for toy) that she had purchased as a gift for him. This was, without comment, lifted by the tail, carried to the wastepaper basket, and ceremoniously dropped in. The mother took it as a sign of forgiveness and restored well-being when her young son, a few days later, finally rescued his toy mouse and played happily with it from then on.

In the sixties and seventies observations similar to those of Bowlby were reported from studies with primates, conducted mainly by Harry Harlow and his colleagues at the Psychology Primate Laboratory of the University of Wisconsin (for reviews, see Harlow & Mears, 1979; Mineka & Suomi, 1978). In one of the early studies Seay, Hansen, and Harlow (1962) observed 6-month-old rhesus monkeys, separated from their mothers for a three-week period. During this time the mother–infant pair could see each other through a Plexiglas barrier but could not contact each other. Seay et al. reported that the infants at first reacted with extreme signs of protest, even trying to break through the barrier. But within a few days the infants' behavior changed; they became lethargic and socially withdrawn.

These findings were replicated in other studies which used a somewhat different procedure. For example, Hinde, Spencer-Booth, and Bruce (1966) raised rhesus monkeys for the first six months of their lives in pens containing mothers, peers, and an adult male. When the mothers were removed from the pen for several days, the infants showed the characteristic biphasic sequence of protest and despair.

According to Bowlby (1971) one of the major functions served by an attachment object, particularly a mother, is that of providing a base of security from which the individual can explore the environment. Whenever an infant is confronted with a frightening stimulus, it not only withdraws but it also retreats toward the attachment object. When the attachment object is gone, there is no longer any secure base to which to retreat in the presence of frightening stimuli. Under these conditions, being separated from one's attachment object can be terrifying. This, according to Bowlby, is the reason why distress is such a universal reaction to the separation from an attachment object.

4.3.2   The biological function of grief and attachment

The observation of grieflike reactions to separation from attachment figures in primates as well as in humans tends to support Bowlby's thesis
that these responses have biological roots. It is indeed plausible that an
aversive reaction to separation would increase the survival chances of
animals that live in herds, since predators tend to attack animals that are
for some reason separated from their herd. Bowlby makes a very persuasive case for this argument:

In the wild to lose contact with the immediate family group is extremely danger-
ous, especially for the young. It is, therefore, in the interests of both individual
safety and species reproduction that there should be strong bonds tying together
the members of a family or of an extended family; and this requires that every
separation, however brief, should be responded to by an immediate, automatic,
and strong effort both to recover the family, especially the member to whom
attachment is closest, and to discourage that member from going away again. For
this reason, it is suggested, the inherited determinants of behaviour (often termed
instinctual) have evolved in such a way that the standard responses to loss of
loved persons are always urges to recover them and to scold them. (Bowlby, 1979,
p. 53)

This attachment behavior is activated by two conditions: *separation*
and *threat*. When the child feels threatened it will run to the mother;
when the child is separated from the mother it will experience separation
anxiety. When the attachment system is intensely activated, nothing but
physical contact with the mother can terminate the chain of behavior.
However, the intensity of distress aroused by a potentially threatening
situation does not only depend on the actual presence or absence of
attachment figure, but also on the person's confidence that an attachment
figure not actually present will nevertheless be accessible and responsive,
should the need arise. Bowlby argued that the confidence of a person in
the accessibility of an attachment figure reflects his or her own past experience. He further suggested that the period between 5 months to 6 years,
during which attachment behavior is most readily activated, is also the
most sensitive for the development of expectations regarding the availability of attachment figures.

4.3.3   Normal and pathological grief

Attachment theory conceptualizes grief as a form of separation anxiety in
adulthood that results from the disruption of an attachment bond
through loss. It thus offers a plausible explanation for several symptoms
of normal grief which are otherwise difficult to understand. Thus, search-

ing for the lost attachment figure and being angry about his or her neglectful behavior, although dysfunctional when a separation is permanent, can
be understood as automatic reactions to separation which in cases of
retrievable loss serve the useful function of establishing and mainitaining
proximity to the lost person. As Bowlby argued, "If . . . the urges to
recover and scold are automatic responses built into the organism, it follows that they will come into action in response to *any* and *every* loss and
without discriminating between those that are really retrievable and
those, statistically rare, that are not" (Bowlby, 1979, p. 53).

Whether an individual reacts to loss with normal grief responses or
develops one of the variants of pathological grief depends, according to
Bowlby (1979, 1981), on certain childhood experiences, in particular the
pattern of parental attachment behavior (see also, Belitsky & Jacobs,
1986). Bowlby distinguished three disordered forms of attachment: *anxious attachment, compulsive self-reliance,* and *compulsive care-giving,*
which he related to "certain common variations in the ways in which
parents perform their roles" (Bowlby, 1979, p. 135). Bowlby (1975) presented evidence from observational studies of children to support the
hypothesis that individuals whose childhood has been characterized by
parental rejection, discontinuities of parenting, threats by a parent to
leave the family or to commit suicide become anxious and insecure. They
are prone to show unusually frequent and urgent attachment behavior in
situations where the behavior does not seem to be justified. They have
lost confidence that their attachment figure will be accessible when
needed and have therefore adopted the strategy of remaining in close
proximity in order to assure that the attachment figure will be available.

Bowlby assumed that the "pathogenic parenting" received by these
individuals has a pervasive influence on their later relationships and also
on the way in which they react to the loss of an attachment figure. Thus,
adults whose childhoods, for the reasons outlined earlier, were characterized by anxious attachment to their parents are particularly likely to be
insecurely attached to, and overdependent on their marriage partners. In
bereavement, these individuals are liable to show a pattern of grieving
which we described earlier (Section 2.2.2) as chronic grief. Recently
Parkes and Weiss (1983) supported this hypothesis with evidence from
their study of a sample of Boston widows.

Individuals who are compulsively self-reliant have problems in accepting care and love from others and insist on doing everything by themselves whatever the conditions. There is little empirical evidence on the
antecedents of compulsive self-reliance. Bowlby suggested that this type
of forced assertion of independence of affectional ties, though in many

ways the opposite of anxious attachment, is caused by some of the same patterns of parenting. But these individuals react to these conditions by inhibiting attachment feeling and behavior and by disclaiming any desire for a close relationship. Compulsive self-reliers, on the other hand, are likely to deny their loss and to delay the onset of grief for months or even years. This period of delay is often characterized by strain, irritability, and episodes of depression.

Compulsive care-giving is a pattern of attachment that is related to compulsive self-reliance. A person showing this pattern may engage in close relationships but always in the role of a giver rather than a receiver of care. As Bowlby admitted, no systematic studies have been conducted of parental behavior which leads to compulsive care-giving. He speculated, however, that such individuals typically had a mother who, due to depression or some other disability, required the child to care for her and even to care for younger siblings. The relationship between compulsive care-giving and pathological grief is not very clear, but Bowlby (1981) suggested that these individuals may also tend toward chronic grief.

4.3.4 Conclusions

By conceptualizing the grief process as a form of separation anxiety, attachment theory offers a plausible theoretical interpretation of many aspects of normal and pathological grieving which have not been explained by other theories. Thus, attachment theory can explain paradoxical symptoms of grief like the urge to search for the lost person, the feeling of the presence of the deceased, or anger about having been deserted. It also allows one to identify antecedents of different forms of pathological grief. Finally, it can offer an explanation for the cross-cultural invariance in the core symptoms of grief (Chapter 3).

In focusing on the biological function of grief, however, attachment theory has little to say about its psychological function. As an aversive reaction to separation, grief is assumed to serve the biological function of assuring proximity with an attachment figure. Obviously, in the case of permanent separation caused by the death of the attachment figure, this response becomes biologically dysfunctional. Nevertheless, Bowlby fully agrees with Freud (1917) and Lindemann (1944) that it is essential for the widowed to work through their grief. Although we would concur with Bowlby in asserting the need for grief work, it is unclear how this prescription can be derived from attachment theory.

4.4 Grief and loss of reinforcement: a behavioral approach

4.4.1 *Behavioral theories of depression*

Behavioral theory, like psychoanalytic theory, has focused on depression rather than grief. However, due to the structural similarity between depression and grief, the behavioral explanations of depression developed by theorists like Ferster (1973), Lazarus (1968), and Lewinsohn (1974) (for a review, see Blöschl, 1978; Eastman, 1976) have much to offer to the theoretical analysis of grief.

Depression, as we described in Chapter 2.3.1, is characterized by a reduced rate of behavior, associated with negative affective states. It is therefore plausible for a behavioral theorist to view depression as the result of a reduction in the rate of response-contingent positive reinforcement (reinforcer-deficit). However, since the frequency of behavior can also be reduced by aversive stimuli, many behavioral theorists (e.g., Ferster, 1966; Lewinsohn, Youngren, & Crosscup, 1979) complement the reinforcer-deficit principle with the additional assumption that the reduction in positive reinforcement is accompanied by a parallel increase in aversive events. Thus, Lewinsohn et al. (1979) suggested that the experience of an increased rate of aversive events makes individuals less willing to initiate interactions and more likely to withdraw from interactions which, potentially, could have led to positive reinforcements.

Finally, to account for the nonbehavioral symptoms of depression, such as fatigue, dysphoria, and other somatic symptoms, Lewinsohn (1974) suggested that both the reduction of response-contingent positive reinforcement and the increase in aversive events act as unconditioned eliciting stimuli for these symptoms.

4.4.2 *The role of reinforcer-deficits and aversive events in grief*

Many of our everyday activities are coordinated with a small number of significant others and if one of these individuals is lost through death, then many of our usual responses will fail to elicit their customary rewards. This is particularly true for marital partners, who are likely to derive a sizeable proportion of their rewards from activities which are mutually interdependent. It is therefore plausible that the loss of a spouse leads to a significant reduction in the rate of positive response-contingent reinforcement for the surviving spouse. A widow may still set the table for two, expect her husband to enter the house, and plan joint activities.

Such behavior will fail to elicit the usual reinforcements and will thus be extinguished. Since extinction can be a painful and frustrating process, even for rats trained in a Skinner box (Amsel, 1962), it is plausible to assume that the extinction of a repertoire of responses which has been built up through years of common experience with a spouse, child, or parent should be exceedingly painful.

While many rewards are no longer available in bereavement, others, while still available, have lost their reinforcing quality. This can be due to endogenous biochemical and neurophysical changes (Costello, 1972), leading to loss of appetite and libido. Alternatively, it is also possible that some aversive environmental cues have become associated with a customary reinforcer and reduced its effectiveness. Thus, formerly favorite places (e.g., a restaurant, holiday resort) or activities (e.g., sailing, skiing) might now remind one of the deceased spouse and elicit sadness and dysphoria.

Finally, the loss of a marital partner is likely to be associated with an increase in aversive events for the surviving spouse. Thus, there will be lonely evenings and long weekends spent alone. There will also be difficulties and failures in dealing with those tasks (e.g., financial affairs, household duties) which had previously been the domain of the spouse and there will be anxiety about the future and one's ability to cope. Some bereaved individuals react to these aversive events with avoidance behavior. Thus, bereavement is associated with increases in the consumption of alcohol and tranquilizers. The most extreme escape behavior, suicide, is also more frequent among the bereaved.

4.4.3 *Variations in normal grief*

The analogy between bereavement and extinction suggested by the behavioral theory of depression offers a plausible explanation for a number of symptoms which are characteristic of grief. Thus, as Averill (1979) pointed out, there is some resemblance between the symptoms exhibited by animals during extinction (e.g., an initial intensification and later reduction of goal-seeking behavior) and the biphasic (protest–despair) response to separation and loss. Furthermore, a reduction of response-contingent positive reinforcement and a related increase in aversive events can serve as an unconditioned stimulus for feelings of sadness, fatigue, and some somatic symptoms. Finally, the reduction in reinforcements can explain the low rate of goal-directed behavior which is characteristic for both clinical depression and grief. The related increase in escape behavior can be accounted for by the assumed increase in aversive events.

Behavioral theory also allows one to identify a number of factors which would tend to modify the severity of a grief reaction. Thus, if grief is to some extent a reaction to the reduction of response-contingent positive reinforcements, its severity should vary with the magnitude of this reduction. Since the amount or quality of positive reinforcements which are lost when a spouse dies are likely to be related to marriage quality, behavioral theory would predict grief to be greater when a marriage was happy rather than unhappy. While this is a very plausible assumption, it is inconsistent with predictions regarding the effects of marital ambivalence, derived from psychoanalytic theory.

The magnitude of the reduction in reinforcement suffered in bereavement is not solely a function of the reinforcement lost but also depends on the availability of alternative sources of reinforcement (e.g., friends, relatives). Thus, it is possible that the survivor of a poor marriage, who has no alternative sources of reinforcement, experiences a more dramatic reduction in reinforcement than an individual whose marriage had been extremely happy but whose loss is alleviated by the loving support of friends, relatives, and neighbors.

The severity of grief responses should further vary as a function of the speed with which the reduction of positive reinforcement occurs. Since an organism is less likely to adapt to sudden loss of positive reinforcement than to a reduction which proceeds in small steps over time, behavioral theory would predict a widowed person to suffer more severe grief when the partner died suddenly (e.g., accident, unexpected coronary) rather than after an extended period of illness which slowly reduced his or her power to reward the partner.

4.4.4 *Determinants of pathological grief*

Since parts of the behavioral repertoire which are no longer reinforced should become extinguished and replaced by other types of behavior, grief reactions should weaken over time and finally disappear completely. As we know, this is the normal sequence of events. But sometimes individuals seem to be unable to cope with their loss and react with pathological patterns of grief. What are the conditions which lead to pathology, according to the behavioral approach, and how can these reactions be explained?

Behavioral theorists discuss a number of mechanisms which could account for the development of pathological grief patterns. Thus, an extended extinction process and an associated increase in aversive events may eliminate large sections of the individual's behavior repertoire to be replaced by escape and avoidance behavior. This would leave the individual with very little reinforcible behavior (i.e., goal-directed actions which potentially lead to positive outcomes). For example, if an individual satisfied nearly all his or her social needs in marital interaction and also dreaded entering social situations without his or her spouse, then bereavement could lead to the extinction of these social responses. Since the bereaved individual will now avoid social interactions, there is no possibility to rebuild his or her repertoire of social behaviors.

Another condition likely to favor the development of pathological grief responses is secondary gain resulting from playing the role of the bereaved. Thus, the social environment of the bereaved individual may positively reinforce behaviors and symptoms which are consistent with the role of the bereaved. If such reinforcement were to continue, it could lead to the development of chronic grief responses. However, it seems likely that after a period of time, when the loss should have been overcome (according to the norms and expectations of a given society), people may end their support for and tolerance of an individual who is still grieving, and thus further accentuate his or her depression.

4.4.5 *Conclusions*

Marriage is typically characterized by a high degree of interdependence between marital partners. It is therefore plausible that bereavement is associated with a significant reduction in positive reinforcements and at the same time, a significant increase in the occurrence of aversive events. According to the behavioral theory developed earlier, the reduction in positive reinforcement and the increase in aversive events have three consequences: They lead to a reduction in goal-seeking behavior, an increase in escape and avoidance behavior, and they act as unconditioned elicitors of feelings of fatigue.

Although the analogy between bereavement and extinction employed by behavioral theory seems to account for a number of the symptoms which are characteristic of the grief syndrome, it also has a basic weakness. Taken as stated by these theorists, there is no place for cognitions within the extinction metaphor. Thus, behavior should be purely a function of schedules of reinforcement and identical changes in these schedules should lead to identical consequences, regardless of the reasons which led to the change. This, however, is clearly not the case in bereavement. For example, individuals who are devastated when their partners die may have been quite able to cope successfully with extended absences of their marital partners, for example absences caused by business trips or hospitalization. And yet, in terms of changes in reinforcement sched- ules, there is no difference between death or absence. The crucial differ- ence between the two situations is in expectations. However, expectations are cognitions which should have no place in a purely behavioral theory.

4.5   Grief and loss of control: a cognitive approach

Extinction, where an organism's responses are no longer followed by the usual rewards, is one example of a situation characterized by an indepen- dence of outcomes and responses. According to the learned-helplessness model developed by Seligman and colleagues (e.g., Abramson, Seligman, & Teasdale, 1978; Seligman, 1975) animals and humans are likely to react to the experience of noncontingency between responses and outcomes with motivational, cognitive, and emotional deficits which bear some similarity to the disturbances observed with depressives. In the following section we will first describe the original and the reformulated version of the learned-helplessness model and then discuss the implications of these models for normal and pathological grief.

4.5.1   *Learned helplessness: the original formulation*

The original formulation of the learned-helplessness model was derived from escape-avoidance experiments conducted with dogs exposed to unavoidable electric shocks (Overmier & Seligman, 1967; Seligman & Maier, 1967). In escape-avoidance experiments, animals are placed in a "shuttle box," a two-sided chamber in which they can escape an electric shock by jumping over a barrier from one side of the cage where the floor is electrified, to the other side, where it is not. Normal dogs learn to escape the shock within a few trials, as do dogs that have been pretreated with escapable shock. But dogs that have been put through a situation in which they were made to experience inescapable shocks behave differ- ently. Such animals run around in panic in the electrified section of the box and finally lie down on the floor and howl. They do not seem to learn to escape over the barrier.

Seligman, Maier, and Solomon (1971) called this *learned helplessness.* They argued that the behavioral deficits of the dogs pretreated with ines- capable shock were due to the fact that, during the exposure to the ines- capable shock, these animals had learned that whatever they did, they could not escape the shocks, that the shocks were uncontrollable. The animals had learned that they were helpless.

To test whether uncontrollability leads to similar consequences in humans, analogous experiments were conducted with human subjects, too (e.g., Hiroto, 1974; Hiroto & Seligman, 1975; Thornton & Jacobs, 1971). Hiroto (1974) developed an adaptation of the triadic design, which was later used in the majority of experiments with human subjects. In the first phase of the experiment of Hiroto (1974), subjects were assigned to one of three groups. In the controllable noise condition, subjects were exposed to loud noise, which they could terminate by pushing a button four times. In the uncontrollable noise condition, they were exposed to comparable noise, which was shut off independently of the subjects' responses. A third group did not receive any noise at all. In the second phase all subjects were tested in a situation in which the noise could be terminated by moving a lever from one side to the other. The behavior of the subjects during this phase was very similar to the behavior exhibited by animals under the analogous conditions. While subjects who had either been exposed to controllable noise or no noise during Phase 1 of the experiment readily learned to terminate the noise during Phase 2, subjects who had previously been exposed to uncontrollable noise frequently failed to learn to escape and passively listened to the noise.

Seligman (1975) developed the learned-helplessness model as a unified theoretical framework, which integrated the data from animal as well as human research. The basic assumption of the model is "that when an animal or person is faced with an outcome that is independent of his responses, he learns that the outcome is independent of his responses" (Seligman, 1975, p. 46). This learning results in motivational, cognitive, and emotional deficits: If persons or animals have learned that the escape from aversive stimulation occurs independent of responses, they will be less motivated to initiate a response, will have great difficulties in learning that responses can produce relief, and will react to the traumatic experience at first with fear and then depression.

On the basis of the similarity in symptoms of learned helplessness and depression, Seligman (1972) later proposed learned helplessness as a laboratory model for the development of reactive depressions. He suggested that learned helplessness and depression are parallel in their symptoms, etiology, cure, and prevention (Klein, Fencil-Morse, & Seligman, 1976). Seligman and his colleagues (e.g., Klein et al. 1976; Miller & Seligman, 1973, 1975) attempted to support this assumption by demonstrating that helplessness induced in nondepressed subjects in the laboratory produced deficits in response initiation and cognitive deficiencies which are comparable to those shown by depressed subjects without helplessness training.

4.5.2   *Learned helplessness: the reformulated model*

The extension of the learned-helplessness model to depression raised a number of problems. Seligman (1975) had originally emphasized that it was the uncontrollability rather than the aversiveness of outcomes which was responsible for the motivational and emotional deficits. It seemed implausible, however, that people would get depressed because uncontrollable good things tended to happen to them. Furthermore, as Abramson and Sackheim (1977) pointed out, the view that depressives feel helpless is inconsistent with their tendency toward self-blame. If individuals believe that their outcomes occur independently of their responses, how, they asked, could depressed individuals feel responsible for these outcomes?

To solve these and a number of related problems, Abramson et al. (1978) suggested a reformulation of the learned-helplessness model, which changed the model from a learning into an attribution theory. Like the original model, the reformulated version assumes that depressed persons have learned that outcomes are uncontrollable. However, according to the reformulated model, mere exposure to current uncontrollability is insufficient for the motivational, cognitive, and emotional deficits to occur. For helplessness to be induced, individuals must also expect that future outcomes are uncontrollable. Whether current uncontrollability will lead to the expectation of future uncontrollability depends on the attributions an individual makes about the causes of the uncontrollability: "In brief, we argue that when a person finds that he is helpless, he asks *why* he is helpless. The causal attribution he makes then determines the generality and chronicity of his helplessness deficits as well as his later self-esteem" (Abramson et al., 1978, p. 50).

Abramson et al. suggested that these attributions could be classified along three dimensions. One dimension, which resolves the paradox raised by Abramson and Sackheim (1977), distinguishes between *personal* and *universal* helplessness. Thus, a father whose child suffered from leukemia and who recognized that there was nothing he or anybody else could do to help his child would experience universal helplessness. A student, on the other hand, realizing that he or she lacked the ability to pass an exam, would experience personal helplessness. Whereas the father should not feel responsible for the death of his child, the student who believed that the failure to pass the exam was due to his or her incompetence would accept the blame for this failure. Thus, the universal–personal distinction can explain an important aspect of depression, that of lowered self-esteem. Although depression can be caused by experiences of personal as well as universal helplessness, only the experience of personal helplessness leads to lowered self-esteem.

A further problem with the original theory was its lack of precision in predicting the range of situations in which helplessness would be felt or the duration of the learned-helplessness experience. To solve this problem Abramson et al. (1978) introduced two additional attributional dimensions, *stability* and *globality*. Stable factors are more or less permanent, whereas unstable factors are transient. Global factors generalize across a great variety of situations, while specific factors are more or less unique to the situation in which helplessness had been induced.

Let us illustrate these differences, using the example of a psychology student who failed the statistics examination. If the student attributed this failure to a lack of intelligence (personal, stable), he or she would expect to fail the next exam as well. If, on the other hand, the failure was attributed to lack of effort (personal, unstable) the student would hope to pass the exam, given sufficient preparation. Lack of intelligence is not only a stable, it is also a very global cause, which will lead the individual to expect failure in a wide range of situations. Alternatively, the problems with the statistics examination could be attributed to a more specific cause, like lack of mathematical ability. The student would then expect to do much better in all examinations which do not involve mathematical ability.

In summary then, the reformulated model suggests that people become depressed when they believe that desired outcomes are unobtainable, that highly aversive outcomes are unavoidable, and that they can do nothing to change this state of affairs. Whether or not they experience this as a blow to their self-esteem will depend on whether they blame themselves for the bad outcome. The generality and chronicity of their depression as well as of their loss of self-esteem will depend on the globality and stability of the characteristic seen as causal. The intensity of the motivational deficits will depend on the degree of certainty with which uncontrollability is expected, while the emotional and self-esteem deficits will depend on the importance of the outcome.

4.5.3   *Learned helplessness and grief*

The implications of the learned-helplessness model for a theory of grief are not hard to derive. When an individual loses a spouse through death, a decreased sense of outcome control is likely to be generated, which in turn will be accompanied by depression and cognitive disorganization. According to the reformulated model, the duration of the depression, and whether it will be accompanied by a lowering of self-esteem, will depend on the surviving spouse's interpretation of the loss. Thus, in the normal course of events, bereaved individuals are unlikely to blame themselves for the death in a global sense. They are likely to believe that there was nothing they or anybody else could have done to prevent the death, although they may sometimes blame doctors or nurses. Thus, the loss experience should result in a feeling of universal helplessness. The bereaved will be depressed but they will not suffer a loss of self-esteem. This, incidentally, is the pattern of grieving described by Freud (1917).

It is not so infrequent, however, that bereaved individuals feel some responsibility for the loss. They believe, sometimes quite irrationally, that there was something they could have done to prevent the death. They may feel, for example, that if only they had persuaded the spouse to go by train rather than car, or to live a more healthy life, or to stick to a diet, or to drink less, the death could have been avoided. This self-blame is typically accompanied by intense guilt feelings.

Bereavement research (e.g., Parkes & Brown, 1972) has uncovered some of the conditions which are particularly likely to induce self-blame. Not surprisingly, self-blame occurs particularly often after a loss due to suicide. Other antecedents of loss which have sometimes been found associated with self-blame and guilt feelings are marital relationships characterized by ambivalence, or the unexpectedness of the loss. The survivor of an ambivalent relationship may feel that he or she did not treat the spouse fairly. If the partner dies after a long illness, rather than suddenly, the spouse has ample opportunity to make up for anything he or she may have done to the spouse by love and care.

Feelings of personal helplessness could occur even if a bereaved individual believed that there was nothing anybody could have done to prevent the traumatic event. This might happen if the surviving spouse was convinced that he or she lacked the ability to cope with life unsupported by the partner. Thus, if the bereaved had been overly dependent on the partner throughout marriage (e.g., the deceased made all the decisions, managed the lives of both partners, and was the gatekeeper for all social relationships), the bereaved may feel unable to cope with life unaided by the spouse. This feeling of personal helplessness would be based on the conviction that without the deceased, he or she could not control the positive outcomes which were previously provided by that partner.

4.5.4 *Conclusions*

The death of a spouse and thus the loss of a large range of positive outcomes, which were previously provided or mediated by the partner, is likely to have a severe impact on the surviving spouse. The recognition that a great number of highly desired outcomes are no longer available, and that there is nothing the individual can do to change this state of affairs, is likely to lessen the surviving spouse's feeling of control. However, in the normal course of events, the widowed will realize in time that life without the partner is possible and that coping alone is possible.

There are a number of conditions, however, which may induce feelings of personal helplessness and thus lead to pathological grief reactions. For example, if the widowed blame themselves for the death of their partners, if they feel that they could have done more, that they were not as kind to their spouse as they might have been, the resulting guilt feelings and loss of self-esteem will make it more difficult for them to work through their grief without complications.

A second set of conditions which tends to induce personal helplessness is related to the partners' independence during their married lives. Individuals who kept some of their independence even during marriage, who had their own friends, participated in family decision making, were well informed in matters relating to family finances, etc., should feel more able to cope with a future without the partner than persons who had been completely dependent on the partner throughout married life.

4.6 Summary and conclusions

With the exception of attachment theory, the models discussed in this section have been developed as theories of depression rather than grief. However, since they all focus on depressions which occur in reaction to some kind of loss, implications for normal and pathological grief reactions are easily derived.

Each of these theoretical approaches is based on a different metaphor. Freud's *psychoanalytic theory* discusses loss and grief in terms of his outdated energy model. The death of a loved person is conceptualized as the loss of an object to which a great deal of energy has been cathected. Since individuals are assumed to have only limited energy resources at their disposal, this cathexis to the lost object has to be abandoned in order to regain the energy bound by it. The psychological function of grief is to sever the ties to the deceased. Grief work achieves a gradual detachment by means of reviewing the past and dwelling on memories of the deceased. Since this struggle to decathect the loved object requires the investment of additional free energy, it forces the grieving individual to turn his or her back to the real world.

Although the concept of grief work is very important, Freud can be criticized for his neglect of the influence of the social environment on grieving. The image of the grieving individual presented by Freud is that of a social isolate who, unaided by friends and family, withdraws from the outside world to work through a painful process of detachment from the beloved who has died. Although this withdrawal certainly describes one side of grief, it disregards another, more "social," side: Bereaved individuals seem often to experience an urge to talk to others about their loss and a need to receive condolence and social support.

Attachment theory discusses grief and loss in terms of an instinct metaphor borrowed from ethology. This theory offers a fascinating fusion of ideas from psychoanalysis and ethology. Like Freud, Bowlby sees grief as the emotional response to the disruption of the bond between the bereaved and the lost attachment figure. He argued that grief was not specific to loss through death but that the same biphasic protest–despair reaction could be observed as a general response to separation. Bowlby speculated that grief, as an aversive emotional response to separation, served the biological function of motivating humans and animals to stay near their primary group.

This assumption can account for several symptoms of normal grief which are otherwise difficult to understand (e.g., searching for the lost attachment figures, being angry about their neglectful behavior). The depressive phase of grieving can be seen as a special case of depression, arising as a result of the disorganization of behavior patterns, consequent to the loss of a significant object or goal in the external world. Since new behavior patterns adapted to new objects can only be built up if the old ones are broken down, the behavioral processes going with the depression can be seen as having an adaptive function.

One of Bowlby's significant contributions to the theory of grief was certainly to demonstrate that many of the important insights of Freud could be incorporated within a theoretical framework which was more acceptable than the antiquated energy model. Furthermore, Bowlby's approach moved the theory of grief from its purely individualistic focus to an interpersonal perspective. One of the implications of his theory is that the impact of loss can be lessened by forming substitute attachments. Thus Bowlby's work offers a theoretical basis for the explanation of the ameliorative function of social support.

By likening the bereaved individual to a rat on an extinction trial, *behavior theory* certainly employs one of the less palatable metaphors used in this area. It has to be admitted, though, that there is some resemblance between the symptoms exhibited by animals during extinction and the protest–despair response to separation and loss. Furthermore, the reduction in reinforcements can explain the low rate of goal-directed behavior which is characteristic of both clinical depression and grief. The related increase in escape behavior (e.g., crying, withdrawal) can be accounted for by the plausible assumption that bereavement is associated with an increase in aversive events.

The problem with the extinction metaphor, however, is that it implies that behavior is purely a function of schedules of reinforcement and that identical changes in these schedules should, regardless of cause, lead to identical consequences. This, however, does not seem to be the case in bereavement. Individuals who grieve when their partners die may previously have been happy when they could leave for a separate holiday or business trip.

For the *learned-helplessness model,* finally, depression or grief are the response to a feeling of loss of control, due to the experience of noncontingency between responses and outcomes. People become depressed when they realize that desired outcomes are unobtainable or that highly aversive outcomes are unavoidable, and that they can do nothing to change this state of affairs. According to the reformulated version of the model, the generality and chronicity of this depression will depend on the globality and stability of the characteristics seen as responsible for the loss of control.

As a cognitive theory, the learned-helplessness model can account for a number of aspects of grief that create problems for behavioral theories. Unlike behavioral theory, the learned-helplessness model can explain the differential behavior of individuals faced with permanent rather than temporary loss. Similarly, since the presence of ambivalence in the relationship to the deceased might affect the attributions surrounding the death event, the learned-helplessness model can also account for the fact that such ambivalence has been shown to increase the risk of pathological grief reactions (e.g., Parkes & Weiss, 1983). Since the deficit in reinforcement resulting from the death of a spouse is likely to be greater when the marriage was happy rather than conflicted, behavioral theory has problems with such findings. And yet, the approach to understanding grief offered by the learned-helplessness model is still very limited. While it is plausible that feelings of loss of control and the ensuing hopelessness play an important role in those forms of pathological grief characterized by depression, the model cannot account for pathological developments such as delay or even absence of grief.

5   Stress models of grief

5.1 Introduction

The death of a spouse is a stressful as well as an emotionally harrowing experience. Thus, by applying depression or stress models to the analysis of partner loss, we are looking at different aspects of the same phenomenon. While depression models construe bereavement in terms of loss and focus on the emotional reaction, stress models view bereavement as a stressful life event, that is, as an experience that overtaxes the coping resources of the individual. The conception of partner loss as a stressful life event integrates the study of bereavement into a body of research which has linked psychosocial stress to a number of health consequences and has isolated various physiological processes assumed to mediate these relationships.

The stress concept has been made popular by Selye's (1936, 1976) seminal work on the General Adaptation Syndrome, a pattern of bodily responses shown to occur whenever the organism is exposed to a stressor (e.g., intensive heat, extreme cold, infection). Although much of the theoretical foundation for this work had been prepared by Cannon (1929), Selye's research, which will be discussed in Section 5.2, has significantly advanced our understanding of physiological reactions to noxious environments.

The second major impetus in the advancement of stress theory came from psychiatrists, who, guided by the teachings of Adolf Meyer, began to study stressful life events as factors contributing to the development of a variety of psychosomatic and psychiatric illnesses. Basic to this work, which will be described in Section 5.3, was the assumption that psychosocial stress leads to some of the same bodily changes which Selye observed as a result of tissue damage. This essentially psychosomatic tradition generated clinical and epidemiological research (e.g., Cobb & Lindemann, 1943; Holmes & Rahe, 1967), which tends to support the assumption that experiences that increase stress also increase the risk of a number of illnesses.

77

The move away from a concept of stressors based on tissue damage raised a number of problems to which neither the physiological nor the psychosomatic approach could offer satisfactory solutions. Neither approach provides theoretical explanations as to why certain psychological experiences are stressful or how the organism recognizes such stressful events. These issues have been addressed by the third major approach, the psychological theories of stress (French & Kahn, 1962; French, Rodgers, & Cobb, 1974; Lazarus, 1966; Lazarus & Folkman, 1984; Lazarus & Launier, 1978; McGrath, 1976) which view stress as the result of the relationship between environmental demands and individual coping resources. In Section 5.4 two psychological theories of stress will be discussed.

5.2   The physiological approach to stress: the work of Selye

In his highly readable book *The Stress of Life* Selye (1976) described how, as a young medical student at the University of Prague, he was impressed by the fact that apart from a small number of symptoms characteristic of a given illness, there appeared to be many signs of bodily distress which were common to most, if not all, diseases. Patients suffering from the most diverse illnesses exhibited strikingly similar symptoms, such as loss of weight and appetite, diminished muscular strength, and motivational deficits.

It was ten years later, while doing physiological research on animals, that Selye discovered a set of nonspecific bodily responses which seemed to occur whenever an organism was exposed to a stressor, whether that stressor was a surgical injury, extreme cold, or a nonlethal injection of formaldehyde. He called this set of reactions the General Adaptation Syndrome (GAS). This is a syndrome of bodily reactions consisting of the following triad of responses: (1) a considerable enlargement of the adrenal cortex, (2) a shrinkage of the thymus, spleen, the lymph nodes and other lymphatic structures, (3) bleeding, and deep ulcers, in the lining of the stomach. Selye assumed that this response syndrome represented a universal pattern of defense reactions which served the function of protecting the organism's integrity (Cox, 1978).

The adrenals are two small endocrine glands situated above the kidneys. They consist of two portions, a central part (medulla) and an outer rind (cortex). Both of these synthesize hormones, though not the same ones. Hormones are special messenger substances produced by endocrine glands, which, released into the bloodstream, direct the functioning of distant organs. The thymicolymphatic system, on the other hand, plays an important role in the immune defense of the body.

Since the various changes of the GAS tend to occur together, suggesting an interdependence, further research focused on the way these glands influence each other and on the consequences of these changes for bodily functions. It appears that stress signals stimulate neurons in the median eminence of the brain to produce a hormone called the corticotropin-releasing factor (CRF), which then causes the production of the adreno-corticotrophic hormone (ACTH) in the pituitary gland. Released into the bloodstream, ACTH stimulates the adrenal cortex to produce and release a set of hormones called corticosteroids (cortisol, aldosterone, and corticosterone). Through a negative feedback loop, the release of corticosteroids normally inhibits the production of further ACTH. This feedback loop is overridden, however, under certain types of stress, and much larger amounts of corticosteroids are produced (Miller, 1980). Such overproduction of corticosteroids can cause an atrophy of the lymphoid structures, and thus lower the immune defenses of the organism. A second effect of stress is on the sympathetic adrenal medullary system leading to an increase in catecholamine secretion.

Selye (1976) suggested that these changes help the organism to cope physiologically with the stressor agent. If we assume that bodily injuries frequently occur in a context in which an animal has to fight or run, the activation of the *sympathetic adrenal medullary system* is indeed adaptive. Activation of this system leads to an increase in the secretion of two catecholamines, norepinephrine and epinephrine. Although qualitatively similar, the two catecholamines have somewhat different effects. Whereas epinephrine causes some structures to contract and others to relax, norepinephrine is nearly exclusively concerned with contraction. Broadly speaking, norepinephrine, which is released from the nerve endings of the sympathetic nervous system, does the routine jobs, such as maintaining a stable blood pressure (by adjusting the resistance of the small arteries). Epinephrine, on the other hand, deals with emergencies, when it can be released in large amounts by the adrenal medulla.

The release of catecholamines stimulates cardiovascular activity and raises the blood pressure. The heart beats faster, increasing the amount of blood pumped out with each beat. By constricting peripheral blood vessels and those leading to the gastrointestinal tract, the blood pressure is raised. At the same time, the arteries serving muscles (including the coronary arteries of the heart muscle) are dilated, thus increasing their blood supply. The pupils of the eye dilate, increasing the amount of light impinging on the retina. Catecholamines also relax the air passages.

Breathing becomes faster and deeper, the bronchioles of the lungs dilate, and the secretion of mucus in the air passages decreases. Thus, more oxygen is available for the metabolism. Catecholamines also cause the liberation of blood sugar from the liver, thus availing the muscles of large energy resources. One further effect, which is quite advantageous in cases of physical injury, is that catecholamines increase the tendency of the blood to coagulate. In summary then, the activation of the sympathetic adrenal medullary system prepares the body for action. At the same time, it inhibits digestion and excretion.

The activation of the *pituitary adrenal cortical system* leads to increases in the secretion and release of corticosteroids from the adrenal cortex. For the physiology of stress reactions, the most interesting corticosteroid is cortisol. Cortisol is important for the energy mobilization of the body. It promotes the synthesis and storage of glucose, which is one of the principal sources of energy in the body. It also, jointly with the catecholamines, mobilizes the fat stores from adipose tissues and increases the level of serum lipids (e.g., free fatty acids, cholesterol), which provide energy for skeletal muscles and myocardium.

A second major effect of the increase in cortisol production is its impact on the immune system. Pharmacological doses of cortisol have been shown to cause an atrophy of the lymphoid structures, and thus act to impair the activity of the body's immune system. The adaptive functions of this immune suppression is somewhat unclear. Since inflammation of the affected areas, one of the painful side effects of an active immune system, would tend to interfere with fight or flight responses, one could speculate that the prevention of such interference might initially be more important than the destruction of the intruding agent.

No organism can stay in a heightened state of arousal indefinitely. Reactions to stress therefore change over time. Selye (1976) distinguished three phases of the GAS. The activation of the pituitary adrenal cortical and the sympathetic adrenal medullary systems described above are characteristic of the first phase, the *alarm reaction.* In the second phase, the *stage of resistance,* the organism seems to have adapted to the stressor and the general activation has subsided. However, an extended exposure to the same stressor, to which the body seemed to have adjusted quite well, may "exhaust" the adaptive energy of the body (Selye, 1976). Then, the symptoms which were characteristic for the first stage reappear. But now they are irreversible and can result in the death of the organism. This last phase is called the *stage of exhaustion.*

There are two ways in which a stressor can harm an organism. It can either cause damage by exceeding its power of adaptation or by leading to the breakdown of an already weakened system of the organism. In the latter case, the harm would be a direct result of the processes marshaled in defense against the stress. Such diseases (in whose development the nonspecific stress effects played a major role) have been termed *diseases of adaptation* by Selye (1976). The ulcers, which form part of the GAS, should be conceived of as such a disease of adaptation. Similarly, the psychosomatic illnesses which seem to be related to an accumulation of stressful life events would rightfully belong into this category.

5.3 The psychosomatic approach

5.3.1 *The impact of stressful life events*

A decade after Selye's first short article on physiological stress responses appeared in print (Selye, 1936), Erich Lindemann (1944) published a classic paper describing the course and management of grief, as well as some of the psychiatric problems likely to develop in individuals who have experienced the loss of a loved person. Lindemann's (1944) study was based on his work with the friends and relatives of the victims of the fire at the Coconut Grove. This tragedy, which cost the lives of 491 persons, took place in the evening following the Harvard–Yale football game, in a Boston nightclub where people gathered to celebrate the occasion.

It is less well known that the first evidence that the loss of a person can be related to medical disease that Lindemann found came from his work with patients who suffered from ulcerative colitis, a severe and chronic inflammation of the colon, of which the cause is still unknown. Lindemann interviewed eighty-seven patients from the gastrointestinal service of the Massachusetts General Hospital and, although his findings were only published in 1950, he gave his first report to the Massachusetts Psychiatric Society in 1942, nine months before the Coconut Grove fire (see Lindemann, 1979, p. 21). In the course of these interviews, Lindemann was struck by the fact "that loss of security, especially the loss of another person of emotional significance, is frequently encountered as the crisis in human relationships which preceded the onset of the illness." He further emphasized that "the rupture of a human relationship may occur not only as a result of death but also as a consequence of being rejected, jilted, or disillusioned regarding the partner in the relationship" (1979, p. 22). Lindemann observed that in terms of this wider definition, seventy-five of his eighty-seven patients had recently suffered a loss experience.

Although it seems somewhat overcritical to suggest that this group of patients did not have more than a normal share of loss experiences, it has to be pointed out that this possibility cannot be ruled out, since a control group is lacking in Lindemann's study. However, even if he had examined a control group of, let us say, sufferers from appendicitis, and indeed reported fewer loss experiences, his results would still have been less than conclusive. The fact that the death of "persons of emotional significance" includes a wide range of people, and that in this retrospective study, the emotional significance was decided upon after the onset of the illness (by a psychiatrist searching for a psychogenic cause), leaves one wondering whether these reports may not have been affected by the expectations of the interviewer or by demand characteristics unwittingly conveyed to the patients.

Although much more sophisticated, most of the research studying the role of cumulative life stress in the etiology of depression (e.g., Beck & Worthen, 1972; Brown & Harris, 1978; Paykel, Meyers, Dienelt, et al., 1969) is retrospective and thus liable to some of the same criticisms. For example, Paykel et al. (1969) compared the frequency of life changes among 185 female and male patients treated for depression with those of 185 matched controls with no psychiatric symptoms. Several weeks after the onset of treatment, when symptoms were much improved, patients were interviewed about any life events occurring in the six months prior to the illness. The control subjects were interviewed in their homes and asked about life events during the six months prior to the interview. It was found that the depressed patients reported nearly three times as many important life events as the control subjects. When life changes were further categorized according to whether they were desirable (e.g., promotion) or undesirable (e.g., demotion), significant differences were found only with regard to undesirable changes.

Obviously, inferences about the noxiousness of stressful life events drawn from interviews conducted with depressive patients after the onset of their illness are problematic. Patients are likely to magnify events in order to justify their illness and interviewers may be biased by their own expectations and search more thoroughly for stressful events in the lives of depressed patients than in those of control subjects.

In a study conducted in London, Brown and his colleagues (Brown & Harris, 1978) attempted to reduce the risk of biased evaluations by a two-step procedure. Interviewers first asked for life events and then inquired extensively after the circumstances surrounding each event. These interviews were tape-recorded and then transcribed, to allow members of the research team (who did not know whether the person interviewed was a patient or a control subject) to evaluate the seriousness of each event. In support of Paykel et al. (1969), Brown and Harris (1978) observed a strong relationship between stressful life events and depression. Of their depressed subjects, 61 percent had at least one severe event in the months preceding the onset of their illness as compared to 20 percent of the control subjects.

5.3.2 *The role of life-event scales in prospective studies of the stress–illness relationship*

It is evident from the above discussion that the findings reported would have been more convincing if this research had been conducted prospectively rather than retrospectively. Since the illness is likely to bias a patient's recollections regarding stressful life events in the period before the illness, this weakness of life-change studies is not even remedied by the inclusion of a control group. Thus, the recommended procedure is to conduct such studies prospectively (i.e., assess life events before the illness onset). However, such prospective studies necessitate the evaluation of life events of a large sample of individuals, who are then followed to check whether those with more stressful life events are also more likely to become ill.

Since interviewing large samples of people is time consuming and expensive, prospective studies of the stress–health relationship became much easier with the development of an objective self-report measure to assess the incidence of critical life events (Holmes & Rahe, 1967). This questionnaire consists of forty-three items describing life-change events, that is, "events that signify transitions in a person's psychosocial adjustments" (Rahe & Arthur, 1978). The events included in this questionnaire range from such major life changes as the death of a spouse or detention in jail to minor breaks in routine like "vacation" or "change in eating habits." Since it was assumed that any event requiring an individual to deviate from his habitual pattern would be stressful, the questionnaire included pleasant as well as unpleasant events.

In the first version of this questionnaire, known as the Schedule of Recent Experience (SRE), the score consisted of the number of items checked, thus giving equal weight to a wide range of experiences (e.g., vacation and death of a spouse). Since it seemed likely that a major loss had more severe effects than a minor break in routine, Holmes and Rahe (1967) had the events included in the SRE scaled according to the magnitude of social readjustment such an event would require. Social readjustment was defined as the amount and duration of change in a person's accustomed pattern of life resulting from the life event, regardless of the desirability of this event. The resulting scale, which became known as the

Social Readjustment Rating Scale (SRRS), is presented in Table 5.1. Not surprisingly, death of a spouse was rated as the event requiring the most intense readjustment, closely followed by divorce. At the other extreme, "Christmas" or "minor violations of the law" were evaluated as rather mild upheavals. Assuming a cumulative effect of these life changes, the values of the events an individual reported for a given period of time were summed, reflecting the total life-change units (LCU) for that period. These life change units could then be related to subsequent periods of illness.

While the SRRS was first used in a great number of retrospective studies (e.g., Rahe & Lind, 1971; Rahe & Paasikivi, 1971; Theorell & Rahe, 1971), the ease with which it could be administered made it feasible to screen large numbers of people and thus encouraged investigators to conduct prospective studies. In one of the most impressive projects of this kind, Rahe (1968), a high-ranking officer with the U.S. Navy Medical Corps, assessed the changes that occurred in the lives of 2,500 Navy officers and enlisted men in the six months previous to tours of duty aboard three navy cruisers. These LCU scores were then related to shipboard medical records at the end of the six-month tour of duty. Individuals with LCU scores in the top 30 percent of the distribution were categorized as a high-risk group, those with the lowest 30 percent, as a low-risk group. Holmes and Masuda (1974) summarized the findings of this study as follows:

In the first month of the cruise, the high-risk group has nearly 90 percent more *first* illnesses than the low-risk group. The high-risk group consistently reported more illnesses each month for the 6-month cruise period and had one-third more illnesses during the follow-up period than did the low-risk group. (p. 65)

Similar results were reported in a study of a large sample of Norwegian sailors (Holmes & Masuda, 1974) and in a study of the crew of a warship on combat duty off Vietnam (Rubin, Gunderson, & Arthur, 1971).

Other prospective studies were, however, less supportive of the assumed relationship between life stress, as measured by the SRRS, and ill health than those cited above. Thus, Theorell, Lind, and Floderus (1975), who studied a sample of over 4,000 Swedish construction workers, found no relationship between stressful life events for a given year and mortality, hospitalization, or times missed from work for the following year. Goldberg and Comstock (1976) were similarly unsuccessful, in a prospective study, relating life events to death and hospitalization in two American communities.

Table 5.1 *The Social Readjustment Rating Scale (from Holmes & Rahe, 1967)*

Rank	Life event	Mean value
1	Death of spouse	100
2	Divorce	73
3	Marital separation	65
4	Jail term	63
5	Death of close family member	63
6	Personal injury or illness	53
7	Marriage	50
8	Fired at work	47
9	Marital reconciliation	45
10	Retirement	45
11	Change in health of family member	44
12	Pregnancy	40
13	Sex difficulties	39
14	Gain of new family member	39
15	Business readjustment	39
16	Change in financial state	38
17	Death of close friend	37
18	Change to different line of work	36
19	Change in number of arguments with spouse	35
20	Mortgage over $10,000	31
21	Foreclosure of mortgage or loan	30
22	Change in responsibilities at work	29
23	Son or daughter leaving home	29
24	Trouble with in-laws	29
25	Outstanding personal achievement	28
26	Wife begin or stop work	26
27	Begin or end school	26
28	Change in living conditions	25
29	Revision of personal habits	24
30	Trouble with boss	23
31	Change in work hours or conditions	20
32	Change in residence	20
33	Change in schools	20
34	Change in recreation	19
35	Change in church activities	19
36	Change in social activities	18
37	Mortgage or loan less than $10,000	17
38	Change in sleeping habits	16
39	Change in number of family get-togethers	15
40	Change in eating habits	15
41	Vacation	13
42	Christmas	12
43	Minor violations of the law	11

5.3.3   *Critique of use of life-event scales in life-stress research*

In a major critique of the research relating cumulative life-stress to ill health, Rabkin and Struening (1976) pointed out that most of these studies reported rather weak associations between life stress and illness, accounting at best for 9 percent of the variance in ill health. Furthermore, these authors discuss a number of psychometric as well as conceptual weaknesses of the SRRS. The one conceptual issue, however, which seems in particular need of empirical clarification is the assumption that it is the amount of life change rather than the desirability of the change that is stress-producing. For example, Item 22 (Table 5.1; change in responsibility at work) refers to promotions as well as demotions. Or, Item 16 (change in financial status) included improvements in one's finances as well as deteriorations. Since, in the true Selye tradition, stress is assumed to be caused by the need to adapt to new situations, including positive as well as negative changes, in a measure of life stress seemed to be quite sensible. However, Gersten, Langner, Eisenberg, and Orzeck (1974), in a study of a large sample of children, presented some evidence that the undesirability of life changes or even balanced scale (sum of undesirable events minus sum of desirable events), rather than the total amount of change, is a better predictor of behavioral impairment.

Another issue which has been raised by Mechanic (1974, 1978) derives from the fact that these studies of the stress–health relationship do not assess amount of stress or number of illnesses directly, but measure self-reported life stress and treatment-seaking behavior (in the case of medical records), or even self-reports of symptoms. Mechanic pointed out that treatment seeking is to some extent the end result of a complex process of inference, in which the prospective patient (or some caretaker) infers from a number of more or less ambiguous clues that a person is ill and that a physician should be consulted. While there are many instances where such symptoms are so clear-cut that everybody would consult a physician, there are numerous instances which leave a high degree of freedom to the individual, to either categorize oneself as slightly off color or as seriously ill.

We probably all know individuals with very low thresholds for treatment-seeking behavior. We tend to consider such persons as hypochondriacs because they consult their doctors for what we would classify as minor complaints. Since, furthermore, the items of the SRRS leave respondents a great deal of freedom in categorizing a given event as stressful (e.g., what kind of change in social activities or trouble with a boss is worth reporting and what is below such a threshold), it seems quite likely that individuals who consult their doctors for every minor health problem also tend to report minor upheavals as major life events.

This line of reasoning suggests that most of the findings indicating health deteriorations following accumulations of stressful life events do not prove a direct causal relationship. It is argued that the relationship observed between reports of stressful life events and visits to the doctor is due to some feature in the personality of the subjects studied (e.g., hypochondriac tendencies). A somewhat different interpretation takes the reports of stressful life events as real, but suggests that the visits to the doctor are motivated not by a physical illness but by a need to find help in coping with life stress. Thus, the physician is not consulted for purely medical counsel.

B. P. Dohrenwend (1979) suggested an even more direct contamination between personality variables and stressful life events as measured with life-event lists. Dohrenwend noted that these lists frequently include items that may reflect the physical and psychological condition of the respondent. If items such as "major personal illness" are used to measure stressful life events, then the event score is directly contaminated with concurrent health. In support of this hypothesis, Schroeder and Costa (1984) demonstrated that the correlation obtained between standard measures of life events and physical illness disappeared when "contaminated items" were eliminated from the life-event scale.

Thus, after the initially enthusiastic reactions with which the development of self-report measures of cumulative life stress had been greeted, researchers in this area have become very skeptical of these instruments. However, although criticism (e.g., Rabkin & Struening, 1976) has been rather devastating, it should always be remembered that these critical remarks are only directed at studies which employ *self-report* questionnaires to measure *cumulative* life stress. Thus, the research on the health consequences of bereavement (see Chapters 7 and 8) still justifies our belief that stressful life events play some role in the occurrence of illnesses.

5.4 The psychological approach to stress

By relating the incidence of illness to specific stressful events or sets of such events, the psychosomatic approach evaded the thorny issue of specifying why certain psychological experiences are stressful, how the organism recognizes stressful events and distinguishes them from positive events, and how interindividual differences in reactions to stress can be explained. These issues were addressed by the psychological approach to stress (e.g., French & Kahn, 1962; French, Rodgers, & Cobb, 1974; Lazarus, 1966; Lazarus & Folkman, 1984; Lazarus & Launier, 1978; McGrath, 1976) which viewed stress as the result of a perceived mismatch between environmental demands and individual coping resources. This section will discuss two theories, one general to all types of stress, namely, the cognitive stress theory of Lazarus and his colleagues (e.g., Lazarus & Folkman, 1984; Lazarus & Launier, 1978), and one specific to bereavement, namely, the deficit model of partner loss (M. Stroebe & Stroebe, 1985; W. Stroebe, Stroebe, Gergen, & Gergen, 1980, 1982; W. Stroebe & Stroebe, 1986).

5.4.1   *The cognitive model of Lazarus*

Stress as a person–environment interaction. According to a definition offered by Lazarus and Folkman (1984), "Psychological stress is a particular relationship between the person and the environment that is appraised by the individual as taxing or exceeding his or her resources and endangering his or her well-being" (p. 19). Thus, the extent of the stress experienced in a given situation neither depends solely on the demands of the situation nor on the resources of the person but on the relationship between demands and resources.

This does not imply that situations do not differ in the extent to which they are likely to be experienced as stressful. For example, driving a car through fog on an icy motorway is likely to be more stressful for most drivers than driving along a country road on a sunny afternoon. However, under each of these driving conditions, an experienced driver will be better able to cope than somebody who has only just passed his or her driving test. Thus, while the demands of driving on a sunny day with little traffic may already tax the resources of the beginner and thus be experienced as stressful, this drive will be a pleasant experience for the veteran driver. Fog and ice, on the other hand, are stressful conditions for most drivers, but while these demands by far exceed the capabilities of the beginner, they may only just tax the resources of the experienced driver.

Cognitive appraisal processes. Cognitive appraisal is an evaluative process which determines why and to what extent a particular situation is perceived as stressful by a given individual. Lazarus distinguishes three basic forms of appraisal, "primary appraisal," "secondary appraisal," and "reappraisal." In primary appraisal, individuals categorize a given situation with respect to its significance for their well-being and decide whether the situation is irrelevant, benign–positive, or stressful.

A situation is considered irrelevant if it has no implications for the person's well-being. Situations which promise to preserve or enhance the well-being of the individual are categorized as benign. If, however, a situation implies harm/loss, threat, or challenge, it is appraised as stressful. Harm/loss refers to a damage which has already occurred (e.g., an accident, in the above example), while threat concerns an anticipated harm/loss situation. Thus, driving on the icy road is stressful because accidents are very likely under these conditions. However, experienced drivers may consider this situation as a challenge to their driving skills and thus view it less negatively than beginners, who are likely to be terrified with anxiety as to what could happen.

Once a situation has been categorized as challenging or stressful, individuals have to evaluate their coping options to decide which strategy will be most effective in a given situation in achieving the intended outcome. Thus, the driver who runs into bad weather conditions has to decide whether to go on as before, to drive more slowly, or even stop at the next parking place to wait for conditions to improve. This assessment of coping resources and options is referred to as secondary appraisal. The extent of stress experienced in a given situation is the combined result of an interaction between primary appraisal of what is at stake and secondary appraisal of coping options.

The notion of reappraisal was introduced to emphasize that cognitive appraisal processes are in a permanent state of flux due to new inputs. Thus, the original appraisal of a situation may change as new information about the situation or about the impact of one's own behavior is received. The realization that one is quite able to cope with the difficult conditions or that the ice was only wetness will lead to a reappraisal of the threat by the unpracticed driver.

Coping process. When a situation has been appraised as stressful, individuals have to do something to master the situation and/or to control their emotional reactions to the situation. These processes of responding to stressful demands have been called coping processes. Lazarus and Folkman (1984) define coping "as constantly changing cognitive and behavioral efforts to manage specific external and/or internal demands that are appraised as taxing or exceeding the resources of the person" (p. 141).

Lazarus and Folkman distinguish two basic forms of coping, problem-focused coping and emotion-focused coping. Coping is problem focused if it is directed at managing and altering the problem that is causing distress. For example, a student who has to pass an examination will do everything to be well prepared. Classes will be attended, the assigned literature read, and other students who have already passed the examination consulted for information about the questions, etc. However, despite all these preparations, the student may be worried to such an extent that he or she begins to suffer from insomnia and lack of concentration. In order to reduce this emotional distress, the student may engage in a range of emotion-focused forms of coping. These may include cognitive operations such as attempting to reappraise the situation as less threatening. But they may also include actions such as taking sleeping pills, or drinking alcohol, to cope with the emotional distress.

Coping resources and coping constraints. The extent to which the situation is experienced as stressful as well as the individual's success in mastering the situation will depend on his or her coping resources. Lazarus and Folkman (1984) distinguish resources that are primarily properties of the person and resources that are primarily environmental. The person-resources include physical resources such as health and energy, psychological resources such as positive beliefs (e.g., positive self-concept, belief in control) and competencies such as problem-solving and social skills. Examples of environmental resources are material resources (e.g., money) and social support.

Individuals do not always make use of coping resources available to them. For example, old people are frequently reluctant to draw on the social support available to them because they are too proud to ask or because they do not want to be a burden to anybody. Thus, they underutilize resources and are therefore less effective in coping with environmental demands than one would have predicted from an analysis of their coping resources. Lazarus and Folkman (1984) introduced the concept of constraints to refer to factors that restrict the ways individuals draw on their resources.

Conclusions. The cognitive stress model developed by Lazarus and his colleagues offers a general framework for the analysis of psychological stress. While the model identifies many important general principles of stress and coping, its high level of generality can be a disadvantage in research that attempts to use the model to derive testable predictions for specific stressful life events. For example, in applying a stress model to bereavement, a researcher would hope to predict the characteristics of individuals who are likely to run a high risk of poor bereavement outcome and to relate these characteristics to strategies of coping that are maladaptive. Unfortunately, the core principle of the cognitive stress model, that "stress is a particular relationship between the person and the environment that is appraised by the person as taxing or exceeding his or her resources" (Lazarus & Folkman, 1984) and the distinction between emotion-focused or problem-focused coping would provide the researcher at best with a very rough indication of where to begin his or her search. To answer questions about risk groups and maladaptive coping, bereavement researchers must identify the aspects of the loss experience that are stressful, the coping resources of the individual which are relevant to these situational demands, and the coping processes that are typically employed by bereaved individuals. Furthermore, their research should be guided by a theoretical understanding of the mechanisms that relate different coping strategies to good or poor adjustment and health outcome. The deficit model of partner loss was developed as an attempt to address these issues.

5.4.2 *The deficit model of partner loss*

The deficit model of partner loss (M. Stroebe & Stroebe, 1985; W. Stroebe et al., 1980, 1982; W. Stroebe & Stroebe, 1986) applies the general psychological stress model to the situation of conjugal bereavement. Based on the interactional definition of stress, the deficit model offers an analysis of the situational demands characteristic of widowhood and of the coping resources needed to deal with these demands. This analysis allows one to account to some extent for individual differences in psychological and physical reactions to loss. It also, as will become evident in the following pages, places bereavement in an interpersonal as well as an intrapersonal perspective.

(i) The demands of the situation

A marital couple can be considered a social group or a small social organization with a differentiated system of roles regulating the division of labor as well as the distribution of rewards. However, marital couples typically far exceed other social groups in the extent of mutual social support. Thus, marital partners are likely to spend more time in voluntary and informal interaction with each other than with other adults. As a rule, their attachment to each other is also stronger than that toward other adults and they are likely to fulfill a wider range of functions for each other than is characteristic for normal social groups. Since bereavement marks the end of this close mutual relationship, the loss is likely to result in a number of deficits in areas in which the spouse had previously been able to rely on the partner. More specifically, the loss of the partner leads to deficits in areas which can broadly be characterized as loss of instrumental support, loss of validational support, and loss of emotional support. Since the role of "spouse" is likely to be central for an individual's self-concept, the death of a partner will also be associated with a loss of social identity.

Loss of instrumental support. Success or failure of the marital group in adapting to the demands from the outside world depends mainly on the adequacy of the group's resources in relation to task demands. Resources include all the relevant knowledge, abilities, and skills possessed by the individuals forming the group (Steiner, 1972). A marital partnership typically performs a number of task functions such as raising children, running a household, and earning the financial resources needed by the family. Marital partners rarely share all these tasks equally, but establish some kind of division of labor. Even today, this division of labor typically follows traditional sex-role boundaries, with the wife acting as the "housekeeper" and the husband fulfilling the role of "provider" (Miller & Garrison, 1982; Stafford, Backman, & Dibona, 1977).

Although loss of the marital partner reduces some of the task demands, it usually results in a much more sizeable reduction of the resources available to respond to task demands. Especially in families with dependent children, these role requirements continue even if one of the partners dies. Thus, the death of a partner forces the surviving spouse either to take over the task functions previously performed by the deceased or to find some kind of replacement. The higher the specialization of task roles in a given marriage, the more stressful is the loss of one partner for the other. Thus, if a husband has never performed any household chores (e.g., cooking, washing, cleaning), the loss of his wife should create a number of problems. While he is likely to be able to solve these more easily if widowhood merely reduces him to his former bachelor status, these problems become almost insolvable if he has to take over the responsibility for small children. For the wife, the death of a spouse frequently implies the loss of a reliable income. Despite life insurance and/or a pension, loss of a spouse is frequently associated with a significant reduction in income for the widow. Although these difficulties may be lessened with the help of an extensive social support system (Kobrin & Hendershot, 1977; Lopata, 1973b; Walker, MacBride, & Vachon, 1977), such problems serve to add to the emotional aspects of the loss.

Loss of validational support. Success or failure in responding to situational demands depends not merely on one's skills but also on whether one is able to assess these abilities and the environmental demands realistically. Thus, people often fail because they overestimate their ability or underestimate the difficulty of a task. According to Festinger (1954), the assessment of the validity of one's beliefs about "reality" as well as about one's own level of ability frequently depends on social comparison processes, particularly when objective criteria are lacking. Marital partners often serve as mutual reference persons for such comparison processes. Loss of a marital partner can therefore lead to drastic instability in such judgments.

Social comparison processes also play an important role in the evaluation of the appropriateness of one's emotional reactions, particularly in novel emotion-arousing situations (Schachter, 1959). Again, it seems likely that marital partners are important reference persons for such evaluations. For most people the death of a spouse is an unprecedented situation which is highly emotionally arousing. Thus, one may be uncertain about what one should be feeling emotionally, and whether one's reaction is still normal. As Glick et al. (1974) have shown, almost 40 percent of the bereaved included in their study were fearful at one time or another that they may lose their sanity. In summary, then, to the extent that the survivor is unable to locate sources enabling a successful definition of reality, the stressful nature of the loss may be increased.

Loss of emotional support. There is broad agreement among the helping professions concerning the central, if not critical, role of emotional support for self-esteem and psychological well-being. A partner's expression of caring and love is likely to augment the partner's feeling of self-worth and thus serve an important function in the maintenance of his or her mental health. Sociologists have been well aware of the importance of this "therapeutic" function partners perform for each other:

One of the major functions of positive, expressive talk is to raise the status of the other, to give help, to reward; in ordinary human relations it performs the stroking function. As infants need physical caressing or stroking in order to live and grow, and even to survive, so also do adults need emotional or psychological stroking or caressing to remain normal. (Bernard, 1968, p. 137)

Deficits in emotional support as a result of the loss of the partner may therefore be partly responsible for the lowered self-esteem often observed with the bereaved.

Loss of social identity. In addition to this indirect impact, the loss of a partner is likely to have a direct effect on the surviving spouse's self-definition. As Tajfel (1978) emphasized, the social groups to which we belong are important determinants of our definition of "self" and form the basis for our social identity.Tajfel offered the following definition of social identity: "Social identity will be understood as that part of an individuals's self-concept which derives from his knowledge of his membership to a social group (or groups) together with the value and emotional significance attached to that membership" (p. 63).

Since membership in a marital group is likely to be central for the individual's social identity, leaving the status of married and entering that of widowed should lead to important changes in the conceptualization of the person's social self. The impact of that reconceptualization on self-esteem will depend to some extent on individual as well a societal evaluations of widowed status. Since married status in Western societies is evaluated more positively than widowed status, the redefinition will result in a lowered self-esteem. The fact that the widowed may be uncertain about their acceptance by others as single individuals rather than as part of a marital group is likely to further contribute to this loss of self-esteem.

(ii) Coping resources: a preliminary taxonomy

According to the interactional definition of stress on which the deficit model of partner loss is based, stress is experienced when a situation is perceived as presenting a demand which threatens to exceed the person's coping resources. Thus, individual differences in coping resources are as important as variations in situational demands in determining bereavement outcome. In an analysis of the resources which are likely to affect the individual's ability to cope with bereavement, we developed the following preliminary taxonomy which distinguishes between *intrapersonal* and *interpersonal* resources. Intrapersonal resources consist of the personality traits, abilities, and skills which enable a person to cope with the loss. All external resources, regardless of whether they are owned by the person (e.g., financial resources) or contributed by others (e.g., social support) are categorized as interpersonal in this taxonomy.

Intrapersonal resources. Probably the most important intrapersonal resources are personality traits, which enable an individual to cope with critical life events such as partner loss without suffering permanent deterioration in mental health. It is almost trivial to suggest that individuals with stable and well-adjusted personalities should be better able to cope with bereavement than people who are unstable and poorly adjusted. Thus, personality traits such as emotional stability (Eysenck & Eysenck, 1964) and ego strength (Cattell, Eber, & Tatsuoka, 1970) are likely to contribute positively to coping ability. Some support for this hypothesis comes from studies of the relationship between cumulative life stress and health (e.g., Henderson, Byrne, & Duncan-Jones, 1981; Smith, Johnson, & Sarason, 1978). Results of studies by Johnson and Sarason (1978) and Ganellen and Blaney (1984) further suggest a positive relationship between internal control beliefs and coping ability. As will be seen later (Chapter 8.3.2) less support has been found in studies of the health consequences of bereavement.

Since we will argue below that the availability of social support is an important (interpersonal) coping resource, personality characteristics (e.g., extraversion, assertiveness) that contribute to an individual's level of relational competence and thus help him or her to access and maintain social support networks should also be considered here (Hansson, 1986a, 1986b). Thus, in a study of elderly subjects (Hansson, 1986b; Jones, 1985), who were asked to indicate the extent to which stressful events (such as retirement, widowhood, or change of residence) had disrupted their social networks, shy individuals reported having experienced such disruptions more often.

Further examples of intrapersonal resources are the abilities, skills, and knowledge which help the individual in the performance of those task functions which had previously been conducted by the deceased (e.g., household chores, financial affairs, upbringing of children). To take over these tasks is likely to be much less stressful if the widowed has the abilities, skills, and knowledge necessary for a successful performance of these functions.

Interpersonal resources. The two major examples of interpersonal resources are financial resources and social support. Of these two, we consider the availability of social support to be more important. Although deficits in task functions could be compensated by paying somebody to help, they can also be mastered when social support from friends or relatives is readily available. In addition, friends and relatives can fulfill some of the bereaved individual's need for emotional support.

Social support can be defined as the "existence or availability of people on whom we can rely, people who let us know that they care about, value, and love us" (Sarason, Levine, Basham, & Sarason, 1983). Since the deficit model implies that the stress of bereavement can only be moderated by the availability of coping resources that correspond to a deficit created by the loss, we distinguish between instrumental, validational, and emotional support. Similar distinctions have been suggested by other authors in the area of social support (e.g., Cohen & McKay, 1984; Cohen & Wills, 1985; House, 1981; Silver & Wortman, 1980). There is also some evidence (e.g., Bankoff, 1983b) to suggest that bereaved individuals need different kinds of support at different time periods during bereavement.

There are several mechanisms by which coping resources moderate the impact of stressful events: First, coping resources determine the extent to which stress is experienced by affecting stress appraisal. For example, the presence of dependent children and the need to care for them will be perceived as less stressful by a widower who is wealthy enough to hire help or has relatives who can be trusted to help with this task than by somebody who lacks these resources. Second, coping resources may intervene between the experience of stress and the onset of pathological outcome. For example, certain personality characteristics (e.g., ego strength; emotional stability) are associated with greater resilience against the impact of stressful life events, or the presence of others who offer emotional support may moderate stress, by directly reducing anxiety and the level of physiological arousal. Third, coping resources can moderate stress by helping the individual to change the stressful nature of the environment.

(iii) Coping processes

Like Lazarus, we distinguish two forms of coping, namely problem control and emotion control (Leventhal, 1970). Problem control refers to those forms of coping which are directed at solving problems created by the loss. Thus, taking over some of the task functions previously performed by the deceased, or finding help from others, are as much part of problem control as are attempts at reconceptualizing one's social identity.

Although the demands of problem control are recognized as important determinants of bereavement stress, research in this area has typically focused on emotion control as a moderator of the health impact of partner loss. Emotion control consists of cognitive (e.g., denial, grief work) and behavioral strategies (e.g., drinking, taking tranquilizers, distractive activities) directed at reducing or suppressing emotional distress. If one categorizes these coping strategies according to whether they involve sensitization or repression, it becomes evident that, with the exception of grief work, they all reduce distress via repression.

Denial, when loss is not acknowledged at all or not fully acknowledged, is the most extreme case of coping by repression. If persistent, it is maladaptive and an indicator of a pathological development. Thus, Ramsay (1979) describes the case of a widow who continued to set the table for two, talk to an empty chair, and describe to others activities jointly undertaken with her husband.

While it is obvious that complete denial of the death of a loved one is not a healthy coping strategy, it would seem plausible that sedation or distraction should help to lessen the emotional impact of loss. After all, time is considered a great healer and by using antidepressants, tranquilizers, or even alcohol during the first few weeks or months after the loss, the painful memories might be made to fade a little and the distress might become more tolerable. This view is firmly rejected, however, by most practitioners in the area of bereavement (e.g., Jacobs & Ostfeld, 1980; Worden, 1982) who consider distraction as well as the more palliative forms of emotion control (tranquilizers, alcohol) as dysfunctional, at least in the early stages of grief, because they prevent the individual from working through his or her grief. Thus, Worden (1982) warns against the use of antidepressant medication for those undergoing grief, since they do not relieve normal grief symptoms and could lead to abnormal grief. Although there have been no clinical studies of the effects of psychotropic drugs for bereaved people (Osterweis, 1985) there are some reports that individuals who have been prescribed sedatives for the first few days of bereavement found these not helpful, since they hindered the realization of loss (Jacobs & Ostfeld, 1980).

Despite the dearth of empirical evidence, there exists a general consensus among bereavement researchers (e.g., Bowlby, 1981; Freud, 1917; Lindemann, 1944; Parkes, 1972) that grief work is the only strategy of emotion control that leads to a healthy resolution of the emotional reactions to loss. It is difficult, however, to assess the validity of this claim, since the concept of grief work has never been clearly defined. Thus, it is somewhat unclear how and why grief work should help to resolve the grief reaction. When Lindemann describes grief work as "the effort of reliving or working through in *small quantities* (our italics) events which involved the now-deceased person and the survivor" (1979, p. 234), he seems to refer to a process of desensitization by repeated exposure to the emotion-arousing stimuli. This conception would be consistent with Freud's (1917) view that the function of grief work is to free the individual of his or her ties to the deceased.

There is some evidence, however, that merely ruminating about the spouse's death does not help individuals to cope with the loss (e.g., Remondet, Hansson, Rule, & Winfrey, 1986; Pennebaker & O'Heeron, 1984; Silver, 1986). In a survey of survivors whose spouses had either died in an accident or by suicide, Pennebaker and O'Heeron (1984) found a positive correlation between the increase in illness rates from before to after the death (reported retrospectively) and ruminating about the spouse's death. Thus, the less people were able to put the death out of their minds and the more they constantly thought about it the greater was the increase in illnesses they suffered after the loss.

The theory of cognitive adaptation to threatening events developed by Taylor (1983) suggests a number of ways in which grief work as an active coping strategy might differ from the more passive process of ruminating about a loss. To be an effective coping strategy, grief work must involve a search for meaning in the experience, an attempt to regain mastery over one's life, and an effort to enhance one's self-esteem. The search for meaning is an effort to understand the event, why it happened and what impact it will have on the person's future life. The theme of mastery centers around regaining control over one's life and strategies to manage life without the partner. The theme of self-enhancement may be less important for bereavement than for the traumatic events mainly studied by Taylor (e.g., cancer patients, rape victims). However, since bereavement is associated with a loss in social identity (i.e., being part of a couple), self-enhancement may be nevertheless a necessary process to encourage the individual to rebuild his or her social life. If one assumes that the search for meaning, the regaining of mastery, and the enhancement of self-esteem are tasks that have to be successfully concluded in order to adjust to a loss, it becomes understandable why sedation by drugs or alcohol would slow down or prevent the resolution of grief.

Although most of these functions of grief work could be performed in social isolation, it seems plausible that social support from relatives and friends should facilitate these processes. Thus, the availability of support figures to whom the bereaved can talk about the loss and express their feelings of despair should aid grief work by encouraging the bereaved to work through events which involved the deceased and to explore the impact the loss will have on his or her future life. Confiding in others might help the bereaved to organize the structure their thoughts about the event, to accept the loss, and to find meaning in the experience. Individuals may also receive social comparison information indicating that others have had similar feelings and problems. Furthermore, the knowledge that there are people who can be relied on for love, esteem, and unconditional acceptance should reduce arousal, anxiety, and feelings of loneliness. Finally, relatives and friends can also assist the bereaved with problems created by the loss by providing them with tangible help as well as information to replace the functions which had previously been fulfilled by the deceased.

In the study of spouses of partners who had died from suicides or accidents described earlier, Pennebaker and O'Heeron (1984) presented some evidence to support the notion that bereaved individuals benefit from talking about their loss. They found that talking to friends about the loss seemed to be positively related to health, an effect that was independent of the respondents' self-reported number of close friends. Since this correlation might merely reflect the fact that people with poor bereavement outcome are less likely to talk about their loss, Pennebaker and Beall (1986) conducted an experimental study in which subjects were randomly assigned to conditions under which they had either to write about trivial topics or about personally traumatic life events for four consecutive days. Pennebaker and Beall reported that writing about both the emotions and facts surrounding a traumatic event was associated with a decrease in health-center visits in the six months following the study.

One final issue concerns the factors that determine an individual's dominant coping strategy. From our perspective one would assume that personality characteristics should be relevant here. Thus, we would expect that individuals who believe in internal rather than external control should be highly motivated to search for the meaning of the loss experience and to regain mastery over their life by engaging in grief work, rather than using sedation or engaging in distracting activities. However, there may also be situational determinants of coping strategies. For example, individuals might be more likely to face loss and engage in grief work if they have a great deal of time to prepare themselves, because the death is the result of a long and terminal illness rather than happening suddenly.

(iv) Conclusions

In offering a framework for the analysis of the demands of the situation that confront a person who has suffered the loss of a partner as well as of the resources needed to cope with these demands, the deficit model of partner loss allows the identification of individuals who are at high risk of poor bereavement outcome. The analysis of situational demands suggests several constellations which are potentially stressful. Thus, the situation with which the widowed individual is faced after the loss should be the more demanding, the closer the relationship between the partners, the greater the role differentiation within the marital group, the more central marriage is to their social identity, or the less warning the individual had of the impending loss. Whether these demands will be appraised as stressful will depend, however, on the availability of coping resources. We argued that a stable, non-neurotic personality and the availability of emotional social support are the most important resources to help the individual cope with personal loss. However, even under stressful conditions, grief can be resolved if the bereaved person engages in a process of grief work rather than denying the loss or seeking distraction (notably, in the early stages of loss) or sedation.

5.5   Stress and depression: two sides of the coin

We argued earlier that, by applying depression or stress models to the analysis of partner loss, we are looking at different aspects of the same phenomena. That stress and depression are frequently reactions to the same experience can be demonstrated most clearly for the case of learned helplessness. According to the learned-helplessness model, the experience of having lost control over one's outcomes leads to depression. At the same time, however, control has also featured centrally in research on stress. It has been demonstrated that having control over an aversive event can greatly reduce the stressfulness of the situation. Thus, Glass and Singer (1972) demonstrated that being subjected to unpredictable noise led to subsequent performance decrements, but only for subjects who believed that they had no control over the noise. These performance decrements did not occur for subjects who had been told that they could stop the noise simply by pushing a button, even though none of them actually used that button. The information that a coping response was possible evidently helped to alleviate the stressfulness of the noise.

We would argue that an individual who perceives a situation as presenting a demand which threatens to exceed the person's coping resources, will, when it is important to meet these demands, feel stressed as well as anxious. Whether depression sets in will probably depend to some extent on the aversiveness of the event which is likely to happen if the individual's efforts at coping are unsuccessful. But it will also depend on the length of the time period during which stress is experienced. Individuals are more likely to react with depression if stress is prolonged rather than brief. Thus, like physical illness, depression can be a disease of adaptation resulting from prolonged exposure to stress.

However, there is more to grief than stress. Stress models focus on the current situation of the individual, to determine whether the bereaved has sufficient personal and interpersonal resources to cope with situational demands. Grief, on the other hand, is a reaction to the loss suffered in the past. Individuals may be grief-stricken over a loss, even though they have ample social support and feel quite able to cope with their present as well as their future situations. One would therefore predict that when stress is added to grief, depression and other pathological grief reactions are likely to develop. Predictions derived from the deficit model, on stress and other factors, will be discussed further in Chapter 8, where the empirical evidence on risk factors for poor outcome is presented.

6   Mediators between stress and illness

Stressful life events like the loss of a job or the death of a spouse do not operate in the same manner on one's bodily system as the entry of some alien bacterium or even the noxious physical or chemical stimuli studied by Selye. And yet, despite some of the weaknesses in the research on cumulative life stress discussed in the last chapter, there can be little doubt that the experience of stressful life events is associated with an increased risk of a wide range of physical as well as mental disorders. Furthermore, it will be argued later (Chapter 7.4) that the widowed have a higher mortality than married individuals from causes such as arteriosclerotic heart (including coronary) disease, cancer, tuberculosis, and even liver cirrhosis. There is also some evidence that bereaved individuals have a higher incidence of infectious disease during the first year after their loss (Maddison & Viola, 1968). Thus, a final and probably most intriguing question still to be answered is how stressful life events can lead to health deterioration.

This chapter will discuss two types of mechanisms assumed to mediate the impact of psychosocial stress on health. First, the experience of stressful life events is likely to lead to a number of behavioral changes (e.g., changes in eating habits and health care, increases in smoking, alcohol and drug intake) which are known to have a deleterious effect on health. Second, it will be argued that the health consequences of stressful life events are likely to be mediated by some of the same changes in the endocrine, immune, and autonomic nervous systems which are responsible for the health impact of physical stressors.

6.1 Behavioral changes

In a persuasive analysis of health behavior, the economist Becker (1976) argued that there is no clear distinction between normal death and suicide:

According to the economic approach ... *most* (if not all!) deaths are to some extent "suicides" in the sense that they could have been postponed if more

101

resources had been invested in prolonging life. . . . Good health and a long life are important aims of most persons, but surely no more than a moment's reflection is necessary to convince anyone that they are not the only aims: somewhat better health or a longer life may be sacrificed because they conflict with other aims. The economic approach implies that there is an "optimal" expected length of life, where the value in utility of an additional year is less than the utility foregone by using time and other resources to obtain that year. Therefore, a person may be a heavy smoker or so committed to work as to omit all exercise, not necessarily because he is ignorant of the consequences or incapable of using the information he possesses, but because the life span forfeited is not worth the cost to him of quitting smoking or working less intensively. (pp. 10–11)

Becker's analysis suggests at least two mechanisms which might be responsible for the association of stress and illness. First, an unhealthy life style could cause both stressful life events and ill health. Thus, aggressive and achievement-oriented businessmen or -women may be so set on their careers that they not only neglect their health, but also their families. Such intense pursuit of a career could lead to life changes like those included in the Social Readjustment Rating Questionnaire (e.g., sexual difficulties, marital separation from mate). At the same time, the neglect of one's health is likely to cause some health deterioration.

More interesting, however, for our purposes, is a second mechanism suggested by Becker's analysis, namely the possibility that the experience of a stressful life event changes the value the individual places on his or her life and thus also the willingness to expend effort on health care. Some support for this notion can be found in the research on health consequences of bereavement. In describing their feelings after the death of their partners, bereaved individuals typically report that, at least initially, life no longer seems worth living. The significant increase in suicides in the period immediately following the loss (e.g., Kaprio & Koskenvuo, 1983; MacMahon & Pugh, 1965) demonstrates the seriousness of these claims.

It seems quite likely that some of the "accidental deaths," which are much more frequent among the bereaved than among the married, are outright suicides as well, while others may be the result of a combination of stress and lack of care. In such emotionally arousing and stressful situations, accidents are likely to happen unless particular care is taken to ensure safety. However, with the value of life significantly reduced, the bereaved are unlikely to make great efforts to attend to their own safety.

Other causes of death in which the widowed rates are excessive could be considered as the result of a slow process of self-destruction (Gove, 1973). Thus, the commonest causes of liver cirrhosis are heavy drinking over many years and malnutrition. Since even advanced cases of alcoholic cirrhosis can be improved by abstention from alcohol and a regular and healthy diet, death from cirrhosis is at least to some extent self-inflicted. Thus, there is some evidence that the experience of stressful life events leads to behavioral changes which could be responsible for some of the health deterioration. A poor diet and a general lack of health care may also aggravate the impact of some of the physiological changes associated with stress, which will be discussed in the next section.

6.2 Physiological changes

This section will present evidence to support the claim that the experience of stressful life events leads to some of the same physiological changes which Selye (1936, 1976) observed in his research on physical stressors. Thus Selye's work on the General Adaptation Syndrome, which we described in the last chapter, will provide the basic framework for our discussion of physiological changes induced by stressful life events. However, going beyond his general perspective, this section will consider the role of psychosocial stress in the development of a number of specific disorders.

6.2.1 Stress and infections

Infections are obviously caused by some infectious agent. But exposure to such agents does not always cause infections. There are numerous factors which affect an individual's susceptibility to disease (e.g., prior exposure to the microorganism and the development of immunity, nutritional status of the host, a wide range of genetic factors). Since Selye's (1936) classic work on the effect of stress on the immune system, exposure to stress has to be included among the determinants of individual susceptibility to infectious diseases. The description of stress-induced effects on the immune system now forms part of the standard repertory of textbooks in physiology (for a review, see Ader, 1981; Jemmott & Locke, 1984; Laudenslager & Reite, 1984). Pharmacological doses of corticosteroids have been shown to lower the immune defense of the body causing an atrophy of the lymphoid structures by suppressing the formation of immunoglobulins and by causing a decrease in the number and toxicity of lymphocytes in the blood. Lymphocytes, which account for 20 to 45 percent of the total white blood cell population (Laudenslager & Reite, 1984), are of central importance for the immune response.

Descriptions like these typically come from studies in which corticosteroids (cortisol) have been administered in pharmacological doses for their anti-inflammatory effect (in the treatment of severe arthritis) or for their effect in reducing the danger of rejection (in cases of organ transplants). What little evidence there is on the effects of natural stress seems to be much less dramatic. Although Hofer, Wolff, Friedman, and Mason (1972a, b) reported evidence of elevated corticosteroids in parents of children who had recently died of leukemia, this finding could not be replicated in studies by Jacobs, Mason, Kosten, et al. (1985) and Bartrop, Luckhurst, Lazarus, et al. (1977). Jacobs et al. (1985) observed no significant difference in the adrenocortical acitivity (urinary and serum free cortisol) of forty-three recently bereaved and a nonbereaved comparison group. Their failure to find evidence of differential adrenocortical activity between the two groups could have been due to the fact that their comparison group consisted of individuals who had been under considerable stress themselves (i.e., nonbereaved persons whose spouses had been admitted to a hospital two months earlier with life-threatening illness and then recovered). However, similar objections cannot be raised against a study by Bartrop et al. (1977) who studied the effect of bereavement on the immune systems of twenty-six widows at two weeks and six weeks after bereavement. Compared to matched controls (nonbereaved hospital staff members), the widowed showed no difference in numbers of lymphocytes (T- and B-cells), the presence of antibodies, nor in the mean serum concentrations of thyroxine, cortisol, prolactin, and growth hormone. Only the response of the lymphocytes to mitogens (phytohemagglutinin; concanavalin A), which is used as a test to assess cellular immunity, was significantly depressed in the widowed group at six weeks after the bereavement. It is interesting that this depression of the immune functions of the T-cell system was found only at six weeks but not at two weeks after the bereavement. This might indicate that a marked immunosuppression occurs mainly after extended periods of stress.

Similar patterns were described by Schleifer, Keller, Camerino, et al. (1983), who measured pre- and postbereavement lymphocyte functions in fifteen men whose wives died from breast cancer. As early as two weeks after the loss a significant suppression of lymphocyte response to mitogens was found relative to prebereavement levels. Continued moderate suppression could be observed at a four to fourteen months postbereavement follow-up. No changes were observed in total lymphocyte count or relative T and B cell numbers. Further evidence comes from a study by Goodwin, Bromberg, Staszak, et al. (1981) who found surgical stress to be associated with depressed lymphocyte function.

Such reports fit well with everyday experiences that individuals who are exhausted, due to excessive stress experiences, are more likely to catch such infections as the common cold or influenza. However, none of the above studies related these indicators of impairment in immune functions to actual incidence of disease. As we will see, the evidence with regard to physical health deterioration following bereavement is less than clear-cut. On one hand, Parkes (1964b) in his longitudinal study of doctors' consultations of forty-four London widows before and after the loss of their spouses reported a significant increase in the number of consultations for psychiatric and chronic conditions (e.g., rheumatism), while the number of acute conditions, such as infections and gastrointestinal disorders, showed little change. Maddison and Viola (1968), on the other hand, who obtained data on the health of 375 widows in Boston and Sidney through a health questionnaire, found that their widowed sample differed significantly from their control group in the reported incidence of "frequent infections." However, the percentage of widows suffering from such infections was rather small. When we look at causes of death, however, we find that widowed indeed die more often from infections than do married controls (Parkes et al., 1969; Klerman & Izen, 1977; Koskenvuo, Sarna, Kaprio & Lönnqvist, 1979).

There is also some evidence that tuberculosis, an infectious disease which is a particularly excessive cause of death among the bereaved, is also affected by other stressful life events. Rahe, Meyer, Smith, et al. (1964) report a study conducted by Holmes and collaborators of twenty employees of a tuberculosis sanitarium who had developed TB during the previous three months. When compared to a matched control group of twenty sanitarium employees who were free of tuberculosis, the tuberculosis group had a higher incidence of recent life events than the control subjects. While nine of the tuberculosis subjects demonstrated "peak frequencies" of stressful life events during the two years previous to illness onset, only one of the control subjects showed a similar frequency for a comparable period. However, since the life-change data were collected retrospectively, depressed mood or knowledge of illness onset could have biased reports.

More persuasive evidence for the effect of stress on susceptibility to infections comes from a prospective study of the effect of stress on the development of glandular fever (infectious mononucleosis). Kasl, Evans, and Neiderman (1979) screened 1,327 cadets entering West Point Military Academy for the presence of Epstein–Barr virus, the antibody for infectious mononucleosis. Those cadets who had already developed an immunity were eliminated from the study. The remainder was followed during the stay at the academy. It was to be expected that a proportion of these cadets would become infected. Of these, some would only develop the antibody without falling ill, while others would come down with the illness as well. The majority, however, would probably not even become infected. Kasl et al. (1979) found evidence that those cadets who developed the disease were under greater academic pressure than other susceptible cadets. Academic pressure was assumed to be great among individuals who were highly motivated to pursue a military career but whose academic performance was poor. Additional evidence on the influence of psychosocial factors on susceptibility to infectious diseases was reported by Jemmott and Locke (1984) who reviewed findings that related stress to an increased incidence of acute respiratory infections (e.g., Hinkle, 1974; Jackson, Dowling, Anderson, et al., 1960; Totman & Kiff, 1979); necrotizing ulcerative gingivitis, commonly known as trench-mouth (Cohen-Cole, Cogen, Stevens, et al. 1981); and herpes simplex (Katcher, Brightman, Luborsky, & Ship, 1973; Luborsky, Mintz, Brightman, & Katcher, 1976).

The clearest demonstration of the immunosuppressive effect of stress comes from animal studies (e.g., Friedman, Ader, & Glasgow, 1965; Monjan, 1981). Miller (1980) summarized these findings as follows:

Mice having to perform a shuttle-avoidance response once every five minutes were found to have involution of the thymus and spleen, reduction in the number of lymphocytes, a delay in the rejection of skin grafts, a decrease in susceptibility to acute anaphylaxis induced by intravenous administration of antigen-antibody complexes, and a reduced level of interferon, which is believed to be important in the defense against viral infections. The same conditions that produced these reduced activities of the immune system increased the susceptibility of the mice to a variety of experimental infections: herpes simplex, poliomyelitis, Coxsackie B, and polyoma virus. (pp. 328–329)

To summarize, there is now convincing evidence that relates psychosocial stress to impairment of immune functions as well as altered susceptibility to infectious diseases (Jemmott & Locke, 1984). The implication of this research for the bereavement area is that the loss experience is likely to be accompanied by alterations in immune functions which, in turn, lower resistance to infectious diseases and increase risk of morbidity and mortality from these causes.

6.2.2   *Stress and cancer*

There is some speculation (e.g., Fox, 1978; Fredrick, 1976) that the immunosuppressive effect attributed to stress, by reducing the organism's chances to recognize and destroy foreign tumor cells, could be responsible for the apparent relationship between life stress and cancer. A similar but more general argument was advanced by Sklar and Anisman (1981), who suggested that the mobilization of resources, or the potential exhaustion of resources due to extended stress experiences, may render the organism less capable of efficiently contending with malignant cells. This speculation, Sklar and Anisman argued, is somewhat supported by the fact that a number of parallels exist in the effect of stress on cancer growth and its effect on other physiological systems. The reader is referred to Sklar and Anisman (1981) for a detailed discussion of this issue.

There is indeed some evidence that cancer is associated with psychological stress, although it comes mainly from retrospective studies (e.g., Bahnson & Bahnson, 1964; Greene, 1966; Horne & Picard, 1979). The obvious weakness of this type of research is that once cancer has been diagnosed, patients are likely to be depressed and dwell on negative experiences. However, Horne and Picard (1979) managed to circumvent the problem by interviewing patients at hospitals after roentgenographic examinations had indicated subacute or chronic lesions, but before any further diagnosis had been made. Thus, the group whose lesions were later found to be due to benign causes could be used as a control group. The interviews focused on five areas: childhood instability, job stability, marriage stability, lack of plans for the future, and recent significant loss experiences. On the basis of these interviews, the authors predicted successfully the diagnosis of 53 (80%) of the 66 patients with benign disease and 27 (61%) of the 44 patients with cancer.

Cancer incidence seems to be particularly marked among individuals who have recently lost an important emotional relationship and who express a sense of hopelessness and inability to cope (Greene, 1966; LeShan, 1961). In a study similar to that of Horne and Picard, Schmale and Iker (1966) demonstrated that a psychiatrist's diagnosis of hopelessness could be used to predict cancer in women who, on the basis of suspicious symptoms found in a routine smear test, had been transferred for further examination. Thus, at this point in time, cancer was merely suspected, and this suspicion could still prove to be unfounded. Patients who viewed themselves as failures, and regarded their futures as hopeless, were diagnosed by the psychiatrists as potential cancer cases, a prediction which proved correct in 31 out of 40 cases.

Even though the type of design employed by Horne and Picard (1979) and by Schmale and Iker (1966) avoids some of the pitfalls of retrospective studies, it does not rule out the possibility that their physical condition affected the patient's behavior during the interview. This is particularly likely in the case of categorization with regard to hopelessness. After all, the cancer was already present at the time of the psychiatric diagnosis, and it seems quite possible that the physiological consequences of cancer do affect the mood state of a patient and may thus be responsible for the depression noted by the psychiatrists.

Unfortunately, a series of prospective studies which compared premorbid depression scores of individuals who later contracted or did not contract cancer yielded contradictory results. Thus, Shekelle, Raynor, Ostfeld, et al. (1981) found that psychological depression (measured with the Minnesota Multiphasic Personality Inventory (MMPI) at a baseline examination in 1957–8 of a sample of more than 2,000 middle-aged men) was associated with a twofold increase in odds of death from cancer during a seventeen-year follow-up. Moreover, this relationship persisted after the investigators controlled for known cancer risks such as age, smoking, and family history of cancer. However, Dattore, Shontz, and Coyne (1980) who compared the premorbid MMPI D scores of groups of male cancer and noncancer patients reported the opposite result. These authors observed significantly lower depression scores among the cancer patients. Finally, Gillum, Leon, Kamp, and Becerra-Aldama (1980) found no relationship between MMPI scores and cancer incidence in a group of 281 middle-aged men who were evaluated in 1947 and followed over a thirty-year period. While the failure of the Gillum et al. (1980) study to find any relationship between depression and cancer incidence could have been due to the small size of their sample, the contradiction in the findings of Dattore et al. (1980) and Shekelle et al. (1981) is more difficult to reconcile. However, one wonders whether the fact that the noncancer control group of the Dattore et al. study included individuals with benign neoplasms, essential hypertension, gastrointestinal ulcers, and schizophrenia could have contributed to the difference in results. Nevertheless, in view of these inconsistencies, it seems difficult to draw firm conclusions about the relationship between premorbid depression and cancer.

Since the study of stress-induced cancer in animals has also yielded contradictory results this body of research does not greatly improve our understanding of the impact of sociopsychological factors on cancer in humans. Although a recent review by Sklar and Anisman (1981) introduced some order into what previously seemed to be a chaos of contradictory findings, the pattern suggested by these authors is still rather complex. Acute physical stress (e.g., a single shock session) tends to accelerate the growth of cancer tumors in mice, if the shocks cannot be avoided. No such effects have been observed for electric shocks that can be avoided. Thus, the impact of a stressor is again shown to be dependent on the availability of a coping response. However, Justice (1985) has cautioned against the extrapolation of these findings to humans. He argued that ongoing exposure to a stressor only accelerates the growth of *viral* tumors and the existence of this type of tumor in humans is as yet unproven. The chemical- or radiation-induced *nonviral* tumors (the type of tumor that is predominant among humans) may even be inhibited by ongoing stress. Justice (1985) further suggested that after stress is terminated there is a rebound response that causes nonviral tumors to grow but inhibits viral tumors (via immune enhancement).

Unfortunately, the implications of this research for the bereavement area are somewhat unclear. Thus, if the facilitative impact of the rebound phase outweighs that of the stress-induced inhibition, the net result of the stress experience might still be an acceleration of growth even for non-viral tumors. Second, Sklar and Anisman (1981) argue that although the evidence is not conclusive there are data suggesting that there are some virus-induced cancers even in humans. Furthermore, as Justice (1985) points out, some clinical cancers seem to be immunoresponsive, "so the viral tumor model is more appropriate to them" (p. 133). Finally, these regularities have only been substantiated for tumor growth but not for metastatic invasion from the primary tumors. Thus, while the conclusions drawn by Justice raise serious doubt about the role of the immune system in cancer in humans, they are not necessarily inconsistent with the view that stressful life events such as bereavement increase cancer risk.

6.2.3 *Stress and coronary heart disease*

There are two major forms of coronary heart disease, angina pectoris and myocardial infarction. The symptoms of *angina pectoris* are periodic attacks of distinctive chest pain, usually situated behind the sternum and radiating to the chest and left shoulder. Attacks of angina pectoris are typically brought on by physical exercise or emotional exertion. They are quickly relieved by rest or by medication aimed at dilating blood vessels and reducing blood pressure. The major cause of angina pectoris is an insufficient supply of oxygen to the heart due to atherosclerosis, a thickening of the innermost walls of coronary arteries. This thickening is caused by the formation of plaques, which are fatty deposits consisting mainly of excess amounts of serum lipids, especially cholesterol. While some plaque formation is quite normal, substantial occlusion can impair the blood supply of the heart. However, attacks of angina pectoris rarely involve permanent damage to the heart muscle.

If the plaque grows at a rate exceeding the blood supply available for the nutrition of its cells, it is likely to rupture and form the basis for a thrombosis, which will then completely block an already narrow passage.

Such ruptures may also be the result of hemodynamic factors, such as high levels of arterial blood pressure (Herd, 1978). The formation of blood clots which obstruct the artery and diminish the blood supply to the left ventricle of the heart are the most frequent cause of *myocardial infarction,* a necrosis (death) of the heart tissue caused by a long-lasting insufficiency in the oxygen supply. Myocardial infarction is one of the major causes of death in most industrialized nations.

At present three mechanisms are recognized by which stress can contribute to coronary heart disease. *First,* stress is likely to accelerate the development of atherosclerosis by increasing the secretion of catecholamines and corticosteroids. Catecholamines, jointly with the corticosteroid cortisol, mobilize fat stores. Thus, increased production of catecholamines and cortisol leads to increased levels of serum cholesterol, a major factor in plaque formation. There is now ample evidence from studies of animals as well as humans which links stress experiences to increases in serum cholesterol (e.g., Friedman, Byers, & Brown, 1967; Pare, Rothfeld, Isom, & Varady, 1973). For example, Pare et al. (1973) found that rats fed on high-lipid diets and also exposed to unavoidable shocks for two to eight days showed higher levels of accumulated serum cholesterol than control rats only fed the lipid diet. Studies by Rahe and his colleagues (e.g., Rahe, Rubin, & Arthur, 1974; Rahe, Rubin, Arthur, & Clark, 1968; Rahe, Rubin, Gunderson, & Arthur, 1971) on Navy personnel exposed to a variety of stressful training situations found elevated serum cholesterol levels when subjects felt overburdened by the demands of the training. Similarly, Friedman, Rosenman, and Carroll (1958), who took repeated blood samples from accountants over a six-month period, reported elevated serum cholesterol levels for the two weeks before the final date for tax returns, an exceedingly demanding time for accountants. *Second,* catecholamines increase the tendency of blood to coagulate. This is a great advantage when an organism is wounded, but it may contribute to the formation of blood clots and consequent blocking of arteries, especially arteries already narrowed down due to the formation of atherosclerotic plaque. *Third,* increases in catecholamine output lead to increases in blood pressure. The pressure produced in the arteries as the heart pumps blood through them will be elevated by any of three changes: increased cardiac output (i.e., the amount of blood pumped out of the left ventricle per minute), by constriction of the blood vessels, and by an increase in fluid volume. The sympathetic nervous system regulates blood pressure by controlling cardiac output and vasoconstriction through the release of catecholamines.

Further strain on an already damaged heart and the risk of sudden death may result from processes described by Engel (1978). He argued that the inability to cope with a negative emotional situation may simutaneously activate two contradictory biological reactions to emergency situations, namely, the fight–flight and the conservation–withdrawal systems. While the fight–flight system mobilizes the body's resources for massive motor activity, activation of the conservation–withdrawal system leads to inactivity, to internal withdrawal from the situation. Normally, the two systems inhibit each other, but Engel (1978) proposed that situations of uncertainty and hopelessness may lead to a simultaneous activation of both systems. For healthy individuals, the result may be vasodepressor syncopes of benign arrythmias, but for people who already suffer from heart trouble, this additional strain may lead to death.

In view of the strong relationship between stress and coronary heart disease, it will hardly be surprising to learn that, at least in longitudinal studies, heart disease is responsible for a large proportion of bereaved mortality. Thus in their study of the mortality of widowers, Parkes et al. (1969) reported that circulatory diseases accounted for two-thirds of the increase in mortality observed during the first six months of bereavement. A somewhat smaller excess was observed by Kaprio and Koskenvuo (1983) for the first months of bereavement.

6.2.4 *Stress and the gastrointestinal system*

The effect of stress on the gastrointestinal system is quite apparent in everyday life. Anxiety-arousing situations (e.g., examinations) lead to a loss of appetite in most individuals, except for a small minority, who overeat. Diarrhea is frequently elicited by the anticipation of danger and has plagued troops before battles since ancient times. However, while these are only temporary afflictions which pass as soon as the crisis is over, stress seems also to play a role in the etiology of two painful diseases of more chronic character, ulcerative colitis and peptic ulcers.

Ulcerative colitis is a chronic inflammation of the colon which can lead to uncontrollable diarrhea and bleeding. It is serious because the continuous diarrhea and its accompanying loss of blood can lead to severe weight loss and anemia. Some patients recover completely from an attack but in many cases the only effective treatment is to surgically remove the affected part of the colon.

The importance of psychogenic factors in ulcerative colitis was first suggested by Murray (1930). Lindemann (1950), in what, despite its weaknesses, is still one of the more conclusive studies in this area, reported tentative evidence that disruptions of close emotional relationships play an important role in the etiology of this disease. This suggestion was further elaborated by Engel (e.g., 1958) who argued that a real or fantasized object loss, or disturbance in a relationship with a person of emotional significance, results in feelings of helplessness and hopelessness which then (presumably mediated by neuroendocrine mechanisms) lead to the inflammation. Fortunately, ulcerative colitis is not a very frequent disease. The fact that neither Parkes (1964b) nor Maddison and Viola (1968) found a significant incidence of ulcerative colitis among their widowed groups does not, therefore, contradict the assumption that psychogenic causes play a role in its etiology.

Peptic ulcers are craterlike holes in the lining of the stomach (gastric ulcers) or the duodenum (duodenal ulcers); occasionally other parts of the digestive tract are affected. The symptoms include stomachache, heartburn, and often nausea and stomach bleeding. The pain is nearly always relieved by food or antacid drugs. It is easy enough to imagine that the stomach lining could be attacked by digestive juices. After all, these juices consist of an aggressive mixture of hydrochloric acid and pepsin, which breaks food down into components that the body can use. However, the inner walls of the digestive tract are normally protected from this destructive mixture by a layer of mucus. Precisely how the lesions of the stomach walls develop is still not known. There is some evidence however, that a reduction in the blood supply to the mucus or an increase in the secretion of hydrochloric acid or pepsin acting on an already damaged mucus are important factors in the formation of erosions (Weiss, 1977). Since activation of the sympathetic nervous system causes a reduction of the blood supply to the gastrointestinal system, it seems quite feasible that intensive and extended stress experiences could lead to a degeneration of the stomach lining.

The secretion of hydrochloric acid and pepsinogen (the precursor of pepsin), on the other hand, is controlled by the parasympathetic nervous system (vagus) which is not normally involved in stress reactions. But the increased secretion of stomach juices might be explained in terms of Engel's assumption that in situations of uncertainty and hopelessness both systems are simultaneously activated, causing an imbalance which might lead to increases in secretion and reduction in blood supply at the same time. Another potential explanation suggests that stress interacts with a physiological predisposition. One such predisposing factor could be a differential level of pepsin. Pepsin is secreted as pepsinogen. It turns into pepsin and becomes active only when mixed with hydrochloric acid.

Since stress leads to ulcers in only a small proportion of individuals, it seems reasonable to suppose that the stress-induced reduction of the blood supply to the stomach lining increases the vulnerability of the lining which then becomes ulcerated in individuals with a chronically high level of pepsinogen.

This hypothesis was indeed supported in an early study by Weiner, Thaler, Reiser, and Mirsky (1957), who selected two extreme groups of individuals with very high or very low pepsinogen levels, from over 2,000 newly inducted draftees of the U.S. Army. A complete gastrointestinal checkup at the beginning of the basic training indicated that neither the high-risk group (sixty-three individuals) nor the low-risk group (fifty-seven individuals) had any incidence of peptic ulcers. In reexaminations of these individuals, which took place during the eighth and the sixteenth weeks of their basic training, nine ulcer cases were found, all in the group with the habitually high pepsinogen level. The fact that none of these draftees, regardless of level of pepsinogen, suffered from peptic ulcers at the beginning of the training would be consistent with the assumption that the disease results from an interaction of an individual predisposition (high pepsinogen level) and environmental stress (basic training).

While Weiner et al. (1957) examined the effect of a differential predisposition on the development of peptic ulcers among individuals who were all exposed to the same stressful environment, Ackerman, Manaker, and Cohen (1981) employed a more common research procedure by comparing the frequency of stressful life experiences among ulcer patients with that of a matched control group of appendectomy patients. Data collected retrospectively, on the incidence of separation or loss among these patients in the year preceding hospital admission, indicated that ten of the twenty-four ulcer patients (44 percent) had suffered instances of separation (6) or loss (4). In comparison, of the twenty-four appendectomy patients there was no incidence of loss and only one incidence of separation (4 percent). However, the authors themselves caution that "the sources and quality of information were not the same for the peptic ulcer disease and appendectomy groups," since the "social history obtained at the time of admission noted in the medical record is likely to be much more extensive for patients with peptic ulcer disease than for patients with appendicitis" (p. 307). Thus, most of the information on appendicitis patients had to be collected by telephone interviews which were sometimes conducted several years after the release of the patient from the hospital. Since we know that individuals remember less and less about critical life events the longer the time between the interview and the period in life examined (Casey, Masuda, & Holmes, 1967), this difference in procedure could account for the findings. Thus, while the above studies are indicative, more evidence, preferably from prospective studies, is needed to confirm the relationship between stressful life events and peptic ulcers.

However, the assumption that stress contributes to the development of peptic ulcers has been consistently supported in animal studies. Since the original report of Selye (1936) that various forms of physical restraint applied to rats produced gastric lesions, it has been shown that ulceration can be induced in rats by various other methods (e.g., electric shocks, psychological conflict, attacks by conspecifics). The most extensive research into this issue has been conducted by Jay Weiss (1977, 1984).

The work of Weiss is particularly interesting because it contradicts one of the most popularized findings in psychology, the myth of the executive monkey who developed ulcers (Brady, 1958). These reports were based on a study of four pairs of monkeys who were strapped into seats and exposed to electric shock. In each pair, one monkey, called the "executive," was able to press a lever that postponed the onset of a shock by twenty seconds. Thus, while continued pressing could postpone the onset indefinitely, any failure to respond within twenty seconds of the last response resulted in a shock. Whenever the executive monkey failed to prevent the shock, the nonexecutive monkey was shocked as well (yoked control). The yoked nonexecutive in each pair therefore received as many shocks as the executive, but had no control. In all four pairs, the executive monkeys died from duodenal ulcers, often still strapped to their seats, while the yoked monkeys stayed healthy and fit.

Nevertheless, the findings fit perfectly with the popular image of the stressed business executive as an endangered species. It is much less consistent with present-day psychological notions about learned helplessness and the beneficial effect of having control (Seligman, 1975). However, the Brady findings not only could not be replicated in more recent studies, but Weiss (1977) observed with rats that it was those that had no control which developed stomach lesions. Weiss used "matched triplets" of animals in these studies. All animals had a wheel in front of them and their tails tied to an electrode. Only one wheel, the wheel of the "executive rat," was connected to the shock apparatus and, if turned, avoided the shock for the executive as well as for the yoked control, whose wheel was not connected. The third animal did not receive any shocks at all. While the yoked animals developed an average of 4.5 mm lesions, the executive rats with 1.5 mm lesions showed hardly more damage than the no-shock controls, with 0.5 mm.

These findings, which once more suggest that it is not the aversive stimulation per se, but the lack of control over it which does the damage, fit nicely with findings on humans, such as the results of Cobb and Rose (1973). These authors reported that ulcers were twice as frequent among air traffic controllers than among pilots. One attractive interpretation of this result is that pilots develop fewer ulcers because they have more control. But, as always with this type of research, there are so many other differences in the work situation, and in the selection of individuals into these groups, that alternative interpretations are hard to rule out. For example, it is quite possible that flying in today's highly automated planes is less stressful than the continual vigilance required from air traffic controllers. A less likely explanation, but one which cannot be ruled out either, is that the job of air traffic controller for some reason attracts more individuals with a predisposition to ulcers (e.g., high pepsinogen secretion).

Since animal studies provide the possibility of eliminating such loose ends by random assignment and by experimental control over conditions, one would expect more clear-cut results from the latter. How, then, can we explain the contradiction between the Brady and the Weiss findings? Surprising though it sounds, it seems that Brady did not assign animals to conditions randomly. True to real life, the executive job was always given to that member of the pair who learned the avoidance response faster. This may have been a fateful mistake, since it has been shown with rats that the ones who learn fastest are also more susceptible to gastric ulceration (Sines, Cleeland, & Adkins, 1963).

6.2.5 Stress and depression

The last decades have seen great progress in the identification of physiological mechanisms assumed to mediate the relationship between stress and depression (Depue, 1979; Depue & Evans, 1981; Willner, 1985). Research into physiological processes associated with depression has focused on deficiencies in the level of neurotransmitters in the brain. As we discussed earlier, the transmission of signals is not based on changes in electrical potential *inside* of nerves, but on chemical substances *between* them. When an electric impulse reaches the terminal button of one nerve axon, it causes the release of a messenger substance (the neurotransmitter) which floods the gap between the terminal button of one neuron and the cell body of another neuron (the synapse) and stimulates an electric impulse in the next neuron. The neurotransmitter is then removed from the synapse by two processes: Most of it is inactivated by a reuptake process, whereby the released transmitter substance is actively transported back into the presynaptic terminal. A small proportion, however, is biochemically deactivated on the spot, rather than being retransported (Depue & Evans, 1981). The level of the neurotransmitter inside the presynaptic terminal is regulated by monoamine oxidase (MAO), which deactivates any of the neurotransmitter substance that leaks out of the vesicles in which it is normally stored.

Two groups of neurotransmitters, both monoamines, have been identified as important for those parts of the brain which are involved in the regulation of mood and emotions: Norepinephrine and dopamine (which are catecholamines) and serotonin (which is an indoleamine). That depressions were somehow related to deficiencies in brain monoamines was suggested in the early fifties by two chance discoveries. These were reports that reserpine, a drug prescribed against high blood pressure, had serious side effects, causing depression in some 15 percent of the patients (Schildkraut, 1978; Willner, 1985). Animal studies suggested that reserpine depleted body cells of norepinephrine and serotonin by impairing storage capacity. At about the same time, it was discovered that a drug originally used in the treatment of tuberculosis (iproniazid) could cause euphoria and had antidepressant properties for some patients. Studies on animals showed that this drug inhibited the enzyme MAO and prevented the deactivation of brain monoamines, thus raising the level of these neurotransmitters in the brain. This resulted in the development of the first antidepressant drug, iproniazid, in 1956. Today, however, the most important antidepressant drugs are the tricyclic antidepressants. These increase the physiological effect of the monoamines by two mechanisms: They interfere with the reuptake process and also with the deactivation of the monoamines inside the terminal by inhibiting the effects of MAO (Depue & Evans, 1981).

These observations led to the formulation of the *catecholamine hypothesis of depression* by Schildkraut (1965) and others (e.g., Bunney & Davis, 1965). The catecholamine hypothesis states "that some, if not all, depressions are associated with an absolute or relative deficiency of catecholamines particularly noradrenaline at functionally important adrenergic receptor sites in the brain" (Schildkraut 1965, p. 509). Other researchers (e.g., Coppen, 1972) have since argued that deficiencies in brain levels of serotonin are equally important.

Due to the inaccessibility of brain tissue and the difficulty of direct measurement, two indirect strategies have been used to examine the validity of the catecholamine hypothesis. One approach tests the assumption that depression involves a catecholamine deficiency in the brain by correcting that deficiency through the administration of the amines in large doses. Since norepinephrine does not pass the blood–brain barrier (Depue & Evans, 1981) these studies used the drug L-dopa, which can enter the brain and should allow a greater amount of catecholamines, including norepinephrine, to be produced. If the catecholamine hypothesis were correct, administering L-dopa to depressed individuals should be therapeutically effective. However, as Depue and Evans (1981) point out, research employing this strategy has found little improvement in the majority of depressed patients studied (e.g., Bunney, Brodie, Murphy, & Goodwin, 1971). This evidence is not considered conclusive, however, since orally administered L-dopa may lead to only marginal increases in the level of norepinephrine in the brain and also has a number of other effects, including a reduction in serotonin (Depue & Evans, 1981; Murphy, 1972).

A second and more indirect strategy aims at measuring the metabolites of these neurotransmitters, the byproducts of the breakdown of norepinephrine found in the cerebrospinal fluid (CSF) or the urine. Since there is evidence that norepinephrine is metabolized within the central nervous system into 3-methoxy-4-hydroxyphenylglycol (MHPG), MHPG concentration in the cerebrospinal fluid and levels of urinary MHPG have been used to assess, indirectly, brain norepinephrine. While CSF studies have been rather inconclusive (Depue & Evans, 1981; Willner, 1985) the studies comparing the urinary MHPG levels of depressed patients (who have not been treated pharmacologically for their depressive disorders) with that of healthy subjects have usually (e.g., Maas, Fawcett, & Dekirmenjian, 1968) but not always (e.g., Agren, 1982) confirmed the hypothesis that depressives have lower MHPG levels.

Despite the fact that support for the catecholamine hypothesis is rather tenuous, it is tempting to speculate about the mechanisms by which stress may lead to a depletion in brain monoamines. It can be assumed that stress causes an increase in the turnover of brain monoamines. In fact, Rubin, Miller, Clark, et al. (1970) showed that naval aviators who had to perform simulated as well as actual carrier landings had MHPG levels which were significantly elevated for the actual day and night landings, but not for simulated landings. Normally, these levels return to base line soon after the cessation of the stress experience. However, one might expect that after extensive periods of stress, and particularly in the presence of some genetic predisposition, a more permanent insufficiency in the level of brain monoamines may ensue. Prange, Wilson, Knox, et al. (1972) presented some evidence which suggests that prolonged stress may impair the postsynaptic receptor sensitivity leading to a compensatory increase in presynaptic norepinephrine. Thus, as stress accumulates, such individuals will not be able to synthesize functionally adequate levels of norepinephrine.

That extensive stress experiences can lead to a depletion in norepinephrine levels was demonstrated in a classic series of studies by Jay Weiss and his colleagues (Weiss, Glazer, Pohorecky, et al., 1979). Using the same equipment as in their studies of ulceration in rats, Weiss and his colleagues showed that rats exposed to an extensive series of electric shocks, which they could not avoid, had lower norepinephrine levels than control animals which were not shocked. Animals which could control the shocks, on the other hand, showed even higher levels of brain norepinephrine than control animals. These results were found regardless of whether the shock control involved physical activity (e.g., turning the wheel) or physical inactivity (e.g., not moving). Since the animals which could control shocks and those which could not were run as yoked pairs, and thus received the same amount of electric shock, the findings again indicate that it is the lack of control over the aversive stimulation rather than the aversive stimulation, per se, which seems to account for the stressful nature of the situation.

Weiss and his colleagues (Weiss et al., 1979) further demonstrated that rats exposed to a stressor (in this case a forced swim of 3.5 and 6.5 minutes was used) showed the same inability to learn an avoidance–escape response as the dogs exposed to unavoidable shocks in the learned-helplessness experiments of Seligman and his colleagues (e.g., Overmier & Seligman, 1967; Seligman & Maier, 1967). Weiss et al. (1979) therefore offered norepinephrine depletion as an alternative explanation for the behavior deficits which Seligman (1975) attributed to learned helplessness.

However, as Glass (1977) pointed out, the two interpretations are not necessarily contradictory: "A possible reconciliation is to accept the notion that subjects learn to give up and treat norepinephrine depletion as a biochemical correlate of this process" (p. 171). While Weiss et al. (1979) would probably agree that norepinephrine depletion is the physiological reflection of some psychological process, they insist that this process is not learned helplessness. Their rejection of learned helplessness as a psychological explanation of these performance deficits is based on the transience of these performance deficits, which typically disappear within forty-eight hours after the exposure to inescapable shock. If the animal had really learned that it cannot control shock exposure, these deficits should be more permanent.

More damaging to a learned-helplessness interpretation of such behavior deficits are the findings of a further study, in which Weiss et al. (1979) demonstrated that behavioral deficits do not appear if animals are injected with a monoamine oxidase inhibitor before being exposed to inescapable shock. Thus, a drug which is known to relieve the symptoms of depression in humans has been demonstrated to alleviate behavioral deficits in rats exposed to uncontrollable stress.

The fact that animals recover within forty-eight hours from norepinephrine depletion induced by exposure to unavoidable shock, while periods of depression last much longer in humans, tends to detract from the value of the studies of Weiss and his colleagues as an analogy of human depression. Unlike animals, human beings have a tendency to internalize threats, and such resentment, regret, and worry cannot as readily be fought or avoided as external threats. It seems reasonable, though admittedly highly speculative, to suggest that the aftereffects of stressful life experiences on our system are much longer-lasting than those observed in rats exposed to electric shock.

Since depression is a psychological rather than a physical impairment, understanding the physical processes that might mediate the stress–illness relationship seem to be less essential. There is therefore less reason to be concerned about the apparent inconsistency in research findings in this area. Furthermore, regardless of whether or not depression in bereavement is characterized by a catecholamine deficiency, we doubt that antidepressant drugs will be helpful in cases of normal bereavement. To cope emotionally with bereavement, it is essential for the widowed to work through their loss, and this grief work cannot be replaced by medication.

6.3 Conclusions

In this chapter on the relationship between stress and health, we tried to go beyond the mere demonstration of the impact of stressful life events on health. Since many individuals become ill without being under stress and similarly, many individuals under stress do not become ill, such general conclusions are of little help in identifying risk groups. Progress in this area can only be made if the behavioral and physiological changes which mediate the relationship of stress and health are successfully identified.

Although, in an attempt to disentangle some of these mechanisms, we discussed behavioral and physiological changes separately, it is likely that the health consequences of stress result from the closely interrelated action of many of these processes. For example, the immunosuppressive effect of stress may be aggravated by poor diet and a lack of health care, and may accelerate the development of infectious diseases. These, in turn, may not only be the result of a lack of care on the part of the individual but also of a lack of instrumental social support from friends or relatives. A case in point is the increased mortality of the bereaved due to tuberculosis. Since tubercular infections are frequently counteracted by the healthy body's natural defences, the increases in these infections may reflect the impact of bereavement on the immune system. However, a poor diet is also a factor contributing to the illness, since tubercle bacilli thrive in the presence of malnutrition and tuberculosis patients require a good, mixed diet with sufficient protein and vitamins. The excess in tuberculosis deaths among the bereaved further suggests that medical treatment may not have been sought in time. Tuberculosis can typically be arrested or even cured by drug treatment.

One question which remains open is whether the loss experience results in health deterioration by accelerating or aggravating existing illnesses or whether it can also be the cause of new illness. We believe that this question is oversimplistic. It is based on the outdated disease model of "one germ, one disease, one therapy" (Engel, 1977). If it is accepted that diseases are typically the result of an interaction between psychological as well as biological factors, one cannot keep on searching for single-cause explanations. Thus, exposure to an infectious agent is a necessary but not a sufficient cause of an infection. For example, it has been reported (e.g., Cornfeld & Hubbard, 1961) that among people colonized with streptococci, only 20 to 40 percent actually become ill. It is not entirely clear why some people have greater resistance than others. If one assumes, however, that an individual who develops an illness would not have done so without the existence of a stress-induced impairment in immune reactions, it would be impossible to decide whether responsibility should be attributed to the pathogen or to the impairment of the immune system.

7   The loss effect: health consequences of marital bereavement

Grief over the death of a spouse is an immensely painful experience. Those who suffer show psychological and physical symptoms which for some considerable period of time are very similar to those of clinical depression. It is comforting to know, however, that after twelve to eighteen months most bereaved begin to recover and ultimately show little sign of psychological or physical damage. Though they may still miss their partners intensely at times, having worked through their grief, they will be ready and able to cope with the demands of everyday life. And yet, the age-old belief that grief can have lethal consequences is more than a myth. As we will show in this chapter, there is a great deal of evidence which links widowhood to an increase in clinical depression, mental illness, physical illness, and mortality from natural as well as unnatural causes such as suicide. This negative impact of bereavement on health has been called the *loss effect* (W. Stroebe et al., 1982). But before we discuss these findings, a brief overview of the methodology used in this area will be provided since, as we will show, an accurate assessment of the extent of health risk has frequently been obscured by a failure to follow methodologically stringent procedures.

7.1   Methodological issues in bereavement research

7.1.1   *The choice of data base: large-scale survey versus in-depth interview*

Investigations of the impact of bereavement on mental and physical health fall fairly clearly into two categories, large-scale epidemiological surveys of representative and often nationwide samples, and studies in which in-depth interviews are conducted with small and nonrepresentative samples of bereaved and nonbereaved subjects. As in all research, the choice of data base will depend on the goals and priorities which led to the planning of the research project.

121

(i) The large-scale survey

If it is the major aim of a study to describe the frequency with which marital bereavement is associated with deterioration in mental and physical health, data are needed from representative samples of widows and widowers. Since representative samples, especially if they are nationwide, are quite expensive, it is fortunate that most governments routinely collect data on vital health statistics and also provide a breakdown of these data according to marital status categories. Thus, if one were interested in the relative mortality of widowers as compared to married men, one would only have to consult mortality statistics published by the National Center for Health Statistics in the United States or by the Office of Population Census and Surveys in Great Britain. A further source of representative data are the self-ratings of health and well-being frequently included in opinion polls, which, if broken down by marital status, allow widowed-to-married comparisons on these variables.

Classic examples of this type of approach are the studies of Farr (1975) and Durkheim (1951) mentioned earlier (Section 1.1). More recently, Kraus and Lilienfeld (1959) conducted a widely cited cross-sectional analysis of mortality among the bereaved, based on comprehensive statistical data on mortality by marital status published by the National Office of Vital Statistics in 1956. Their analysis, which took into account marital status, age, sex, race, and cause of death, found clear differences in mortality risk between the widowed and those remaining married. For all age groups and for both sexes the mortality risk of the widowed was consistently higher than that for married individuals of the same age and sex.

It is evident that the secondary analysis of large bodies of epidemiological data provides valuable information on the prevalence of health problems in the bereaved. They do avoid certain pitfalls of small in-depth investigations. For example, even when survey data are collected by interview, demand characteristics in health assessments are generally less problematic than is the case for in-depth studies of samples of bereaved individuals, since a connection between widowhood and the variables measured is not usually made (widowed subjects are not interviewed in their status and role as "widowed"). Further, when vital health statistics are used, sampling bias through self-selection is circumvented. Also, data are usually collected from representative samples, and thus permit more generalization than small-sample studies.

Unfortunately, there are also a number of disadvantages which considerably weaken the validity of any conclusions based on such data (M.

Stroebe, 1984; M. Stroebe et al., 1981). First, the widowed are rarely subdivided according to length of widowhood. Most agencies do not even
collect this information. Thus, in most publications of vital health statistics, the duration of widowhood of the widows and widowers from whom
health data are collected is unknown. Since the health consequences of
bereavement are worst during the first year of bereavement (e.g., Glick,
Weiss, & Parkes, 1974; Parkes, Benjamin, & Fitzgerald, 1969), these
effects are likely to have been diluted by the presence of a large proportion
of widowed whose loss experience may date back more than a year, and
sometimes even more than a decade. Furthermore, the proportion of
recently bereaved in the widowed category of such large-scale statistics is
likely to be positively associated with age (i.e., longer durations in the
higher age categories). This correlation could contribute to the finding
that the health deterioration of the widowed is greatest for the younger
age groups (Kraus & Lilienfeld, 1959).

Another weakness of these statistics is that they do not allow one to
keep track of individuals who remarry. These individuals are simply
moved from the widowed to the married category. Because bad health
may lower the chances of marriage in a competitive marriage market, it
seems reasonable to believe that the healthy are more likely to remarry
than the unhealthy. This differential selection of the healthier individuals
out of the widowed into the married category could contribute to the
health difference between widowed and married typically observed in this
type of study. This artifact is particularly critical in the interpretation of
mortality statistics (see 7.4.1).

Finally, the limitations in quality and range of information collected in
large-scale surveys must be mentioned: Government agencies or opinion
pollsters rarely gather in-depth information on psychological process or
state variables. Few national surveys of the general population are interested in, or ask questions about, grief.

(ii) The small in-depth study

Researchers interested in a more fine-grained analysis of predictors of
health risk and processes of coping with bereavement have little choice
but to conduct their own in-depth interviews with small samples of
recently bereaved individuals. The advantage of this method is that it
allows researchers to evaluate a great many variables of theoretical interest to them, their choice being constrained only by ethical concerns and
by the time the bereaved are willing to devote to the interview. Further-

more, investigators are usually able to reinterview their subjects and thus can provide a detailed description of the recovery process.

In the typical study of this type (e.g., Clayton & Darvish, 1979; Gallagher, Breckenridge, Thompson, & Peterson, 1983; Glick et al., 1974; W. Stroebe, Stroebe, & Domittner, 1985) lengthy interviews are conducted with samples of widows and widowers who are often interviewed several times after their bereavement to evaluate coping processes as well as grief symptoms and health consequences of bereavement. These interviews typically collect information about the nature of the marriage, about the events that preceded the spouse's death, about the circumstances of the death, about the respondent's current situation, his or her physical and mental health status and personality characteristics. The widows and widowers are usually matched with a control group of married women and men of the same age, sex, race, family size, and social class.

Although it will become apparent that a great deal of knowledge about the deterioration in physical and mental health following bereavement can be gained by this approach, it also suffers from a number of weaknesses: Due to the extensive time requirements for the in-depth interviews, usually only small samples of bereaved individuals can be studied. Thus, this type of investigation is inappropriate for the study of consequences of bereavement which are relatively infrequent (e.g., mortality at a given age, or the incidence of infrequent psychosomatic illnesses such as ulcerative colitis). However, even if resources were made available to conduct in-depth interviews with large samples of the recently bereaved, drawn to be representative on a nationwide scale, the high refusal rate typical for this type of research would rule out the possibility that the sample actually interviewed was still representative.

This reduction in sample size would be less problematic if it could be assumed that the selection was unrelated to any of the dependent measures studied. This is not very likely, however. It seems plausible that the willingness to participate in such a study is associated with the health status of the widowed. One might argue that it is the poorly off widowed who refuse to be interviewed (the loss is too painful for them to talk about) while those who are coping well are willing to talk about their bereavement. On the other hand, it seems equally reasonable to assume that those who suffer most feel the greatest need to talk about their experience, and one could as well imagine that those who have got over their grief do not want to be reminded of it by being interviewed.

In the Tübingen Longitudinal Study (W. Stroebe et al., 1985) the attempt was made to assess potential health differences between the widowed who agreed to participate in the interviews and those who refused.

The widowed individuals who declined participation by phone were asked whether they were willing to complete a short questionnaire. Fifteen percent of the widowed refusers agreed to perform this task. Furthermore, a much larger percentage of the refusers were willing to give informal reports on their health status by telephone. A comparison of the widowed interview refusers to the participants indicated an intriguing interaction between sex and participation status on the depression measures. While the widows who refused the interview were less depressed than the widows who agreed to be interviewed, the opposite difference was observed for the widowers. Since there is evidence to suggest that this selection effect reflects a general sex difference in the use of social contacts to cope with stressful life events (Section 8.2.2), it is likely that self-selection should follow different criteria with different methods of data collection (e.g., interview versus written response).

Finally, an issue should be mentioned which has, with the exception of a recent study by Caserta, Lund, and Dimond (1985), received little attention in the bereavement literature, namely, the possibility that by their very presence interviewers alter aspects of the situation that they are trying to study. Thus, in the course of in-depth interviews, especially when the same individual has to be interviewed repeatedly, the interviewer enters into an intense interaction with the bereaved. In their attempts to establish a rapport with respondents, interviewers may become a source of social support and thus help to reduce the stress of bereavement. Furthermore, by encouraging these recently bereaved to talk about their loss and their attempts at coping with grief, the interview itself could have therapeutic effects. Although this ameliorative impact is laudable on humanitarian grounds, the fact that a health measure leads to health improvement creates methodological difficulties which, if taken seriously, would necessitate the introduction of an additional control group. This control group would consist of bereaved individuals who are not interviewed but merely asked to fill out a questionnaire containing some of the health measures employed in the interview. This strategy was adopted by Caserta et al. (1985), who assigned elderly bereaved subjects to a personal interview or a postal questionnaire condition. Group assignment had no effect on depression, life satisfaction, or bereavement-related measures at six measurement periods across the first two years of bereavement. Replication with other subgroups of the bereaved, and including a control group which neither participated in interviews nor filled out postal questionnaires prior to the time of final measurement (which might also have been "therapeutic"), would help to establish the generality of these findings.

Any ameliorative effects on health measures may, however, be counterbalanced by subtle demand characteristics created in the interview situation. In interviewing recently widowed individuals about their feelings toward the deceased, their ways of coping and their health and well-being, one cannot help but make salient the widowed role. Since, at least in Western societies, depression and despair are part of the widowed role, widowed individuals who have made a speedy recovery may still report a great deal of despair in compliance with these role expectations. After all, to admit to well-being may be taken as an indication of lack of love for the deceased spouse.

The weaknesses characteristic of in-depth investigations described above need careful monitoring, but may not be as critical as they appear at first. There are a number of reasons for this: First, assessment of bias can be made to some extent by drawing comparisons with the results of the large-scale epidemiological surveys. Second, as the Tübingen study illustrates, attempts can be made to assess bias directly (e.g., accepter–refuser differences). Third, this type of design permits not only careful matching with nonbereaved controls but also longitudinal and prospective investigations (points which will be elaborated in the following sections), so that the selection bias within the bereaved sample may not be as critical as it appears to be. The main advantage of this type of study is that it provides a wealth of data on psychological variables, which, as we noted, are typically not provided by large-scale surveys.

7.1.2   *The choice of a comparison group*

Grief is not associated with any specific and distinct cause of death. It is assumed by most researchers in this area to act by aggravating or accelerating existing health problems. The impact of grief on health can therefore only be demonstrated by showing that the incidence and prevalence of certain illnesses is higher in a group of bereaved individuals than in an otherwise comparable nonbereaved comparison or control group. Thus, statements about the impact of bereavement on general health should be based on a comparison of bereaved to nonbereaved individuals. Frequently, however, one finds studies in the literature which do not include a nonbereaved control group (e.g., Caserta, Lund, & Dimond, 1985; Lund, Dimond, Caserta, et al., 1986; Smith, 1978; Stern, Williams, & Prados, 1951; Valanis & Yeaworth, 1982; Wretmark, 1959; Zisook & Schuchter, 1986). Some, but by no means all, of these studies make an assessment of the impact of bereavement on health by comparing health status at different points in time in relation to the loss event. But even in the rare case when prebereavement health measures are available, such a one-group, pretest–posttest design (Campbell & Stanley, 1963) does not allow one to control for numerous sources of invalidity such as "maturation" (e.g., a higher rate of illness after bereavement could be due to aging), "history" (a higher rate of illness after bereavment could be due to some external event unrelated to loss, e.g., to some epidemic) or "testing" (filling out tests repeatedly might have an influence on test scores).

There are some aspects of bereavement that can be investigated without inclusion of a nonbereaved control group into the design of the study. Thus, research that assesses psychological and physical bereavement reactions at several times after the loss experience without nonbereaved controls can be useful for the description of phases and symptomatology of grief over time, or for the comparison of recovery rates after different types of loss. Furthermore, comparison with nonbereaved control groups makes little sense if bereavement-specific symptoms (e.g., feelings of the presence of the deceased, acquisition of symptoms resembling those suffered by the deceased, yearning for the deceased) are studied rather than depression or somatic complaints. However, as will be discussed further in Chapter 8, the failure to compare health differences among subgroups of bereaved with that of corresponding groups of nonbereaved individuals often leads to the erroneous interpretation of population main effects as bereavement-specific risk factors. For example, if widows of lower social class are found to have poorer health than those of higher socioeconomic standing (e.g., Amir & Sharon, 1982; Sheldon, Cochrane, Vachon, et al., 1981), this difference could be due to the inverse relationship between social class and illness found in the general population rather than to social class differences in adjustment to loss.

How can one make sure that the individuals comprising the control group are really comparable to the bereaved sample in all important respects, except for the bereavement? Depending on one's professional background, different solutions to this problem will come to mind. Researchers trained in experimental psychology will think of random assignment as the most powerful tool of assuring the equivalence of comparison groups. Sociologists, on the other hand, are likely to suggest comparing representative samples of bereaved and nonbereaved individuals. While the first solution is impracticable for obvious reasons, the second is likely to be insufficient as the following example will show: Suppose we compared the physical health of a nationwide representative sample of widowed to that of a representative sample of married individuals and found a relative excess of health problems for the widowed. Would that justify the conclusion that marital bereavement increases the risk of ill health? Since the two samples differ in many other aspects associated with health in addition to bereavement, such a conclusion would definitely be unwarranted. The married sample is likely to be much younger than the widowed sample and this age difference alone could account for the health differential. There is also likely to be a greater proportion of women than men in the widowed rather than the married sample, since, due to the traditional age difference between marital partners and to the greater longevity of women, women are more likely to become widowed than men.

Thus, regardless of the representativeness of one's sampling, it will always be necessary to increase the equivalence of "treatment" and "comparison" groups by matching bereaved and nonbereaved individuals on all characteristics which are known to be associated with health status. In studies using large-scale epidemiological data, matching is achieved by comparing "adjusted" or "specific" (e.g., age- and sex-specific) rather than "crude" rates. In small-scale studies using in-depth interviews, the comparison group is typically matched to the bereaved sample on an individual basis.

The major weakness of the matching procedure is that the validity of any conclusions drawn from matched samples depends on the investigator's evaluation of what are plausible confounding variables. Obviously, this evaluation will only be as good as the state of our knowledge permits. Thus, while at present it is plausible that bereaved and nonbereaved individuals should be matched with regard to sex, age, and socioeconomic status, future research may point to other variables associated with health outcomes which are at present neglected in our matching procedures.

One matching problem which is specific to bereavement research is the decision *which* marital status to chose for the comparison group. Some researchers (e.g., Briscoe & Smith, 1975) have compared the widowed to the divorced. Although such comparisons are useful if one is interested in the differential consequences of different types of marital dissolution, they tell us nothing about the impact both kinds of dissolution have in common. Furthermore, if divorced individuals are found to suffer from psychiatric problems or poor physical health, their health problems could have been a cause of the divorce rather than an effect. The single, though similar to the widowed in being alone (at least by definition), may not be an ideal comparison group for reasons of selection. From middle age onwards, most people are married, and it is possible that individuals who are not married are in some way less fit for marriage (cf. Carter & Glick, 1976). To avoid this problem, most bereavement research uses married individuals as controls, because both the widowed and the married have been selected into marriage and remained married. Thus, both groups should be similar with regard to factors necessary for being chosen into marriage and for maintaining a relationship.

7.1.3 *Strategies of design*

(i) Longitudinal versus cross-sectional designs

The difference between a longitudinal and a cross-sectional design is in some ways similar to that between a snapshot and a motion picture: While the snapshot portrays the situation as it was at the moment at which the picture was taken, the film allows us to see how the situation unfolds through time. But the analogy is less than perfect, because cross-sectional studies can assess the dependent measure not only at one point in time but also across a certain duration of time (e.g., number of illnesses during the last six months). In longitudinal studies, on the other hand, the same set or cohort of individuals is studied repeatedly. Since both designs require the inclusion of a control group, both longitudinal and cross-sectional types of design involve cross-sectional comparisons of the health of bereaved and nonbereaved samples. But in addition to the cross-sectional analysis of differences between the control and bereaved sample at a given point in time, longitudinal designs permit us to examine health change over time.

Longitudinal investigations of the bereaved are typically undertaken from the time of the spouse's death (or as soon as possible thereafter) and include periodic follow-up examinations. Since they are the most suitable method for investigators interested in the relationship between processes of coping with the loss and outcome variables, it is not surprising that the majority of longitudinal studies employ in-depth interviews, whereas cross-sectional investigations typically use secondary data. There are exceptions, however, particularly in the area of mortality studies (e.g., Parkes et al., 1969).

(ii) Prospective versus retrospective designs

The distinction between a prospective or retrospective strategy refers to the difference between starting an investigation with the presumed cause and moving forward in time, as compared to starting at some later point in time and looking backward. A prospective study of the health consequences of bereavement will begin soon after the partner loss and then follow the cohort of bereaved individuals for a period of time to examine whether the incidence of ill health is greater in the bereaved rather than the nonbereaved sample. A retrospective study, on the other hand, will take a sample of individuals who have been widowed for some time, evaluate their health, and then search backward to see whether poor health is associated with certain risk factors such as the unexpectedness of the loss or low social support.

Retrospective studies are typically considered less valid than prospective studies. The major objection to retrospective investigations is that information collected after the event and based on subjects' recollections is likely to be affected by the time lag and colored by subsequent events. It is thus less trustworthy than information gathered beforehand. For example, if a group of clinically depressed individuals remember more negative life events for the previous two years than do nondepressed controls, this difference could merely reflect the biased memory processes typical for depression. Thus, given the same number of negative events, depressed individuals may recall negative instances forgotten or not perceived as critical life events by the nondepressed controls.

However, if a retrospective study is concerned with a cause which can be assessed objectively, such as the death of a spouse (e.g., Cottington, Matthews, Talbott, & Kuller, 1980), a retrospective design does not necessarily lead to less valid conclusions than a prospective strategy. The great advantage of retrospective studies is that they enable one to examine the role of bereavement in the etiology of relatively rare illnesses without using exceedingly large samples. For example, since very few individuals develop ulcerative colitis, one would need very large samples of bereaved and nonbereaved subjects to study prospectively the effect of bereavement on that illness. If, on the other hand, a sample of individuals who suffer from ulcerative colitis were identified and the proportion of bereaved individuals among them compared with the proportion among a group of individuals suffering from some other disease, for which psychosocial stressors are not assumed to be important (e.g., appendicitis), one might be able to demonstrate the causal role of bereavement in the etiology of ulcerative colitis using samples of no more than 80–100 individuals (e.g., Lindemann, 1950). Thus, the normal problems of retrospective studies may not always apply in bereavement research: To answer certain specific questions, such as the one just illustrated, they may be very useful.

7.1.4 *Measures of health*

In our analysis of the impact of bereavement on health we will depend on a number of different measures which vary in the degree to which they reflect bodily conditions. These measures should be interpreted with great care, since both medical diagnoses as well as self-reports are the product of a decision-making process which is likely to be influenced by a patient's personality as well as by social context variables. Thus, to be diagnosed as ill by a doctor, an individual has to go through a process which usually begins with some kind of self-diagnosis. The individual must first perceive some symptoms and define them as serious enough to reflect a medical condition which requires treatment. He or she must then act upon this diagnosis by seeking medical help. Finally, the medical practitioner must agree with the patient's evaluation and diagnose the presence of some ailment.

The probability that an individual notices a given physiological symptom will not only depend on the intensity of that symptom, but also on the presence or absence of competing symptoms or of distracting environmental events (Pennebaker, 1982). Since the stress of bereavement and the resulting activity of the autonomous nervous system are typically associated with a number of psychosomatic symptoms, cues signaling the development of some illness should be more difficult to notice. It also seems plausible to assume, at least in the case of the recently bereaved, that the process of grief work should distract the individual from paying much attention to physiological symptoms. However, in a small proportion of his bereaved patients, Parkes (1986) observed the opposite tendency. These women complained of aches and pains similar to those prominent during the last illness of the person for whom they grieved. The symptoms could be considered hypochondriacal since they did not reflect true illness. This would suggest, then, that the "alarm system," which helps to distinguish illness cues from other bodily sensations, is frequently impaired during bereavement. Physiological symptoms signaling the presence of some "real" illness are less likely to be noticed, either because the individual is still too preoccupied with grief work or because of the presence of competing symptoms, which may be the result of somatic arousal or of hypochondriacal processes.

It would seem rational to assume that the use of medical facilities should closely reflect the patient's medical needs. It is well known, however, that help-seeking behavior is only partly determined by illness cues. In our secular age, physicians are often forced into the role of psychological counselor, previously enacted by the cleric. Thus, controlling for "objective health status," Tessler, Mechanic, and Dimond (1976) found that individuals who were psychologically distressed were more likely to visit their physicians than nondistressed individuals. This would suggest that, given comparable health status, bereaved individuals should be more likely to see their doctors than individuals who have not recently suffered a loss. We would further expect this tendency to be more marked in health systems where medical services are either paid by the state or covered by compulsory health insurance schemes.

Finally, medical diagnoses and treatment recommendations are not based exclusively on symptomatology but also take into account the past history and present circumstances of the patient. There has even been evidence of subjective adjustment in diagnoses: Psychiatrists have been found to underrate the severity of symptoms reported by women (who complain of many more ailments than men) and attach greater weight to the same symptoms if reported by a man (Langner & Michael, 1963). Similarly, one might expect that the information that a patient has recently suffered marital bereavement could affect the diagnosis. For example, physicians may tend to devalue certain symptoms as due to grief and prescribe some form of mild tranquilizers. If, on the other hand, they diagnose some serious complaint, they might be more likely to decide on hospitalization in the case of a widowed rather than a married patient, unless it is known that the widowed individual has relatives or friends to provide care. Clearly, hospitalization is not an accurate measure of the severity of a disease, particularly if comparisons are to be made across marital status groups, which differ systematically in the availability of persons to assist with home care.

Thus, in interpreting health measures based on self-reports or medical diagnoses, we must always be aware of the possibility that the differences between samples of bereaved and nonbereaved individuals may partly reflect the direct effect of bereavement on self-perceived health or on treatment-seeking behavior rather than differential rates in physical or mental illness.

7.1.5   *Conclusions and implications*

For social psychologists used to experimental research plans which allow them to assign subjects randomly to social environments of their own design, doing bereavement research is a sobering experience. Not only has one no control at all over the social context, but one is also an intruder into the world of the bereaved, and must fully respect their decision, if they do not wish to participate in a research project. This precludes representative sampling in any investigation attempting the in-depth analysis of processes of coping with bereavement. With very few exceptions (e.g., Lopata, 1979) representative samples have only been studied in investigations based on secondary data. As we have pointed out earlier, however, the use of secondary data does not permit an in-depth study of the personality of the bereaved, their coping processes, or the pattern of their recovery from grief.

To counterbalance the problems associated with either methodology, we have always favored a convergent strategy in drawing conclusions about determinants of bereavement outcomes. We have argued (e.g., M. Stroebe & Stroebe, 1983) that since the biases of the large-scale epidemiological studies and of the small-scale interview studies somewhat compensate for each other and since different areas of bereavement reactions are vulnerable to different threats to validity, one has to examine results from both types of studies for all major areas of bereavement reactions. In the following review of the evidence on bereavement consequences, we will base our conclusions mainly on findings which have been replicated across different designs and different bereavement reactions.

7.2 Mental health

7.2.1 *Depression in bereavement*

Since sadness and despair are core symptoms of grief, a major proportion of the research on health consequences of bereavement has focused on the frequency and intensity of depression among the bereaved (e.g., Bornstein, Clayton, Halikas, Maurice, & Robins, 1973; Carey, 1977, 1979; Gallagher, Breckenridge, Thompson, & Peterson, 1983; Glick et al., 1974; Radloff, 1975; van Rooijen, 1979; Stroebe, Stroebe, & Domittner, 1985). These studies provide convincing evidence for the assumption that recent bereavement is associated with depression.

One relatively comprehensive source of data is a household survey conducted between 1971 and 1973 in two communities in the United States by the Center for Epidemiological Studies (CES) of the National Institute of Mental Health (Radloff, 1975). In this survey, 2,829 residents, constituting 75 to 80 percent of a sample drawn to be representative for the two communities, were administered the CES-D, a twenty-item depression scale. Since preliminary analyses suggested that data from whites and nonwhites should not be combined and since the number of nonwhite residents was too small to be analyzed separately in any detail, data were only reported for the 2,514 white residents, of whom 315 were widowed and 1,710 married.

Table 7.1 presents the average depression scores for the married and widowed, separately by sex. The depression scores for the total sample show the typical pattern (see Lehmann, 1971; Silverman, 1968; Weiss-

Table 7.1 *Average depression scores of a community sample by sex and marital status (adapted from Radloff, 1975)*

Status	Men	Women
Married	7.33[a]	9.53
	(779)	(931)
Widowed	12.80	10.34
	(45)	(270)

Note: Sample size indicated in brackets.
[a]Higher numbers indicate higher levels of depression.

man & Klerman, 1977) with women being more depressed than men. Surprisingly, however, a comparison of the married and widowed suggests that widowhood is associated with heightened depression only for men but not women. Although we have argued elsewhere (M. Stroebe & Stroebe, 1983) that if there is a sex difference in conjugal bereavement reactions, it is the men who suffer more, it is somewhat atypical to find that women do not seem to be affected at all.

One reason for this failure to find any indication of increased depression among the widows may have been the composition of the widowed sample studied by Radloff (1975). A large proportion of the sample consisted of widowed of long standing, who had had a great deal of time to recover from their loss experience. Certainly the thirty-three widowed who had lost their partners within one year of the study showed signs of much more marked depression (CES-D score of 18.36). Perhaps women are as depressed as men initially, but take less time to adjust to loss. Unfortunately, Radloff did not separate the data for the recently bereaved by sex and it is thus not possible to check this hypothesis.

As so often in this area, there are alternative interpretations of the data pattern which are equally plausible but theoretically much less intriguing. Since widowers have a much higher remarriage rate than widows, the average duration of widowhood in a representative sample of widowed is likely to be shorter for men than for women. With the emotional impact of bereavement lessening over time, a difference in duration of widowhood could account for the higher depression scores of widowers as compared to widows. Furthermore, if we assume that it is the healthier wid-

Table 7.2 *Average depression scores of a sample of Boston widows and widowers after fourteen months of bereavement (adapted from Parkes & Brown, 1972)*

Status	Men	Women
Married	2.84[a]	4.63
	(19)	(49)
Widowed	4.89	6.57
	(19)	(49)

Note: Sample size indicated in brackets.
[a]Higher numbers indicate higher levels of depression.

owed who remarry, differential selection due to remarriage may have led to a widening of the sex difference in average depression scores.

Some support for the assumption that women need less time to recover from loss than men comes from the Harvard Bereavement Study of Parkes and his associates (Glick et al., 1974; Parkes & Brown, 1972; Parkes & Weiss, 1983). In this investigation, a sample of widows and widowers, matched individually to a control group of married women and men of the same age, sex, race, family size, and social class, were interviewed repeatedly during the first few years following the loss. Among many health measures, an eighteen-item depression scale (constructed by the authors) was administered to forty-nine widows and nineteen widowers, fourteen months after bereavement. This group of sixty-eight widowed, with whom interviews could be completed during the first year, constituted 30 percent of those who were initially contacted and found eligible. In a long-term follow-up, this scale was readministered to an even smaller proportion of the original sample at two to four years after bereavement.

A comparison of the depression mean scores of the sixty-eight widowed subjects at fourteen months of bereavement with those of sixty-eight married controls (Table 7.2) suggests two main effects, one for sex and one for bereavement. Women show higher depression scores than men and bereaved individuals are more depressed than nonbereaved individuals. There is no indication of a sex by marital status interaction. The widowed to married difference in depression scores is practically identical for both sexes.

It is only in the long-term follow-up at two to four years that a sex difference in bereavement reactions seems to have emerged. Although widowed depression scores showed a steady decline for both sexes during that period, an analysis combining the data for the second, third, and fourth years still yielded a significant married-to-widowed difference for men but not for women. Thus, the failure of Radloff to observe a marked widowed-to-married difference for women, while at the same time finding a difference for men, would be entirely consistent with the pattern reported by Parkes and his associates (e.g., Parkes & Brown, 1972).

Since differences in mean depression scores, though statistically significant, could merely reflect minor variations within the range of good health, such differences say very little about the severity of the depression suffered by the bereaved. Therefore, Carey (1977, 1979), Clayton and associates (Bornstein et al., 1973; Clayton & Darvish, 1979), Gallagher et al. (1983), van Rooijen (1979), and W. Stroebe et al. (1985) went beyond the comparison of depression levels and attempted to assess the proportion of their samples of recently bereaved for whom the experience of partner loss was associated with marked depression.

Carey (1977) interviewed a group of 78 widows and 41 widowers at thirteen to sixteen months after the deaths of their partners. The sample consisted of every widow and widower of 70 years or younger whose spouse died in a general hospital during the first eleven months of 1974. Of the 221 possible respondents, 119 (54 percent) agreed to participate, 38 (17 percent) refused, and 64 (29 percent) could not be contacted. The comparison group consisted of 100 married people who were approached randomly in and around the hospital.

Carey used an eight-item Adjustment Scale which elicited self-reports of feelings of loneliness, depression, and unhappiness. Scores ranged from 8 to 24, with a mean at 18.9 and a standard deviation of 4.8. Depression was defined somewhat arbitrarily as a range between a score of 8 and 15. According to this criterion, 25 percent of the widowed were depressed as compared to only 3.5 percent of the married, a difference which is highly significant. Although these data clearly demonstrate that even thirteen to sixteen months after the loss of their partners, these widows and widowers were more depressed than their married controls, the intensity of their depression is difficult to evaluate due to the use of a newly constructed measure and the arbitrary nature of the criteria for defining depression.

Similar problems arise in interpreting the findings of a study of widowed depression in women, which was conducted in the Netherlands by van Rooijen (1979). Van Rooijen mailed questionnaires to 340 women residing in Amsterdam, whose husbands had died sixteen to eighteen months earlier. Of the 210 questionnaires (62 percent of the total) which were returned, 194 (59 percent) were usable. Nonusable questionnaires were discarded mainly because of too many missing responses. The non-bereaved control group consisted of 73 married, divorced, or single women who were residents of two nearby towns. Depressive mood was measured in both samples with the Dutch version of the Depression Adjective Check List (Lubin, 1965; van Rooijen, 1979). Van Rooijen used a cut-off score of 2 standard deviations above the mean of his control group as a criterion of extreme depression. In a normal distribution, such a cut-off score would separate the 2.3 percent of cases with extremely high values from the 97.7 percent of cases with lower values. Although nearly half of his control group consisted of divorced and single women, van Rooijen found that only two of the control group (2.8 percent) received scores of 18 or above as compared to 36 percent of the widowed sample. Thus, more than one-third of the widowed sample suffered from an extreme level of depressive mood.

Clayton and associates (Bornstein et al., 1973; Clayton & Darvish, 1979) avoided the problem of arbitrariness in defining depression by using the widely accepted criteria for clinical depression developed by Feighner et al. (1972) described earlier (Chapter 2.3.2). Subjects in Clayton's investigation were 109 white widowed (76 female, 33 male), who were either chosen on the basis of obituaries in the local newspaper or from death certificates. The overall acceptance rates for these methods was 58 percent. The first interview was conducted with 92 members of the original sample. While 35 percent of the widowed could be categorized as probable or definite depressions at one month after the loss, this was true for only 17 percent one year later.

W. Stroebe et al. (1985) and Gallagher et al. (1983) defined depression in terms of criteria suggested for the Beck Depression Inventory (BDI) which is widely used in screening for psychiatric interviews. According to these criteria, BDI scores of 11 and above can be classified as mild to severe depression. A score of 19 is suggested as the lower cut-off point for moderate depression.

In the Tübingen Longitudinal Study of Bereavement (W. Stroebe et al., 1985) thirty widows and thirty widowers under the age of 60 were given the BDI at four to six months after bereavement. In terms of Beck's criteria 42 percent of the widowed fell within the range of mild-to-severe depression as compared to 10 percent of the married. Even the more stringent criteria for moderate-to-severe depression were still fulfilled by 14 percent of the widowed but only by 5 percent of the married. Thus, their recent bereavement was associated with a significant increase in mild to moderate depression. At the second interview at thirteen to fifteen months after the loss, there was only moderate improvement in the BDI scores of the widowed sample.

Similar findings were reported by Gallagher et al. (1983; cf. also Breckenridge, Gallagher, Thompson, & Peterson, 1986), who compared samples of 113 widows and 98 widowers over the age of 55 to matched married controls (acceptance rate: 30 percent) on the BDI and other health measures. Controlling for sociodemographic differences between the bereaved and the married samples, the odds for mild-to-severe depression at two to four months were found to be approximately 1.50 times higher for the bereaved than the married controls, a difference which was highly significant.

What then is the "true" rate of depression after one year of bereavement? Is it 36 percent, as van Rooijen's findings would lead one to believe, or is the estimate of 16 percent suggested by Clayton and Darvish nearer to the truth? This question cannot be answered from the evidence presented, since these studies used different criteria in their definition of depression and sampled different populations. Furthermore, in view of the high refusal rates, it is even doubtful whether the rates reported in these studies reflect the actual distribution of depressive symptoms in the widowed populations from which these samples were drawn. However, despite variations in the estimates of the proportion of widowed individuals to be classified as depressed, these studies are consistent in finding bereavement associated with significant increases in depression.

To our knowledge there is only one study which has not reported a significant increase in depression following bereavement. Heyman and Gianturco (1973) found that emotional stability characterized the adaptation of a sample of elderly widowed at twenty-one months after loss. The report does not include nonbereaved controls but, as subjects were drawn from the Duke University Study of Aging and Human Development, ratings before and after bereavement were available for comparison. The authors discussed a number of reasons for the lack of distress and depression in this sample. These relate to characteristics of the particular group of widowed persons studied, such as relief at the ending of prolonged suffering, a lessening of the sheer physical exhaustion of caretaking which these aged survivors had undertaken, the presence of ample social support structures in the particular community, and psychological preparation for the death of the partner and for the role of widowhood. While a number of these factors are to be found in other studies, this study is probably the only one in which so many ameliorative factors appear together. It is quite likely that this accounts for the good adaptation and low level of depression.

There seems little doubt that recent bereavement is associated with a heightened risk of depression and that it may reach the criteria for diagnosis of clinical depression. Similar conclusions were reached by Paykel (1985), who reviewed the literature on recent separations on bereavement and depression. His conclusion was, however, cautious: "There is some relationship between depression and interpersonal losses, but these also precede other disorders, and many depressions are not preceded by them" (1985, p. 329). With respect to the duration of depression after bereavement, it is by now well accepted (cf. Osterweis, Solomon, & Green, 1984) that symptoms may endure for far longer, often very unevenly, than the calendar year commonly expected for recovery.

7.2.2 Mental illness

The category of "mental illness" is a residual category combining many diverse and unrelated disorders. As Gove (1979) criticized, to "treat all phenomena that receive a psychiatric label as the same disorder makes about as much sense as a doctor treating all persons admitted to a general hospital (including those admitted to the psychiatric ward) as suffering from the same disease" (p. 23). However, since in this section we are interested in marital status differences in the rates of psychiatric problems severe enough to need medical treatment, it seems justifiable to group together diverse psychiatric illnesses according to their severity, disregarding for the moment differences in etiology or symptomatology.

Although patterns may be changing in the 1980s, a gender main effect in the occurrence of psychiatric disorders has consistently been reported: Women are more likely to be mentally ill than men (see Gove & Tudor, 1973; Hammen & Padesky, 1977; Phillips & Segal, 1969). This sex difference has been found in a variety of different types of study (community surveys, inception rates to in- or outpatient psychiatric care, census information, etc.). This main effect is important to remember when considering the effect of bereavement on mental illness, because it means that more widows than widowers are likely to be found in psychiatric care, even if the effect of bereavement is similar on males and females.

The literature comparing mental illness rates of married and widowed samples has presented a very consistent pattern (see, e.g., Bachrach, 1975; Bloom, Asher, & White, 1978; Crago, 1972; Gove, 1972a; Redick & Johnson, 1974). Compared to married women and men, widows and widowers have typically been found to be overrepresented among psychiatric patients. Thus, Gove (1972a) in a review of studies of marital status and the incidence of mental disorder, found that the widowed were overrepresented relative to the married in nine out of ten studies and that this was true regardless of the severity of the illness. Similarly, the literature on stressful life events and life-change events (see Dohrenwend & Dohrenwend, 1974; Paykel, Myers, Dienelt, et al., 1969; Rahe, 1979) has consistently confirmed loss as a powerful predictor of mental disorder.

Comparable results have been reported in a number of studies conducted in Great Britain (Parkes 1964a; Robertson, 1974; Stein & Susser, 1969). Thus, Robertson (1974) analyzed data from all patients from the Northeast Region of Scotland who entered psychiatric care for the first time in their lives between 1963 and 1967. A comparison of referral rates of married and widowed individuals clearly indicated that the widowed were overrepresented in the patient sample.

Similarly, in a study of 3,245 psychiatric patients admitted to the Bethlem Royal and Maudsley Hospitals in London during the years 1949 to 1951, Parkes (1964a) reported that the number of patients whose illness followed the loss of a spouse was six times greater than expected. Expected rates of recent bereavement in the hospital population were obtained by applying the mortality tables for England and Wales covering the years of the study to the age–sex distribution of spouses of patients. This procedure is somewhat problematic since it is based on the dubious assumption "that the national death rate is applicable to the subpopulation from which Maudsley patients are drawn" (Stein & Susser, 1969, p. 107).

However, Stein and Susser (1969) replicated Parkes's findings in a study of inception rates of widowed and married individuals entering psychiatric care for the first time between 1959 and 1963 in Salford, a small town in England. The study of Stein and Susser is particularly interesting because it not only showed that the widowed were overrepresented compared to the married, but that this difference was mainly due to an excess of the recently widowed among psychiatric patients. Thus, comparing the duration of widowhood of their psychiatric patients with data from a random sample of households in the community conducted in 1963, Stein and Susser found the samples of patients to show a "significant clustering in the earliest time-interval after loss of the spouse, that is, in the first year" (1969, pp. 109–10).

Although these findings suggest that the experience of losing a marital partner through death leads to a deterioration in the mental health of the surviving spouse, differences between married and widowed individuals in the availability of domestic support would offer a plausible alternative hypothesis. Since widows and widowers are less likely than married individuals to have somebody willing to care for them at home, they might be more readily admitted to mental hospitals, while the married might be more frequently treated outside the institution. This implies, however, that the loss-of-domestic-support hypothesis could only account for those findings which are based on inception rates to inpatient facilities.

Stein and Susser (1969), who evaluated this interpretation for their data, concluded that loss of domestic care could be placed very low on the list of potential causes of the association between widowhood and inception rates found in their study, since only one-quarter of their subjects received residential care. The others were treated as outpatients or received treatment from the mental health services of the local authority. Similarly, of studies of admission rates to outpatient psychiatric clinics in the United States for the years 1961, 1969, and 1970 (Kramer, 1966; Taube, 1970; Redick & Johnson, 1974), only Kramer (1966), whose study is also the single exception reviewed by Gove (1972a), failed to find an excess of widowed over married rates. However, this can hardly be accounted for in terms of "loss of domestic support," since Kramer did find an excess for the divorced and the single (who should also be lacking in home care) as compared with the married.

A study by Frost and Clayton (1977) did not find support for the hypothesis that bereavement is a precipitating factor in admission to a psychiatric hospital. Consecutive admissions to a hospital, 249 patients, were compared with an equal number of matched subjects, all of whom were inpatients at the orthopedic or obstretric units of the hospital, and with a psychiatric hospital survey group of 95 patients (to establish the incidence of recent bereavement). There were no significant differences between the samples in the occurrence of loss of a close relative in the six months or one-year periods prior to admission. Although it is possible, if bereavement leads to an excess risk of physical illness too, that bereaved persons were also overrepresented among the control subjects, this was thought less likely with orthopedic and obstetric than with other patients.

Despite these negative findings, Frost and Clayton (1977) did find a large preponderance of affective disorders among patients with recent bereavement. There was also a suggestion that alcoholic patients were at particularly high risk of a worsening of their problem (increased intake of alcohol) during the bereavement period. The actual numbers of cases for affective disorders or alcoholism was, however, too small for this to be substantial evidence.

Although few of the studies described above provide diagnostic specific information, those that do suggest that the most consistent widowed excess is in depression rates, which would be in line with the excess in affective disorders indicated by the Frost and Clayton (1977) study. Similarly, in a number of studies, loss has been linked in various ways to alcoholism (initiation or increase in consumption). In a small-scale study by Blankfield (1983), twelve out of a total of fifty consecutive admissions to an inpatient alcohol treatment center had suffered the loss through death of a significant person in their lives. While this seems a high proportion, one would need to know how many nonalcoholics with the same sociodemographic characteristics had also suffered losses in their lives, to conclude that it is excessive.

There is some indication that it is particularly widowers, rather than widows, who show an excess in alcoholism. Robertson (1974) observed that "among widowed referrals under 65 years, neurotic depression accounted for almost 30 percent of male referrals and over 40 percent of female referrals" (p. 194). For widowers, the second most frequent disorder was alcoholism (28 percent). Unfortunately, these rates were not compared with those of the married comparison group. However, Stein and Susser (1969), who compared married and widowed rates, report a similar pattern: Widows were excessive in depressive illness, widowers in "addictions (most often alcoholic psychoses)." Consistent with this differential effect of bereavement on the sexes, Mor, McHorney, and Sherwood (1986), in a large-scale study which will be described shortly, found that bereaved men were twice as likely as bereaved women to increase their alcohol consumption in the first four months of bereavement. Women were at significantly increased risk for using antianxiety medications. These findings are suggestive of a sex difference in the use of drugs and medication for coping with the problems of bereavement.

Parkes (1964a) observed that 28 percent of his bereaved group but only 15 percent of the nonbereaved patients had been diagnosed as reactive or neurotic depressives. He did not confirm the pattern regarding male alcoholism, but this is hardly surprising, since his sample included only six widowers. This sex difference in depression and alcohol-related psychiatric problems is consistent with the hypothesis proposed by Seligman (1975) that depression is the female equivalent of alcoholism in males as a reaction to events such as bereavement. Similarly, M. Stroebe and Stroebe (1983) suggested that more men might use alcohol to cope with bereavement and thus, rather than being diagnosed as depressed, might end up in the category of alcoholics.

In summary, then, there is a great deal of evidence suggesting that the widowed have higher inception rates to psychiatric care than the married and that the excesses are associated most closely with recent rather than long-term bereavement. Although few studies give diagnostic specific information, there is some evidence that females show an excess in depressive illness, while males exceed in depressions as well as alcohol-related problems. The finding that widowed individuals are overrepresented among patient samples cannot be explained in terms of a differential availability of domestic support, since these differences have been observed for inception to outpatient as well as inpatient facilities.

7.3 Physical health

It will be demonstrated later that the evidence which links bereavement to increases in mortality risk is fairly convincing. Since death is usually preceded by more or less extended periods of ill health, it would seem plausible that bereaved individuals should be more prone than the nonbereaved to suffer from physical illness. Thus, relative to the married, recently bereaved individuals would be expected to complain more of symptoms of physical illness, they should have a higher rate of disability, and they should show an increased utilization of medical services (i.e., doctors' visits, hospital stays). As we will see, the evidence presented in this section offers reasonable, though not unqualified, support for this assumption.

7.3.1 *Physical symptoms*

In a mail survey conducted in Boston and Sydney, Maddison and Viola (1968) evaluated the health of a sample of 375 widows under the age of 60 who had been bereaved thirteen months previously. With 25 percent outright rejections and 25 percent who could not be traced or were unsuitable, this constituted 50 percent of the total sample potentially available. The responses of these widowed on a self-report health questionnaire were compared to that of 199 matched married controls. As expected, significant differences between widowed and nonwidowed controls were observed in the prevalence of somatic symptoms suspected to be associated with recent bereavement, such as headaches, dizziness, fainting spells, skin rashes, excessive sweating, indigestion, difficulty in swallowing, and chest pain (Table 7.3).

To assess whether the bereaved had suffered a genuine deterioration in health status, Maddison and Viola constructed a health index by weigh-

Table 7.3 *Prevalence of somatic symptoms and complaints in samples of bereaved and nonbereaved women (adapted from Maddison & Viola, 1968)*

Symptom or complaint	Total widows N = 375 (%)	Total control N = 199 (%)	P[a]
Psychological symptoms			
General nervousness	41.3	16.1	0.001
Depression	22.7	5.5	0.001
Requiring medical treatment	12.8	1.0	0.001
Requiring hospitalization	1.3	0	0.05
"Fear of nervous breakdown"	13.1	2.0	0.001
Feelings of panic	12.0	2.5	0.001
Persistent fears	12.0	3.0	0.001
Repeated peculiar thoughts	8.5	2.0	0.001
Nightmares	8.8	1.0	0.001
Insomnia	40.8	12.6	0.001
Trembling	10.4	1.0	0.001
Neurological			
"Migraine"	4.8	3.0	n.s.[b]
Headache	17.6	9.0	0.01
Dizziness	9.1	4.5	0.05
Fainting spells	1.3	0	0.05
Blurred vision	13.7	7.5	0.02
Facial pain	1.9	0.5	n.s.
Dermatological			
Skin rashes	6.1	2.5	0.05
Excessive sweating	9.3	5.0	0.05
Gastrointestinal			
Indigestion	9.9	4.5	0.01
Difficulty in swallowing	4.8	1.5	0.02
Peptic ulceration	2.1	2.0	n.s.
Colitis	0.5	0	n.s.
Vomiting	2.7	0	0.01
Excessive appetite	5.4	0.5	0.001
Anorexia	13.1	1.0	0.001
Weight gain	8.5	9.0	n.s.
Weight loss	13.6	2.0	0.001
Genitourinary			
Menorrhagia	3.4	0.5	0.05
Cardiovascular			
Palpitations	12.5	4.0	0.001
Chest pain	10.1	4.5	0.01

Table 7.3 *(cont.)*

Symptom or complaint	Total widows N = 375 (%)	Total control N = 199 (%)	P[a]
Respiratory			
Dyspnea	12.0	4.5	0.001
Asthma	2.4	1.5	n.s.
General			
Frequent infections	2.1	0	0.01
General aching	8.4	4.0	0.001
Reduced work capacity	46.7	26.1	0.001
Gross fatigue	29.6	11.6	0.001
Neoplastic growth	0.8	0	n.s.
Diabetes mellitus	0.8	0.5	n.s.

[a]Probabilities calculated by chi-square analysis with 1 degree of freedom.
[b]Chi-square value does not reach 0.05 level of significance.

ing all symptoms (physical and psychological) according to the seriousness of the complaint. For example, relatively simple symptoms such as sleeplessness received a score of 1, whereas major diseases such as asthma received a score of 4. On inspection of the data it was decided somewhat arbitrarily that a score of 16 or more reflected a "substantial deterioration in health." According to this criterion, 28 percent of the widowed had suffered a marked health deterioration as compared to 4.5 percent of the married controls.

These findings were not replicated in the Harvard Bereavement Study (Glick et al., 1974; Parkes & Brown, 1972; Parkes & Weiss, 1983) which used a newly constructed physical health questionnaire listing approximately fifty symptoms of somatic complaints. Although widows reported a greater number of symptoms than widowers fourteen months after bereavement, only the scores of the widowers differed significantly from those of the matched controls. Clayton (1979), who did not report separate analyses for widows and widowers, did not find any difference in the prevalence of physical symptoms between her sample of ninety-two widows and widowers at thirteen months of bereavement and a matched sample of married controls. However, in a recent study by Ferraro (1985) with a sample of elderly bereaved, widowhood was found to lower perceived health shortly after loss, although long-term consequences were minimal.

How can we account for the discrepancies in the results of these studies? Obviously, with the small samples employed in these investigations, any differences between studies could be due to chance fluctuations. Furthermore, the fact that the samples studied by Clayton (1979) and Glick et al. (1974) were less than half the size of that of Maddison and Viola (1968) could account for the failure of the former studies to find significant widowed-to-married differences in physical symptomatology for their total sample. However, a significant impact of bereavement on physical health can be found even in studies using small samples. This has been demonstrated in two studies in which interviews were conducted in close temporal proximity to the loss experience (two to six months). Thus, Thompson, Breckenridge, Gallagher, and Peterson (1984), in the study of elderly widowed described above in the section on depression (Gallagher et al., 1983), found that recent bereavement adversely affected the health of the surviving spouses. When interviewed two months after the loss, widows as well as widowers reported more instances of the development of new illnesses or the deterioration of existing ones, than the control group. The illnesses were also slightly more severe than those of the controls. Furthermore, the bereaved reported increased or new medication usage relative to the controls. Similar findings were reported by W. Stroebe et al. (1985) from the Tübingen Longitudinal Study. Interviewed at four to six months after their loss, the 60 widows and widowers reported a significantly greater number of somatic symptoms and also rated their health less positively than the married controls.

Is there a somatic basis to this health deterioration? Since all of the findings discussed so far are based on self-report measures, the possibility remains that these bodily complaints are a reflection of the depressed mood state of these bereaved. After all, bodily symptoms are an integral part of the symptomatology of depression. To assess whether an impact of bereavement on physical health could be demonstrated over and above its effect on depression, W. Stroebe et al. (1985) conducted analyses of covariance on their measures of physical health using the BDI as a covariate. This analysis permits a statistical control for the potential effect of depression on the health measures by removing its influence from the comparison group. When differences in depression between married and widowed groups were controlled, there was no significant difference in self-reported physical health between the two groups. Although suggestive, the finding that it is the same people who suffer from both depression and physical symptoms does not eliminate the possibility that there is a somatic basis to the physical complaints. After all, if marital bereavement is considered a stressful life event it would follow that higher stress levels should be associated with both higher levels of depression and a greater number of physical symptoms.

7.3.2 Disability

That rates of disability are higher among the widowed than the married was found in a health survey of 88,000 households which was conducted by the National Center for Health Statistics (1976a) in 1971–1972. Disability was measured in two ways: (1) short-term disability, reflected by days of restricted activity during which a person had to reduce normal activities as a result of illness or injury and (2) long-term disability, defined as inability to carry on the major activity for one's age and sex group (e.g., working, keeping house, going to school).

A comparison of age- and sex-adjusted measures of debility suggests that the widowed have higher rates of short-term and long-term disability than the married. However, the survey report does not allow one to differentiate between causes of disability. It is thus possible that part of the difference is due to differences in mental rather than physical health.

7.3.3 Utilization of medical services

If bereavement is a cause of health deterioration, then the widowed should be overrepresented in physicians' consultation rooms and hospital wards. And indeed, the data from the National Health Survey conducted by the National Center for Health Statistics (1976a) indicate a somewhat higher rate of physician visits among the widowed than the married. While the age-adjusted rate for the widowed is 6.2 visits per year, the annual average is at 5.6 for the married. Again, there is no information on the kinds of illness for which the physicians were consulted. Thus, the higher rate of the widowed may be due to psychiatric rather than physical problems.

A study by Parkes (1964b) presents some evidence, however, that consultations for *physical* problems increase following bereavement. Parkes (1964b) analyzed the medical records for the time period before and after bereavement of forty-four widows living in London. A comparison of the consultation rate for the six months before and the six months after the bereavement showed an increase from a rate of 2.2 consultations before to 3.6 consultations after the death of the spouse, a difference which is highly significant. Although a large proportion of the increase in consultations was due to psychiatric complaints, the difference remained significant when only consultations for nonpsychiatric symptoms were considered.

To the uninitiated this demonstration that bereavement is associated with an increase in the use of medical services would seem powerful evidence for the deleterious effect of grief on health. However, as we implied above, there are several reasons apart from illness which can contribute to such differences in the utilization of medical services. An obvious motive in the case of the recently widowed is loneliness and a need to talk to somebody about one's problems. Such an explanation would seem particularly plausible for British data, since in Britain medical services are provided free of charge by the National Health Service. In the United States, on the other hand, where medical services are expensive and individuals typically take out insurance coverage only for inpatient but not outpatient treatment, the recently bereaved should be reluctant to consult physicians. If there was an increase in physical illness subsequent to the experience of loss, it would be more likely to be reflected in increased frequency of inpatient treatment.

Since many forms of physical illness only get worse if not treated in time, one would expect an increase in inpatient treatment among the U.S. widows. It is interesting, therefore, that both studies which examined rates of physicians' visits among small samples of recently bereaved in the United States did not find a difference comparable to that of Parkes (1964b) but instead observed an increase in the frequency of hospitalization. Thus, in the Harvard Study, four times as many bereaved as nonbereaved spent some time in the hospital during the year following their bereavement (Glick et al., 1974). Clayton (1979) did not find any difference for her total sample but reported that her young widowed had significantly more hospital stays during their first year of bereavement than did the married controls of the same age during an equivalent time period. Since the study of Glick et al. (1974) was restricted to young widowed, Clayton's findings are consistent with those of Glick et al.

A recent U.S. study by Mor et al. (1986) reported that physician rates were somewhat higher, but hospitalization, lower, among a large sample of recently bereaved compared to age- and sex-adjusted national norms. This data, then, at first sight appears to contradict the explanation of patterns found in England the United States presented above. Interview data from the National Hospice Study (see Greer, Mor, & Sherwood, 1983) were analyzed to assess the rate of medical care use of bereaved persons. The interviewees were drawn from a broad range of sociodemographic groups and were not limited to the conjugally bereaved. They were compared, not with a matched control group, but with rates reported in the existing literature (some of the studies reviewed in this section) and with national averages (from the National Center of Health Statistics, 1983). The study was of 1,447 persons identified as "primary care persons" of terminally ill patients in hospice care who died at some time after inception of the study (thus, prebereavement measures of health would be available, although they were not focal in Mor et al.'s report). Acceptance rate for paticipation was very high (82.5 percent). Annual rates of visits to physicians and hospitalizations were extrapolated from the rates found at four months, to be comparable with year-long studies. This is a somewhat dubious extrapolation, since rates within the first four months of bereavement might be expected to differ significantly from the following eight months. However, the rates were reported to be comparable with those in the Clayton (Clayton, Halikas, & Maurice, 1971; Clayton, 1974; Clayton & Darvish, 1979) and Parkes (Parkes & Brown, 1972) studies. Compared with the national rates, the bereaved had higher mean rates of physician visits than the national rates, whereas the hospitalization rates for the bereaved were generally below national rates, for both males and females, and particularly in the oldest age groups.

A plausible explanation of the high rate of physician visits among the bereaved in this study could be that they neglected making such visits in the prebereavement period, when they were intensely involved in the care and well-being of the terminal patient. It should also be noted that "previous health problems" was one of the strongest predictors of health care use. Mor et al. (1986) explain the surprisingly low hospitalization rate of the bereaved in terms of sample composition, and this explanation does seem to explain the apparent contradiction between these results and those reported above. When restricted only to spouses (55 percent of the sample) the rate of hospital use among both sexes was almost double that of other relatives. Had these been compared with rates of matched married controls, then, it is possible that they would have been excessive, particularly as the national rates are elevated by the inclusion of women of childbearing age and the oldest and sickest members of society who, as Mor et al. (1986) noted, contribute so highly to hospital use. Such a married control group would generally have provided a more appropriate comparison group than the ones used. We have elsewhere (M. Stroebe et al., 1981) given further reasons for caution in using national statistics for establishing base-line rates.

It should also be noted that the "primary care persons" who comprised the bereaved in this study are likely to be relatively low risk for physical ill health. Intensive caretaking of a terminally ill patient requires a healthy person: Because of this, the sample may have been biased toward healthier individuals from the outset. Furthermore, bereavement was expected, and the circumstances surrounding the death (in hospice care) easier than many other situations (see Chapter 8). The subjects were also monitored before and after bereavement: This could have some of the positive effects of intervention (see Chapter 9). Nevertheless, the increase in visits to physicians and, we suspect, for hospitalization among bereaved spouses, still testifies to the stresses of terminal care and bereavement among this sample and suggests the possibility that while fulfilling the role of primary care person, they themselves may have neglected their health.

7.3.4 *Drug and medication use*

Utilization of drugs and medication can be viewed as providing some, although indirect, indication of the impact of bereavement on health, and this aspect will be briefly considered here. Medication and drugs are, in fact, frequently prescribed by doctors for the bereaved, and most studies report increases in intake among them, even though medication as an antidote to grief should be used with great caution (see Chapter 9). Increased use by the bereaved ranges from antianxiety medications, such as sedatives or minor tranquilizers, to sleeping pills (hypnotics) and anti-depressants (see Osterweis et al., 1984; Osterweis, 1985). For example, some investigators (e.g., Parkes & Brown, 1972; Clayton, 1974; Clayton & Darvish, 1979) reported that as many as a third of their subjects used tranquilizers in the first year of bereavement, a clear excess over the non-bereaved. As was indicated earlier (7.2.2) there is evidence to show that use of drugs such as the antianxiety ones may be increased more among bereaved women than among bereaved men, who may turn to alcohol instead. Again, in the case of medication use, the sex difference may be linked to sex roles in society (Mor et al., 1986).

7.3.5 *Conclusions*

Although many of the findings reported in this section supported the thesis that bereavement is associated with a deterioration in physical health, it is apparent that the empirical evidence for this relationship was somewhat weaker than that linking bereavement to problems in mental health. While this might merely be an indication that the impact of bereavement on physical health is less powerful than that on mental health, one must still consider the alternative that, since the findings reported in this section are mainly based on behavioral measures of physical illness (e.g., self-reports, doctors' visits), these physical health measures may merely be secondary reflections of the depressive mood state of the bereaved. However, this explanation becomes less plausible in the light of the findings on bereavement and the most extreme physical consequence, namely, mortality.

7.4 Mortality

Perhaps the most convincing evidence of a relationship between bereavement and health comes from the mortality area. However, even this area is not without problems. In the following detailed discussion of findings, we therefore highlight methodological issues (research design, validity of conclusions, etc.).

7.4.1 Cross-sectional research

National death statistics provide some of the most consistent evidence for marital status differences in mortality. As long ago as 1858, Farr (1975) noted the low mortality rates of the married as compared with the unmarried (single), and the even more marked difference between the married and the widowed. Some years later, March (1912) published data showing a similar pattern for the age-specific mortality rates for 1886–95 in France, Prussia, and Sweden. Since then, these findings have been repeatedly confirmed in investigations and national death statistics publications (e.g., Carter & Glick, 1976; Ciocco, 1940; Fox & Goldblatt, 1982; Kitagawa & Hauser, 1973; Klebba, 1970; Office of Population Censuses and Surveys, 1986; Registrar General, 1971; Shurtleff, 1955, 1956; Kraus & Lilienfeld, 1959; Statistisches Jahrbuch für die Bundesrepublik Deutschland, 1978). For example, Shurtleff (1955) in an analysis based on the death rates of adults in the United States from 1949–51, which was overshadowed by the later paper of Kraus & Lilienfeld (1959), described the classic pattern (Figure 7.1): (1) For both men and women, death rates are lower for the married than for the single, widowed, and divorced; (2) the excess risk for the widowed is highest for the younger age groups; (3) the excess risk of widowers as compared to married men is greater than that of widows as compared to married women. Comparable results can be found in many different countries (Table 7.4).

Although the cross-national consistency of marital status differences in mortality is quite impressive, the historical stability of the pattern is even more surprising. After all, mortality rates have undergone dramatic changes since the time when Farr conducted his analysis. Even during

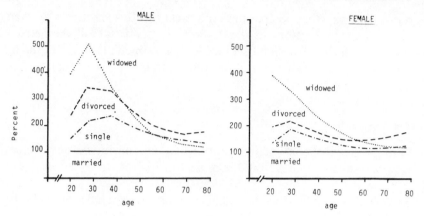

Figure 7.1. Age-specific death rates for each marital–sex class as percentages of death rates for married persons of corresponding age and sex; United States, 3-year average, 1949–51 (from Shurtleff, 1955).

this century life expectancy for white males in the United States rose from 48.2 years in 1900–2 to 67.6 years; and for white females from 51.1 years to 74.2 years (Spiegelman, 1960). Since then, life expectancy has risen even further (Crimmins, 1981).

Can these differences in the mortality of married and widowed individuals be attributed to the loss experience? There are two issues involved in this question: First, one can doubt that there is an increase in the conditional probability of one spouse dying, given the death of the other. Second, one can accept the increase but question that it has been caused by the psychological impact of the loss. There are a number of alternative explanations which either challenge the notion that widowhood is associated with an increase in mortality risk (selection, statistical artifacts) or that the increase is due to the loss experience (homogamy, joint unfavorable environment).

Selection. An interpretation in terms of differential selection questions the assumption that partner loss is associated with increased mortality among the widowed and suggests instead that it is the individuals of lower health status who remain widowed rather than becoming married again. Thus, health is considered one of the determinants rather than a consequence of marital status.

The selection argument is based on the assumption that the choice of a marital partner takes place in a competitive marriage market and that poor health lowers the chances of marriage (and remarriage). Applied to the mortality difference between married and never-married individuals,

Table 7.4 *Ratios of the mortality rate of the widowed to the corresponding married group by sex (from M. Stroebe et al., 1981)*

Country	Sex	Age 25–34	35–44	45–54	55–64
Canada	Males	7.8	1.5	2.1	1.4
1966	Females	2.3	1.7	1.4	1.3
USA	Males	4.3	2.9	2.0	1.5[a]
1950	Females	2.7	1.8	1.4	1.2[a]
Australia	Males	3.5	3.1	1.7	1.5
1961	Females	1.4	1.9	1.4	1.2
Japan	Males	7.1	4.5	2.9	2.0
1965	Females	3.6	1.6	1.4	1.3
France	Males	7.5	3.2	2.4	1.7
1965	Females	2.7	2.0	1.5	1.2
Holland	Males	2.0	2.9	1.9	1.5
1965	Females	2.8	1.1	1.3	1.3
Sweden	Males	2.6	1.8	2.0	1.6
1965	Females	4.2	2.6	1.5	1.3
England & Wales	Males	6.4	2.8	1.9	1.6
1966	Females	3.5	2.3	1.5	1.4
Germany	Males	6.5	4.2	2.5	1.8
1976	Females	3.1	2.2	1.6	1.3

Note: Coefficients are formed by the ratios (age- and sex-specific widowed mortality rate)/ (corresponding age- and sex-specific married mortality rate). Thus a coefficient of 2.0 means that the mortality rate of the widowed is twice as high as that for the married.
[a]Age group 55–59 and not 55–64 (white Americans only).
Sources: Registrar General (1971) for all countries except United States (Kraus & Lilienfeld, 1959) and Germany (Stat. Jahrb. für die BRD, 1978).

a selection interpretation would suggest that the ill health of the never married both lowered their chances of marriage and increased their mortality risk. Let us hasten to add that we know of no data to either support or refute this hypothesis. Furthermore, if this interpretation were correct, then the slow decrease in rates of first marriages evident since 1950 (Carter & Glick, 1976), which indicates a societal change in marriage preference, should lessen the gap in the mortality risks of married and single individuals.

Given a competitive marriage market, remarriage is likely to be as competitive as first marriage. Thus, differential selection could also account for the higher mortality rates of the widowed. According to this interpretation, the widowed mortality rate is higher than that of the married because the healthier widowed are continually drained from the widowed and reselected into the married category through remarriage. Such differential selection should lead to a decrease in the average health of the widowed and to an increase of the health of the married. With remarriage rates being higher in the younger age groups, and higher for widowers than for widows, differential selection could account for the higher mortality of the younger widowed, and particularly the males. Thus, an interpretation in terms of differential selection offers a parsimonious explanation for the total pattern of marital status differences in mortality. Although Helsing, Szklo, and Comstock (1981) found that the mortality rates among the widowed males (but not the females) of their sample who remarried were much lower than among those who did not remarry, they were unable to rule out the possibility that the health advantage of the widowers who had remarried was due to the social support provided by the new marriage.

Statistical artifacts and biases. In a critical review of mortality studies, M. Stroebe et al. (1981) discussed a number of statistical biases which could exaggerate differences in the mortality of the widowed as compared to the married. For example, mortality statistics typically collapse age groups into large age-range categories, for example, 35–44, 45–54, 55–64. It is therefore possible that the marital status categories differ from each other in average age within these broad categories. In fact, close analysis reveals that in many cases the average age of the widowed is one year older than the married populations with which they are compared (e.g., Kraus & Lilienfeld, 1959). With the close relationship between age and mortality, the higher average age of the widowed is likely to contribute somewhat to their higher mortality rate.

There is also a tendency for widowed persons to be underrepresented during the collection of census data which are used to estimate the widowed population, and overrepresented in the collection of mortality statistics. In one case, a comparison of census records with death registers indicated a discrepancy of the order of 6 percent for males, and 2 percent for females (Registrar General, 1971). This bias would exaggerate the true mortality associated with widowhood.

Homogamy. An interpretation in terms of homogamy (the similarity of marital partners in sociological, psychological, and physical traits), would accept that the death of one spouse raises the probability of the death of the other. Such an interpretation would question, however, whether this increase was due to the psychological impact of loss.

Homogamy has typically been studied as a result of differential availability (e.g., due to residential propinquity). More relevant in our context is the homogamy with regard to socially valued traits due to the competitive nature of the marriage market. If each marriageable individual were out to get the most desirable spouse possible, one would expect marital partners to be highly similar to each other on valued characteristics (W. Stroebe & Frey, 1980; W. Stroebe & Stroebe, 1984). To the extent that good health is a valued characteristic on the marriage market, one would expect the healthy to marry the healthy and the sick to marry the sick. This similarity in health status would increase the probability of both partners dying closely together in time. However, at least for first marriages, it seems somewhat implausible that physical health should be a determinant of marital choice in view of the young entrance age. Since similarity in attitudes and values has also been shown to increase interpersonal attraction (e.g., Byrne, 1971; Kerckhoff & Davis, 1962; Levinger & Breedlove, 1966; W. Stroebe, Insko, Thompson, & Layton, 1971), it is possible that similarities in attitudes toward danger, or in behavior patterns that may be risky to one's health (e.g., smoking, alcohol, skiing) affect the marital choice.

Joint unfavorable environment. Since marital partners to some extent share the same environment, the presence in their environment of factors detrimental to health would shorten the lifespan of both partners and thus increase the conditional probability of one spouse dying, given the death of the other. Thus, married partners living under conditions of high stress due to poverty or minority status might be likely to die more rapidly and more closely in time than those not sharing such experiences (M. Stroebe et al., 1981). Another aspect of the shared environment which might serve to increase the temporal proximity in the death dates of married individuals are family habits with regard to eating and drinking. For example, since habitual high intake of alcohol and fat is associated with high coronary risk, shared eating and drinking habits could shorten the lifespan of both spouses.

A joint accident can be considered an extreme example of a couple sharing the same harmful environment. If both suffer a fatal accident, and one outlives the other, if only by hours, he or she is nevertheless categorized as widowed in official statistics. Since car accidents are a relatively frequent cause of death among the younger age groups, joint accidents could contribute to the relatively higher mortality rates of the younger widowed.

As each spouse is also part of the other's environment, mutual infection could be considered a case of joint unfavorable environment. If one spouse dies of some infectious disease it would be likely for the other spouse to be infected as well. However, the control of infectious diseases having increased considerably during this century, this is unlikely to be a major factor in contributing to the increased mortality risk of the bereaved.

In view of the plausible alternative interpretations of the marital status differences in mortality, the evidence from cross-sectional studies cannot be considered conclusive support for the loss effect. Although there seem to be grounds for the view that none of these alternative interpretations can fully account for the married-to-widowed differential in mortality risk, the extent to which all of these alternatives in combination contribute to the increases is hard to assess. Thus, although their individual contributions to the mortality patterns may be minor, the possibility remains that each contributes to the pattern, and that in combination they make up the total excess in widowed mortality rates.

7.4.2 *Longitudinal research*

Longitudinal studies, in which a given cohort of individuals is systematically examined over time, provide a more adequate form of investigation of the impact of bereavement on the mortality of the surviving spouse. One of the major advantages of longitudinal investigations is that, in contrast to cross-sectional studies, they provide information on the length of time that the widowed survive their spouse. It is thus possible to examine mortality at different time intervals after bereavement. According to an interpretation in terms of a loss effect, the impact of bereavement should diminish with increasing duration of widowhood.

A very careful early longitudinal investigation of the mortality risk of the widowed conducted by Young, Benjamin, and Wallis (1963) focused on widowers only. They studied the death rate of a sample of 4,486 widowers aged 55 and over in England and Wales whose wives had died in 1957. Mortality rates for the widowers were compared for a period of five years with those of married men of the same age. An excess in the mortality of the widowed sample over that of the married controls was observed for the first half-year of bereavement only. During this period, the widowed mortality rates showed a 40 percent increase compared to the rates of the married. During the second half of the first year, the mortality rates of the widowed returned to the level of the married controls.

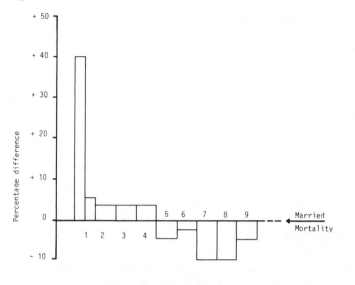

Figure 7.2. Percentage difference between mortality rate of widowers over 54 and that of married men of the same age, by year since bereavement (from Parkes et al., 1969).

Results of a nine-year follow-up of the widowers in the Young et al. study conducted by Parkes et al. (1969) showed that the mortality rate in the subsequent years remained at, or even slightly below, the level of the married men (Figure 7.2.). Thus, according to these results, the excess mortality rates reported cross-sectionally would be accounted for by the recently bereaved.

The study by Cox and Ford (1964), which focused on the mortality risk of widows, would have nicely complemented the evidence from Young et al. (1963) were it not for a number of methodological weaknesses (M. Stroebe et al., 1981). Cox and Ford (1964) examined the mortality rates of 60,000 British widows below the age of 75, who had been awarded a widow's pension in 1927. The mortality rates of these widows in each of the first five years of bereavement was compared with the rates of those same widows taken for the five-year period as a whole. Although details of statistical tests are not given, the authors concluded that there was an excess in widowed mortality during the second year of bereavement. After this peak the rates became comparable to expected rates.

For a long time these results, which suggested the possibility of a sex difference in the period of high risk, were discounted. It was argued that since only widows who had applied for a widow's pension were included in the sample, the study might have excluded those who died in the first year and thus had no time to submit their application. However, a similar sex difference in the period of highest risk was reported by McNeill (1973). In this unpublished study, the mortality rates of 9,247 males and females, residents of Connecticut whose partners had died in 1965, were computed for the first three and a half years of bereavement. Mortality of this sample was compared with the mortality of the general population of Connecticut for the years 1959–61.

The McNeill study is somewhat problematic because in contrast to all cross-sectional and to other longitudinal findings the expected mortality figures exceeded the widowed rates for ages over 60 in the case of widowers and 55 in the case of widows. For widowers under 60, McNeill reported a particularly high risk of death for the first half-year of bereavement. After this period the morality risk declined to the level of the control group. The excess mortality of the younger widows reached statistical significance only for the second, but not the first or third year of bereavement.

This sex difference in the period of risk for the widowed seems to confirm the difference suggested by Cox and Ford (1964). The failure of the study to find an excess in widowed mortality for the older age groups is inconsistent, however, with the findings of Young et al. (1963) that the risk of mortality for widowers over 59 years of age is significantly excessive. This discrepancy could have been due to the composition of the comparison group used by McNeill (1973). He compared his widowed sample with the total (age- and sex-specific) population, which included widowed, divorced, and never married and thus had a higher mortality rate than the married controls employed by Young et al.

Further evidence for a sex difference in mortality risk following bereavement comes from a study by Helsing and Szklo (1981) conducted in Washington County, Maryland. The authors identified a sample of 1,204 widowers and 2,828 widows, all white persons aged 18 and over, who had become widowed from 1963 to 1974. The married controls were matched to the widowed persons according to sex, age, and geographic area of residence. Both populations were followed until 1975, resulting in a potential time in the study ranging from twelve months to twelve years, depending on the date of widowhood. The authors found that widowers of all age groups had a mortality rate in excess of that of the matched married controls, but the difference was only significant for the age groups between 55 and 74 years. Although there were indications that the excess risk was even higher for the younger age groups, the difference did not reach statistical significance, probably due to the small number of younger widowed included in the sample. Surprisingly, no significant excess in mortality was found for widows, although the higher rates for the younger widows were "suggestive." Even more surprising was the failure of the Helsing and Szklo study to find a duration effect. Rates during the first six months were not more excessive than during any other time and the increased mortality risk for the widowers persisted for many years after the spouse's death. This result is in marked contrast with the peaks reported in all studies reported above.

The findings of Helsing and Szklo are also inconsistent with the results of two recent longitudinal studies conducted in Scandinavia (Kaprio & Koskenvuo, 1983; Kaprio, Koskenvuo, & Rita, 1986; Mellström, Nilsson, Oden, et al., 1982). Mellström et al. (1982) studied the effect of bereavement on mortality for all individuals who were widowed in Sweden between 1968 and 1978. The 360,000 individuals between 50 and 90 years of age who had become widowed during this period were observed from the day of bereavement until the end of 1978, or until the day of their own death if it occurred earlier. Mellström et al. reported that life expectancy at age 50 showed a difference of 3.1 years between married men and widowers, the latter having the lower expectancy. With 1.3 years, the corresponding difference was smaller for women. A detailed analysis, possible with the more numerous widowed at the ages of 60 and above, indicated a peak in the mortality risk during the first nine months for widowers. For widows the peak was less marked and occurred only for the first three months.

In the large-scale study of Kaprio and Koskenvuo (1983; Kaprio et al., 1986), the mortality of 95,647 persons, widowed from 1972 to 1976, was followed up to the end of 1976. Expected numbers of deaths were based on national annual age- and sex-specific mortality rates. Consistent with previous findings, the authors reported a significant increase in widowed mortality for both sexes. However, inconsistent with the pattern emerging from previous studies, Kaprio and Koskenvuo did not observe any sex difference in the period of highest risk. For both sexes, the greatest increase in widowed mortality occurred during the first four weeks of bereavement. After that, the widowed mortality rates were not notably different from those of the total population.

While these discrepancies cannot be explained, it is much less difficult to account for the failure of a number of small-scale studies (Clayton, 1974; Shepherd & Barraclough, 1974; Ward, 1976; Ekblom, 1963; Niemi, 1979) to find a significant difference in the mortality of widowed and non-widowed groups. Clayton's failure to find mortality differences is hardly surprising, since she only studied a sample of 109 widowed. Even if her results had paralleled those of Young et al. (1963), who found a mortality rate of 4.8 percent among the widowed as compared to 3.2 percent among the married controls, with her sample only five deaths could have been expected in the widowed group as compared to three in the married control group. Shepherd and Barraclough (1974), with their sample of forty-four persons whose spouses had committed suicide, had even less possibility of finding a significant difference, despite the fact that loss due to suicide is likely to be associated with bad outcome.

Ward's (1976) more sizeable sample consisted of 87 widowers and 279 widows (mean age, 64) whose spouses had died of cancer. This may have contributed to his failure to find an increase in widowed mortality, since, as we will see later, a loss following an extended illness seems to lead to somewhat better outcome than a sudden and unexpected loss. Furthermore, Ward computed expected mortality rates from life tables of the similarly aged population of England and Wales, which included widowed as well as never married, to derive expected mortality figures.

Two studies that used somewhat larger samples reported an impact of bereavement which was marked but did not reach an acceptable level of statistical significance. Thus Ekblom (1963), in a study of 351 widowers and 283 widows aged 75 conducted in Sweden, found that compared to the age- and sex-specific death rates of married controls, widowed mortality rates showed a 36 percent increase during the first six months following bereavement. After this period the rates dropped rapidly: For the second six months and the second year of bereavement the observed rates were in fact lower than the expected rates. It is interesting to note that widows but not widowers showed a considerable excess in mortality rates during the third year of bereavement.

In a more recent study of the mortality of 939 retired men, of whom 174 had lost their spouses after retirement, Niemi (1979) reported an excess in mortality for the widowers during the first six months after their wives' death, but the excess was not sizeable enough to reach statistical significance. Thus, though generally supportive of the findings of previous research, the studies by Ekblom (1963) and Niemi (1979) do not add substantially to the available evidence.

We know of only one prospective study of the mortality risk of the bereaved which found a statistically significant difference in widowed to married mortality with a sample of less than 1,000 and this is the classic study of Rees and Lutkins (1967). This investigation, which included not only bereaved spouses, but also other near relatives, seemed to demonstrate that not only the loss of a spouse, but also the death of other close relatives can lead to an increase in mortality risk. The authors compared the mortality of 903 inhabitants of Llanidloes, a small market town in Wales, who had all lost a spouse or a close relative (a total of 371 deceased persons) to that of a comparison group comprised of the spouses and near relatives of 371 inhabitants still living in the town. During the first year of bereavement significantly more individuals in the bereaved (a total of 43 persons) than in the control group (a total of 6) died, and the difference is significant for spouses as well as other relatives. However, as only 156 of the relatives were spouses, the absolute death figures are very small (19 widowed versus 2 controls). Furthermore, the rate of 12.2 percent mortality for the widowed seems unusually high and a mortality rate of 0.68 percent for the control group rather low.

The problem of sample size can be circumvented by using a retrospective design. A study by Cottington et al. (1980) followed this procedure, using cause of death expected to be excessive among the bereaved as their starting point. They examined the circumstances of eighty-one white women aged 25 to 64 in Allegheny County, Pennsylvania, who had died suddenly from arteriosclerotic heart disease. Each case was matched to a neighborhood control on the basis of age, race, and sex. Results indicated that relative to matched controls, the women who had died from heart disease were six times as likely to have experienced the death of a significant other within the last six months.

7.4.3 The evidence combined: Is there a loss effect?

Taken together, the cross-sectional and longitudinal studies reviewed in this section provide convincing support for the loss effect. With the exception of a few studies which employed small samples, findings from longitudinal studies substantiated the evidence from cross-sectional research indicating significant increases in mortality following marital bereavement.

Except for the study by Helsing and Szklo (1981), all longitudinal studies of widowers and some studies of widows found excess mortality to be greatest during the first six months of bereavement. This pattern is rather crucial for an interpretation in terms of the loss effect (or rather, for the exclusion of alternative interpretations). We will argue that the finding that partner loss had the greatest impact on mortality during the first six months (Ekblom, 1963; Niemi, 1979; McNeill, 1973; Mellström et al., 1982; Young et al., 1963) or even the first month of bereavement (Kaprio & Koskenvuo, 1983) does not only rule out differential selection; it is also inconsistent with interpretations in terms of statistical biases, homogamy, and joint unfavorable environment (with the exception of joint accidents, which will be discussed below).

Remarriage of the fittest could not explain the peak in excess mortality, unless it were argued that substantial remarriage occurred during the first six months of bereavement. This is unlikely, however, because from all we know about patterns of grief, widowed persons do not feel inclined to remarry shortly after the death of their spouse. But even if they wanted to, very few widowed would consider violating social norms to such an extent as to marry within the first six months or even the first 30 days of bereavement.

A peak in mortality within the first six months following bereavement is also difficult to explain in terms of homogamy. Even if similarity in health status were a determinant of partner choice, it seems unlikely that this similarity at a fairly young age would cause partners to die in such close temporal proximity several decades later. The same is true for similarities in dietary habits or alcohol comsumption. Although these interpretations have not been completely ruled out by findings of a peak in excess mortality among the widowed, they seem at this point to have become rather unlikely.

There is still one alternative to the loss effect which would also be fully consistent with the peak pattern, and that is "joint accidents." If both spouses are involved in a car accident and one is killed outright while the other, though injured, survives for a few hours or days, that death would contribute to a peak excess during the first month of bereavement. An analysis of the causes of death of the widowed would not lead to an identification of all of these cases, because they would not necessarily be classified as accidental, unless the death occurred within a few days of the accident. As far as we know, there is only one investigation which eliminated widowed persons who died as a result of the same accident that killed their spouses, namely the study by Helsing and Szklo (1981). Since this is also the one study which did not observe a peak in excessive mortality for the bereaved, one might wonder whether their findings could not be attributed to selection. However, the pattern of results reported by Helsing and Szklo is also inconsistent with a selection interpretation. Since widowed remarriage rates are positively associated with duration of widowhood, differential selection would lead to a widening over time of the difference in the mortality of widowed and married individuals. The finding of Helsing and Szklo that the excess mortality persisted at the same level for several years after the loss is therefore inconsistent with an interpretation in terms of differential selection.

7.4.4 Causes of death in the widowed

(i) Broken heart: reality or myth?

Is the "broken heart" more than a poetic image for loneliness and despair, is it really a "medical reality" as Lynch (1977) claimed in his popular book? Or, expressed more technically, do widowed rates in coronary heart disease show a significant excess over that of married persons of the same age and sex? Since numerous investigators have detailed psychological and social precursors of heart disease (e.g., Friedman & Rosenman, 1974; Glass, 1977; Jenkins, 1971; Lynch, 1977), it would provide support for the loss effect if a considerable share of the excess mortality of the widowed could be attributed to death from cardiovascular disease.

One of the most detailed accounts of cross-sectional evidence on causes of death for the different marital status groups was published by the National Center for Health Statistics (NCHS) in 1970. This report presents information on the leading causes of death for the married and the widowed. It is interesting to note that the rank order of the three leading causes of death is identical for married and widowed persons: Coronary heart disease is the major killer, followed by strokes, and then cancer of the digestive organs and peritoneum.

The picture changes, however, if one inspects ratios in widowed-to-married mortality rates for specific causes of death to identify those causes which show the greatest *excess* for the widowed (Table 7.5). The NCHS (1970) published standardized marital status–mortality ratios for white women and men on a number of cases of death, using U.S. rates for the years 1959–1961. If one rank-orders these ratios according to magnitude, it becomes evident that the two leading causes of death (arteriosclerotic heart disease, including coronary heart disease and vascular lesions of the nervous system) do not show the greatest excess. In widows, coronary heart disease and vascular lesions rank behind violent causes of death (accidents, suicide, and homicide). In widowers, they are even preceded by homicide, liver cirrhosis, suicide, accidents (motor vehicles and others), and tuberculosis and closely followed by the various forms of cancer, which are also excessive in the widowed.

It should be emphasized, however, that the magnitude of widowed over married excess for a given cause of death is frequently quite unrelated to the relative contribution of that cause to the overall widowed-to-married difference in mortality. Since widowed-to-married excess is expressed as a ratio of widowed-to-married rates of mortality due to a given cause of death, rare causes of death, if they are affected by stress,

Table 7.5 *Mortality ratios of widowed to married. Standardized marital status–mortality ratios for white persons for selected causes of death[a] in order of relative excess ratios of widowed to married, USA, 1959–61 (from W. Stroebe et al., 1982)*

Widowers		Widows	
1. Homicide	2.69	1. Accidents (other than motor vehicle)	1.84
2. Liver cirrhosis	2.42		
3. Suicide	2.39	2. Suicide	1.66
4. Accidents (other than motor vehicle)	2.27	3. Arteriosclerotic heart, including coronary, disease	1.48
5. Tuberculosis	2.17	4. Lesions of CNS	1.47
6. Motor accidents	1.99	5. Tuberculosis	1.43
7. Vascular lesions of central nervous system (CNS)	1.50	6. Liver cirrhosis	1.31
		7. Homicide	1.28
8. Arteriosclerotic heart, including coronary, disease	1.46	8. Cancer of digestive organs and peritoneum	1.23
9. Diabetes	1.41	9. Cancer of cervix	1.18
10. Cancer of digestive organs and peritoneum	1.26	Cancer of respiratory system	1.18
Cancer of respiratory system	1.26		

[a]The "selected causes" are composed, for the most part, of categories which contribute to the four leading causes of death (ICD nos. 400–402, 410–443, 140–205, 330–334, E800–E962). Also included are liver cirrhosis, diabetes, suicide, homicide, and tuberculosis. For further details see NCHS (1970), p. 2.
Source: NCHS, 1970 (Series 20, no. 8A, compiled from Tables 2, 10, 37, and 47).

are more likely to become excessive than causes such as coronary heart disease or cancer, which have a very high base rate in the general population. Therefore, if one is interested in assessing the relative contribution of each cause to the overall widowed-to-married difference in mortality, the widowed-to-married *difference* in mortality due to this cause should be considered. Thus, although the excess mortality of widowers from homicide, liver cirrhosis, and suicide is more than twice that of married men, these three causes contribute very little to the overall widowed-to-married difference in mortality. For example, in 1959–1961 only 56 widowers per 100,000 died from tuberculosis as compared to 3,171 who died from coronary heart disease. Since tuberculosis is even rarer in married individuals, it outranks cardiovascular disease when standardized marital status–mortality ratios are considered. But despite its smaller widowed-to-married ratio, cardiovascular diseases account for a much greater share of the overall widowed-to-married difference in mortality.

One would expect that mortality from cardiovascular diseases should be even more excessive in longitudinal studies than when cross-sectional data are considered. Although we assume that bereavement merely aggravates or accelerates existing disease processes, a myocardial infarction is a faster-acting cause of death than tuberculosis, liver cirrhosis, or cancer. Thus, in a longitudinal study of recently bereaved, coronary disease should be a more excessive cause of death than in cross-sectional samples where individuals have typically been widowed for several years. Consistent with this expectation, Parkes et al. (1969) reported that heart and circulatory diseases accounted for two-thirds of the increase in mortality observed during the first six months after bereavement. Although coronary heart disease accounted for a smaller proportion of death in their study, Kaprio and Koskenvuo (1983) found coronary disease to be mainly excessive during the first month of bereavement. A recent report focusing on bereavement and cancer by Jones, Goldblatt, and Leon (1984) provides further support for the hypothesis that the recently bereaved are at a greater risk of cardiovascular disease than of cancer, although the authors point out that, as the latent period for many cancers is several years, longer periods of follow-up would be required to further clarify the relationship of widow(er)hood to cancer.

Some other discrepancies between longitudinal and cross-sectional studies in reports on causes of death, such as the failure of Parkes et al. (1969) to find any excess for violent causes of death among the bereaved, may have been due to sample size. Since, particularly in the older age groups studied by Parkes et al., violent deaths are much less frequent than death from natural causes, the sample of widowed investigated by Parkes et al. may have been too small to register increases in violent death among the bereaved.

In summary then, we would argue that the evidence from both cross-sectional and the longitudinal studies tends to support the assumption that cardiovascular diseases are to a large extent responsible for the excess in the mortality of the widowed. Thus, as the poets always knew, the experience of losing one's spouse can be heartbreaking.

(ii) Suicide

Although suicide accounts for a relatively small proportion of the overall difference in the mortality of widowed as compared to married individuals, it deserves special attention, because nothing reflects more clearly

Table 7.6 *Ratios of the suicide rate of widowed to the corresponding married group, by sex (adapted from Gove, 1972b)*

		Age-specific coefficient							
Sex	Status	25–29	30–34	35–39	40–44	45–49	50–54	55–59	60–64
Males	Widowed SR[a]								
	Married SR	9.823	6.283	6.298	4.063	3.173	2.855	2.392	2.325
Females	Widowed SR								
	Married SR	2.475	2.700	1.934	1.750	1.850	1.648	1.711	1.585

[a] SR = suicide rate.

the absolute and total despair of bereavement than this choice of death over life. Furthermore, suicide is one of the causes of mortality for which the widowed-to-married ratio is most excessive.

That the rate of suicide is considerably higher among the widowed than among the married was demonstrated nearly a century ago, in 1897, in the pioneering work of Durkheim (1951). As Table 7.6 shows, this pattern is still apparent in more recent suicide statistics (NCHS, 1970).

Suicide rates are generally higher for males than for females (Carter & Glick, 1976), a difference that holds for a wide range of countries (WHO, 1968). As can be seen from Table 7.6, there is also a sex by marital status interaction. The widowed excess in suicide rates is greater for males than for females. In one of the most extensive analyses of marital status differences in suicide, Gove (1972b) demonstrated comparable sex differences in widowed-to-married ratios for a number of other Western countries in addition to the United States.

If suicide is to be taken as a behavioral indicator of despair, the suicide risk of the widowed should be greatest for the period immediately following the loss. This has been demonstrated in a number of longitudinal studies (e.g., Bojanovsky, 1977, 1980; Bojanovsky & Bojanovsky, 1976; Bunch, 1972; Kaprio & Koskenvuo, 1983; MacMahon & Pugh, 1965). MacMahon and Pugh (1965) examined the death certificates of a sample of widowed persons who committed suicide in Massachusetts between the years of 1948 and 1952. Their control group consisted of widowed individuals who died from other causes. MacMahon and Pugh (1965) reported that the suicide risk among the widowed was highest during the first year of bereavement and subsequently decreased over the next few years. These findings have been replicated by Bunch (1972) in England

and by Bojanovsky (1977, 1980; Bojanovsky & Bojanovsky, 1976) in Germany.

The most impressive support for the association between loss and suicide comes from the study by Kaprio and Koskenvuo (1983) which we described earlier. In a comparison of the widowed suicide rates with the sex- and age-adjusted rates of the general population, the authors reported a peak in widowed suicide rates for the first week after bereavement. This excess was 66-fold for men and 9.6-fold for women. After this period, the excess mortality was of the same order for both sexes.

In summary then, cross-sectional and longitudinal studies comparing suicide rates of widowed and married individuals consistently reported higher rates for the widowed. Furthermore, as expected from an interpretation in terms of a loss effect, longitudinal analyses of the relationship between duration of widowhood and risk confirmed that the suicide risk of the widowed is greatest in close temporal proximity to the loss experience.

7.5 Conclusions

In this chapter we reviewed evidence from a great number of studies of the health consequences of bereavement. Although much of this research is marred by methodological problems, the convergence of these findings is quite impressive. Whether one looks at the rate of psychiatric disorders, physical illness, or mortality, comparisons of married and widowed individuals typically find the widowed to be worse off. It will be evident that, while reporting figures presented in individual studies, we have been cautious in making general statements about percentages of bereaved at risk for specific ailments, of the precise duration of symptoms or debility, of risk periods following bereavement, and so on. There is good reason for this: Studies differ from one another in many ways, such as sample composition (e.g., sociodemographic features, extent of bias through attrition) or in procedure (e.g., interview versus postal techniques, dependent variables employed, duration of bereavement at measurement) and also in methodological sophistication. Thus, while the convergence of findings enables one to establish general patterns of debility following bereavement, it would be misleading to make general quantitative statements about precise rates. We can say that the evidence from longitudinal and cross-sectional studies across all major areas in which normal and pathological grief reactions have been manifested all support the conclusion that the experience of partner loss is associated with health deterioration.

8 Risk factors in bereavement outcome

8.1 Introduction

In the last chapter empirical evidence was presented to support the thesis that the experience of losing a partner increases the probability of mental and physical illness. Having thus established bereavement as a health risk factor, it is the aim of this chapter to identify those subgroups of bereaved individuals who suffer the most severe health detriments. There are practical as well as theoretical reasons for this type of analysis. On the practical side, the analysis of risk groups is probably the best way toward an early identification of individuals likely to need professional help, as there are few grief symptoms which could reliably be used as early signals of an impending pathological development. From a theoretical point of view, the analysis of risk factors plays an important role in developing and testing theoretical explanations of the health impact of bereavement. Since theories of bereavement identify a number of situational and/or personal characteristics likely to be associated with poor bereavement outcome, the study of these risk factors can be used as a method of testing such theoretical predictions. But even in the absence of specific hypotheses, empirical evidence that certain characteristics of the bereaved are associated with greater health risk is likely to stimulate theoretical speculation about mediating processes, which can then be pursued in further research.

One methodological caution should be added, however, before entering into the discussion of research on this topic. The focus on risk factors in bereavement outcome has tempted many researchers either not to collect data from a matched, married, control sample (e.g., Stern, Williams, & Prados, 1951; Wretmark, 1959) or not to use such data in the analysis of risk factors although they had been collected (e.g., Carey, 1977). For example, Carey (1977) interpreted the finding that the widows in his sample had higher depression rates than the widowers as indication of a gender difference in *adjustment* to loss. Since gender is also related to depres-

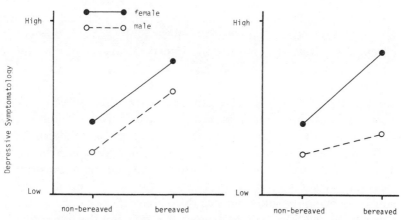

Figure 8.1. Hypothetical example depicting additive and nonadditive combinations of the effects of gender and bereavement on depression.

sion in the general population, this is certainly unfounded, on the basis of his data. To illustrate this, Figure 8.1 depicts two patterns of sex differences in depression of bereaved and nonbereaved individuals. The left panel shows an additive combination of the effects of sex and bereavement (two main effects). Although widows are more depressed than widowers, this sex difference cannot be attributed to better adjustment to loss, because it is of the same magnitude as the sex difference in depression among nonbereaved individuals. To reflect a difference in adjustment, the sex difference in depression would have to be greater for bereaved than for nonbereaved individuals. This is shown in the right panel of Figure 8.1. If one only analyzes data for bereaved subjects (and that for only one point in time), it is not possible to distinguish between a sex main effect and a sex by marital status interaction.

There are conditions, however, under which valid conclusions about the role of risk factors in moderating the impact of bereavement can be made without use of a nonbereaved comparison group. Thus, comparisons with a nonbereaved control group make little sense if risk factors specific to bereavement (e.g., the mode of the spouse's death) and/or symptoms specific to bereavement (e.g., feelings of the presence of the bereaved, yearning for the bereaved) are studied. However, research in this area has typically focused on the impact of bereavement on general health (e.g., depressed mood, somatic complaints, physical and mental illness, mortality) and has studied risk factors (e.g., gender, social class) that are known to be related to these health measures in the general population. Under these conditions, unless a longitudinal design is used, the failure to include a nonbereaved control group makes it impossible to distinguish between the nonspecific effects of these risk factors (i.e., main effects) and those that modify the impact of loss on the health of the bereaved (i.e., risk-factor × marital status interactions). In longitudinal studies, when health outcome is measured several times after bereavement, differential adjustment can be inferred from differences in the recovery rates of different groups of widowed individuals. But even then, the inclusion of a nonbereaved control group is always advisable.

We have grouped risk factors into *personal* and *situational* variables. The personal variables are further subdivided into sociodemographic factors (social class, sex, age, and ethnic group) and individual factors (religiosity, personality, and prior health). Three categories of situational factors are distinguished, namely those that affected the individual before the loss (antecedent stresses, bonds to the deceased), the mode of death (duration of terminal illness, causes of death), and the circumstances after the loss (concurrent stresses, social support). Whenever known, the main effect of a potential risk factor (i.e., its impact on the general population) is described before discussing its impact on the bereaved.

8.2 Sociocultural factors

8.2.1 *Social class*

(i) Social class differences in morbidity and mortality

In the general population, there is an inverse relationship between mental illness and socioeconomic status (SES). The greater prevalence of psychiatric problems among individuals of lower SES is one of the oldest and most accepted findings in psychiatric epidemiology (e.g., Faris & Dunham, 1939; Hollingshead & Redlich, 1958; see also Dohrenwend & Dohrenwend, 1969; Kessler, Price, & Wortman, 1985; Liem & Liem, 1978).

There is also a great deal of evidence to indicate that individuals of low socioeconomic status have a greater frequency of illness, disability, and restriction of activity because of health problems than do those of higher status (for a review, see Mechanic, 1978). Furthermore, there is an inverse relationship between socioeconomic status and mortality (e.g., Kitagawa & Hauser, 1973).

The association between social class and ill health has been explained in terms of selection as well as social causation theories (Liem & Liem, 1978). Selection theorists assume that health problems cause downward mobility and/or prevent upward mobility. Social causation theorists, on the other hand, emphasize the role of class-linked social factors as determinants of mental illness.

One of the major causes assumed to be responsible for the relationship between social class and mental illness has been the exposure to stressful life events. Moderate but significant positive correlations between SES and life-change scores (e.g., Myers, Lindenthal, & Pepper, 1974; Dohrenwend, 1973) indicate that stressful life events are overrepresented in the lower classes. There is also evidence that exposure to undesirable life events is more likely to evoke mental health problems in low rather than high SES individuals (Dohrenwend, 1973; Langner & Michael, 1963). This greater vulnerability of lower class individuals seems to a large extent to be due to a differential availability of social support. Thus, Brown and Harris (1978) found that lower class people have fewer confidants than those in the middle class, and that this contributed importantly to the greater impact of undesirable life events. The possibility that class-linked differences in coping styles may be responsible for part of the differences in vulnerability has been less explored.

Although differences in the availability of social support and the exposure to stressful life events are likely to contribute to the association between social class and physical health, status-related differences in patterns of living (e.g., poor nutrition, housing, restricted access to health care, unhealthy jobs) are typically given greater weight in explaining the poorer health of low-SES individuals.

(ii) Social class differences in bereavement outcome

It follows, from the findings reported above, that the widowed of lower SES should be more likely to have health problems than those of higher SES. This could either be due to the fact that low-SES individuals are already less healthy at the time of their bereavement or that they are at greater risk as a consequence of loss (i.e., loss leads to greater health *deterioration* for low- as compared to high-SES individuals). It is, however, somewhat unclear whether the interpretations of the association between social class and health offered above would lead one to assume that the effects of social class and bereavement combine additively (two main effects) or that the impact of bereavement is modified by the social class of the widowed (social class × bereavement interaction). If the inverse relationship between health and social class is attributed to class-linked differences in vulnerability, an interaction between social class and bereavement could be expected (e.g., buffering). If the greater prevalence of health problems among the lower classes is explained in terms of their greater exposure to critical life events, then the effect of bereavement as an additional stressor might merely be added to the social class effect (two main effects).

Mental health. A number of studies have linked low SES with poor mental health outcome among the bereaved, without using a nonbereaved control group. For example, Sheldon, Cochrane, Vachon, et al. (1981) examined social class differences among a sample of Canadian widows. They used a multiple regression analysis approach, and found that low SES accounted for a large part of the variance on their main health measure (General Health Questionnaire). The combination of the sociodemographic factors of age and SES accounted for 22 percent of the variance in health scores of the widowed. However, since this analysis did not include their nonwidowed sample, these findings may reflect a main effect of social class. The same interpretation applies to the findings of Amir and Sharon (1982). These authors reported a significant difference in the adjustment of war widows in Israel depending on whether their socioeconomic situation before they lost their husbands was good or poor. The former adjusted much better (on measures of social, emotional, and work functioning) than the latter.

Parkes (1975a), avoided this problem by defining poor outcome mainly in terms of bereavement-specific symptoms (e.g., acquisition of symptoms resembling those suffered by the bereaved, overactivity without a sense of loss, pronounced ascription of self-blame). He examined the differential effects of SES on outcome among the sample of young widowed in the Harvard Study. People of low social class (low income and low occupational class of the husband) were more likely to be found in the bad-outcome group.

There are only a few studies which used nonbereaved controls to examine whether the impact of bereavement on psychological health is modified by social class (Bahr & Harvey, 1980; Gallagher et al., 1983; Morgan, 1976; Sanders, 1980). Bahr and Harvey (1980) looked at morale among young widows of miners, bereaved through a mining disaster in 1972. The study included two control groups, namely, wives of survivors of this disaster, and wives of miners in the area who had not been involved. The effect of bereavement on morale (personal happiness ratings) and on the perception of quality of life was measured. The relative strength of the relationship between two components of socioeconomic status (income and education) and morale was assessed using separate stepwise multiple regression analyses conducted on each of the three groups. Although Bahr and Harvey found that education explained more of the variance in the morale scores of the widowed than in those of the nonwidowed controls, the interpretation of this pattern is somewhat unclear.

More clear-cut results were reported in a study by Morgan (1976), who examined "morale" among 232 widowed and 363 married women, aged 45–74 in Los Angeles County. Morale was measured by a six-item scale comprised of questions related to sadness and depressed mood, boredom and loneliness. Only one component of SES, family income, was measured. Low income was related to lower morale for the widowed as well as for the married. There was no interaction between marital status and income.

Further data on this point were provided by Gallagher et al. (1983) and Sanders (1980). In a study described earlier (7.2.1), Gallagher et al. found that lower SES was significantly associated with higher scores on measures of psychological distress for both widowed and nonwidowed controls and that the relationship between SES and distress measures did not differ significantly between the two groups.

Similarly, Sanders (1980), in her study of bereavement reactions among spouses, children, and parents, found that bereaved and control (i.e., nonbereaved) participants lower in income showed more repression on the Grief Experiences Inventory and higher depression, social isolation, and lowered ego strength. She noted, however, that there was "no evidence to suggest that the death experience exaggerates or exacerbates these differences" (p. 313). In fact, the controls manifested even greater differences than the bereaved.

Maddison and Walker (1967) failed to find any relationship between social class and bereavement outcome in a sample of 132 widows in Boston, Massachusetts. No further information on the range of social classes sampled is available, though Maddison and Walker noted that only 48 percent, of the sample originally approached, participated in their postal questionnaire. Thus, it is possible that the lower social classes were selected out of the sample.

Conclusions. There is a great deal of evidence to indicate that widowed of low SES are less healthy than bereaved of high SES. Since studies which employed nonbereaved controls (Gallagher et al., 1983; Morgan, 1976; Sanders, 1980) tend to show that the health differential due to social class is the same for bereaved and nonbereaved groups, it can be assumed that the social class differences observed in studies which failed to employ appropriate controls are merely a reflection of the pervasive inverse relationship between social class and health.

This absence of an interaction between social class and marital status on health is inconsistent with interpretations of the relationship between social class and health in terms of class differences in vulnerability. If stressful life experiences had a greater capacity to provoke mental health problems in the lower class than in the middle class, then bereavement should have a greater effect on the health of low rather than high SES individuals. Since the greater vulnerability of lower class individuals was assumed to be due to a lack of social support, the failure to find a social class by marital status interaction is also inconsistent with predictions about the moderator role of social support in bereavement which were derived from behavior theories of depression (Chapter 4) and our deficit model of partner loss (Chapter 5).

Mortality. The few studies that looked at mortality risk by marital status and social class typically included married control groups. Thus, Parkes et al. (1969) analyzed the mortality rate of their sample of 4,486 widowers over 55 years of age (in England and Wales, for the year 1957) by social class, comparing the rate during the first six months of bereavement with that of comparable married men. There was a suggestion that the largest widowed-to-married men excesses occurred in the highest SES group and the smallest in the group with the lowest SES. However, as the authors pointed out, the numbers in the extreme groups are very small so that the differences do not reach statistical significance.

This suggestion of a greater impact of bereavement on high SES individuals does not only run counter to the theoretical interpretations of the social class effects discussed earlier, it is also not confirmed in a national, cross-sectional investigation also conducted in Great Britain by the Office of Population Censuses and Surveys (1978). The direct age-standardized death rates for men of widowed and married status by social class are shown in Figure 8.2. It appears from this that the lower the social class, the greater the excess risk of mortality for widowers. This suggests that the Parkes et al. (1969) results were idiosyncratic to the small sample of older widowers. It remains unclear, however, why the impact of social class and marital status on health should be additive for mental health but nonadditive for mortality.

(iii) Is the loss effect due to social class differences?

There have been speculations in the literature that, for widows, the health deterioration following bereavement could be due to a sudden drop in income after the death of the major wage earner. The fact that there is little evidence for a class-related difference in vulnerability to loss does not invalidate this explanation, which relies on the well-documented

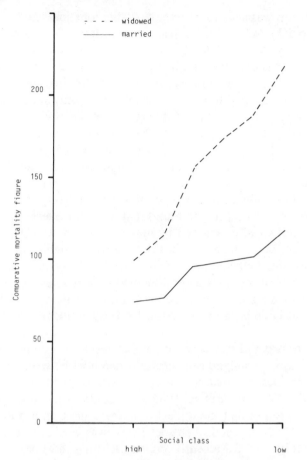

Figure 8.2. Mortality by social class and marital status for men (adapted from OPCS Series DS, No. 1, 1978).

inverse relationship between social class and health. If people are less healthy the lower their social class, and if bereavement leads to a drop in social class, then this drop could be responsible for the lower health of the widowed.

A study by Atchley (1975) is frequently cited in the literature as evidence for this assumption. The impact of widowhood on elderly males and females (widowed and married) of different occupational groups in the Midwest, United States, was examined. Widowhood was reported to have a pronounced social impact (as measured by social-participation, car-driving, and income-adequacy questionnaire items) on working class widows. This group was also noted to have higher loneliness and anxiety (the so-called social psychological impact) than widowers or married persons. Unfortunately, Atchley (1975) gives no detailed results of the social class by marital status patterns, and it is possible that the widow-to-widower differences reflect the main effect of gender rather than marital status changes. For social psychological variables it is only reported that " ... there were as many significant differences between widowers and widows as between widowed and married persons of either sex" (p. 177). Thus, it is difficult to assess the validity of Atchley's conclusion that economic circumstances were a powerful factor influencing the social situation of widows.

Some supporting evidence is provided, however, by Morgan (1976) in the study described earlier. Morgan found that when the effect of income differences was statistically removed by means of an analysis of covariance, the impact of bereavement on health became nonsignificant. Thus, when income was held constant by this method, there was no difference between the morale of the married and the widowed women in his sample. Morgan (1976) suggested that "the lower morale generally attributed to widows should have been attributed instead to low income level" (p. 692).

This assumption could not account for the results of studies which demonstrated major and significant health differences between married and bereaved samples that had been matched with regard to social class (Glick et al., 1974; W. Stroebe et al., 1985) or of studies such as Gallagher et al. (1983), who found that the impact of bereavement on health measures was only slightly reduced when social class was used as a covariate. Furthermore, Morgan (1981) recently reported findings that challenge the assumption that bereavement is generally associated with a loss of income. In this study cross-sectional and longitudinal analyses were compared in a national sample of women widowed in midlife. While the cross-sectional analysis replicated previous findings of a lowered income among the widows, the longitudinal comparisons failed to demonstrate a significant decline in income due to the death of a spouse. Instead, the longitudinal findings suggested that many sample members were already poor prior to widowhood. Thus, the difference in income of married and widowed women typically reported in cross-sectional studies could have been a consequence of the inverse relationship between social class and mortality. If members of the lower classes have a shorter life expectancy than members of the higher classes, then women who have been poor all their lives are also more likely to become widowed. In generalizing these findings it should be remembered, however, that they are specific to middle-aged women living in a relatively affluent country during a period of fairly low unemployment.

There can be no doubt that the death of a spouse is associated with a severe drop in income for *some* widows and that the financial difficulties resulting from the loss of the major wage earner will serve as an *additional* source of stress and thus contribute to the negative health impact of bereavement. But since it is only one of many stresses of bereavement which, in addition, happens to only some of the bereaved, financial stress cannot serve as a general explanation of the loss effect.

8.2.2 Gender

(i) Sex differences in morbidity and mortality

Women (at least in Western societies) have higher distress and depression rates than men (National Center for Health Statistics, 1976b; Weissman & Klerman, 1977) and in general report symptoms of both physical and mental illness and utilize physician and hospital services for these conditions at a higher rate than men (Nathanson, 1975). Men, on the other hand have higher mortality rates than women (National Center for Health Statistics, 1970; Office of Population Censuses and Surveys, 1986; Registrar General, 1971). This is true for mortality from natural causes as well as accidents and suicides. That men have a higher suicide rate than women is particularly noteworthy, because women have a higher rate of attempted suicide.

There are a number of processes which have been made responsible for the gender difference in morbidity. From an extensive review of the evidence, Wingard (1984) concluded that sex differences in *illness behavior* (i.e., women may have more time than men to adopt the sick role and stay at home or in bed); *service utilization* (women have more time to utilize health services, and each visit to a doctor increases the likelihood of an illness being detected); and *physicians' behavior* (physicians may be more willing to attribute psychogenic illnesses to women than to men) may all influence the detection and reporting of illness. There seems to be little support, however, for the assumption that women report more illnesses because it is culturally more acceptable for them to be ill. Gender differences in mortality have typically been attributed to differences in life style (e.g., cigarette smoking, Type A behavior). There is also evidence that biological factors influence male/female mortality differences, particularly in infancy and prenatal life.

(ii) Sex differences in bereavement outcome

Since our extensive review of the available evidence on differential health consequences among widows and widowers (M. Stroebe & Stroebe, 1983), a few more recent studies have contributed some further information on this issue. But there is still a lack of reliable information on sex differences. In the majority of studies only widows have been included (e.g., Ball, 1977; Blanchard, Blanchard, & Becker, 1976; Hobson, 1964; Lopata, 1973b; Maddison & Viola, 1968; Marris, 1958; Morgan, 1976; Parkes, 1964b; van Rooijen, 1979). Because widows are more numerous, and due to some of the main effects of sex on mental and physical health treatment, the conclusion is often reached that widows are at higher risk than widowers (e.g., Carey, 1979; Greenblatt, 1978). Others (e.g., Lund, Caserta, & Dimond, 1986) have drawn the conclusion, in the absence of nonbereaved male and female controls, that there are no substantial differences between elderly males and females in bereavement outcomes: "Their bereavement-related feelings and behaviors were found to be at similar levels of intensity and their changes over time were also alike" (Lund et al., 1986, pp. 318–319). Our conclusion was different: If there is a difference (and evidence is not entirely conclusive) it is the widowers who are at higher risk, for when widows and widowers are compared with same-sex, nonbereaved comparison persons (thus controlling for the main effects of sex on health) widowers are found to suffer greater detriments compared with married men than are widows compared with married women. In fact, it has sometimes been found that depression among samples of widowers is greater than among widows even when nonbereaved controls were not included (e.g., Richards & McCallum, 1979).

Why should men suffer more? After considering a number of alternative interpretations, we suggested that the sex difference in the health consequences of bereavement are due to a differential availability of alternative sources of social support to men and women. This assumption is plausible in view of the large body of research that demonstrates that social support can protect individuals against the deleterious effects of critical life events (e.g., Brown & Harris, 1978; House, 1981). It would also allow for an interpretation of sex difference findings in terms of behavior theories of depression (e.g., Ferster, 1973; Lazarus, 1968) and stress theory (e.g., Lazarus & Folkman, 1984; M. Stroebe & Stroebe, 1985; W. Stroebe & Stroebe, 1986). According to behavior theory, the severity of grief responses is related to the reduction of response-contingent positive reinforcements suffered by the widowed. Since friends and relatives can serve as alternative sources of reinforcement, the availability of social support should replace some of the reinforcements previously provided by the partner. Similarly, the deficit model of partner loss considers social support as an interpersonal resource, which by replacing some of the deficits in task support, validational support, and emotional support created by the loss would help the bereaved to cope with the stress of bereavement. Furthermore, the availability of others to whom one can openly express one's feelings of grief and despair is likely to encourage and facilitate grief work.

There are a number of reasons why widowers should be less likely than widows to find alternative sources of social support. It is much less acceptable in our culture for men than for women to express personal feelings or verbalize intimate thoughts with regard to feelings of loneliness or a need for companionship. Due to these constraints, men are more likely to rely exclusively on their wives as confidants, while women frequently have confidants outside their households. As a consequence, widowers are less likely than widows to have somebody to whom they can talk freely about their anguish and pain and who, by merely listening, helps them to work through their grief. There is some evidence in the data of the Tübingen study to suggest a general sex difference in the use of social support in coping with traumatic life events. While stressful life experiences motivate women to actively search for emotional support, men seem to react by trying to distract themselves through their work.

Depression and mental illness. Much of the evidence on sex differences in depression following bereavement has been discussed earlier (Chapter 2.1). Strong support for the hypothesis that men adjust less well to bereavement than women is provided by the studies of Radloff (1975) and Glick et al. (1974). In a community survey of depression, Radloff (1975) observed a sex by marital status interaction on depression. While married women were more depressed than married men, widowed men were more depressed than widowed women. Thus, despite the higher depression rates of females, males become relatively more depressed on bereavement. Glick et al. (1974) found, two to four years after bereavement, that widowers had taken longer to recover than widows. Although widows had higher depression scores one year after bereavement, at the later follow-up they were no more depressed than the married women, whereas widowers remained significantly more depressed than married men.

In contrast, Gallagher et al.(1983) found no sex by marital status interaction on depression. In this study widows and widowers showed similar excesses compared with same-sex controls. However, since the depression measures were administered two months after bereavement (i.e., at a time when there was no sex difference in the Harvard study either), these findings do not contradict those of Glick et al. (1974). Furthermore, the sex difference in selection observed in our own investigation (W. Stroebe et al., 1985) raises the possibility that the failure of these studies to find a sex by marital status interaction on the immediate impact of bereavement could have been due to a selection effect. As reported earlier (Chapter 7.1), the Tübingen data indicate an interaction between sex, and willingness to participate, on depression (BDI). While widows who refused to be interviewed were less depressed than those who agreed, the opposite difference was observed for widowers. This sex difference in selection might be a reflection of the sex difference in coping styles mentioned earlier: While women cope by searching for social support to facilitate grief work, men prefer to distract themselves through work. A related explanation of the sex difference in selection (which might also be at the root of the sex difference in coping styles), could be the existence of sex-specific norms about self-control of emotions. To cry during an interview is more embarrassing for a man than a woman. Thus, although the more emotionally distressed widowed would feel in greater need than the less distressed to talk to an interviewer who was an expert in the area of bereavement, the fear of an emotional breakdown could have led those widowers who felt most depressed and most likely to break down during the interview to refuse participation.

This normative interpretation, which was further validated by sex differences in the reasons given for declining participation, has two important implications. On one hand, it suggests that this type of bias should be most likely in interview studies. Depressed men might be more willing to reply when written responses are required. More importantly, however, this sex difference in selection indicates that, without selection, interview studies such as Glick et al. (1974), Gallagher et al.(1983), and W. Stroebe et al. (1985) might have observed a sex by marital status interaction on depression at the time of the first interview. Thus, in the Tübingen study, while a two-factor analysis of variance on the scores of the Beck Depression Inventory yielded main effects for marital status and gender with the data of the "accepters" (Figure. 8.3, left panel), such an analysis results in a sex by marital status interaction when the married are compared with the "refusers" (Figure 8.3, right panel).

Information on the incidence of *mental illness* following bereavement is consistent with the findings for the less severe measures of depression

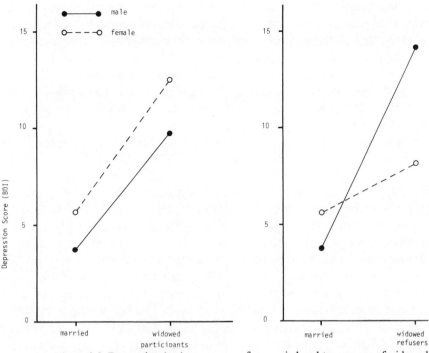

Figure 8.3. Depression (BDI) mean scores for married and two groups of widowed by sex in the Tübingen study.

described above. Gove (1972a) reviewed studies of mental illness by marital status and came to the conclusion that, while rates of mental illness were higher for the widowed than for the married, the difference between being married and being widowed was greater for men than for women. This was confirmed in a later review (Bloom et al., 1978). Bloom (1975), for example, examined diagnostic specific admission rates into psychiatric facilities and included analyses by sex and marital status. While the admission rates for psychoneurotic illnesses (of which depression constitutes a large proportion) were twice as high for married women as for married men, for the widowed this large sex difference was not evident: Widows had only slightly higher rates than widowers.

It is interesting to note that the rates for this category are actually lower than those for the married. This could be because the rates given are those for first admissions to inpatient facilities. We would hypothesize that this may be due to the fact that if depression occurs for the first time in bereavement it is probably less severe and thus less likely to require inpatient treatment. But a further problem, that relatively more widowers than widows may be assigned to inpatient care because they are less able to take care of themselves, cannot be clarified in this cross-sectional investigation, and the possibility remains that the rates reflect this sex difference in addition to illness per se. Despite limitations of cross-sectional studies for present interests, findings on mental disorder are quite consistent: Bereavement appears to have more extreme effects on the mental health of men than of women.

Apparent contradictions to this conclusion from some early longitudinal studies (Stern, Williams, & Prados, 1951; Wretmark, 1959) are probably attributable to a failure to consider main effects of sex on psychiatric treatment variables. However, a further early study by Parkes (1964a) compared inception rates into psychiatric care of bereaved and nonbereaved patients and still attested to a higher vulnerability among widows than widowers. This study was based on data obtained from the case-note summaries made by psychiatrists on each patient. It is problematic for a number of reasons (see Stein & Susser, 1969; M. Stroebe & Stroebe, 1983) and, in addition, seems inconsistent with the depression findings from the more recent Harvard study (Parkes & Brown, 1972). The latter study employed more appropriate control groups and found the sex difference to be in the opposite direction. It also contradicts the findings of a further study, specifically on mental illness. Stein and Susser (1969) examined inception rates among the bereaved from 1959–63 in Salford, England, and found the ratio of widowers to married men (2.74) to be greater than that for widows to married women (1.66). The most pronounced differences were found for the younger bereaved (20–39 year olds) and in the months immediately following loss. Since the study population was drawn from all types of psychiatric care and was not limited to resident populations (who comprised only just over a third of the total inceptions) it is unlikely that the sex difference was due to a greater loss of care among widowers than among widows.

Physical health. With regard to physical health, some information on sex differences is available in the large-scale household survey conducted by the National Center for Health Statistics (1976a). The widowed in general were found to have higher short-term and long-term disability scores than the married. There was a somewhat higher rate of visits to physicians among the former. The pattern of findings also suggested that these effects are stronger for widowers than for widows.

There are two main limitations to the usefulness of this information:

(1) Differentiation is not made between causes of disability, some of which could be psychological problems, and (2) the data are not presented according to the duration of bereavement. Thus, the healthier widowed could have remarried. However, longitudinal studies with better control over these factors have generally confirmed the marital status pattern, but with regard to sex differences, findings are not completely consistent across the few studies available. Thompson et al. (1984), though reporting physical effects of bereavement on a variety of indices (medication use, self-reported illnesses, etc.) of physical health among the elderly sample, found no significant marital status by sex interactions on any indices. On the other hand, Glick et al. (1974) found a sex difference on their specifically constructed physical health questionnaire: Though widows had higher scores on the physical health measure than widowers fourteen months after bereavement, only the scores of the widowers differed significantly from those of married controls. A third longitudinal study of an older sample by Gerber and colleagues (Gerber, Rusalem, Hannon, et al., 1975a; Gerber, Wiener, Battin, et al., 1975b) found a similar sex difference to the Harvard study results, but since no married controls were used this study does not provide strong support for a sex difference in physical symptoms.

Mortality. The most unequivocal support for the sex difference in bereavement outcome comes from cross-sectional mortality data (see Kraus & Lilienfeld, 1959; National Center for Health Statistics, 1970; Office of Population Censuses and Surveys, 1986; Registrar General, 1971; M. Stroebe et al., 1981). These studies, which were discussed earlier (Chapter 7.4), show that widowers have more excessive mortality rates from all causes taken together than do widows compared with married women.

The evidence from longitudinal studies is less consistent. Of the four studies which employed sizeable samples of both sexes (Helsing & Szklo, 1981; Kaprio & Koskenvuo, 1983; McNeill, 1973; Mellström et al., 1982), Helsing and Szklo and Mellström et al. found a sex difference, Kaprio and Koskenvuo did not, and McNeill's data are difficult to interpret, due to the problems with the control group. With regard to sex differences in the period of highest risk, there are some indications that widowers are most at risk in the first six months of bereavement (Niemi, 1979; Parkes et al., 1969; Young et al., 1963) whereas for widows the peak in risk appears to occur during the second year (Cox & Ford, 1964; McNeill, 1973).

Studies of the incidence of *suicide* among the bereaved provide strong corroboration of the findings for mortality from other causes. Thus, Gove (1972b), in a cross-sectional investigation, computed age-specific widowed-to-married suicide ratios for each sex, for the U.S. national statistics 1959–61 and found greater excesses for widowers compared with married men than for widows compared with married women. Of particular interest in this investigation is Gove's analysis of attempted suicides, which exceed by far the number of completed suicides. Here there is a reversal in the sex main effect: Women are more likely to attempt suicide than men. But it is noteworthy that, despite this reversal, the pattern for the widowed is comparable to that for actual suicides. The widowed-to-married ratio for attempted suicides is greater for men than for women. Longitudinal studies of the distribution of suicides over the time period after loss (Bojanovsky & Bojanovsky, 1976; MacMahon & Pugh, 1965) indicate that widowers are more at risk during the first few months, whereas for widows the risk spreads more evenly over a longer period.

Conclusions. The evidence on sex differences in the health consequences of bereavement is generally still consistent with the conclusion drawn in our previous review (M. Stroebe & Stroebe, 1983) that men seem to suffer more than women. Studies of the impact of bereavement on a wide range of health measures demonstrated that, compared to matched married controls, widowers have more problems with their health than widows. The consistency of this pattern is impressive in view of the fact that it could be replicated for measures of health as well as mortality, even though women have higher rates of health complaints while men have a shorter life expectancy.

The explanation of this pattern in terms of sex differences in the availability of social support offers an interpretation which can be based on predictions from behavior theory of depression as well as stress theory. There is some indication, however, to suggest that men are also less motivated than women to use social support to cope with traumatic life events. Since most of the evidence on the role of social support differences as mediators of sex differences in bereavement outcome has been indirect, it is not possible at present to distinguish between these two interpretations. If it could be demonstrated, however, that the sex difference in bereavement outcome can be eliminated, or at least significantly reduced, by matching widows and widowers with regard to availability of social support, this would be more consistent with an interpretation in terms of sex differences in the availability of, rather than the preference for, social support.

8.2.3 *Age*

(i) Age differences in morbidity and mortality

The most typical finding of research in this area is that of a positive association between age and illness. It is a less frequent finding, however, in studies of mental rather than physical health. Thus, statements about the relationship between age and depression have been less than consistent (for a review, see Boyd & Weissman, 1982). There seems to be a positive relationship between age and moderate depression for men but not for women. Depression in women appears to reach a peak at the age range of 35 to 45 years, but there may also be an increase over the age of 55. This sex difference is also reflected in suicide rates, which show a positive relationship with age for men but not for women. For mortality from all causes, rates begin to increase with age for both sexes after adolescence. Up to approximately the age of 35, accidents are the most important cause of death. In the age group of 35 and older heart disease, cancers, and, later on, strokes account for most of the deaths (Mechanic, 1978).

(ii) Age differences in bereavement outcome

Since the negative health impact of bereavement is generally attributed to the fact that it aggravates or accelerates existing health problems, one would expect older bereaved persons to be more vulnerable to detrimental effects after such a stressful life event as loss of a spouse, than younger, more healthy persons. It is therefore rather puzzling to find that most of the empirical evidence supports the opposite conclusion: It is the younger bereaved who appear to suffer more severe health deterioration.

The reasons for the negative association between age and bereavement outcome are unclear. One plausible interpretation is in terms of age-related differences in the expectedness of loss. Since evidence to be discussed later (Section 8.5) has shown unexpected death to carry a higher risk for the survivor than an expected death, a negative correlation between age and expectedness of loss could account for the greater health risk of the younger bereaved. Other authors (e.g., Berardo, 1970; Blau, 1975; Heyman & Gianturco, 1973; Silverman, 1972) suggest that the supportive social network of similarly widowed friends, more available among the elderly, lessens the impact of bereavement. Lopata (1973b) noted that friendships are not as disrupted among the elderly since others are becoming widowed too: There is less couple orientation than among younger groups.

One of the studies that isolated the age variable and looked specifically at whether it was easier for widowed to cope at an older than at a younger age has been conducted by Ball (1977). The sample of widows had been bereaved between six to nine months. The widows were divided into young (aged 18–46), middle aged (47–59) and old (60–75) age groups. Subjects were asked to fill out a grief-symptoms questionnaire, which included psychological and somatic items. They were also asked to evaluate their present adjustment to loss (grief intensity). Age was significantly related to reported intensity of grief, with young widows experiencing a stronger overall grief reaction. There was a tendency for age to be related to total number of symptoms reported (the younger reporting more) although this result did not reach significance. When severity of these symptoms was measured, however, the young widows were found to have more severe grief reactions than the older.

It is interesting to note that there was a tendency for young widows of sudden bereavements to have more severe reactions than those of expected deaths. From Ball's data presentation it would appear that the young, sudden-bereavement group accounts for a large proportion of the age difference in severity. The interaction does not, however, reach an acceptable level of significance. Nevertheless, it points to the possibility that the age variable is confounded by expectedness of death.

Maddison and Walker (1967) examined how illness scores (psychological and physical symptoms) were related to age. They found that young widows had higher illness scores and greater health deterioration following loss than older ones. These differences were observed despite the fact that the age range was relatively small: Husbands of these widows had died between the ages of 45–60 years.

Similar results have also been reported by other investigators. In the study by Morgan (1976) age was one of five covariates examined with widowed and married women between the ages of 45–74 years on a six-item morale scale. Whereas younger widows were found to have considerably lower morale than the married controls, the older widows had similar or higher levels of morale than their married counterparts. Sheldon, Cochrane, Vachon, et al. (1981) also observed that the younger widowed had higher scores than the older on the General Health Questionnaire. Similarly, Carey (1977) found that the widowed under a median age of 57 years were more poorly adjusted than those over this age. Stein and Susser (1969) reported the younger bereaved as being worse off than the older, mental illness excesses of widowed to nonbereaved controls being greatest at younger ages. Bahr and Harvey (1980) noted a similar pattern in a follow-up investigation. Clayton (1974, 1979) concluded from her own study and from a review of the literature that the increase in morbidity and visits to physicians was greater among the younger rather than the older bereaved.

One study which failed to find an age effect was that of van Rooijen (1979), although, apart from the youngest age group of widowed (25–35 years old), there does seem to be a trend toward less depressive mood with increasing age, which is not apparent for the nonbereaved controls. In the Tübingen study there was no tendency for an age effect on any of the health measures. However, since the study focused on the younger bereaved, the age range may have been too restricted for significant correlations to occur. It is also possible that the fact that, for our sample, expectedness of loss was unrelated to age may have worked against an age effect on bereavement outcome.

That the majority of the studies on age and bereavement outcome documented the relatively good adjustment of older widowed compared with younger does not imply that the older do not suffer detriments to their health and symptoms of distress following bereavement. Recent studies focusing specifically on older age groups have confirmed this (Gallagher et al., 1983; Thompson et al., 1984). A longitudinal study by Sanders (1981) comparing the bereavement outcomes of older and younger widowed even indicates that under certain conditions older samples may have more persisting problems in adjustment than the younger. Sanders (1981) interviewed bereaved spouses approximately two months after the death and again eighteen months to two years later. Subsequently, the participants were divided into older (over 65; $n = 21$) and younger (under 63; $n = 24$) age groups. The Grief Experience Inventory (GEI; see Sanders, Mauger, & Strong, 1979), a self-report questionnaire designed to assess experiences, feelings, symptoms, and behavior during bereavement, was administered. Matched controls were included in the study. Duration of bereavement was found to be differentially related to grief intensity and symptomatology for the two age groups. Soon after bereavement the younger widowed manifested greater grief intensities. Later on, after the lapse of eighteen to twenty-four months, however, it was the older bereaved who showed exacerbated grief reactions. While younger spouses manifested higher elevations on the guilt subscale of the GEI, older spouses were higher on denial. Sanders (1981) interpreted the elevation on denial among older spouses as a defense mechanism against anxiety, for these widowed had high scores on the social isolation, depersonalization, death anxiety, and loss of vigor scales.

Sanders's (1981) study of age as a risk factor is important in several respects. It focuses attention on the multidimensional nature of grief symptomatology, examining how the pattern is different for younger and older widowed at different time points after loss. Younger spouses responded initially with greater shock, confusion, anxiety, and guilt, but they were able to readjust over time. For older spouses the trend was different: While initially denial mechanisms diminished grief expressions, after the lapse of eighteen to twenty-four months grief reactions were exacerbated. Sanders (1981) related this to the persistence of extreme loneliness and deprivation, and to the minimal social support from others that these older widowed persons received. So it seems that, while bereavement was less disorganizing for older than for younger widowed in Sanders's sample, it was not age per se but the persisting situation of extreme isolation and loneliness of this particular older group that was responsible for the exacerbated grief reactions. Clearly, the circumstances of the elderly vary from sample to sample, such that the pattern found by Sanders will not necessarily be observed elsewhere. In fact, Brown (1960) noted that the number of social contacts increased rather than decreased among a sample of widowed individuals sixty years and over. Similarly, Heyman and Gianturco (1973) reported no before- and after-bereavement differences in health status and social involvement, and attributed this to the stability of the life style of these elderly people, even after their bereavement.

The Sanders (1981) study also implies that the widowed of different age groups are vulnerable to different types of debility. Others have argued that the younger may be worse off with regard to emotional problems, whereas for the older there is a preponderance of physical problems. In an early study Stern, Williams, and Prados (1951) observed that there was a preponderance of somatic symptoms among widowed "in later life," arguing that there was a tendency for the replacement of an emotional grief reaction by somatic equivalents. However, the sample of "elderly" ranged in age from 53 to 70, and neither younger widowed nor non-widowed controls were included for comparison.

More systematic evidence for this comes from Parkes's studies. He reported (1964b) that following bereavement the widowed under 65 years gave psychiatric symptoms as the reason for visiting physicians far more often, compared with prebereavement rates, than those over this age. However, the older had a greater increase in physical symptoms. While the younger had increased rates for these nonpsychiatric consultations too, the increase was not nearly so striking. In a later study Parkes (1975a) found that the younger bereaved suffered more from psychological problems. They had a greater increase in the intake of sedatives, whereas the older bereaved had predominately physical health symptoms. It is not quite clear why this pattern should be found. Could it be that the older confuse grief reactions with the health problems of old age?

As with the study of sex differences, the most consistent evidence for age differences in bereavement outcome is obtained from cross-sectional data on *mortality*. Relatively more excessive widowed-to-married ratios are found in cross-sectional statistics for the younger compared with the older groups (Kraus & Lilienfeld, 1959; M. Stroebe et al., 1981). These data are not conclusive, since a number of artifacts could account for the pattern. For example, accidents are a more frequent cause of death among younger than among older adults. If a married couple were to be involved in a fatal accident and one outlived the other by any length of time, this person would be classified as "widowed" at death (Registrar General, 1971). This alternative interpretation could not account for the fact that the same age pattern as for mortality of all causes can also be found for mortality from suicide (Gove, 1972b), although the widowed-to-married ratios for suicide decrease less with age for women than for men.

Possibly of greater impact on mortality rates is selection into remarriage. More of the younger than the older widowed remarry and if one assumes that the healthier are selected into remarriage (Carter & Glick, 1976), the younger sample would likewise be biased toward the unhealthy. However, this age pattern has also been confirmed in a number of longitudinal studies which controlled for remarriage. Thus Helsing and Szklo (1981) reported excess mortality among widowed males between the ages of 55 and 74, but an even greater excess in the younger age groups, though the small numbers meant that the latter were not significantly different from the married controls. In this study the age effect did not pertain for women, but widows in no age group were found to have excessive rates compared with married women.

Conclusions. There is a great deal of evidence to suggest that age is a predictor of bereavement outcome: The younger widowed are at higher risk to their health than the older and, possibly, suffer a greater risk of emotional problems than the older. The reasons for the negative association between age and bereavement are less clear. Although interpretations in terms of age-related differences in expectedness of loss and/or availability of social support are plausible, there is a lack of studies that directly assessed the mediating role of these variables.

8.2.4 *Race and ethnic group*

(i) Race and ethnic differences in morbidity and mortality

Much of the research on race differences in morbidity and mortality has focused on black–white differences in the United States. The pattern of findings on mental health variables has been somewhat inconclusive (for a review, see Kessler, Price, & Wortman, 1985). Thus, there seems to be no difference in overall treatment rates, but blacks report higher levels of distress than whites in community surveys. The higher distress of the blacks can be accounted for by black–white differences in socioeconomic status (Kessler et al., 1985). Death rates for blacks are higher than those for whites in the United States (Carter & Glick, 1976; Kraus & Lilienfeld, 1959).

Studies of ethnic differences have mostly focused on the comparison between Americans of Mexican heritage with Anglos. Americans of Mexican heritage are typically underrepresented in treatment statistics relative to their proportions in the population. For levels of psychological distress, no consistent evidence has been found (Kessler et al., 1985).

(ii) Race and ethnic differences in bereavement outcome

There is a lack of reliable information on race and ethnic differences in bereavement outcome, although the sociological research of Lopata (1973a, b; 1979) provides insightful background material on responses to widowhood among blacks and whites, from which testable hypotheses could be derived. Most samples selected for bereavement research are ethnically homogenous, or contain subsamples of minority groups too small to permit analysis of this variable. But even when bereaved samples are of mixed racial or ethnic composition, it is frequently difficult or even impossible to disentangle the confounding of the minority group status with other variables such as social class. Thus, Amir and Sharon (1982), in their study in Israel, found ethnic group differences in the adjustment of widows (those of Western being better adjusted than those of Middle Eastern origin), but these could not be separated from the confounding effect of social status (the former being high and the latter low status).

By using analyses of covariance, Morgan (1976) overcame some of the problems inherent in making ethnic group comparisons. This technique permits a statistical control for a suspected confounding variable on the dependent measure by removing its effect from the comparison group. Morgan examined specific ethnic group patterns in a study of morale among 232 widowed and 363 married women between the ages of 45 and 74 in Los Angeles County. The three ethnic groups were black, Mexican American, and white. The major variables utilized as covariates were age, income, employment, and family interaction. It was found that in all three ethnic groups the widows had lower morale than their married counterparts (although the difference was significant only for whites), and that, in general, most ethnic group differences were not significant. Income was found to explain differences in morale by marital status for white women only, but this could be partially an artifact of the differences in sample size, as the author notes. Most striking was the finding that family interaction was crucial to the morale of widowed Mexican American women. Among this group, but not the other two ethnic groups, the widowed have lower morale than the married when family interaction is low. Morgan (1976) speculated that this may reflect heightened social isolation among Mexican Americans. It may also suggest the importance of ethnic differences in the impact of family interaction on morale.

Differences between black and white Americans with regard to the mortality risk of the bereaved have been examined by Kraus and Lilienfeld (1959), who based their investigation on statistics of all deaths in the United States in 1949–51. The widowed-to-married ratios for white widowed were substantially lower than those for nonwhites over the age of 35. Under this age, the opposite pattern was found, with whites having relatively higher widowed-to-married ratios. However, widowhood in this age group is a comparatively rare event and subject to more artifacts than the older groups. Carter and Glick (1976) also reported very high death rates for nonwhite widowed persons, who were also relatively more at risk than white widowed, compared with their married peers. This pattern held for males and females (see Carter & Glick, 1976, Fig. 11.1).

Conclusions. In view of the limited evidence and the problems of interpretation outlined above, no clear conclusions can be drawn about the impact of bereavement on the health among members of different ethnic or racial groups. But even when such differences have been identified, as in the black–white comparisons of the mortality risk of the bereaved, it is unclear how these findings should be explained. Racial or ethnic group comparisons reflect complex combinations of demographic, biological, social, and economic characteristics. These groups differ in the percentage of widowed in their marital statuses, due to differing mortality and remarriage rates. They differ in economic welfare, religion, and, notably for the United States, in immigration histories, assimilation rates, and even in the misreporting of marital status (cf. Carter & Glick, 1976). In addition, cultural variations in mourning customs and grieving patterns, which we discussed in Chapter 3, are relevant to ethnic or racial group differences in bereavement outcome.

8.3 Individual factors

8.3.1 *Religiosity*

Whereas people's religious affiliation (e.g., Catholic, Anglican) is a socio-demographic variable, the intensity of their beliefs and practices (their religiosity) can be considered an individual characteristic. The potential influence of differences in religious affiliation on bereavement has been discussed briefly in the chapter on cultural influence (Section 3.6.1). In this section on individual factors we will focus on the influence of religiosity as a moderator of bereavement outcome. Over the years many have argued that, in various ways, religious beliefs help bereaved persons to overcome their loss (e.g., Alexander & Adlerstein, 1959; Eliot, 1946; Gorer, 1965; Krupp & Kligfeld, 1962). Some empirical support can be found for this view.

Glick et al. (1974) reported that 59 percent of their Boston sample thought religion had been a source of great comfort to them during their bereavement. Similarly, among an elderly sample of both widows and widowers, Heyman and Gianturco (1973) found that emotional strength and comfort was derived from church affiliation. Clearly these studies report purely subjective feelings. They do not investigate the relationship specifically between religiosity and outcome. However, a study by Bornstein, Clayton, Halikas, et al. (1973) found such an association. These investigators reported a significant difference between their depressed and nondepressed groups in church attendance. Of the depressed group, 50 percent had never attended church, whereas this was true for only 17 percent of the nondepressed group.

Obviously, religiosity is a multifaceted concept. Religions not only offer systems of beliefs which may be comforting to the bereaved (e.g., the belief in life after death), they also offer a religious community and thus a social support network likely to protect the individual against the adverse effects of life stress. It is not clear from the above studies whether social or spiritual features of religion are critical. Yamamoto (Yamamoto, Okonogi, Iwasaki, & Yoshimura, 1969; Yamamoto, 1970) argued specifically that, in Japan, it is the religious concepts which have a bearing on adaptation to loss. In their study, Yamamoto and his colleagues compared the course of grief among a small sample of Japanese widows, all of them bereaved from sudden, unexpected deaths, with published data from two studies in Britain (Parkes, 1965 and Marris, 1958). Since sampling techniques and sample characteristics differed between these studies it is rather doubtful whether any comparative inferences about bereavement outcome should be made. However, since their conclusions are widely cited, it should be mentioned here that Yamamoto et al. (1969) found comparatively good adjustment among the Japanese widows compared with the other samples. This the authors attributed to the belief in both Shinto and Buddhist religions, to which most of the widows adhered, that contact can be maintained with the deceased, who become ancestors. The deceased person is therefore not lost to the survivor: Experiences can still be shared. The deceased must be revered and fed at the family altar, where a photo is placed. Thus, the idea of his or her presence is cultivated and the tie remains.

One might argue that this cultivation of the presence of the deceased might hinder rather than help recovery, and it is not hard to imagine that it could fixate the bereaved in the grief process and lead to chronic grief, the bereaved failing to relinquish the tie. Yamamoto et al. (1969) argue that this does not happen: The bereaved "look at the picture and feel he is alive, and look at the urn of ashes and realize he is dead" (p. 1,665).

Bahr and Harvey (1980), in their study of young miners' widows, reported that religious beliefs and activity were positively associated with happiness and high quality of life in their widowed sample. Church involvement was far less relevant to the happiness of women in the two control samples (wives of survivors and wives of miners not involved in the catastrophe). Unfortunately, as with their findings on socioeconomic status, the methodology employed in analyzing their data makes it difficult to interpret their results.

Some insight into the relationship between religiosity and bereavement outcome can be derived from a study by Sanders (1980). She measured the influence of church attendance on outcome by dividing participants in her study of bereaved spouses, parents, and children into those who regularly attended church and those who did not. Church attendance made a difference on certain scales of the Grief Experience Inventory and the MMPI. Frequent attenders had higher scores on the optimism and the social desirability scales. They also showed more repression of grief responses than the less-frequent attenders. When similar analyses were made on nonbereaved controls, only the social desirability scale showed significant differences according to church attendance.

Sanders's (1980) results have to be interpreted with some caution since regular and nonregular church attenders showed significant differences on only four subscales. Thus, for the majority of scales (including despair, guilt, loss of control, rumination) there were no significant differences between them. It cannot be argued, therefore, that church attendance makes a major difference to grief intensity. Since social desirability was the only scale to show a significant difference due to attendance for the nonbereaved controls, the differences found between bereaved attenders and nonattenders could reflect a weak interaction between bereavement and church attendance.

Other studies have not found any association between religiosity and bereavement outcome. In one of his studies, Parkes (1971b) reported that "faith in God" and regular attendance at church were not good predictors of outcome. The same was true for our Tübingen sample, where we used church attendance, self-rated religiosity, and belief in an afterlife as a measure of religiosity. Purizman and Maoz (1977) tried to establish the importance of religiosity for a sample of bereaved parents in Israel. As it happened, good adjustment and high level of education were highly correlated, this factor being responsible for most of the variance. Since the majority of their subjects fell into the "more educated, less religious" or into the "less educated, more religious" categories, Purisman and Maoz (1977) were unable to clarify the impact of religion.

Similarly negative findings were reported in a further study in Israel. Amir and Sharon (1982) found that nonreligious functioned better than religious widows in emotional, social, and domestic activities, and in their relations with their children. The religious in this sample were mostly Middle Eastern, whereas the nonreligious were Western. Again in this study, it is likely that the religious variable is confounded with other variables. The Western widows were more educated and had fewer children than the Middle Eastern. Attitudes toward widowhood also vary between the two ethnic-origin groups. Further, we have no way of knowing how religiosity is related to effective functioning among the nonbereaved in these communities.

Conclusions. The studies reviewed in this section do not lead to clear-cut conclusions about the effect of religious beliefs on bereavement outcome. At best, religion has only been shown to be a weak predictor of bereavement outcome, and it is still debatable whether it can be regarded as one at all. Furthermore, even if widowed who are highly religious had been found to adjust better to bereavement than those who are not, it would have been unclear whether to attribute such a finding to the spiritual or the social support offered by most religions. Since believers tend to be well integrated into their religious communities, the two aspects are difficult to separate.

8.3.2 *Personality*

Intuitively, personality variables would seem to be among the most important determinants of adjustment to loss. It is reasonable to assume, for example, that individuals with stable and well-adjusted personalities should be better able to withstand the impact of stressful life events such as bereavement than people who are unstable and poorly adjusted. Although there is some support for this hypothesis in studies of the association between unspecific critical life events and health (e.g., Ganellen & Blaney, 1984; Henderson, Byrne, & Duncan-Jones, 1981; Johnson & Sarason, 1978; Smith, Johnson, & Sarason, 1978; Wheaton, 1983), evidence from bereavement research has so far been not very conclusive.

Thus, Parkes (1985; Parkes & Weiss, 1983) described the "grief-prone personality" as a major characteristic contributing to poor outcome. In his study of London widows, Parkes (1986) found that those widows who reported excessively severe reactions to previous losses were among the most disturbed after loss of their husbands. He concluded that "previous excessive grief and depression prognosticate a poor outcome following bereavement"(p. 153). Parkes and Weiss's (1983) more recent empirical study in Boston also found grief-prone individuals, who were intensely clinging and who pined deeply for their spouses, to be at high risk of poor outcome. Other personality variables identified by Parkes (1975a; Parkes & Weiss, 1983) as characteristic of poor outcome were insecure, overanxious persons with low self-esteem; excessively angry or reproachful persons; or those who are unable to express their feelings.

Although indicative, caution must be used in interpreting the results of a study by Vachon, Sheldon, Lancee, et al. (1982). These authors reported a plausible relationship between personality measured with the 16 Personality Factor Questionnaire (Cattell, Eber, & Tatsuoka, 1970) and the level of distress reported after two years, using the General Health Questionnaire (Goldberg, 1972). Vachon et al. (1982) found that their "enduring high distress group" had lower scores on Ego Strength and higher scores on Guilt Proneness and Anxiety than the widowed characterized as "enduring low distress group" on the basis of the GHQ. However, since these personality scales are likely to be related to the GHQ in nonbereaved populations as well, these findings may merely reflect the general correlation between the GHQ and the 16 PF (i.e., a personality main effect). In the absence of a nonbereaved control group, this interpretation is hard to rule out.

Lund, Dimond, Caserta, et al. (1986) attempted to avoid these problems by relating personality to bereavement-specific variables (e.g., shock, disbelief) as well as somatic complaints and depression. In their two-year longitudinal study of the elderly ($n = 138$), low self-esteem in early bereavement was found to be predictive of poor coping (on a scale combining perceived stress, coping, and depression) at two years after bereavement. However, since this difference seems to have been mainly due to items which are not specific to bereavement and which are likely to be related to self-esteem in nonbereaved samples as well, it is doubtful whether these results can be interpreted in terms of self-esteem differences in adjustment to loss.

To avoid this kind of ambiguity, the relationship between personality and health measures was tested for bereaved as well as nonbereaved samples in the Tübingen study. Emotional stability and locus of control were assessed as two personality variables likely to affect bereavement outcome. Emotional stability has been conceived of as an intrapersonal coping resource in our deficit model of partner loss. Individuals who are emotionally stable should be better able than those who are unstable to withstand the onslaught of stressful life events such as bereavement. Emotional stability was measured with the German version of the neuroticism scale of the Eysenck Personality Inventory (EPI; Eggert, 1983). High scores on the EPI-N indicate low emotional stability. As one would expect, bereavement was associated with higher neuroticism scores in our study. Furthermore, individuals who scored high on neuroticism (i.e., low emotional stability) were more depressed than those who scored low, regardless of marital status. However, a regression analysis did not support the predicted interaction. There was no evidence during the first year that the stress of loss affected the highly neurotic individuals more than those with low neuroticism scores.

Differences in locus of control were assessed because, according to learned-helplessness theory, control beliefs should play an important role as stress moderators. There is some discrepancy, however, in predictions of the nature of the relationship between individual control beliefs and reactions to stress. Some researchers (e.g., Ganellen & Blaney, 1984; Johnson & Sarason, 1978) argue that since the state of learned helplessness is characterized by a belief in the inability to control important aspects of life, people who already believe that they have little control should be more likely to react with depression to loss than those who have high control beliefs. Research on critical life events typically supported this prediction (e.g., Ganellen & Blaney, 1984; Johnson & Sarason, 1978). In contrast, Pittman and Pittman (1979) have argued, on the basis of the integration of the learned-helplessness model and reactance theory proposed by Wortman and Brehm (1976), that individuals who expect control will be affected more severely by uncontrollable situations, once they realize that they truly have no control. Using an experimental induction of learned helplessness, Pittman and Pittman (1979) were able to support this prediction.

In the Tübingen study, locus of control was measured with the German version of the Interpersonal Control Scale of Levenson (1973; Mielke, 1979). The Interpersonal Control Scale (IPC) provides three fairly independent scores indicating the extent to which the individual believes that what happens to him or her is either under his or her own control (IPC-I), or externally controlled, by chance (IPC-C) or by powerful others (IPC-P). While bereavement was associated with an increased belief that events are controlled by chance, there was no difference between bereaved and nonbereaved on the other two measures. As expected, the bereaved and individuals with low internal control beliefs were more depressed than the married and individuals with high internal control beliefs. A regression analysis provided no evidence, however, for an interaction between control beliefs and marital status on depression during the first year of bereavement. However, when expectedness of the loss was entered as an additional variable into the regression, a highly significant interaction between expectedness and control beliefs (IPC-I) emerged: Individuals with low internal control beliefs reacted with greater depression to unexpected loss than those who believed that they had control over their environment. There was little difference in the depression levels of the two groups when loss was expected. Since there is some evidence that sudden and unexpected loss is associated with greater feelings of helplessness, this finding tends to support the predictions of Johnson and Sarason (1978) and Ganellen and Blaney (1984) rather than those of Pittman and Pittman (1979). However, depression was first measured four to six months after the loss experience in the Tübingen study. Thus, the better adjustment of individuals who believe in internal control could have been the result of a differential effort to regain control. This assumption could also reconcile the discrepancy between findings of experimental (Pittman & Pittman, 1979) and nonexperimental studies (Ganellen & Blaney 1984; Johnson & Sarason, 1978).

Conclusions. The studies reviewed in this section offer only limited evidence for the assumption that personality traits modify the impact of loss. However, very few personality traits have as yet been examined in the context of bereavement. Furthermore, many of the studies reported are problematic because they lack nonbereaved control groups. It is difficult, therefore, to draw any conclusions about the importance of personality factors as moderators of bereavement reactions. This dearth of empirical evidence is surprising as most theories of bereavement predict personality-related differences in individual reactions to loss.

8.3.3 Health prior to bereavement

A person's health before the death of a spouse is another characteristic of the individual likely to moderate bereavement outcome. Since stress is assumed to aggravate or accelerate existing health problems, it seems plausible that those in poor mental or physical health prior to bereavement should be more vulnerable than those who were mentally and physically fit. Individuals who already suffer from psychiatric impairment at the time of bereavement might also be less able to cope effectively with the loss experience. An example of this would be the increased risk of suicide among alcoholic patients with recent loss (cf. Murphy & Robins, 1967). There is very little evidence on the relationship of health prior to bereavement and subsequent outcome, and few of these studies actually compare nonbereaved persons in poor health with those who have been bereaved, to examine relative adjustment.

At first glance, the relatively higher mortality risk and general health debilities of the younger rather than the older widowed appears to run counter to this hypothesis, for one would assume that older groups, being more infirm, would suffer relatively greater risks, which the statistics do not support. However, it must be remembered that age is confounded with other factors (e.g., unexpectedness, untimeliness of the death of the spouse). This cannot be taken as strong evidence against the assumption that physical health status is a risk factor.

In support of the hypothesis, Perlin and Schmidt (1975) reported that the physically disabled and physically ill were more vulnerable to poor bereavement outcome. Similarly, Vachon et al. (1982) found that health problems correlate with enduring high distress, although the health problem may have appeared after bereavement and therefore not have entailed a previous condition. Mor et al. (1986) reported that the bereaved who utilized health services the most tended to be those persons who had poor physical health before bereavement, too.

With regard to mental illness, the study by Bunch (1972), which examined the relationship of recent bereavement to suicide among bereaved spouses and adult children, provides important information. Previous psychiatric breakdown was more frequently found to have occurred among the bereaved who committed suicide than among those bereaved who did not. Further, the work of Parkes (see, e.g., 1975a) has consistently confirmed the link between previous mental illness and poor bereavement outcome. In his early work (Parkes, 1962; see also Parkes and Weiss, 1983) a high incidence of previous depressive illness was found among bereaved psychiatric patients. In a more recent study by Wahl (1970) it was also reported that bereavement may exacerbate antecedent neurotic symptoms.

It seems justified to conclude that prior mental illness is a high-risk factor for poor outcome to bereavement: The mental problems are likely to be intensified. With regard to physical health, the data are not so clear-cut, but there is some supportive evidence which appears indicative.

8.4 Antecedent situational factors

8.4.1 *Antecedent stresses*

This first section on the influence of a person's situation before the loss on bereavement outcome examines whether individuals whose lives have been marked by an accumulation of stressful life events or who, more specifically, have suffered previous losses of loved persons in their lives are more vulnerable to bad outcomes during bereavement.

Prior unspecific stresses. Multiple life crises, particularly those involving disturbance of the marital relationship, was one of the factors which Parkes (1975a) reported as a predictor of poor outcome. In the Harvard study, "other life crises preceding bereavement" was one of three classes of intercorrelated predictors of outcome to emerge at one year after bereavement. The other two were low social class and lack of preparation for loss. The particular crises associated with poor outcome were infidelity, loss of a job, pregnancy, or previous divorce affecting the respondent.

Different interpretations of these findings are possible. For example, it could be that disturbance of the marital relationship, such as infidelity, is related to bad outcome because of feelings of guilt or ambivalence. Similarly "loss of a job" could be related to bad outcome for a number of reasons (financial difficulties, loss of a sense of self-esteem, status change, or other related changes). Thus, the mechanisms by which these variables have an impact on outcome are not completely clear. Furthermore, it is conceivable that depression or poor coping abilities of the bereaved person may have been responsible for the occurrence of "multiple life crises" such as divorce or marital conflict.

Further evidence that prior stresses are related to poor bereavement outcome comes from a study of a different type of loss, namely, that of a parent. A longitudinal study by Elizur and Kaffman (1983) of twenty-five Kibbutz children who had lost their fathers during the October War of 1973 examined pathological grief reactions (defined by two criteria, namely, the presence of persistent clinical symptomatology and the need for psychological care) in relation to three types of variables: (1) child variables (e.g., dependency, withdrawal, stubbornness), (2) family variables (prebereavement separation/loss, marital disharmony, negative father–child relations, maternal personality), and (3) circumstantial variables (remarriage of mother, no "surrogate father," stressful events). A significant relationship was found between prior long-term (though not short-term) separation from the father, or previous deaths in the family and "pathological bereavement" in the first six months. Similarly to Parkes's (1975a) findings for adults, children of families with longstanding conflict and marital discord reacted to loss with intense and pervasive problems. It is important to note that prebereavement factors were most influential in the early months of bereavement, whereas concurrent bereavement circumstances exacerbated bereavement reactions over the years of measurement. Indicative though these findings are, it is unfortunate that the design omitted a matched control group of nonbereaved children.

Prior bereavements. Whether antecedent loss through death of a loved person plays an etiological role in affective disorders has been strongly debated over the years. Much of this research has focused on the effect of parental loss. Whereas some reviewers (e.g., Birtchnell, 1980; Birtchnell & Kennard, 1981; Crook & Eliot, 1980; Granville-Grossman, 1968; Tennant, Bebbington, & Hurry, 1980) conclude that the death of a parent during childhood has not been established as a factor of etiological significance in later affective disorders, such as depression, others (e.g., Brown, 1982; Lloyd, 1980) have argued persuasively that there is now considerable evidence that early loss of a parent does increase the risk of depression in adult life. In an empirical investigation of depression among women in London, Brown and Harris (1978) reported that losing one's mother before the age of 11 was a significant factor in coping with later stressful life events. Those who had been maternally bereaved experienced greater depression. Brown's (1982; Brown & Harris, 1978) carefully conducted investigations provide convincing support for the link between early loss and depression.

Less extensive are investigations of the more specific question whether persons who have suffered an early loss through death respond to a later bereavement more poorly than those who had experienced no earlier loss. In fact, such evidence as is available suggests the *facilitation of good outcome* following earlier experiences with bereavement. Bornstein, Clayton, Halikas, Maurice, and Robins (1973) reported that their depressed subsample had few if any previous bereavement experiences. Of this group, 25 percent, but only 4 percent of the nondepressed group, reported no previous experiences of death among relatives in their lifetime. In accordance with these findings, Huston (1971) and Vachon (1976) also suggested that coping with a prior bereavement experience facilitates adjustment to the death of a spouse. The above studies are not as contradictory in their conclusions as may appear at first sight. Antecedent loss is likely to have differing effects on bereavement outcome depending (a) on whether it occurred during childhood or adulthood and (b) on the frequency and type (relationship to the deceased) of antecedent experiences of loss.

Following Brown (1982) one would hypothesize that an antecedent bereavement experience would increase the risk of poor outcome if it entailed the loss of a key attachment figure, such as the mother, during childhood. If, on the other hand, the antecedent death or deaths had occurred during adulthood, it is possible that this experience could "prepare" the bereaved for subsequent bereavement. It is not hard to imagine that such an acquaintance with one's own grief reactions and pattern of recovery could be helpful. But a third hypothesis is also possible: Someone who has suffered multiple losses of very close persons, possibly in close succession, as happens in wartime, could be at particularly high, rather than low, risk. Such cumulative experiences might lead to loss of the feeling of control over events, to hopelessness and depression, to a withdrawal from persons for fear that they too might die, and to consequent loneliness. This pattern would be similar to the "bereavement overload" among the elderly, to which Kastenbaum (1969) drew attention. In short, in assessing the impact of prior losses on bereavement reactions, one needs to look at the specific type and timing of these experiences. The three hypotheses suggested above remain to be tested systematically.

8.4.2 *The marital relationship and bond with the deceased*

The closeness or happiness of the marital relationship which was disrupted by the death of a spouse is another aspect of the situation before the loss which is likely to affect bereavement outcome. The romantic notion of the broken heart implies that the more intensely loved a partner was, the more that person will be grieved for after death. This prediction is in line with expectations from both the behavior theory of depression as well as our deficit model. According to behavior theory, grief is a reaction to the reduction of response-contingent positive reinforcements. Thus, the severity of grief should vary with the magnitude of this reduction. Since the amount of positive reinforcement which is lost when a spouse dies is likely to be related to the closeness and happiness of the marital relationship and to the degree to which partners used to engage in joint activities, behavior theory would predict grief to be greater after a marriage that was characterized by closeness and happiness rather than conflict and unhappiness. For similar reasons, the deficit model would expect a negative association between marital happiness and magnitude of loss.

As these assumptions may appear even too plausible, we would like to point out that the opposite prediction can be derived from psychoanalytic theory. According to Freud (1917), it is the existence of ambivalence in marital relationships which is likely to lead to poor bereavement outcome. It is interesting to note that for certain conditions of ambivalence, a similar prediction can also be derived from the learned-helplessness perspective. As we pointed out in our discussion of this theory (Section 4.5), if we assume that marital ambivalence will make it more likely that the widowed react with feelings of personal helplessness to the loss (because they may feel that they could have done more, that they were not as kind to their spouse as would have been possible), the resulting guilt feelings and loss of self-esteem will make it more difficult for them to work through their grief without complications.

Ambivalence refers to a relationship in which elements of love and hate coexist. It does not mean that attachment is no longer present, but rather that it may be insecure. Parkes and Weiss (1983) noted that when attachment no longer appeared to have existed between the marital partners and investment had been withdrawn from the marriage, grieving was brief and recovery accordingly rapid. On the other hand, Lindemann (1944) found that most severe grief reactions often occurred following an ambivalent relationship, and this was supported by Parkes and Weiss (1983) who reported that difficulties in recovery occur more frequently " ... following the loss of marriages which were conflict-ridden, thoroughly troubled, in which one or the other spouse may well have contemplated separation or divorce" (pp. 97–8).

Since widows and widowers whose marital relations were characterized by ambivalence might have been psychologically unstable even before their bereavement, it is important to note that this assumption could hardly explain the differences in patterns of recovery found between survivors of ambivalent and nonambivalent marriages by Parkes and Weiss (1983). Initially the survivors of ambivalent marriages seemed to adjust much better to the loss than those widowed after a happy marriage. It was only at the follow-up interviews, two to four years after bereavement, that the survivors of ambivalent marriages showed signs of maladjustment and poor recovery from grief.

While these findings tend to support psychoanalytic reasoning, the results of a study of Chicago widows by Lopata (1973b; 1979) seem to be more in line with expectations derived from behavior theory and our deficit model. Lopata found disorganization in widowhood to be related to previous marital roles: Those widows who had been intensely involved in their husbands' lives and who were not only psychologically but also socially dependent on them had greater problems in adjustment during bereavement than those who were more autonomous.

These findings are not necessarily inconsistent with those of Parkes and Weiss (1983), since preoccupation with the partner, which Lopata found so characteristic of widows who adjusted poorly to widowhood, may be unrelated to marital conflict and ambivalence. In fact, Parkes (1975a) also noted that an overdependence on the marital partner was related to poor outcome. Since overdependence referred to a clinging relationship, one which is marked by lack of autonomy in the partner who survives, it could be considered an extreme form of marital involvement and preoccupation with the partner.

Conclusions. The work of Parkes and Lopata suggests two characteristics of the marital relationship which may be related to poor bereavement outcome: dependency and ambivalence. Thus, in line with predictions from behavior theory and the deficit model, spouses whose lives were completely devoted to marriage and who were socially and psychologically dependent on their partner are likely to have greater problems in bereavement than those who were fairly autonomous. That partners who have happy marriages and loving relationships with each other may have better health outcomes in bereavement than those who are intensely involved and dependent, or whose marriages are full of conflict, may not be as paradoxical as it seems. As Parkes (1975a) pointed out, it makes sense when viewed from a developmental perspective: Children who are securely attached to their mothers do not cling to them, requiring permanent presence (see also Bowlby, 1975). On the contrary, a well-established relationship is one in which separation is tolerated because the person is trusted to return. Overdependent or ambivalent relationships are ones in which an element of insecurity exists. This they have in common with the clinging attachments of small children and similarly, too, an intolerance for separation.

8.5 Mode of death

Most people would agree that the circumstances of the death of a spouse are likely to affect the course of bereavement. Thus, the situation of a person whose spouse dies in a car accident on his or her way to work differs in ways that are likely to affect the course of bereavement from that of an individual who loses his or her partner after an illness lasting for several years. Recent studies have gone some way toward unraveling different aspects connected with mode of death that may mitigate or intensify grief. In the following sections we look at the length and nature of terminal illness, at causes of death, particularly the data on violent versus natural deaths, and at the special cases of suicide and of wartime bereavement.

8.5.1 *Duration of terminal illness*

Sudden, unexpected, untimely deaths are generally believed to result in poorer adjustment and higher risk of mental and physical debilities during bereavement than bereavements that have been anticipated. The prediction that the abruptness of the change and the period of time that the individual has to adjust to the loss should affect health outcomes can be derived from depression as well as stress theories. Thus, according to the behavior theory of depression, the severity of a grief response should vary as a function of the speed with which the reduction of positive reinforcements occurs. Stress theories like the deficit model would argue similarly: Adjustment to a change which takes place over a lengthy period of time (i.e., death after a long illness) should be less stressful than adjustment to a sudden change of the same magnitude. From a learned-helplessness perspective, one could argue that individuals are more likely to respond to aversive events with feelings of helplessness if these occur suddenly and unexpectedly rather than following a period of forewarning. Finally, on the basis of psychoanalytic theory, one could argue that the forewarned individual should be able to avoid guilt feelings by having the opportunity to make restitution. This should be particularly important for marital relationships characterized by ambivalence. Furthermore, individuals who expect their partners to die are likely to engage in "anticipatory grief" and thus begin their grief work at an earlier time than those who lose their partners unexpectedly.

Evidence that sudden, unexpected deaths result in poorer adjustment among the bereaved comes from the Harvard study (Glick et al.,1974; Parkes & Weiss, 1983). Parkes (1975a) divided the sixty-eight bereaved males and females, who were all under 45 years of age, into good and bad outcome on the basis of a larger number of outcome measures derived from interviews shortly after bereavement. Mode of death was found to be one of the major predictive factors of outcome. The following were found to correlate significantly with bad outcome on mental and physical health indices: Cause of death *not* cancer, short duration of terminal illness, and lack of opportunity to discuss death with partner. When the widowed were divided according to the length of time they had to prepare themselves for the impending death of their spouses, only 6 percent of those who had had a "short preparation" before the spouse's death were categorized as good outcome at two to four years after bereavement, but 65 percent of the widowed with "long preparation" were classified as good outcome.

While Parkes (1975b) concentrated on establishing the effects of type of death on a cumulative measure of outcome, assessing the combined psychological, social, and physical health consequences, a recent study conducted by Lundin (1984a) in Sweden provides some useful information on the effect of type of death on physical and mental health separately. Lundin compared health outcomes among a sample who had suffered sudden and unexpected bereavement with that of a matched control group whose deaths had been expected. The bereaved from sudden deaths were forty-five spouses or parents of persons under 65 whose deaths had occurred without preceding illness and quite suddenly. Controls were relatives of two persons for each proband, whose deaths were expected, and who were matched for age, sex, and relationship to the deceased. The relatives in this group had died of a long and serious illness, which was most frequently cancer. For the final analysis, thirty-two probands and fifty-five controls were available.

Lundin's (1984a) outcome measures were derived from registers of illness kept by the general insurance office. As it is possible to be registered as sick for one week without consulting a doctor, registrations do not necessarily reflect medical treatment or consultation. Records were used for all subjects for the two-year period before and the two years following bereavement. Psychiatric and somatic diagnoses could be analyzed separately, although Lundin did not differentiate types of illness other than into these two general categories.

An increase in the frequency of sickness was found among probands following sudden and unexpected deaths, but not among the control group of survivors of longer terminal illness deaths. There was an increase for both somatic and psychiatric illness among the probands, but the rate of psychiatric illness was especially high. Although the control group showed no increase in registered sickness after bereavement, this could have been because their rates were already above that of the general population before bereavement.

To summarize, it seems that the health status of the proband (sudden bereavement) group was fairly comparable with that of the general population before bereavement but worsened considerably after it, particularly with regard to psychiatric ailments. The health status of the control group (expected bereavement) was already poorer than the general population before bereavement, and did not show a further decline after the death of the spouse or child. Probands had a high risk of psychiatric ailments after death of their relatives, whereas this excess risk appeared before loss for the controls.

A follow-up to this study (Lundin, 1984b) provides some information on the longer-term effects of the two types of bereavement and on the question whether the impact of loss was the same for the two groups, except for the fact that it was anticipated (and thus resolved sooner after the death) in the case of expected loss. Eight years after bereavement the same sample were asked to fill out the Expanded Texas Inventory of Grief (see Zisook, Devaul, & Click, 1982). Of the original sample, 60 percent returned the questionnaire. Although there were some differences in responses to individual items which suggested that the two groups differed with regard to the specific "grief syndrome" manifested, no significant differences between relatives of sudden versus expected deaths were found in an analysis of subsets of items that related to good versus poor outcome.

Ball (1977) reported that longer preparation time diminished the intensity of the grief reaction. Among a sample of eighty widows in Sacramento County, California, those who had less than five days warning of their husband's death had more intense grief reactions, as measured on a comprehensive grief-reactions questionnaire, than those with longer forewarning. There was a tendency for the impact of loss to be stronger for the younger than the older bereaved, but this interaction did not reach an acceptable level of significance. Ball (1977), like Parkes (1975b), concluded that anticipatory grief was a mitigating influence on postdeath grief. Carey (1977) also reported that the widowed in his study who had had forewarning of the death of their spouses reported better adjustment thirteen to sixteen months after bereavement than those who had had no forewarning. Forewarning was a main predictor of adjustment, being more important than education or income. Similarly, Richards and McCallum (1979) found unexpected death to be associated with more depression (a nonstandardized measure was used) than if death was expected. The sample was 100 bereaved spouses aged 65 and over, who were interviewed six to seven months after loss. Finally, as mentioned earlier, depression rates were higher after expected rather than unexpected loss in the Tübingen study, but only for individuals who believed that they had little control over their environment (low IPC-I; Levenson, 1973).

A study by Sanders (1983) attempts to disentangle the effects of forewarning from those of duration of illness. Sanders (1983) divided the eighty-six bereaved participants in her study into three groups, according to the mode of death by which the close family member had died (this analysis was not restricted to the conjugally bereaved). Three categories were used: sudden death, short-term chronic illness (defined as less than six months), and long-term chronic illness. While the three groups showed similar levels of grief intensity at the first time point shortly after bereavement, after eighteen months differences were evident. The short-term chronic illness group tended to make the most favorable adjustment to bereavement, while the other two groups sustained higher intensities of grief, as measured on the Grief Experience Inventory. Sanders (1983) noted qualitative differences between the groups too. The sudden-death group exhibited more intrapunitive responses ("anger-in" and guilt) accompanied by longer-lasting physical repercussions, whereas the long-term chronic illness survivors showed greater feelings of isolation and alienation, and emotional upset. These results partially support the findings from the other studies reviewed above, that deaths which have occurred unpredictably and with no anticipation lead to greater problems for survivors than those which are expected. However, the relationship appears more complex: If the terminal illness had been very protracted the usefulness of preparation time is obliterated, and survivors appear to have as great a problem, though of a different nature, as those surviving a sudden death of a loved one. Reasons for this are likely to be that social support from others is not sustained throughout a very lengthy terminal illness, that anger toward others is felt, that contacts with others have been broken off during the extended period of terminal illness, and that the physical and emotional strain of caring for a very ill person over a protracted period is likely to take its toll.

Useful though these results are in understanding the impact of different types of death on survivors, further replication of Sanders's (1983) findings would be needed, because length of preparation time was confounded by type of relationship to the deceased. The short-term chronic illness group had a larger percentage of parent over spouse deaths, the sudden-death group had the largest percentage of child deaths. Thus, an alternative explanation could have been in terms of type of relationship to the deceased: Death of a parent is not generally so traumatic as the sudden death of a child.

While the above studies support the hypothesis that expected deaths lead to better adjustment than unexpected ones, one study (Bornstein, Clayton, Halikas, et al.,1973; Clayton, Halikas, Maurice, & Robins, 1973) failed to find differences in depression between those who had had sudden bereavement and those for whom death of the partner had been expected. Subjects had been interviewed shortly after bereavement and again after thirteen months. Criteria for depression were derived from Feighner et al.'s (1972) diagnostic criteria for depression. Bornstein et al. (1973) reported that a short terminal illness of less than five days preceding the death did not predict depression at follow-up.

Parkes (1975b), who applied Bornstein et al.'s criteria for depression to his Boston sample and still found that the short-preparation group were depressed compared with the long-preparation group, attributed the differences to the fact that nearly half of the subjects of the Bornstein study were over the age of 60. For this age group sudden deaths, he argued, could hardly be completely unexpected and were not as untimely as those which occurred without warning among younger adults. He concluded that for the effect to be detrimental to the survivor, as he found in his own study, not only suddenness but also untimeliness must occur. This interpretation could also account for the failure of the study by Breckenridge et al.(1986) to find a difference in depression levels due to expectedness of loss for their sample of elderly bereaved.

There is one study, however, that did not find a relationship between illness score and a widow's report that she had "little or no warning of her husband's death" for a sample of younger widows (Maddison & Walker, 1967). Although it is somewhat unclear whether the question enquiring about forewarning of death did divide subjects into sudden versus expected deaths or rather into groups with more or less forewarning, this finding does seem to be inconsistent with those of the studies by Parkes (1975b) and Ball (1977).

On balance, the evidence indicates that sudden, unexpected deaths lead to greater intensities of grief and health risks than expected deaths. It is noteworthy that the studies that found this effect were practically all conducted with younger bereaved. While this is possibly because even "sudden" death is not a completely unexpected or unprepared-for event at older ages, it is also likely that the experience of caring for a terminally ill person has negative effects which outweigh the positive ones for older survivors. Gerber et al. (1975a) found that the physical health of elderly widows and widowers was worse after a lengthy chronic illness than widowed whose spouses had died of a shorter chronic illness. Gerber et al. attributed this difference to the strain of being a caregiver during an illness of long duration, and the neglect of personal health while caring for the critically ill partner. Lundin's (1984a, b) findings, indicating elevated sickness ratings among the expected bereavement group before the death of the relative, are also in line with an interpretation in terms of health detriments due to the strain of caregiving. Thus, while preparation time is important for adjustment to bereavement, if this is associated with extended caregiving on the part of someone who is vulnerable to physical ill health (such as the elderly) then this may be detrimental at least to the *physical* health of the survivor.

8.5.2 *Cause of death*

In many cases, causes of death are associated with the length of terminal illness. For example, deaths from cancer or tuberculosis are typically more expected than heart attacks or strokes. Violent deaths are usually, though not always, unexpected and untimely. The effects of length of illness and cause of death are thus frequently confounded. However, for the purpose of understanding why the type of death can affect bereavement outcome, it is useful to consider the duration of death forewarning and the cause of death separately. It is easy to see that while suicide and death from a stroke may differ little in their suddenness and lack of forewarning for the survivors, the impact on survivors of these two types of death might differ greatly. Little systematic evidence isolating the impact of length of preparation time from the nature of the terminal illness and cause of death exists, but some studies have looked at the relationship between different types of death and bereavement outcome.

(i) Violent versus natural causes

The literature on bereavement counseling attests that survivors of violent deaths have a high risk of poor bereavement outcome and it is with these bereaved that much therapy has been undertaken. Singh and Raphael

(1981), for example, organized a preventive psychiatry program for relatives of a rail disaster in Sydney, Australia, in which eighty-three people were killed. The study, aimed at developing an effective therapy program and assessing postbereavement morbidity, did not compare outcome with that of survivors of natural deaths, but it is apparent from their account that the bereaved from this disaster suffered enormous loss and intense grief reactions, from which recovery was exceedingly difficult and prolonged for many persons. It is not difficult, when reading such accounts, to accept the hypothesis that disastrous deaths of this kind lead to exceptionally hard adjustment and possibly high risk to health among the bereaved.

Some evidence to support this assumption comes from a recent longitudinal study conducted in Los Angeles by Vargas, Loya, and Vargas (1984). These investigators attempted to examine the effect of mode of death on grief experiences, differentiating between natural, accident, suicide, and homicide deaths. Results suggested that homicide survivors, followed closely by accident survivors, experienced more intense grief than suicide or natural death survivors. Vargas et al. (1984) acknowledge the possibility of a confounding variable, namely, that for accidents and homicides most of the bereaved were parents, for natural death they were spouses, whereas for suicides they were siblings or offspring. Since there is some evidence (cf. Gorer, 1965; Raphael, 1984) that the loss of a child, including or even especially an adult child, is the most difficult bereavement to bear, while adjustment to loss of a parent or sibling during adulthood is comparatively less traumatic than either loss of a child or spouse, the differences between bereavement reactions in this study could be due to the type of relationship with the deceased. Admittedly, however, it is very plausible that homicide deaths lead to exceptionally high risk of poor outcome among survivors. The complexity of adjustment to the murder of a loved person has been described by Burgess (1975) and Pouissaint (1984).

(ii) Suicide

For a number of reasons, suicide is a unique type of loss. Most importantly, although it is sudden, the death is not always unexpected. In part this is because the decision to take one's life is frequently preceded by depression and by the occurrence of diverse stressful life events. It is not only likely that the relationship between the deceased and survivor was affected by these factors before death, but that coping after death will be complicated by them also. Further, if one is trying, as we are, to establish health risk to the survivor of a sudden death, it is important to remember that cause and effect sequences in suicide are more difficult to establish than those for other causes of death. The most extreme example (as indicated in the study of Shepherd and Barraclough described below) is the harrowing case where a spouse takes his or her own life in the face of the terminal illness of the partner, who outlives him or her only for a short time. Although mortality of the couple occurs in this instance in close proximity, a causal interpretation in terms of the effect of suicide on mortality risk of the bereaved would be spurious.

Clinical studies of survivors of suicide deaths (e.g., Cain, 1972; Rudestam, 1977; Wallace, 1973) generally emphasize problems in adjustment during bereavement, elaborating on aspects such as the guilt and bewilderment of those left behind. Many of these accounts present only case descriptions of survivors of spouses who died of suicide, without employing nonsuicide control groups. However, Sheskin and Wallace (1976) compared the case study data on twelve widows from suicide deaths reported in Wallace (1973) with the forty-eight widows of nonsuicide (natural and accidental) deaths reported in Glick et al. (1974). This must be regarded as an exploratory investigation, as the samples, though similar on a number of sociodemographic variables, were not matched, nor were the research procedures identical. Nevertheless, Sheskin and Wallace (1976) highlighted a number of features which distinguished bereavement reactions following suicide from those following nonsuicide deaths. They reported that widows from suicide search for explanations of the death far more intensely and feel more blameworthy than nonsuicide survivors.

In contrast to the conclusions of Sheskin and Wallace (1976), Shepherd and Barraclough (1974) minimized the effects of death by suicide on survivors, arguing that mortality and remarriage rates did not differ significantly from expected rates, and that outcome of bereavement was evenly divided into "better off" and "worse off" than the situation at the time of the suicide. Examination of their report, however, raises some doubt about the validity of this conclusion. Of the forty-four widowed (seventeen widowers and twenty-seven widows) approached for interview, ten had died in the interim since bereavement. Five of these had been terminally ill before the suicide. Shepherd and Barraclough report that this observed mortality rate is not significantly different from an expected rate derived from national tables of widowed and married mortality rates. As we have noted elsewhere (M. Stroebe et al., 1981) such comparisons with small samples are dubious, and although mean age is not given, the number of deaths seems excessive for such a small sample. Similar arguments apply for the assessment of remarriage.

A second drawback of the study is that the assessment of bereavement outcome was based on the spouses' evaluation of their current situation as better or worse than their situation at the time of the suicide. Clearly, these ratings are subject to changing perceptions of events over the five-to-seven-year period between loss and interview. Furthermore, it is likely that the bereaved's situation at the time of suicide was more harrowing and traumatic than that of nonsuicide bereaved. An improvement over time could still mean that the suicide sample would be much worse outcome than a sample of nonsuicide survivors.

Suicide survivors are confronted with a number of critical problems in addition to the normal burden of grief and bereavement, the effect of which should not be underestimated. Facing an inquest, reading accounts of one's own very personal troubles in the public press, the stigma attached to suicide, and dealing with such matters as life insurance policies, which the suicide has put into jeopardy, are all additionally stressful, and may often have to be handled with little support from others. Calhoun, Selby, and Walton (1986; see also Calhoun, Selby, & Abernathy, 1984) gave evidence of this. They investigated the reactions of others to spouses, of different types of death, including a group of suicide survivors. The latter were viewed as being more to blame, as having had a greater chance of preventing the death, and as being more ashamed of the death than survivors of other types of death. Cumulative evidence from many accounts (see McIntosh, 1986, for a comprehensive bibliography) leads us to the conclusion that coping with bereavement following a suicide is perhaps the most stressful of all.

(iii) War bereavement

Loss of a loved person through active service in a war may be considered a further "special case" of bereavement for here, too, but in a very different manner, a sudden death may come not completely unexpectedly to survivors. Information on this comes from Israel, for, tragically, the frequency of recent wars in which Israel has been involved has led to war loss becoming a first-hand experience for many Israelis. The need to provide counseling and support for the grief-stricken and the need to understand the complexity of war-bereavement reactions has resulted in an accumulation of literature on adjustment to war loss in this country, not only among widows, but also parents, children, and siblings (e.g., Barinbaum, 1976; Golan, 1975; Purisman & Maoz, 1977; and a collection of papers in Spielberger, Sarason, & Milgram, 1982).

These studies draw attention to a number of critical features of war loss, for example, to the different bereavement problems that losing a son, a husband, a father, or an older sibling present. They mention too the "acute problem of wives whose husbands were either missing in action or critically wounded, and then become widows after a most painful period of anxiety and hope" (Katz, 1982, p. 204). But as yet, to our knowledge, only one study (Shoham-Salomon, Vakstein, & Kruglanski, 1986) has directly compared the adjustment of the war bereaved in Israel with that of persons bereaved from other causes, although some of the studies do report systematic differences in adjustment patterns between widows of different wars.

In a small pilot study, designed along the lines of the Tübingen one, Shohan-Salomon et al. (1986) found adjustment among war widows (*n* = 12) to be better, and depression lower (using the BDI) than it was among a matched sample of civilian widows (*n* = 12). However, both widowed samples were more poorly adjusted and more depressed than a nonbereaved matched control group (*n* = 12). Shoham-Salomon et al. (1986) related these differences to differences in economic support, in patterns of interaction with family and friends, and in the meaning of the loss for the widows in the two groups.

Two factors have frequently been suggested in studies of war bereavement as having an impact on subsequent reactions and intensity of grief: first, the meaning ascribed to war loss (e.g., whether it is viewed as an absurd and useless sacrifice or as a noble, heroic act in defense of one's country) and second, the support received after loss of a loved person through war. Following these suggestions, one would predict that, provided the war and the loss of life were perceived as purposeful ("He died for his country," etc.), adjustment would be easier than to other types of violent death (accidents or homicides). One reason is that it is very difficult to find any justification or to rationalize in any way loss through an accident or from murder. Further, besides financial support to war widows (if available) other mitigating factors aiding adjustment to war loss include widowhood status (it is more heroic than non-war loss) and the availability of similar others (other war widows) for social support. Obviously, these ameliorative factors are not always present for those bereaved in war, and there are other factors, such as the untimely loss of a newly wedded husband or anguish over the horrendous nature of a death in battle, which combine to complicate adjustment, and to hinder recovery in comparison with a natural or more timely death.

8.5.3   *Why does forewarning help?*

One popular explanation of the greater impact of unexpected loss is in terms of "anticipatory grief" (cf. Schoenberg, Carr, Kutscher, et al., 1974). This interpretation implies that neither the intensity nor the pattern of grief is affected by forewarning, but that people who are forewarned start grieving already at the time when they learn of their spouse's terminal illness. Thus the impact of loss would be seen as comparable following sudden or anticipated bereavement, but the latter group recover on average sooner after the death than the former, because grieving began before this event.

A second view holds that grief takes a different course, regardless of the time differences in onset and resolution. There are a number of aspects of forewarning which might modify the impact of loss. One is that grief can be shared with the terminally ill person. There can be a gradual leave-taking. This also gives the surviving spouse an "opportunity to make restitution for any deficiencies in relationship with the deceased person" (Parkes, 1975b, p. 129). To some extent, any guilt felt about behavior toward the spouse may be assuaged, for example, through loving care and attention in the terminal phase of illness. Indirect support for this view is provided by the results of Carey's (1977) study. Forewarning of death was found to be a significant factor in good adjustment to widowhood only for those who had undergone some period of unhappiness in their marriage.

Forewarning should also help to reduce the stress of loss by giving the surviving spouse a much longer time in which to adjust. It is, however, not just that gradual realization is more likely to lead to fewer problems in acceptance and adjustment: The meaning of a death to the bereaved, as has been seen not only for cancer and cardiovascular heart disease, but also for suicide and wartime deaths, is critical to outcome. Justification, that "It is better for him" if the spouse no longer suffers from a lingering and painful terminal illness, can be made for cancer deaths, but not so easily for homicide or suicide. Further, the loss of the person's self may be gradual, in the sense that the dying person may slowly withdraw and relinquish his or her tie with the partner: He or she may no longer be the same, may fade away. Finally, in the case of sudden, unexpected deaths, the shattering abruptness with which death occurred may cause a lasting fear that such an event could happen without warning again, to some other loved person.

The different interpretations outlined above are not completely incompatible with each other. There seems good reason to argue that forewarning is likely to start the grief process earlier, so that for this reason it will ultimately be resolved nearer in time to the actual death, but that, for the reasons given above, the course of grief may also be modified. As yet, few studies have looked at the nature of cognitive or behavioral preparation for bereavement directly, most inferring, from the fact that death is expected, that preparation and anticipatory grief work will begin. A retrospective study by Remondet, Hansson, Rule, et al. (1986) did, however, look directly at the impact of certain dimensions of rehearsal on adjustment to widowhood and found that whereas "behavioral" rehearsal (social comparison, planning and making changes) was associated with better adjustment, "cognitive" rehearsal (ruminating) appeared to be associated with increased emotional disruption. As the authors recognized, there are problems of interpretation of this correlational, retrospective data. Their examination of the nature of anticipatory grief processes is nevertheless illustrative of the direction that research needs to go to clarify why there are differences in outcome following expected versus unexpected bereavements.

8.6 Circumstances after the loss

8.6.1 *Social support*

(i) Social support and health

Whether bereaved individuals can rely on their families and friends to stand by and help them in their distress is likely to be an important moderator of bereavement outcome. As most of this book has been dealing with the health effects of interpersonal loss, it seems hardly necessary at this late stage to convince the reader of the beneficial effect of interpersonal relationships on health. And yet marriage is a very special relationship and the effects of interpersonal loss may not be symmetrical to those of availability of support. It should therefore be mentioned that evidence has accumulated in recent years to indicate a positive relationship between the availability of social support and health (for reviews, see Berkman, 1984; Cohen & Wills, 1985; House, 1981). There are even several prospective epidemiological studies that demonstrate a relationship between social support and mortality (Berkman & Syme, 1979; House, Robbins, & Metzner, 1982; Blazer, 1982).

Interactionist approaches to stress (e.g., Cohen & Wills, 1985; Lazarus & Folkman, 1984; W. Stroebe & Stroebe, 1986) conceive of social support as a resource which helps people to cope with the demands of their environment. According to what has become known as the *Buffering Hypoth-*

esis (e.g., Cohen & Willis, 1985; House, 1981) the availability of social support protects individuals to some extent against the deleterious effect of stressful life events. Persuasive evidence for this assumption comes from studies of the relationship between critical life events and depression. For example, Brown and Harris (1978) found that the impact of stressful life events on the mental health of a sample of London women was moderated by social support (stress × social support interaction). Although critical life events were related to a significant increase in psychiatric disorders for women who had a low level of social support (no confidant), no such increase was found for women with high levels of support (availability of a confidant). The level of support was unrelated to psychiatric disorders among women who did not experience critical life events. Similar findings have been reported by Eaton (1978) and Surtees (1980).

There are also studies, however, that observe main effects of social support and stress with no evidence of buffering. For example, Schaefer, Coyne, and Lazarus (1981) found that both stress and social support had direct and additive effects on level of depression and morale. Findings such as these suggest that social support may also have a generalized beneficial effect on health.

(ii) Social support and bereavement outcome

To demonstrate that the availability of alternative sources of social support reduces the surviving spouse's vulnerability to the stress of bereavement (buffering), one is again confronted with the necessity to test for an interaction between marital status and a risk factor. As we have argued previously, this can only be done in factorial designs which vary marital status in addition to social support. When studies merely show that the availability of support is positively associated with health in samples of the bereaved, it is impossible to tell whether this relationship reflects buffering or a generalized positive relationship between health and social support.

It is very tempting to interpret main effects as interactions in this type of study. This was brought home to us recently when we analyzed the impact of the presence of young children on the health of our widowed sample in the Tübingen study at a time when this information was not yet coded for the married. The fact that widowed who had small children were less depressed and had fewer somatic complaints than those who had adult children seemed to suggest that small children help the bereaved to cope with their loss by distracting them or offering them something to live for. However, when the information on children became available for the married, this interpretation had to be abandoned, because the same health difference was found for the married.

Investigations of the association between living arrangements and health are relevant in this context, since those widowed who live alone lack the potential support of a cohabiter. Thus, Clayton and her colleagues (e.g., Clayton et al., 1972; Bornstein et al., 1973; Clayton, 1975) examined the impact of living alone on depressive symptomatology. Thirteen months after bereavement the widowed living with families had lower depression rates than those living alone (Bornstein et al., 1973). Similarly, Lopata (1973b) reported that widows whose adult children lived in the same city recovered from bereavement much better than those who had none living locally. However, conclusions must be tempered by the point made above, and by the possibility that the widowed who live alone may differ systematically in certain respects (health, sociability, personality factors, etc.) from those who live with others (M. Stroebe & Stroebe, 1985).

The study by Bunch (1972) gives evidence that the presence of social ties and interactions among the bereaved is related to a reduction in suicide risk. Bereaved persons who committed suicide seemed to have been receiving less support from their relatives. They had also experienced more social disruption as a consequence of bereavement and were more likely to have been living alone. Support from the family group was taken to be one of the important determining factors in the occurrence of suicide among the bereaved. Similar findings and interpretations were reported in two further studies of suicide among the bereaved (Wenz, 1977; Bock & Webber, 1972). However, without nonbereaved controls, these findings may reflect a general association between social support and suicide risk.

A few studies have looked at patterns of interaction following bereavement (e.g., Morgan, 1984; Rosenman, Shulman, & Penman, 1981), or, more critically here, at the mediating effects of the source (notably, the relationship of the person providing support, such as relative, friend, etc., to the bereaved) and the quality or type of support (emotional, companionship, advisory, etc.) on well-being and depression among the bereaved. Lowenthal and Haven (1968), who examined the impact of having a confidant or intimate relationship generally, reported that of the widowed in their study, 45 percent of those who said they had a confidant were depressed, compared with 73 percent who said they had none. Unfortunately, interpretation of this result remains unclear: It could mean that having a confidant to support one during bereavement is important, but it could as well be interpreted as showing that those bereaved who are depressed are less likely to seek or to acknowledge a close relationship.

It is possible that different persons, for example, relatives rather than friends, are differentially useful in ameliorating psychological distress. Bankoff (1981, 1983a & b) examined the utilization of the social network by young widows at different periods of time following loss of the spouse. She found that parents were of most help in reducing distress early in bereavement, whereas later on single or other widowed friends were most helpful. It appeared to be more important *who* gave the support than *what type* of help was actually given. Although, again, no nonbereaved control group was used, the fact that the sources of support that were most helpful changed during the recovery period suggests that this is a bereavement-specific effect.

Other studies have supported the view that the relationship with family members is critical to outcome. Maddison (1968) found that bad outcome was related to nonsupportiveness of the widow's mother, and Glick et al. (1974) pointed to the benefits of a supportive family: 70 percent of their young widows said that they had received more support from their family than from their friends and had benefitted from this. Similarly, Bahr and Harvey (1979, 1980) and Morgan (1976) confirmed that contact with relatives and friends is positively associated with the level of life satisfaction and morale among widows.

Clearly, family contact might appear particularly important in the Bankoff (1981, 1983b) and Glick et al. (1974) samples because the widows were relatively young. Parents are more likely to be still alive than in the case of older widows, and to be particularly supportive in these cases since some at least are likely to be widowed themselves. Further information on the differential impact of persons in the support network is provided by Arling (1976) who compared various sources of social support (including family members, friends, and neighbors) on the morale of the elderly widowed. Arling found that "contact with family members, especially children, does little to elevate morale, while friendship–neighboring is clearly related to less loneliness and worry" (p. 757). Similarly, Pihlblad and Adams (1972) found that interaction with friends was more closely related to life satisfaction than was interaction with children and relatives.

To summarize, these studies provide suggestive evidence that (1) the presence and interaction with others appears to ameliorate the negative effects of bereavement, that (2) different persons may be most helpful at different times following loss, and (3) different persons may be helpful to younger versus older widowed. However, the lack of nonbereaved controls makes these conclusions rather tentative.

To clarify the role of social support in bereavement, our Tübingen study included measures of perceived social support as well as of social network. Perceived social support was assessed by a scale developed to reflect the various areas of support outlined by W. Stroebe and Stroebe (1986). As a social network index, participants were asked to name all the individuals with whom they had frequent contacts and also rate the quality of these relationships on a good–bad scale.

Since the subscales of our measure of perceived social support proved to be highly interrelated, subjects were divided into groups of high and low perceived social support by a median split on their total support scores. A social support by marital status by sex analysis of variance resulted in a main effect of all three factors on depression and somatic symptoms but showed no trace of the expected buffering effect (i.e., social support by marital status interaction). Although individuals who enjoyed high social support were less depressed than those who did not, this was equally true for both marital status groups. The same pattern emerged when subjects were divided into groups on the basis of the subscales, or according to the quality of their contacts. A division according to number of contacts did not result in any difference, suggesting that it is not the fact that one has relationships at all, but that one has good relationships, which is helpful. (The same set of results emerged when regression analyses were used rather than analyses of variance.)

This failure to find a buffering effect, though inconsistent with all of the theoretical interpretations of the role of social support in bereavement discussed earlier, seems, at first sight, exceedingly problematic for our deficit model of partner loss. However, the high level of social support which all members of our sample enjoyed could be partly responsible for our failure to find a buffering effect. Similar results have also been reported in the Lund et al. (1986) study. No differences in social support variables were found to exist between poor copers and other bereaved elderly persons. In this study, too, participants had fairly good social support networks, both quantitatively and qualitatively. Since one confidant has sometimes been found sufficient to eliminate the impact of stressful life events (e.g., Brown & Harris, 1978), the buffering effect is likely to be found most clearly in samples which include individuals who have very little social support. There were very few individuals who would fit this description either in our own sample, or in that of Lund et al. (1986). But this is at best a partial explanation, as one would have expected the bereaved to have a greater need for support than the married. Thus, if differences in the level of social support enjoyed by either group were associated with differential depression, these differences in depression should have been greater for the bereaved than for the married. The fact that we found a main effect of social support on mental health but no interaction is difficult to reconcile with our model.

(iii) Conclusions

In this section a number of studies were discussed which showed that bereaved individuals who enjoy a high level of social support suffer fewer depressive symptoms and somatic complaints than those who are not so well supported. However, such findings are difficult to interpret in the absence of nonbereaved controls. There are at least three plausible interpretations. In addition to the explanation preferred by bereavement researchers, that social support helps the bereaved to adjust to their loss, these findings might reflect a general main effect of social support on health or they might indicate that people who are depressed and angry behave in ways which are likely to alienate their sources of social support. The failure of our Tübingen study to find evidence of a buffering effect of social support would be consistent with an interpretation in terms of a main effect of social support on health.

8.6.2   *Concurrent stresses*

Many of the variables implied under the broad heading concurrent stresses have already been discussed in the preceding sections. We have considered the potential negative effects of such factors as low socioeconomic status, financial worries, the presence of dependent children, and lack of social support. Despite the absence of adequate data on many variables, the overall impression from the review of specific factors is that concurrent circumstances of the bereaved person are critical in determining the course and outcome of bereavement. Some indication comes from a study of bereaved relatives (the sample was not limited to the conjugally bereaved) and friends of victims of the volcanic eruption of Mt. St. Helens in the United States in 1980, conducted by Cowan and Murphy (1985). Subjects ($n = 69$) were matched with nonbereaved controls ($n = 50$). Measures of depression, somatization, and physical health were taken (the Life Experience Survey, the Symptoms Checklist-90-R, the Physical Health Index, and the Coppel Index of Social Support). Concurrent negative life stress was reported to be the most important single predictor in all three health outcomes. However, this was the case not only for the bereaved, but also for the nonbereaved. This therefore suggests a main effect of stress on health, rather than an interaction with bereavement.

Some researchers have also taken a more cumulative approach, looking at the relative effects or combined effects of concurrent stresses. Parkes (1975a), reporting on the Harvard study, noted that "secondary effects" of bereavement, such as problems with children, home, jobs, and financial difficulties, were all more likely to be mentioned by those whose outcome rating was poor. But, as he commented, "To what extent they caused poor outcome and to what extent they simply reflect emotional disturbance is hard to say" (p. 319). In a more recent paper Parkes (1985) ranked "social circumstances" according to their approximate order of importance for risk. Six contributory factors were listed, in order from greater to lesser importance: (1) absence of family or perceptions of their unsupportiveness; lack of a confidant; (2) detachment from traditional cultural and religious support systems (notably among immigrants); (3) unemployment; (4) presence of dependent children (although, possibly, of long-term help); (5) low socioeconomic status; (6) other losses.

In contrast to Parkes's emphasis on social factors, some investigators (e.g., Atchley, 1975; Bahr & Harvey, 1980; Harvey & Bahr, 1974; Morgan, 1976) have argued that poor adjustment to bereavement is largely attributable to the secondary economic effects of loss, such as sudden financial insecurity or lowering of income, and not to the change in marital status or widowhood status per se. Harvey and Bahr (1974) even claimed that the influence of socioeconomic factors can account for much, if not all, of the variance: "The negative impact sometimes attributed to widowhood derives not from widowhood status but rather from socioeconomic status" (p. 106).

As we pointed out earlier (Section 8.2.1) the financial-drop hypothesis cannot account for married-to-widowed health differences in studies in which groups were matched according to income. It seems reasonable to conclude, however, that concurrent stresses, such as financial burdens, will exacerbate adjustment problems. The reasons for this may be more complex than anxiety alone about "making both ends meet." Such factors as the limiting of social participation that lowered income may cause (cf. Atchley, 1975) and the consequent social isolation may be as critical.

8.7 Conclusions

Given that some individuals will come through the stress of bereavement relatively unharmed while others will suffer severe health problems and even develop psychiatric illness, one purpose of this review has been to identify characteristics of the bereaved or of the bereavement situation which are predictive of poor bereavement outcome. Certain regularities across studies have emerged from the survey of the literature. Thus gender, age, and forewarning of the loss were quite consistently found to be moderators of bereavement outcome in a number of studies. Although we found no indication for a social support by marital status interaction on health measures in our Tübingen data, we would tend to add social support to this list of risk factors, in view of the extensive evidence for buffering effects in the social support literature on nonspecific stress. Since the average level of social support was exceedingly high in our sample, one should reserve judgment on this factor until our findings have been replicated in further research.

While we could readily identify the unfortunate individual who combines many of the risk factors for poor outcome, it would be hard to say, if we had to predict whether a woman whose husband committed suicide and who had a great deal of social support was likely to have a better or worse outcome than a man whose spouse died after an extended illness and who had no friends or relatives to help him through his grief. This prediction would require knowledge of the relative importance of the various risk factors. As we would not only have to consider the main effects on bereavement outcome but also potential interactions between risk factors, it is not possible on the basis of available data, and in the absence of large-scale multivariate studies, to predict this kind of relative risk.

There is some evidence to suggest that (perhaps jointly with personality factors) differences in the availability of social support and the time period available for the adjustment of the loss are likely to account for most of the variation in bereavement outcome. However, most of the evidence on these theoretically important mediating variables has been indirect. For example, the interpretation of the age differences in bereavement outcome in terms of age-related differences in expectedness of loss rely on two separate pieces of evidence: (1) Expected losses are associated with better bereavement outcome than unexpected losses and (2) unexpected losses are likely to be more frequent in younger age groups, since accidents account for a greater proportion of deaths in the younger than older age groups. One would feel more confident about this interpretation if expectedness of loss had been assessed in the studies of age-related differences in bereavement outcome and if it had been demonstrated that by keeping expectedness constant across different age groups, the effect of the age variable could be removed.

Although stress theories like our deficit model and some of the depression theories (e.g., behavior theory) integrate the body of research on risk factors quite well, there are also some findings which are inconsistent with theoretical predictions. The most puzzling inconsistency, as noted above, is the failure of our Tübingen study to support the buffering hypothesis. Another is the fact that in most studies social class did not interact with bereavement outcome. However, this latter inconsistency might be due to the fact that our assumption about the positive association between social class and coping resources is wrong. Nevertheless, we were able to identify a number of fairly stable associations between potential risk factors and bereavement outcome and the overwhelming majority of these findings were consistent with our theoretical predictions.

9 Reducing the risk of poor bereavement outcome

9.1 Introduction

In a popular book of etiquette published in England in 1929 the author, a Lady Troubridge (1979), wrote on the customs to observe on the occurrence of a breavement: "One chief rule to remember . . . is that sorrow is sacred, and that it is one of the most unforgivable breaches of good behaviour to intrude upon it. . . . The members of the bereaved family should be left as much alone in their grief as possible" (1979, p. 55).

Failure to follow the rule of leaving the bereaved to their own devices was censored by Lady Troubridge as inconsiderate and very ill bred. Indeed, she stated, the bereaved should be left to themselves precisely because they are in danger of breaking down and showing unseemly emotion: "It is difficult to keep a firm hold over the emotions at such a time, and it is therefore wiser to see no one if there is a chance of breaking down" (1979, p. 57). The view that the bereaved must be left well alone by all but their closest circle of similarly grieving relatives is no longer a firm rule of contemporary Western society. It has become well accepted that others can help the bereaved and alleviate their psychological and physical suffering. On a more formal level, this follows from our own theoretical perspective (see Chapter 5), which argued that interpersonal variables are critical not only as determinants of the intensity of symptoms and duration of grief, but also of the ultimate health outcome following bereavement.

In this final chapter we take this argument a step further, to consider whether interpersonal factors can actually be demonstrated to reduce risk, and to discuss the implications for those who come into contact with bereaved persons.

9.2 Assessing the impact of interaction and support

Clearly it is difficult to assess the effectiveness of the informal social network in reducing risk, for one cannot randomly assign the bereaved into

224

those who receive or do not receive this type of support. We do know that perceived lack of social support is one of the risk factors (see Chapter 8), which could lead one to assume that a supportive informal network is effective in reducing risk. However, as we noted in the last chapter, these findings are ambiguous with regard to causal sequences. One of the most plausible alternative interpretations of the association of poor bereavement outcome and low social support is that it is due to some personality trait, such as neuroticism. Thus, neurotic persons might be more likely both to have (or to perceive themselves as having) nonsupportive social environments and, at the same time, to be more likely to have breakdowns under the stress of bereavement. To establish whether risk is reduced through social support, more conclusive evidence is needed.

Some such evidence is available from the various types of intervention programs that have been developed in recent years for the purpose of helping the bereaved who feel in need of support. These have included self-help groups (such as Cruse in England, or the Widow-to-Widow programs in the United States) and professionally organized intervention programs, which operate either on an individual or a group basis, and which may or may not employ trained volunteers (cf. Parkes, 1980).

The efficacy of both self-help and professional counseling programs has been the subject of systematic research in recent years, and it is this research which provides data on the question whether others can mediate to reduce risk and enhance well-being of the bereaved. The advantage of these investigations is that subjects can be randomly assigned to treatment or control groups, which precludes systematic differences between conditions with regard to such factors as subjects' personality traits. The results of these studies are evaluated below, following a discussion of the distinctions between grief counseling and grief therapy (in order to clarify the scope and objectives of these different types of support) and consideration of certain methodological issues which are pertinent to the evaluation of intervention programs.

9.3 Grief counseling and grief therapy: distinctions

When considering how to lower risk among the bereaved, it is necessary to draw the distinction between grief counseling and grief therapy. Grief counseling has been defined as "helping people facilitate uncomplicated, or normal, grief to a healthy completion of the tasks of grieving within a reasonable time frame" (Worden, 1982, p. 35). As Raphael (1980) stated, "The background to all bereavement counseling is general support, support that offers human comfort and care and that accepts and encourages appropriate grief and mourning" (p. 162). This type of assistance to the bereaved generally covers some or all of the different aspects of social support described in the deficit model, with particular emphasis on emotional support. Grief therapy, on the other hand, refers to ". . . those specialized techniques . . . which are used to help people with abnormal or complicated grief reactions" (Worden, 1982, p. 35). Thus, generally speaking, grief counseling would be appropriate for normal grief, while grief therapy would be indicated for pathological grief. Clearly, at times this distinction is not an easy one to judge, and expert knowledge may be needed to assess whether the special techniques of therapy are necessary in a particular case, or whether the bereaved person's grief will be alleviated with the aid of counseling. Most experts see grief *therapy* as appropriate in cases where the grief process itself has "gone wrong," when grief work fails to be undertaken and completed successfully, that is, when "the 'normal' reactions of shock, despair, and recovery are . . . distorted, exaggerated, prolonged, inhibited, or delayed" (Ramsay, 1979, p. 225). This then is a problem distinct from those discussed in the previous chapter: We identified persons at high risk of poor bereavement outcome, in terms of mental or physical ailments and debilities. In these latter cases, it may very often be that the grief reaction itself is "normal" (though possibly very intense), although the person is at high risk of developing some health problem. In order to lower this risk, grief *counseling* would be the appropriate technique.

It is evident from this discussion that our concern is with the effectiveness of counseling, and not therapy, as defined above. Thus, we will not consider the effectiveness of professional therapy in alleviating pathological or complicated grief reactions. Indeed, this task would be hard to undertake. Evaluations of psychiatric intervention with the bereaved rely largely on reports of limited numbers of case studies (e.g., Hodgkinson, 1982; Ramsay, 1977, 1979) or, in focusing on the efficacy of particular therapies, are frequently not concerned to make comparisons of outcome with a nonintervention condition (e.g., Horowitz, Marmar, Weiss, et al. 1984; Mawson, Marks, Ramm, & Stern, 1981). Some studies that do make only the comparison of those who have sought treatment for pathological grief with normally bereaved who have not, such that one cannot directly compare the effect of intervention versus nonintervention for pathological grief (cf. Horowitz, Weiss, Kaltreider, et. al., 1984). Random assignment of patients with morbid grief reactions to guided mourning treatment or to control groups is rare, since it is difficult, for ethical reasons, to assign needy patients to a nontreatment condition.

9.4 Methodological issues in the evaluation of intervention programs

9.4.1 *The inclusion of control groups*

How can one assess the effectiveness of counseling in reducing risk? Frequently, such judgments are made by the organizers or the participants of intervention programs themselves (cf. Davis & Jessen, 1982; Hiltz, 1975; McCourt, Barnett, Brennen, et al., 1976; Silverman & Cooperband, 1975) or in terms of the demand for and utilization of a particular service by the bereaved (e.g., Abrahams, 1972). While it may be useful for other purposes, this type of assessment cannot be used as evidence for intervention effectiveness. To illustrate this point, while it is of some value to know that 85 percent of those participants who made an assessment reported beneficial effects of a bereavement service (McCourt et al. 1976), this information tells one very little about the impact of the intervention program per se, because it does not draw the comparison of the outcome of participants with those of similar (preferably matched) bereaved who have, on a random basis, been excluded from the counseling program.

Why should it be so critical to include a control group? For one thing, one cannot be sure, given the complexity of the course of grief, that bereaved persons would not get *worse* without participation in a particular therapy program. Thus, even if self-help or psychotherapy intervention appears to be of very limited effectiveness in *improving* outcome (e.g., Videka-Sherman & Liebermann, 1985), without random assignment of matched subjects to a nonintervention control group, one cannot know whether or not intervention prevented deterioration. Second, participation in such programs is also typically voluntary, and it is very likely that there are important differences between those who choose to participate and those who do not.

9.4.2 *Selection biases*

There are, in fact, a number of selection biases that are critical. First, participants are likely to be those bereaved who feel they need and want this type of support in the first place, and who have stayed in the program long enough for assessment because they find it effective: There is likely not only to be selection into the program of those who feel it could help them, but also selection out of those who have found it unhelpful. Vachon, Lyall, Rogers, et al. (1980) argued that programs that rely on the bereaved responding to announcements of the service in the media are likely to be joined by those who are less passive and more receptive to an offer of help. Further, there are some indicators (see, e.g., Silverman & Cooperband, 1975) that the bereaved who choose to participate in counseling programs may be the ones who lack informal social support, although some inconsistent findings have been reported by Lund, Dimond, and Juretich (1985). Burdette-Finn (1980) found that members who had joined a group for widowed people were in fact the most physically and psychologically distressed of any bereaved groups contacted. Similarly, Lund et al. (1985) who, at the conclusion of a two year longitudinal study of bereavement, asked their sample of bereaved elderly persons if they would have been willing to participate in an intervention program, observed that those who indicated willingness had higher levels of depression and perceived their coping abilities less positively than those who were unwilling. With regard to factors that influence selection out of these programs, conflicting hypotheses have been proposed: While Burdette-Finn suggested that members who drop out of a support group may be the healthier and better recovered, Vachon et al. (1980) argued that those who drop out of intervention may actually be the ones with fewer social supports and worse off generally. Without empirical testing of these hypotheses one cannot draw any further conclusions.

For most practical purposes to do with counseling, the selection biases we have just discussed are not very important, and they are typically very difficult to control. It is sometimes impossible, even when outcome assessment is a key question, to allocate the bereaved randomly to participation versus nonparticipation in intervention conditions (e.g., Liebermann & Videka-Sherman, 1986). Nevertheless, to examine the effect of an intervention program in reducing the risk of bad health outcome, random assignment of the bereaved to either an intervention condition or to a control group that receives no counseling is necessary. Ideally, quantitative assessment of health should be made before, during, and after intervention and at equivalent times for the control group. The following review of the effectiveness of intervention focuses on those studies which conform to these methodological criteria.

9.5 Empirical studies of the effectiveness of bereavement intervention

A number of studies attest to the view that risk of bad outcome in bereavement can be reduced. These range from self-help program evaluation to those employing volunteers, or those conducted solely by professional counselors (psychiatrists, social workers, etc.). The studies reviewed here are those which focus on the "normally" (though frequently high-risk) bereaved, according to the criteria which have been set out above.

Exemplary of the self-help groups are the Widow-to-Widow-programs developed in the United States by Phyllis Silverman (e.g., 1969). The guiding principle behind such programs is that recently bereaved persons will be best helped by others who have been through bereavement themselves, who have recovered, and who can share their experience to the benefit of the recently bereaved. Some (e.g., Blau, 1975) are skeptical of the efficacy of using untrained persons to help the bereaved, and of the motives and personality characteristics of people who offer themselves as aides in such programs. Others (e.g., McNeill-Taylor, 1983) have expressed fears that participation would have the negative effect of concentrating thoughts on bereavement and on the past, hindering development beyond the "widow" role. However, the positive value of such programs was unequivocally stated by Silverman and Cooperband (1975):

The evidence points to another widow who has coped and accommodated as the best caregiver. Very often the first question a widow helper is asked is, "How am I going to manage?" The second question is, "How did it happen to you?" The new widow seems to be seeking a role model, someone with whom to identify. This other widow can be a friend, a neighbor, or a relative. She offers an opportunity to talk with someone who indeed really understands. She can provide perspective on feelings; she provides a role model; she can reach out as a friend and neighbor – not someone defined as concerned with abnormal or deviant behavior. (p. 11)

There are very few studies which provide empirical examination of the impact of self-help intervention on bereavement outcome. However, in one controlled study, Vachon et al. (1980) evaluated the effectiveness of intervention conducted by a widow of longer standing. These widow–counselors had been trained to help the recently bereaved by a professional psychiatrist. As such, they were not quite typical of those who generally work in self-help intervention programs, and they may have been more effective because they had received training (Parkes, 1980). Vachon et al. (1980) assigned participants from a larger investigation (see, e.g., Vachon, 1979; Vachon, Rogers, Lyall, et al., 1982) either to an experimental condition ($n = 68$), or to a nonintervention control group ($n = 94$). Vachon et al. (1980) described the intervention as providing emotional, cognitive, and practical support, categories which are similar to those of the deficit model. Perhaps one distinctive feature in the provision of help from other widowed persons is that counseling is conducted by someone who, having been through the bereavement experience him- or herself, can validate the bereaved's reactions to the various aspects of loss. Furthermore, intervention was not limited to a number of sessions. The widow was free to contact the intervenor as or when she wished.

Results indicated beneficial effects of intervention. Whereas at one month after bereavement (i.e., before intervention) the bereaved in both groups were similar on an overall measure of psychological disturbance, the Goldberg General Health Questionnaire (GHQ), at six months the two groups differed on intrapersonal items. For example, intervention subjects were more likely to feel better than they had. At twelve months interpersonal items such as the initiation and resumption of social ties distinguished between the two groups, in favor of the intervention group. Finally, at twenty-four months, intervention subjects had fewer symptoms on the GHQ, the only time at which a difference in overall disturbance between the groups was apparent.

There is some evidence that participation not only accelerated recovery, as these results imply, but also reduced risk. After two years, significantly fewer women in the intervention group who had high distress scores on the GHQ at one month were still in this high-risk category, as compared with nonintervention controls. One problem was a fairly high attrition rate after two years, over a third in each group having been lost from the sample by this time.

Vachon et al. (1980) were cautious about extrapolating from these data and urged replication. Nevertheless, the results do indicate that social support both reduces the risk of bad outcome among widows and shortens the duration of grief. Intervention seemed to be most effective for high-risk persons.

Similarly effective results were reported by Cameron and Parkes (1983). In a study in Montreal, Canada, they evaluated the effect of the service provided by a Palliative Care Unit (PCU) on surviving relatives of patients who had died. Bereavement outcome was compared with that of a group of subjects (twenty persons matched with each PCU relative) whose close relatives had died in other wards of the same hospital. PCU relatives had a number of services available to them, both before and after bereavement. After the death an informal counseling program conducted by nurses on the staff of the unit was available, the support from which "varied from reassurance and active listening to referral to a specialist for more in depth assistance as required" (p. 74). The relatives of patients who had died in other wards did not have the benefit of this counseling program. Health and recovery from bereavement assessments were made one year and two weeks after bereavement. Relatives of PCU patients had better health ratings, fewer psychological symptoms, and were making less use of psychotropic medication than the relatives of patients from other wards. One particularly notable difference was that the latter group expressed far more persisting irritability and anger than the former.

It is, as Cameron and Parkes (1983) noted, not possible to say exactly which aspects of the total care program explain these differences. Not just counseling after bereavement, but also certain treatment differences before loss were thought to have contributed, particularly the provision of adequate pain relief for the patient (this factor is likely to be related to the persistence of anger toward the doctors, which hampered recovery in bereavement, and will be discussed later) and knowledge of the imminence of death. Both these aspects were given greater attention in the PCU group. One further aspect, which might have introduced some bias, is that patients were not randomly assigned to the two types of care. This was naturally beyond the control of the investigators.

One study in which it was possible not only to include care before and after bereavement but which, in addition, managed to assign subjects randomly to treatment versus nontreatment conditions was conducted by Parkes (1979). The provision of support was given to a group of high-risk bereaved in London, England. In this study, care was not provided by other bereaved or by the nursing staff, but by well-informed individuals who had been selected and trained by professionals. The project was part of a larger provision to dying patients and their families at St. Christopher's Hospice in London. Criteria for selection of high-risk individuals for inclusion in the study included lack of supportive families, low socioeconomic status, young age, certain psychological reactions (clinging or pining, anger, and self-reproach), length of preparation time for bereavement, and an evaluation by the nursing staff at the hospice of probable coping. A few potential participants were judged to be at "imperative need" of counseling, and these were given support but were excluded from the controlled investigation. Other high-risk individuals were assigned either to an intervention ($n = 32$) or to a nonintervention ($n = 35$) condition. Low-risk individuals did not receive intervention (unless, as in a few cases, they requested it). Similarly to Vachon et al.'s (1980) procedure, the support offered was quite comprehensive and not limited to a certain number of sessions. The bereaved were visited in their homes, and besides offering friendship, various other sources of support were offered as necessary (e.g., referral to a general practitioner, social worker, clergy, or social security office).

Measures of change in health in the four years following bereavement were made. Differences between the intervention and control groups were not apparent during the first year, but thereafter the overall scores on health outcome were better for the intervention than for the control group. Two out of three measures of change in health favored the intervention group. The results of this study clearly support the view that risk of poor outcome can be reduced: High-risk individuals who received no support had significantly worse health scores than the low-risk (nonintervention) group. But high-risk persons who had received counseling had health scores similar to those of the low-risk group.

A study by Raphael (1977, 1978) in Australia also provides evidence that high-risk bereaved individuals can be helped by intervention. In this study counseling was conducted by a professional psychiatrist, and support was more formalized than in the above studies. The sample was limited to bereaved widows. The study was designed specifically to test the effectiveness of a crisis-intervention technique in improving the general health of the widows. Two hundred bereaved widows, who had lost their spouses within the previous seven weeks, were interviewed and examined for criteria of high risk. The four factors devised to define high risk were (1) perceived nonsupportiveness of the social network, (2) "traumatic" death of the partner, (3) ambivalent marital relationship with the deceased, and (4) presence of additional concurrent life stresses.

High-risk individuals (defined as those showing one or more of the above risk factors) were randomly assigned either to a treatment group ($n = 31$) to receive intervention, or to a control group ($n = 33$) which did not. Raphael's technique followed her own model of the bereavement process (see Raphael, 1971) and involved primarily encouragement of the expression of grief affects and facilitation of review of both positive and negative aspects of the relationship with the spouse. Intervention took place in the widow's home, each session lasting at least two hours, and the average number of sessions being four. Sessions were completed within three months of bereavement, and assessment was made at thirteen months. This was done by means of a general health questionnaire, sent independently (to minimize the chance of demand characteristics influencing responses) to the widows.

Significantly more of the treatment, than of the control, group had good, rather than bad, outcome. Furthermore, the high-risk intervention group were not significantly different from the low-risk widows who had not met the criteria for high risk at the initial assessment, and who had received no intervention. The high-risk control group, on the other hand, had significantly poorer health scores than the low-risk group.

It is interesting to note that "perceived nonsupportiveness" was the most accurate predictor of those likely to do well after the crisis intervention. Providing social support for those who apparently lacked it appears to be instrumental in improving general health ratings. This factor may be more important in a sample which was essentially self-selected, and might have been in greater need of support than the widowed population in general, but nevertheless, the provision of social support has been linked to improvement in health ratings.

Somewhat similar results were reported in a study by Gerber, Wiener, Battin, et al. (1975b) among a sample of elderly bereaved in New York. Again, the objective was to evaluate the effects of crisis intervention by trained psychiatric workers. Random assignment to treatment ($n = 116$) and nontreatment ($n = 53$) was also possible in this investigation. In addition to emotional support, companionship support was organized. The elderly were also helped with legal and financial matters and with household chores. Thus, although just over half of the interviews were conducted over the telephone, support was very comprehensive, and covered the different types which we have identified as important in the deficit model. Intervention was terminated after the first half-year of bereavement, but assessment was made at approximately three, five, eight, and fifteen months.

Even though subjects were not selected according to a high-risk criterion, the intervention offered to the bereaved had a positive impact on medical outcome: They received fewer drug prescriptions, consulted with doctors less frequently and reported feeling ill without consultation less often than those not in the intervention program. Possibly even low-risk bereaved among the elderly in this sample had many unfulfilled needs with which the intervention program succeeded in dealing.

While the subjects in the above studies were mostly (though not entirely) conjugally bereaved, it is likely that intervention is similarly effective with those bereaved from other types of loss. In a small study of the effectiveness of support after perinatal death, Forrest, Standish, and Baum (1982) found significant differences between supported (counseled) and unsupported groups, the former having a lower incidence of psychiatric disorder at six months after loss than the latter. Undoubtedly, there are many other types of loss (e.g., loss of a limb, infant death), some of which are ambiguous (Rosenblatt & Burns, 1986), or that receive little acknowledgment or support from others (e.g., giving a child for adoption, abortion) for which support or intervention programs could usefully be developed.

One outstanding question is, What is it that helps? While we have described in as much detail as possible from the published accounts, what "counseling" or "intervention" in the various studies was comprised of, the precise nature and extent of the support given, and what made it effective, remains ill defined. As the descriptions of the relevant studies show, few attempts have as yet been made to examine mediating variables. Perhaps indicative are the findings of a very small intervention study by Mawson, Marks, Ramm, and Stern (1981) with pathologically bereaved individuals.

This was a controlled study of different techniques of treating pathological grief in twelve patients (eleven of whom were female) with morbid grief reactions. They were randomly allocated to "guided-mourning treatment" or to control treatment. In the former condition they were encouraged to face cues concerning their bereavement, in the latter they were instructed and encouraged throughout to avoid such cues. Treatment comprised six half-hour sessions over two weeks. Guided-mourning patients showed significant improvement on most measures (including pathology of grief, depression, anxiety, and social adjustment) two weeks after the termination of treatment, and improvement was maintained at a ten to twenty-eighth week follow-up. Control subjects did not improve. While treatment of pathological grief, as we noted earlier, is very different from helping the normally bereaved, these findings are suggestive for the latter: Perhaps it is the encouragement of grief work in intervention that makes a critical difference to outcome.

9.6 Negative results: a consideration

While the above studies give a consistent picture of the beneficial effects on health of providing support programs to the bereaved (especially those at high risk), a few other studies have found intervention to be on the whole ineffective (Polak et al., 1975; Barrett, 1978; Walls & Meyers, 1985). For example, Polak et al. (1975), who reported that crisis intervention had little effect on risk of psychiatric illness and disturbed family functioning, administered crisis intervention to family groups who had experienced the sudden death of a relative, rather than to individuals. Such a procedure is clearly very different from intervention to single individuals (e.g., family dynamics may hamper the effectiveness of intervention). Matching of intervention and control groups was also problematic (although analysis of covariance was used to try to deal with this problem):

Data analysis of the sampling characteristics of the treated and untreated bereaved groups revealed more suicidal deaths . . . and a higher degree of suddenness of death in the treated group. It appears that the deputy coroner unwittingly selected a greater proportion of families in which the death was suicidal or accidental . . . for clinical investigation by the project staff. (Polak et al., 1975, p. 147)

According to all we know about risk factors, this surprising mismatch would mean that the treatment group would be at much higher risk than the nontreatment group. Further criticisms of this study have been made by both Parkes (1980) and Raphael (1977). In view of the problems, it cannot be argued that Polak et al.'s study is a convincing demonstration that intervention does not work.

Two studies (Barrett, 1978; Walls & Meyers, 1985) have attempted, on the whole unsuccessfully, to evaluate the relative impact of different *types* of intervention on outcome. Both these studies used group treatment rather than individual counseling. Barrett (1978) compared three group treatments and a nontreatment (waiting-list) control condition. The treatment conditions were a self-help group, a "confidant" group, and a women's consciousness-raising group. Outcome measures were personality, attitude, and behavioral changes and self-ratings of health. Treatment was for a seven-week period, followed by post-testing and a fourteen-week follow-up. Participants in all treatment groups showed significant improvement in ratings of future health, although the actual index of physical complaints had not changed at post-test. Not only was there little to choose between the treatment groups on most measures, but on some indices the control group changed too: Thus in all groups including the control group, post-test scores on self-esteem were more positive. Grief intensity was also *higher* at post-test for all four groups.

Promising though this design may seem (although the results are puzzling), since the length of widowhood ranged from one month to twenty-two years, with a mean length of four years and nine months, this was not a controlled investigation of acute grief. The study provides little relevant evidence either on reducing risk among recently bereaved, or on the relative effectiveness of different treatment conditions on health outcomes, even among the bereaved of longer-standing.

Walls and Meyers's (1985) study was designed to evaluate three therapeutic group interventions for normally grieving widows. The groups were a cognitive-restructuring group similar to Beck's (cf. Beck, 1976), a behavioral skills group, and a self-help group. These were compared with a delayed-treatment control group. Ten ninety-minute sessions were organized for each experimental group. The three group-therapy interventions were found to have "little effect on adjustment to widowhood" (p. 139), although the cognitive-restructuring group did report a qualitative reduction in depression. Most surprising was the finding that the control group reported an increase in overall life satisfaction, in contrast to the treatment groups, which did not. The authors concluded that cognitive therapy emerged as somewhat better than the other treatments, and could usefully be combined with behavioral skills training as an intervention technique for bereavement.

Sample sizes in this study were extremely small (pre–post-test follow-up data are presented for seven behavior skills subjects, the largest sample, and four controls, the smallest) and could be responsible for some of the nonsignificant differences. It is also possible that Walls and Meyers's (1985) basically negative findings concerning the impact of intervention on health measures are due to the fact that the bereaved were low-risk individuals in the first place: pretest means on the BDI range from 5.28 in the behavioral skills group to 9.60 for the self-help (the differences were not significant). It is possible that, had these subjects been at high risk, the usefulness of the different programs could have been better evaluated.

In conclusion, the few studies which have reported little or no impact of intervention do not seriously call into question the effectiveness of such programs. Apart from the methodological points raised above, certain idiosyncratic features of the studies seem responsible for the negative results. What these studies do lead one to conclude is that, to be effective, intervention must be comprehensive (i.e., covering those aspects of support for which there are deficits), that it must be fairly extensive, that it is likely to be most effective on an individual (rather than group or family) basis, and, finally, that it is most appropriate for high-risk bereaved.

9.7   Does intervention reduce risk?

The answer to the general question set at the beginning of this chapter is in the affirmative: Risk of psychological or physical debility following bereavement can be reduced. Evidence from studies designed to alleviate symptoms shows that participants have better ratings on health measures and recovery ratings than those who were allocated randomly to nonparticipation.

The more specific issue as to which bereaved can most be helped requires further consideration. Authors of the studies reviewed have fairly consistently identified high-risk groups as benefiting from intervention. It is important to remember that perceived lack of social support was one of the main criteria used to establish high risk and, in the study that looked at risk factors separately (Raphael, 1977), it was the most accurate predictor of those whose outcome would improve. In other words, risk can be reduced by providing intervention for those bereaved whose informal social network does not (or cannot) provide support. Perceived lack of support was not, however, the only criterion: Sudden unexpected death, for example, was also frequently used as a predictor. It did seem that counseling persons at high risk, not because of a nonsupportive environment, but because of circumstances of loss (i.e., much less directly related to support), is also effective.

While this argues the case that outcome can be improved for bereaved at high risk for different reasons (different risk factors), there is one major constraint in making this general conclusion. One cannot conclude from the intervention studies reported above that the same positive impact of counseling would have been found for those who did not choose to participate in intervention. Even when assignment to treatment versus non-treatment groups is random, participation is still largely based on self-selection. Thus, one can say very little about the impact that counseling would have on those who choose not to participate or on those who drop out of the program before evaluation. We can only say, then, that the provision of social support is effective in reducing risk of poor outcome among those who actually lack the necessary support (and there may be a very high need for this among groups who have, for example, suffered a particularly traumatic loss) or who perceive their environments as being deficient in this respect, and who, in addition, are willing to accept another source of support.

Nevertheless, if one assumes that the perception of a lack of social suppport reflects an actual deficit caused by loss of support from the spouse, the finding that intervention programs were particularly effective for high-risk groups would be consistent with the deficit model of partner loss. According to this model, the availability of an additional source of social support should further recovery from bereavement *only* if some support deficit occurred due to loss, for which compensation was provided from an alternative source. Since one major criterion for considering subjects low risk was that they did not perceive any support deficits, the finding that intervention did not significantly affect their health outcome is also consistent with the deficit model. Thus, in addition to supporting the general conclusion that social support furthers recovery and lowers risk, the pattern of findings so far is also consistent with more specific predictions derived from the deficit model of partner loss.

Under the conviction that the suffering of bereaved persons can be reduced with the help of others, in the concluding part of this book we for once go beyond our empirical data, drawing on the intuitions of experienced clinicians and on accounts by the bereaved themselves, to make specific suggestions about how the bereaved can be helped, either in the informal social setting or more formally in intervention. For detailed treatment of the wide range of issues that are of concern to those in grief counseling, the reader is referred to Margolis, Raether, and Kutscher et al. (1981), Raphael (1984), Rando (1984), Schoenberg (1980), Spiegel (1978), and Worden (1982).

9.8 Guidelines for supporting the bereaved

At the outset it must be emphasized that counseling for many recently bereaved may require no more than sympathetic company and reassurance, and the patience to listen and let the bereaved person talk over the loss. Very often, however, attempts to give advice, state opinions, or intervene in any way are resented and consequently rejected. This is a problem that is not specific to the area of bereavement. It has been recognized in research on recipients' reactions to help that receiving aid can elicit negative as well as positive reactions (see Fisher, Nadler, & Witcher-Alagna, 1982). The offer of aid will be perceived as supportive to the extent that apart from being helpful, it transmits the positive message of sympathy and care. Thus, in the Tübingen study, when asked to say what they found "helpful" behavior of others, the widowed mentioned offers of specific practical support, expressions of sympathy and the sharing of grief, concern of persons from whom this had not been expected, the simple presence of close persons, condoling remarks about death and bereavement.

Research on recipients' reactions has suggested that the major reason why an offer of aid frequently elicits a negative reaction is the implied inferiority, inadequacy, and dependency inherent in the role of someone needing help (Brickman, Rabinowitz, Karuza, et al., 1982; Nadler & Fisher, 1986). This may be less applicable in the case of the bereaved, since it is generally accepted that recently bereaved individuals are in need of help due to the occurrence of a tragic event for which they cannot be made responsible. However, the existence of powerful social norms that oblige friends and relatives to offer their support makes it very difficult for the bereaved to distinguish sincere from insincere offers of help. Thus, "platitudes" and "ungenuine offers of help" were frequently mentioned as examples of "unhelpful" behavior by the widows and widowers interviewed in the Tübingen study. Paradoxically, the absence of condolences from those from whom they were expected is also deplored. This is in fact consistent with expectations based on attribution theory (e.g., Bem, 1972; Kelley, 1973; W. Stroebe, Eagly, & Stroebe, 1977) that behavior patterns consistent with a norm (i.e., condolences) are perceived as being caused by the norm rather than by personal motives, while violations of the norm (i.e., failure to offer condolences) are attributed personally.

The sensitivity of the bereaved to insincerity is sharpened by the fact that many bereaved individuals have themselves had some experience as half-hearted donors of support at funerals and are therefore doubtful whether others really try to understand their grief. Thus, remarks like "I know exactly how you feel" are often resented, not only because the bereaved tend to believe that nobody really knows how they feel, but also because such statements imply that their grief is typical or normal. Remarks such as "you are standing up to it very well" also evoke annoyance because they are interpreted as indicating that the bereaved is falling short of the level of suffering that could be expected. This resentment is likely to be particularly strong in cases where the relationship between the spouses had been ambivalent and the grieving marked by feelings of guilt.

It is apparent from this discussion that the line between what is perceived as helpful and what is unhelpful is very hard to draw. Furthermore, what is found helpful by some has quite the opposite effect on others (e.g., while most bereaved welcome verbal condolences, a few list this as the hardest thing that they had to endure from others). There is no easy set of rules to apply in helping the bereaved, and much will depend on the tact and intuition of the helper. The following guidelines are intended rather to help a potential supporter gain insight about the problems faced by the bereaved, rather than providing a set of rules to observe when interacting with them.

9.8.1 *Preparation for impending death and bereavement*

Sharing the knowledge of death. Some couples choose to talk openly with one another (and/or with others) about the impending death of one of them, whereas other couples prefer not to. Survivors who have spoken about death with their deceased spouses invariably say that this helped considerably in their adjustment to the loss, and that it helped the dying patient to come to terms with death. Thus, rather than treating death as a forbidden topic which is upsetting to mention, if a couple have been told that the illness of one of them is terminal, they should be gently encouraged to talk it over. Sometimes, however, the reality of death may be too much for one or for both partners to bear and they may cling to a slender hope that death will not occur and prefer to avoid discussing the possibility. As Paulay (1977) commented, "Sometimes the denial in the family is its only defense to help it get through the crises, to give it time to integrate an unhappy truth" (p. 175). Interference would be wrong in such cases: Doctors and others concerned should allow denial.

Forewarning of bereavement reactions. As was described in Chapter 2, bereavement is accompanied by unusual and unexpected symptoms, which often seem bizarre to the bereaved person him or herself. If the possibility arises, it is helpful to give some forewarning of what to expect, so that the bereaved person is not completely taken by surprise, or is even frightened, by the psychological and physical manifestations of grief. However, since no two persons react identically, it is important to indicate the range of possible symptoms, rather than simply listing expected manifestations.

It can be particularly alarming to the bereaved if they seem to be developing symptoms similar or identical to those of the spouse during the final illness (e.g., local pain or heart fluttering) for this sometimes leads them to think that they themselves are dying. Forewarning that this is a common manifestation of grief is reassuring. On the other hand, since the bereaved are at health risk, it is advisable for them to consult a doctor if they have symptoms which disturb them.

Terminal care and interaction with medical staff. It cannot be emphasized enough how very significant for bereavement outcome are the events and interactions with people during the time leading up to the death. The study by Cameron and Parkes (1983) made this point very clear. They argued forcibly on two specific aspects: (1) Bereaved persons who have watched a dying person suffer severe, unrelieved pain are left with a tremendous legacy of anger against the responsible doctors. Cameron and Parkes argue strongly for the provision of adequate pain relief for the dying patient through "meticulous attention to the individual needs of each patient, continuous monitoring of drug responses, and frequent use of narcotic drugs in 4-hourly dosages in order to keep the patient free of pain" (p. 76). Administered in this way, they argue, anesthetic doses to get the pain under control (which is often necessary if drugs are administered only "as required") can be avoided, and much suffering not only of the patient, but of his or her loved ones, spared. (2) Communications between doctors and relatives concerning the imminence of death are also critically important to the outcome of the bereaved person. Relatives who are informed that an illness has reached its terminal stage and that death is to be expected within a foreseeable time period are helped in the adjustment to loss.

It is perhaps helpful at this point to mention that further advice for those who come into contact with relatives in specific capacities is to be found in the counseling literature, for example, advice for those in nursing practice (e.g., Dimond, 1981; Sen, 1980); family physicians (e.g., Brown & Stoudemire, 1983; Stack, 1972); clergy (Preston, 1980); funeral directors (Dalton, 1981; Hausmann, 1981); and the military (Noll, 1981).

9.8.2 *After the death*

Providing information about the death. Particularly if death was sudden and unexpected, and the bereaved person was not present when it occurred, an overriding need may be felt for detailed information. It is very natural, and not morbid, for the bereaved to want to know minute details about what happened, and they should be told if they ask. This will reduce rather than increase anxiety. The actual breaking of the news of a death is critical since the bereaved will remember the circumstances under which they received the news vividly. Rabin and Pate (1981) give some useful advice on this issue.

Whether or not the bereaved person chooses to view the corpse is a very personal decision, and depends too on the circumstances of death. It is inadvisable to persuade the bereaved either to view or not to view the corpse against his or her will. Generally, it helps survivors to accept the finality of death to see the body. Exceptions to this would be cases where the deceased did not die a natural death, and viewing the corpse would be harrowing for the bereaved. In such cases it is better to live with the memory of the deceased as he or she had been when alive.

Support at the funeral. Grueling though it may be, attendance at the funeral has a number of benefits for the bereaved (see, e.g., Goldberg, 1981), which may be realized with the help and support of others. After the first days of shock and numbness, the funeral service can help make real the fact that the loved person has died and will not return. It can provide release and catharsis. As McNeill-Taylor (1983) said, "It takes much longer to recover from a death if there is no funeral ritual, no coffin to cry over or ceremony to go through" (p. 21). The funeral provides the opportunity to talk openly about the deceased, to express thoughts and feelings, although, as Worden (1982) cautions, there is a great tendency to "overidealize and overeulogize a person at a funeral" (p. 50). Since idealization of the deceased by the bereaved is closely related to chronic grief, it is advisable to try to maintain a more balanced view, difficult though this may be at a funeral service. It is interesting to note that saying not only positive but also negative things about the deceased is quite acceptable at the Irish wake, and one would suppose that this situation would foster adjustment among the bereaved.

Over the past two decades the elaborateness of funeral services has been much censored, particularly in the United States, since the publication of Jessica Mitford's *The American Way of Death* in 1963. Mitford harshly criticized the commercialism of the funeral industry, citing at one point from the National Funeral Service journal: "It seems highly probable that the most satisfactory funeral service for the average family is one in which the cost has necessitated some degree of sacrifice. This permits the survivors to atone for any real or fancied neglect of the deceased prior to his death" (p. 33).

One has to agree with Mitford's outrage at such an exploitation of the bereaved, but no doubt for some, feelings of guilt can be assuaged by the arrangement of a very fine funeral (this clearly should be the decision of the bereaved and his or her advisors and not that of the funeral director). Most importantly, funerals and other mourning rituals provide a situation in which the bereaved can be shown emotional support from comforters, which facilitates their grieving. Whatever the current views on funeral customs, presence at the funeral is beneficial, and those close to the bereaved should be there to provide support.

Condolences. The problem what to say to someone recently bereaved was expressed many years ago by Gorer (1965): "Nowhere is the absence of an accepted social ritual more noticeable than in the first contacts between a mourner and his neighbours, acquaintances or work-mates after a bereavement" (p. 57).

Anyone who has extended contact with bereaved persons knows that not only are remarks intended to be helpful often perceived as unhelpful (cf. Wortman & Lehman, 1985), but that they may even be taken as a slight or insult by the recipient and responded to aggressively. Bereaved persons are intensely sensitive. McNeill-Taylor (1983) makes this apparent in reporting on the reactions of a bereaved man whom she interviewed: "One widower, who in all other respects was the soul of reason, told how he felt that every nerve was ultrasensitive and liable to spark off into resentment after his wife's death" (p. 38).

Worden (1982) advises on a simple expression of sympathy: "People in pain make us feel helpless. This helplessness can be acknowledged as a simple statement like 'I don't know what to say to you'" (p. 49). Others (e.g., McNeill-Taylor, 1983) have found physical expressions of sympathy one of the most reassuring signs of genuine concern. In Germany tradition provides the formula "Mein herzliches Beileid" (my sincere condolences), accompanied by a handshake. This custom overcomes the initial

Table 9.1. *Condoling the bereaved: unhelpful statements that were meant to be helpful*

"You're standing up well to it."
"It is the will of God."
"I know just how you feel."
"Keep a stiff upper lip."
"You'll be fine."
"This will soon end."
"Life is for the living."
"It is time you got over it."
"You're lucky to have the children."
"You're lucky the children are grown up."
"At least you're young and can remarry."
"Time heals everything."
"You had a good life with him/her."
"One can't live with the dead."
"You are lucky to have had him for so long."

problem of what to say, and provides an opening for further conversation if desired.

However difficult it may be to find the right expression in condoling the bereaved, platitudes must be avoided. Quite consistently these elicit resentment and annoyance where they are meant to help. Examples of unhelpful statements that were meant to be condoling are given in Table 9.1, many of which were made to the bereaved in the Tübingen study but which can also consistently be found from other sources. There is a fair consistency with which certain well-intentioned remarks misfire and have the opposite of the intended effect on the bereaved.

Pessimistic remarks such as "Things will be worse before they are better" or "It will be at least five years before you feel yourself again" are also unhelpful. So is the recitation of accounts of tragedies in the life of the condoler: Comparing tragedies does not help the recently bereaved person. Generally speaking, sympathy should not be withheld because of a fear of intruding on the bereaved's private grief. It helps to have the loss acknowledged, and this can be done by letter, a telephone call, or a visit, whatever is appropriate given the individual circumstances and closeness of the relationship.

Advice on the use of medication. Extreme caution should be observed in administering medication to the recently bereaved who have no abnormal symptoms (see, e.g., Jacobs and Ostfeld, 1980; Osterweis et al., 1984; Worden, 1982). The general view is that drugs should not be used to suppress the normal emotional reactions to loss, and yet they are prescribed with alarming frequency by doctors for this purpose.

Many who have been prescribed sedatives for the first few days of bereavement find these to be no help at all, since they muffle reactions and hinder the realization of loss. They may, however, be useful in cases where arousal is excessively high (Jacobs & Osterfeld, 1980), but should be prescribed for a short time only. Worden (1982) cautions against the use of antidepressant medication for those undergoing grief, since they take a long time to work, do not relieve normal grief symptoms and could lead to abnormal grief responses. If the bereaved person is suffering from persistent insomnia, such that normal functioning is further impaired by persistent exhaustion, administering hypnotics (sleeping pills) in the smallest effective dose is considered appropriate (Hackett, 1974; Osterweis et al., 1984).

Finally, it is worth remembering that providing social support for the bereaved could possibly minimize the need for medical aid. This conclusion is suggested by two of the intervention studies reviewed above (Cameron & Parkes, 1983; Raphael, 1977) which reported that use of psychotropic medication and visits to physicians decreased under conditions where intervention counseling was given.

9.8.3   The first few days and weeks

Instrumental support. Usually there are many areas for which the bereaved need specific help, notably those tasks for which the spouse had been responsible, for the organization of the funeral, and for the rearrangement of financial and other personal affairs due to the death. Besides emotional support, instrumental help is probably of most importance to the bereaved person in the first few weeks. Since the bereaved will be reluctant to do the asking, it is important to make the offer of help specific and not sound like an empty gesture. Perhaps the best help that can be offered is to assist the bereaved person to acquire the skills for coping on his or her own. Acquiring competence in areas for which the spouse had been responsible is likely to be the best way of overcoming helplessness and the feeling of inability to cope.

Emotional support. The first concern in providing emotional support is to try to help the bereaved to *accept the reality of death*. But just as news of a terminal illness may be seemingly denied, so may the realization of actual death take time. This lack of acceptance in the first few days after loss can be protective against a reality that is too hard to bear. The bereaved may continue to talk of the deceased as if he or she were still alive, and to consider his or her needs and wishes. It is advisable to tread very gently in forcing the actuality of the death on the bereaved. Only if prolonged is this a symptom of pathological grief: The recently bereaved move between apparent acceptance and utter disbelief at their loss.

When the denial of loss is a defense against an overwhelming affect rather than the suppression of a healthy affect, psychotherapeutic intervention designed to break down these defense mechanisms may be counterindicated. This has been suggested by Ramsay (1979), who described the case of a widow whose husband had died suddenly after fifty years of marriage. She did not acknowledge his death, but continued to set the table for two, talk to an empty chair, and describe to others activities jointly undertaken with her husband. Since these minor peculiarities did not seem to impair the widow's ability to cope with the demands of everyday life, Ramsay argued that her denial should not be broken down in psychotherapy. Such an intervention could unleash an emotional reaction of such intensity as to lead to a complete breakdown of her coping ability.

The major task during the early days of bereavement in providing emotional support is, however, to *encourage grief work*. It follows from the theoretical analyses and empirical findings discussed in the previous chapters that being able to talk over the loss, to be able to identify and express feelings of grief, helps the bereaved to come to terms with the death and to ultimately make a better adjustment. This entails being able to admit feelings of anger and guilt as well as sadness and distress. It is part of grief work to dwell on the events leading up to the loss, and to repeatedly recount these to listeners, who may be tempted to lose patience with this constant repetition. One of the most important tasks of the supporter is to tolerate repetitive accounts of the loss and to recognize that this is part of the healing process. McNeill-Taylor (1983) made this point: "If I had not told the story so often in an almost unending monologue I doubt if I would be able to believe it, even now" (p. 33). At the same time, it must be remembered that ruminations about loss, as discussed earlier (Section 5.4.2), are closely associated with poor bereavement outcome (Pennebaker & O'Heeron, 1984; Remondet et al., 1986).

It takes time to accommodate to loss, longer than family members and friends often permit. While overprotection can prevent the bereaved from making an effort to recover by themselves, a frequent irritation for the bereaved is to be told that it is "time they got over it." Although acute grief and depression usually abate within the first few months, suffering continues for much longer and may be renewed in intensity around such times as birthdays, anniversaries, and so on. The bereaved continue to need emotional support for months and even years after the loss.

Validational support. It helps the bereaved to know *what is normal* in grief reactions. Knowledgeable others can play an important role in providing appraisal (of personal responses, of situations, etc.). For example, the bereaved themselves might expect a faster recovery and return to normal life than they are experiencing. They can be shattered to find a recurrence of intense grief just when they thought that the worst was over. To be told that this is a usual ramification of grief is very often reassuring. They may doubt that it will ever "get better" when, having gone through a phase of calm, they are suddenly harrowed by feelings of deep loss and anguish all over again. A skilled comforter can reassure the bereaved that such times are likely to become more widely spaced and ultimately less devastating.

Similarly, some bereaved are afraid, given certain symptoms (such as intense rage against someone, or hallucinations of the deceased), which they do not understand or are surprised by, that they are "going crazy," that their responses are in fact far from normal. It helps to know that the feeling of "going out of one's mind" is a frequent manifestation of grief, shared by many others in the acute phase. Likewise, a bereaved person may be surprised and distraught by the physical pain of grief, and worry that physical illness is overtaking him or her. Interpretation of symptoms (hair loss, heart flutters, hot and cold flushes, etc.) in terms of grief can reassure the bereaved, although as we noted before, persistent physical symptoms should be checked by a doctor. The complexity and range of bereavement symptoms is shown in Table 2.1.

Finally, in providing both emotional and validational support it is essential to recognize *individual differences* in grieving and in coping styles. Thus, not all the bereaved can be helped in the same way. To take the example of bereavement-counseling services: These help some to assuage their grief. The sympathetic listening of another bereaved person who has got over his or her grief may make all the difference, as indeed the evaluation of such programs shows. But it is by no means the best method for everyone.

9.8.4 *Recovery and adjustment*

Aiding in the development of a new social identity. As time goes on, more social aspects of support become important to the bereaved. As acute grief subsides, the bereaved need encouragement to *withdraw from the deceased* and invest their time and energy in other relationships. Some bereaved persons are very reluctant to do this, since they feel it implies a disloyalty to the deceased person, or they reject the possibility of enjoying new friendships, since they feel no one can replace the lost spouse. Sometimes it helps the bereaved to be given "permission to stop grieving," as one counselor put it; in other words, to be told that it is not a dishonor to the memory of the deceased to put the past behind and invest in new, but different, relationships.

Advice on making life changes. Adjusting to the changed environment is a long and gradual process. The bereaved may be tempted to make drastic changes in their lives during this recovery phase. It is tempting for some to move from the place which is full of memories and reminders of the deceased, in the hope of making a fresh start. This should be discouraged: Those who have made such a move invariably regret it. Not only does it not help to diminish grief, but the bereaved person is displaced from his or her social support group and is left even more alone than would have been the case in the familiar environment. Judgment is often erratic when one is grief-stricken, and what seemed to be a good decision at the time may, in the long term, be very impractical. The same caution in making other life-changing decisions (e.g., changing jobs, decisions for the children, remarriage) needs to be advised too: In general, unless special circumstances dictate otherwise, a couple of years is not too little time to let lapse before planning a major upheaval. However, acquiring a job in the case of a widow who has spent much time at home caring for the deceased spouse, and who is thus left lonely and without a purpose to life, would clearly be good advice.

9.9 Implications

Undoubtedly, one of the most valuable aspects of talking to the bereaved in our own study was to learn how very different the reactions to loss are from one person to another. It soon became evident to us that what would be appropriate in trying to help one particular person could be quite inappropriate for another. This, combined with the fact that interactions with the grief-stricken are often perceived as difficult or awkward, can lead to a feeling of utter helplessness among those who wish to provide support. One general suggestion has emerged from our consideration of ways to lessen this bewilderment and increase the effectiveness of help, and that is for supporters to encourage the bereaved to take an active role in deciding how others behave toward them. Since it so often happens that offers of help are found to be unhelpful, or are misperceived by the recipient in some way, a more acceptable alternative might be to ask the bereaved person what he or she feels is most necessary and appropriate, rather than relying on one's own judgment as to what is appropriate. More concretely, the suggestion might take the following form: The supporter expresses concern and willingness to help, but admits to being at a loss concerning how to go about this (even to the point of finding condolences difficult to make). The bereaved can then be asked more specifically if, for example, they prefer to talk about the deceased (e.g., the events leading up to the death, joint experiences, etc.), or whether they would rather no reference were made to certain painful, or personal, or harrowing events. The same strategy can be followed with regard to other types of support: For example, one might ask the bereaved if they would like help with a specific task which had been undertaken previously by the partner, and for which it is likely that there is a deficit subsequent to the death. This avoids, on the one hand, a too unspecific type of offer, such as "Tell me if I can help," which many bereaved find hard to act upon, or, on the other hand, a too direct approach whereby the helper goes ahead and carries out some chore only to find that this is resented by the bereaved.

It is easy to visualize the advantages that this approach would have. For example, some bereaved express negative attitudes toward the clergy for visiting too soon after the death, others say that too much time had passed before they were visited, even though the actual duration of bereavement was similar in the two cases. Clearly, this is one of the situations that is very difficult to judge correctly in every case, but the angry reactions could probably have been avoided had the pastor approached the bereaved (at the funeral, if opportune, or by telephone) and simply asked if and when a visit would be desirable. Such an approach puts the bereaved person *in control* of what happens, and he or she is less likely to be resentful or angry in response to offers of assistance.

This suggestion is obviously not a general solution to all the complex tasks of helping the bereaved, and one should point out a number of potential difficulties: First, such openness is not always easy or appropriate; second, the bereaved in their distress may not always be the best judges of what will most help them, and third, there is the possibility that the strategy could lead to dependency on the supporter, instead of encouraging self-reliance which is ultimately desirable.

9.10 Final remarks

We have, throughout the book, drawn on the expertise and wisdom of very many researchers. One of the foremost of these is undoubtedly Erich

Lindemann, whose monumental contribution is so well documented in *Beyond Grief*, a collection of his classic papers. The final chapter of Lindemann's (1979) book is entitled "Reactions to One's Own Fatal Illness," for, tragically, Lindemann died in 1974, following a long and painful illness. Nowhere is Lindemann's depth of vision clearer than in this last talk, which he gave two years before his death to the radiation workers at Stanford Medical School, where he was both a professor and, at the time of the talk, a patient. Lindemann's fundamental belief in the therapeutic role of others, the need for their companionship, sharing, and openness, unfolds in these pages, as he transcends his own grief at impending death to suggest ways that may help others to come to terms with prospective death. The message that he offered is one that summarizes the underlying theme of our book. Just as the suffering of a dying patient may be relieved through the care and understanding of others, so may that of someone grieving for another. Lindemann eloquently termed this relationship the formation of a "therapeutic alliance," a phrase which conveys the nature of appropriate behavior most succinctly. It recognizes the other's suffering, gives affirmation for his or her individual style of coping, supports with companionship the effort at recovery, and avoids treating the griever as the "target of our ministrations." The health consequences of bereavement that we have described in the foregoing pages will, we believe, be reduced if it is possible to develop such therapeutic alliances.

References

Ablon, J. (1971). Bereavement in a Samoan community. *British Journal of Medical Psychology*, 44, 329–37.

Abrahams, R. B. (1972). Mutual help for the widowed. *Social Work*, 17, 54–61.

Abramson, L. Y., & Sackheim, H. A. (1977). A paradox in depression: Uncontrollability and self-blame. *Psychological Bulletin*, 84, 838–51.

Abramson, L. Y., Seligman, M. E. P., & Teasdale, J. D. (1978). Learned helplessness in humans: Critique and reformulation. *Journal of Abnormal Psychology*, 87, 49–74.

Ackerman, S. H., Manaker, S., & Cohen, M. I. (1981). Recent separation and onset of peptic ulcer disease in older children and adolescents. *Psychomatic Medicine*, 43, 305–10.

Ader, R. (Ed.). (1981). *Psychoneuroimmunology*. New York: Academic Press.

Agren, H. (1982). Depressive symptom patterns and urinary MHPG excretion. *Psychiatric Research*, 3,185–96.

Aguilar, I., & Wood, V. (1976). Therapy through a death ritual. *Social Work*, 21, 49–54.

Akiskal, H. S., & McKinney, W. T., Jr. (1973). Depressive disorders: Towards a unified hypothesis. *Science*, 182, 20–29.

Alexander, I. E., & Adlerstein, A. M. (1959). Death and religion. In H. Feifel (Ed.), *The Meaning of Death*. Maidenhead: McGraw-Hill.

Amir, Y., & Sharon, I. (1982). Factors in the adjustment of war widows in Israel. In C. D. Spielberger, I. G. Sarason, & N. A. Milgram (Eds.), *Stress and Anxiety* (Vol. 8). Washington D. C.: Hemisphere.

Amsel, A. (1962). Frustrative nonreward in partial reinforcement and discrimination learning. *Psychological Review*, 69, 306–28.

Anderson, C. (1949). Aspects of pathological grief and mourning. *Internal Journal of Psychoanalysis*, 30, 48–55

Arling, G. (1976). The elderly widow and her family, neighbors and friends. *Journal of Marriage and the Family*, 38, 757–68.

Atchley, R. C. (1975). Dimensions of widowhood in later life. *The Gerontologist*, 15, 176–8.

Averill, J. (1968). Grief: Its nature and significance. *Psychological Bulletin*, 70, 721–8.

Averill, J. (1979). The functions of grief. In C. E. Izard (Ed.), *Emotions in Personality and Psychopathology*. New York: Plenum.

Averill, J. R. (1982). *Anger and Aggression*. New York: Springer Verlag.

Bachrach, L. L. (1975). *Marital Status and Mental Disorder. An Analytic Review* (D.H.E.W. Publication No. ADM 75-217). Washington D.C.: U.S. Government Printing Office.

Bahnson, C. B. & Bahnson, M. B. (1964). Denial and repressions of primitive impulses and of disturbing emotions in patients with malignant neoplasms. In D. M. Kissen, & L. L. LeShan (Eds.), *Psychosomatic Aspects of Neoplastic Disease*. London: Pitman.

250

Bahr, H. M., & Harvey, C. D. (1979). Correlates of loneliness among widows bereaved in a mining disaster. *Psychological Reports,* 44, 367–85.

Bahr, H. M., & Harvey, C. D. (1980). Correlates of morale among the newly widowed. *Journal of Social Psychology,* 110, 219–33.

Ball, J. F. (1977). Widow's grief: The impact of age and mode of death. *Omega,* 7, 307–33.

Baltes, M. M. (1977). On the relationship between significant yearly events and time of death, random or systematic distribution. *Omega,* 8, 165–72.

Bankoff, E. (1981). The informal social network and adaptation to widowhood. Unpublished doctoral dissertation, University of Chicago.

Bankoff, E. (1983a). Aged parents and their widowed daughters: A support relationship. *Journal of Gerontology,* 38, 226–30.

Bankoff, E. (1983b). Social support and adaptation to widowhood. *Journal of Marriage and the Family,* 45, 827–39.

Barinbaum, L. (1976). Death of young sons and husbands. *Omega,* 7, 171–5.

Barrett, C. J. (1978). Effectiveness of widows' groups in facilitating change. *Journal of Consulting and Clinical Psychology,* 46, 20–31.

Barrett, C. J., & Schneweis, K. M. (1980). An empirical search for stages of widowhood. *Omega,* 11, 97–104.

Barth, F., (1974). On responsibility and humanity: Calling a colleague to account. *Current Anthropology,* 15, 99–102.

Bartrop, R. W., Luckhurst, E., Lazarus, L., Kiloh, L. G., & Penny, R. (1977). Depressed lymphocyte function after bereavement. *Lancet,* 97, 834–6.

Beck, A. T. (1967). *Depression: Clinical, Experimental, and Theoretical Aspects.* New York: Hoeber.

Beck, A. T. (1976). *Cognitive Therapy and the Emotional Disorders.* New York: International Universities Press.

Beck, J. C., & Worthen, K. (1972). Precipitating stress, crisis theory and hospitalization in schizophrenia and depression. *Archives of General Psychiatry,* 26, 123–9.

Becker, G. S. (1976). *The Economic Approach to Human Behavior.* Chicago, IL: University of Chicago Press.

Beilin, R. (1981). Social functions of denial of death. *Omega,* 12, 25–35.

Belitsky, R., & Jacobs, S. (1986). Bereavement, attachment theory, and mental disorders. *Psychiatric Annals,* 16, 276–80.

Bem, D. J. (1972) Self-perception theory. In L. Berkowitz (Ed.), *Advances in Experimental Social Psychology* (Vol. 6). New York: Academic Press.

Berardo, F. (1970). Survivorship and social isolation: the case of the aged widower. *The Family Coordinator,* 19, 11–25.

Berkman, L. F. (1984). Assessing the physical health effects of social networks and social support. In L. Breslow, J. F. Fielding, & L. B. Lave (Eds.), *Annual Review of Public Health.* Palo Alto, CA: Annual Reviews Inc.

Berkman, L. F., & Syme, S. L. (1979). Social networks, host resistance, and mortality: a nine-year follow-up of Alameda County residents. *American Journal of Epidemiology,* 109, 186–204.

Bernard, J (1968). *The Sex Game.* Englewood Cliffs, N.J.: Prentice Hall.

Bindra, D. (1972). Weeping: A problem of many facets. *Bulletin of the British Psychological Society,* 25, 281–4.

Birtchnell, J. (1980). Women whose mothers died in childhood. *Psychosocial Medicine,* 10, 699–713.

Birtchnell, J. (1981). In search of correspondence between age at psychiatric breakdown and parental age at death – "anniversary reactions." *British Journal of Medical Psychology,* 54, 111–20.

Birtchnell, J. & Kennard, J. (1981). Early-mother-bereaved women who have, and have not, been psychiatric patients. *Social Psychiatry,* 16, 187–97.

Blanchard, C. G., Blanchard, E. B., & Becker, J. V. (1976). The young widow: Depressive symptomatology throughout the grief process. *Psychiatry,* 39, 394–9.

Blankfield, A. (1983). Grief and alcohol. *American Journal of Drug Alcohol Abuse,* 9, 435–46.

Blau, D. (1975). On widowhood. Discussion. *Journal of Geriatric Psychiatry,* 8, 29–41.

Blazer, D. G. (1982). Social support and mortality in an elderly community population. *American Journal of Epidemiology* 115, 684–94.

Bloom, B. L. (1975). *Changing Patterns of Psychiatric Care.* New York: Behavioral Publications.

Bloom, B. L., Asher, S. J., & White, S. W. (1978). Marital disruption as a stressor: a review and analysis. *Psychological Bulletin,* 85, 867–94.

Blöschl, L. (1978). *Psychosoziale Aspekte der Depression.* Bern: Huber.

Bock, E. W., & Webber, I. L. (1972). Suicide among the elderly: Isolating widowhood and mitigating alternatives. *Journal of Marriage and the Family,* 34, 24–31.

Bojanovsky, J. (1977). Morbidität und Mortalität bei Verwitweten. *Fortschritte der Medizen,* 95, 593–6.

Bojanovsky, J. (1980). Wann droht der Selbstmord bei Verwitweten? *Schweizer Archiv Neurologische Neurochirurgie Psychiatrie,* 127, 99–103.

Bojanovsky, J., & Bojanovsky, A. (1976). Zur Risikozeit des Selbstmordes bei Geschiedenen und Verwitweten. *Nervenarzt,* 47, 307–9.

Bornstein, P., Clayton, P. J., Halikas, J. A., Maurice, W. L., & Robins, E. (1973). The depression of widowhood after 13 months. *British Journal of Psychiatry,* 122, 561–6.

Bowlby, J. (1960). Grief and mourning in infancy and early childhood. *Psychoanalytic Study of the Child,* 15, 9–52.

Bowlby, J. (1961). Processes of mourning. *International Journal of Psychoanalysis,* 42, 317–40.

Bowlby, J. (1971). *Attachment and Loss* (Vol. 1): *Attachment.* Harmondsworth: Pelican Books.

Bowlby, J. (1975). *Attachment and Loss* (Vol. 2): *Loss.* Harmondsworth: Penguin Books.

Bowlby, J. (1979). *The Making and Breaking of Affectional Bonds.* London: Tavistock.

Bowlby, J. (1981). *Attachment and Loss* (Vol. 3): *Loss: Sadness and Depression.* Harmondsworth: Penguin Books.

Boyd, J. H., & Weisman, M. M. (1982). Epidemiology. In E. S. Paykel (Ed.), *Handbook of Affective Disorders.* London: Churchill Livingstone.

Brady, J. P. (1958). Ulcers in "executive" monkeys. *Scientific American,* 254, 95–100.

Breckenridge, J., Gallagher, D., Thompson, L., & Peterson, J. (1986). Characteristic depressive symptoms of bereaved elders. *Journal of Gerontology,* 41, 163–8.

Brickman, P., Rabinowitz, V. C., Karuza, J., Coates, D., Cohn, E., & Kidder, L. (1982). Models of helping and coping. *American Psychologist,* 37, 368–84.

Briscoe, C. W., & Smith, J. R. (1975). Depression in bereavement and divorce: relationship to primary depressive illness: a study of 128 subjects. *Archives of General Psychiatry,* 32, 439–43.

Brown, G. W. (1982). Early loss and depression. In C. M. Parkes & J. Stevenson-Hinde (Eds.), *The Place of Attachment in Human Behavior.* New York: Basic Books.

Brown, G. W., & Harris, T. (1978). *Social Origins of Depression: A Study of Psychiatric Disorder in Women.* New York: Free Press.

Brown, J. T., & Stoudemire, G. A. (1983). Normal and pathological grief. *Journal of the American Medical Association,* 250, 378–82.

Brown, R. G. (1960). Family structure and social isolation. *Journal of Gerontology,* 15, 170–4.

Bunch, J. (1972). Recent bereavement in relation to suicide. *Journal of Psychosomatic Research,* 16, 361–6.

Bunney, W. E., Jr., & Davis, J. M. (1965). Norepinephrine in depressive reactions. A review. *Archives of General Psychiatry* 13, 483–94.

Bunney, W. E., Jr., Brodie, H. K. H., Murphy, D. L., & Goodwin, F. K. (1971). Studies of alpha-methyl-para-tyrosine, L-dopa, and L-tryptophan in depression and mania. *American Journal of Psychiatry,* 127, 48–57.

Burdette-Finn, P. M. (1980). Evaluation of a model for prevention of maladjustment in young widows. *Dissertation Abstracts International,* 40, 5–99.

Burgess, A. (1975). Family reaction to a homicide. *American Journal of Orthopsychiatry,* 45, 391–8.

Burton, R. (1977). *The Anatomy of Melancholy.* New York: Random House. (Originally published 1621).

Byrne, D. (1971). *The Attraction Paradigm.* New York: Academic Press.

Cain, A. C. (1972). *Survivors of Suicide.* Springfield, IL: Thomas.

Calhoun, L., Selby, J., & Abernathy, C. (1984). Suicidal death: Social reactions to bereaved survivors. *Journal of Psychology,* 116, 255–61.

Calhoun, L., Selby, J., & Walton, P. (1986). Suicidal death of a spouse: The social perception of the survivor. *Omega,* 16, 283–8.

Cameron, J., & Parkes, C. M. (1983). Terminal care: evaluation of effects on surviving family of care before and after bereavement. *Postgraduate Medical Journal,* 59, 73–8.

Campbell, D. T., & Stanley, J. C. (1963). Experimental and quasi-experimental designs for research and teaching. In N. L. Gage (Ed.), *Handbook of Research on Teaching.* Chicago, IL: Rand McNally.

Cannon, W. B. (1929). *Bodily Changes in Pain, Hunger, Fear, and Rage.* New York: Appleton.

Cantril, H., & Hunt, W. A. (1932). Emotional effects produced by the injection of adrenalin. *American Journal of Psychology,* 44, 300–7.

Carey, R. G. (1977). The widowed: A year later. *Journal of Counseling Psychology,* 24, 125–31.

Carey, R. G. (1979). Weathering widowhood: Problems and adjustment of the widowed during the first year. *Omega,* 10, 163–74.

Carter, H., & Glick, P. C. (1976). *Marriage and Divorce: A Social and Economic Study.* Cambridge, MA: Harvard University Press.

Caserta, M. S., Lund, D. A., & Dimond, M. F. (1985). Assessing interviewer effects in a longitudinal study of bereaved elderly adults. *Journal of Gerontology,* 40, 637–40.

Casey, R. L., Masuda, M., & Holmes, T. H. (1967). Quantitative study of recall of life events. *Journal of Psychosomatic Research,* 11, 239–47.

Cattell, R. B., Eber, H. W., & Tatsuoka, M. M. (1970). *Handbook for the 16 Personality Factor Questionnaire.* Champaign, IL: Institute for Personality and Testing.

Cawte, J. E. (1964). Australian ethno-psychiatry in the field: A sampling in North Kimberly. *Medical Journal of Australia,* 1, 467–72.

Chapman, L. J. (1967). Illusory correlation in observational report. *Journal of Verbal Learning and Verbal Behavior,* 6, 151–5.

Ciocco, A. (1940). On mortality in husbands and wives. *Human Biology,* 12, 508–31.

Clayton, P. J. (1974). Mortality and morbidity in the first year of bereavement. *Archives of General Psychiatry,* 30, 747–50.

Clayton, P. J. (1975). The effect of living alone on bereavement symptoms. *American Journal of Psychiatry,* 132, 133–7.

Clayton, P. J. (1979). The sequelae and nonsequelae of conjugal bereavement. *American Journal of General Psychiatry,* 136, 1,530–4.

Clayton, P. J., & Darvish, H. S. (1979). Course of depressive symptoms following the stress of bereavement. In J. Barrett, R. M. Rose & G. L. Klerman (Eds.), *Stress and Mental Disorder.* New York: Raven Press.

Clayton, P. J., Desmarais, L., & Winokur, G. (1968). *American Journal of Psychiatry,* 125, 168–78.

Clayton, P., Halikas, J., & Maurice, W. (1971). The bereavement of the widowed. *Diseases of the Nervous System,* 32, 597–604.

Clayton, P. J., Halikas, J. A., & Maurice, W. L. (1972). The depression of widowhood. *British Journal of Psychiatry,* 120, 71–8.

Clayton, P., Halikas, J., Maurice, W., & Robins, E. (1973). Anticipatory grief and widowhood. *British Journal of Psychiatry,* 122, 47–51.

Cobb, S., & Lindemann, E. (1943). Neuropsychiatric observations after the Coconut Grove fire. *Annals of Surgery,* 117, 814–24.

Cobb, S., & Rose, R. M. (1973). Hypertension, peptic ulcer, and diabetes in air traffic controllers. *Journal of the American Medical Association,* 224, 489–92.

Cohen, S., & McKay, G. (1984). Social support, stress, and the buffering hypothesis: A theoretical analysis. In A. Baum, J. E. Singer, & S. E. Taylor (Eds.), *Handbook of Psychology and Health* (Vol. 4). Hillsdale, N.J.: Erlbaum.

Cohen, S., & Wills, T. A. (1985). Stress, social support, and the buffering hypothesis. *Psychological Bulletin,* 98, 310–57.

Cohen-Cole, S., Cogen, R., Stevens, A., Kirk, K., Gaitan,E., Hain, J., & Freeman, A. (1981). Psychosocial, endocrine, and immune factors in acute necrotizing ulcerative gingivitis ("trenchmouth"). *Psychosomatic Medicine,* 43, 91 (Abstract).

Coppen, A. (1972). Indoleamines and affective disorders. *Journal of Psychiatric Research,* 9, 163–71.

Cornfeld, D., & Hubbard, J. P. (1961). A four-year study of the occurrence of beta-hemolytic streptococci in 64 schoolchildren. *New England Journal of Medicine* 264, 211.

Costello, C. G. (1972). Depression: Loss of reinforcer or loss of reinforcer effectiveness. *Behavior Therapy,* 3, 240–7.

Cottington, E. M., Matthews, K. A., Talbott, E., & Kuller, L. H. (1980). Environmental events preceding sudden death in women. *Psychosomatic Medicine,* 42, 567–74.

Cowan, M., & Murphy, S. (1985). Identification of postdisaster bereavement risk predictors. *Nursing Research,* 34, 71–5.

Cox, P. R., & Ford, J. R. (1964). The mortality of widows shortly after widowhood. *Lancet,* 1, 163–4.

Cox, T., (1978). *Stress.* London: Macmillan.

Crago, M. A. (1972). Psychopathology in married couples. *Psychological Bulletin,* 77, 114–28.

Crimmins, E. (1981). The changing pattern of American mortality decline, 1940–1977, and its implications for the future. *Population and Development Review,* 7, 229–54.

Crook, T., & Eliot, J. (1980). Parental death during childhood and adult depression: A critical review of the literature. *Psychological Bulletin,* 87, 252–9.

Culwick, A. T., & Culwick, G. M. (1935). *Ubena of the Rivers.* London: Allen & Unwin.

Dalton, B. W. (1981). The funeral director as grief counselor. In O. S. Margolis, H. C. Raether, A. H. Kutscher, J. B. Powers, I. B. Seeland, R. Debellis & D. J. Cherico (Eds.), *Acute Grief: Counseling the Bereaved.* New York: Columbia University Press.

Dattore, P-J., Shontz, F. C., & Coyne, L. (1980). Premorbid personality differentiation of cancer and noncancer groups: a test of the hypothesis of cancer proneness. *Journal of Consulting and Clinical Psychology* 48, 388–94.

Davis, G., & Jessen, A. (1982). A clinical report on group intervention in bereavement. *Journal of Psychiatric Treatment and Evaluation, 4,* 81–8.

Depue, R. A. (Ed.) (1979). *The Psychobiology of Depressive Disorders.* New York: Academic Press.

Depue, R. A., & Evans, R. (1981). The psychobiology of depressive disorders: From pathophysiology to predisposition. In B. A. Maher & W. B. Maher (Eds.), *Progress in Experimental Personality Research.* New York: Academic Press.

Deutsch, H. (1937). Absence of grief. *Psycho-Analytic Quarterly, 6,* 12–22.

Dimond, M. (1981). Bereavement and the elderly: a critical review with implications for nursing practice and research. *Journal of Advanced Nursing, 6,* 461–70.

Dohrenwend, B. P. (1979). Stressful life events and psychopathology: Some issues of theory and method. In J. E. Barrett & R. M. Rose (Eds.), *Stress and Mental Disorder.* New York: Raven Press.

Dohrenwend, B. P., & Dohrenwend, B. S. (1969). *Social Status and Psychological Disorder.* New York: Wiley.

Dohrenwend, B. S. (1973). Social status and stressful life events. *Journal of Personality and Social Psychology, 28,* 225–35.

Dohrenwend, B. S., & Dohrenwend, B. P. (1974). *Stressful Life Events: Their Nature and Effects.* New York: Wiley.

Durkheim, E. (1951). *Suicide: A Study in Sociology.* Glencoe IL: The Free Press. (Originally published, 1897).

Durkheim, E. (1976). *The Elementary Forms of Religious Life.* Great Britain: Allen & Unwin. (Originally published, 1915).

Eastman, C. (1976). Behavioral formulations of depression. *Psychological Review, 83,* 277–91.

Eaton, W. W. (1978). Life events, social supports, and psychiatric symptoms: A reanalysis of the New Haven data. *Journal of Health and Social Behavior, 19,* 230–4.

Eggert, D. (1983). *Eysenck-Persönlichkeits-Inventar.* Göttingen: Hogrefe.

Eisenbruch, M. (1984a). Cross-cultural aspects of bereavement. I: A conceptual framework for comparative analysis. *Culture, Medicine, and Psychiatry, 8,* 283–309.

Eisenbruch, M. (1984b). Cross-cultural aspects of bereavement. II: Ethnic and cultural variations in the development of bereavement practices. *Culture, Medicine, and Psychiatry, 8,* 315–47.

Ekblom, B. (1963). Significance of psychosocial factors with regard to risk of death among elderly persons. *Acta Psychiatrica Scandinavica, 39,* 627–33.

Ekman, P. (1971). Universal and cultural differences in facial expressions of emotion. In D. Levin (Ed.), *Nebraska Symposium on Motivation.* Lincoln, Neb.: University of Nebraska Press.

Ekman, P., & Friesen, W. V. (1971). Constants across cultures in the face and emotion. *Journal of Personality and Social Psychology, 17,* 124–9.

Eliot, T. D. (1946). War bereavements and their recovery. *Marriage and Family Living, 8,* 1–5.

Elizur, E., & Kaffman, M. (1983). Factors influencing the severity of childhood bereavement reactions. *American Journal of Orthopsychiatry, 53,* 668–76.

Engel, G. L. (1958). Studies of ulcerative colitis. V. Psychological aspects and their implications for treatment. *American Journal of Digestive Disease, 3,* 315–37.

Engel, G. L. (1977). The need for a new medical model: A challenge for biomedicine. *Science, 196,* 129–36.

Engel, G. L. (1978). Psychologic stress, vasodepressor (vasovagal) syncope, and sudden death. *Annals of Internal Medicine, 89,* 403–12.

Erdman, G., & Janke, W. (1978). Interaction between physiological and cognitive determinants of emotions: Experimental studies of Schachter's theory of emotion. *Biological Psychology*, 6, 61–74.

Eysenck, H. J., & Eysenck, S. B. G. (1964). *Manual of the Eysenck Personality Inventory*. London: University of London Press.

Faris, R., & Dunham, H. W. (1939). *Mental Disorders in Urban Areas*. New York: Hafner.

Farr, W. (1975). Influence of marriage on the mortality of the French People. In N. Humphreys, *Vital Statistics: A Memorial Volume of Selections from Reports and Writings of William Farr*. NY: Methuen: The Scarecrow Press (Originally published 1858).

Faschingbauer, T. R., Devaul, R. D., & Zisook, S. (1977). Development of the Texas inventory of grief. *American Journal of Psychiatry*, 134, 696–8.

Feighner, J. P., Robins, E., Guze, S. B., Woodruff, R. A., Jr., Winokur, G., & Munoz, R. (1972). Diagnostic criteria for use in psychiatric research. *Archives of General Psychiatry*, 26, 56–73.

Ferraro, K. F. (1985). The effect of widowhood on the health status of older persons. *International Journal of Aging and Human Development*, 21, 9–25.

Ferster, C. B. (1966). Animal behavior and mental illness. *Psychological Record*, 16, 345–56.

Ferster, C. B. (1973). A functional analysis of depression. *American Psychologist*, 28, 857–70.

Festinger, L. (1954). A theory of social comparison processes. *Human Relations*, 7, 117–40.

Firth, R. (1961). *Elements of Social Organization*. London: Tavistock Publications.

Fisher, J. D., Nadler, A., & Whitcher-Alagna, S. (1982). Recipient reactions to aid. *Psychological Bulletin*, 91, 27–54.

Flesch, R. (1969). The condolence call. In A. H. Kutscher (Ed.), *Death and Bereavement*. Springfield, IL: Charles C. Thomas.

Forrest, G. C., Standish, E., & Baum, J. D. (1982). Support after perinatal death: A study of support and counselling after perinatal bereavement. *British Medical Journal*, 285, 1,475–9.

Fox, A., & Goldblatt, P. (1982). *Longitudinal study: Sociodemographic Mortality Differentials 1971–1975*. Office of Population Censuses and Surveys. Series L.S., No. 1. London: Her Majesty's Stationery Office.

Fox, B. H. (1978). Premorbid psychological factors as related to cancer incidence. *Journal of Behavioral Medicine*, 1, 45–133.

Fox, S. S. (1985). Children's anniversary reactions to the death of a family member. *Omega*, 15, 291–306.

Frankel, S., & Smith, D. (1982). Conjugal bereavement among the Huli people of Papua, New Guinea. *British Journal of Psychiatry*, 141, 302–5.

Frazer, J. G. (1911). *The Dying God. The Golden Bough, Part III*. (3rd Edition). London: Macmillan.

Frazer, J. G. (1914). *Adonis, Attis, Osiris. The Golden Bough, Part IV* (Vol. 1; 3rd Edition). London: Macmillan.

Frazer, J. G. (1923). *Folk-Lore in the Old Testament*. New York: Tudor Publishing Company.

Fredrick, J. F. (1971). Physiological reactions induced by grief. *Omega*, 2, 71–5.

Fredrick, J. F. (1976). Grief as a disease process. *Omega*, 7, 297–305.

French, J. R. P., Jr., & Kahn, R. L. (1962). A programmatic approach to studying the industrial environment and mental health. *Journal of Social Issues*, 18, 1–47.

French, J. R. P., Jr., Rodgers, W., & Cobb, S. (1974). Adjustment and person–environment fit. In G. V. Coelho, D. A. Hamburg, & J. E. Adams (Eds.), *Coping and Adaptation*. New York: Basic Books.

Freud, S. (1917). Trauer und Melancholie. *Internationale Zeitschrift für ärztliche Psychoanalyse,* 4, 288–301.

Freud, S. (1923). *Das Ich und das Es.* Leipzig: Internationaler Psychoalytischer Verlag.

Freud, S. (1959). Mourning and Melancholia. *Collected papers* (Vol. 4). New York: Basic Books.

Friedman, M., & Rosenman, R. H. (1974). *Type A Behavior and Your Heart.* New York: Knopf.

Friedman, M., Byers, S. O., & Brown, A. E. (1967). Plasma lipid response of rats and rabbits to an auditory stimulus. *American Journal of Physiologiy,* 212, 1,174–8.

Friedman, M., Rosenman, R. H., & Carroll, V. (1958). Changes in serum cholesterol and bloodclotting time in men subjected to cyclic variation in occupational stress. *Circulation,* 17, 852–61.

Friedman, S. B., Ader, R., & Glasgow, L. A. (1965). Effects of psychological stress in adult mice inoculated with Coxsackie B viruses. *Psychosomatic Medicine,* 27, 361–8.

Frost, N. R., & Clayton, P. J. (1977). Bereavement and psychiatric hospitalization. *Archives of General Psychiatry,* 34, 1,172–5.

Gallagher, D. E., Breckenridge, J. N., Thompson, L. W., & Peterson, J. A. (1983). Effects of bereavement on indicators of mental health in elderly widows and widowers. *Journal of Gerontology,* 38, 565–71.

Ganellen, R. J., & Blaney, P. H. (1984). Stress, externality, and depression. *Journal of Personality and Social Psychology,* 52, 326–37.

Geertz, C. (1973). *The Interpretation of Cultures.* New York: Basic Books.

van Gennep, A. (1977). *The Rites of Passage.* London: Routledge and Kegan Paul. (Originally published, 1909).

Gerber, I., Rusalem, R., Hannon, N., Battin, D., & Arkin, A. (1975a). Anticipatory grief and aged widows and widowers. *Journal of Gerontology,* 30, 225–9.

Gerber, I., Wiener, A., Battin, D., & Arkin, A. M. (1975b). Brief therapy to the aged bereaved. In B. Schoenberg, A. C. Carr, A. H. Kutscher, D. Peretz, & I. Goldberg (Eds.), *Bereavement: Its Psychosocial Aspects.* New York: Columbia University Press.

Gersten, J. C., Langner, T. S., Eisenberg, J. G., & Orzek, L. (1974). Child behavior and life events: Undesirable change or change per se? In B. S. Dohrenwend & B. P. Dohrenwend (Eds.), *Stressful Life Events.* New York: Wiley.

Gillum, R., Leon, G. R., Kamp, J., & Becerra-Aldama, J. (1980). Prediction of cardiovascular and other disease onset and mortality from 30-year longitudinal MMPI data. *Journal of Consulting and Clinical Psychology,* 48, 405–6.

Glass, D. C. (1977). *Behavior Patterns, Stress, and Coronary Disease.* Hillsdale, N.J.: Erlbaum.

Glass, D. C., & Singer, J. E. (1972). *Urban Stress.* New York: Academic Press.

Glick, I., Weiss, R. S., & Parkes, C. M. (1974). *The First Year of Bereavement.* New York: Wiley.

Golan, N. (1975). Wife to widow to woman. *Social Work,* 20, 369–74.

Goldberg, D. P. (1972). *The Detection of Psychiatric Illness by Questionnaire.* Maudsley Monograph No. 21. London: Oxford University Press.

Goldberg, E. L., & Comstock, G. W. (1976). Life events and subsequent illness. *American Journal of Epidemiology,* 104, 146–58.

Goldberg, H. S. (1981). Funeral and bereavement rituals of Kota Indians and Orthodox Jews. *Omega,* 12, 117–28.

Goodwin, J. S., Bromberg, S., Staszak, C., Kaszubowski, P. A., Messner, R. P., & Neal, J. F. (1981). *Journal of Immunology,* 127, 518–22.

Gorer, G. D. (1965). *Death, Grief and Mourning.* New York: Doubleday.

Gove, W. R. (1972a). The relationship between sex roles, marital roles, and mental illness. *Social Forces,* 51, 34–44.

Gove, W. R. (1972b). Sex, marital status, and suicide. *Journal of Health and Social Behavior,* 13, 204–13.

Gove, W. R. (1973). Sex, marital status, and mortality. *American Journal of Sociology,* 79, 45–67.

Gove, W. R. (1979). Sex differences in the epidemiology of mental disorder; Evidence and explanations. In E. S. Gomberg & V. Franks (Eds.), *Gender and Disordered Behavior: Sex Differences in Psychopathology.* New York: Brunner/Mazel.

Gove, W. R. & Hughes, M. (1979). Possible causes of the apparent sex differences in physical health: An empirical investigation. *American Sociological Review,* 44, 126–46.

Gove, W. R. & Tudor, J. F. (1973). Adult sex roles and mental illness. *American Journal of Sociology,* 78, 812–35.

Gove, W., Hughes, M., & Style, C. (1983). Does marriage have positive effects on the psychological well-being of the individual? *Journal of Health and Social Behavior,* 24, 122–31.

Granville-Grossman, K. L. (1968). The early environment of affective disorder. In A. Capen & A. Walk (Eds.), *Recent Developments in Affective Disorders.* London: Headley Brothers.

Greenblatt, M. (1978). The grieving spouse. *American Journal of Psychiatry,* 135, 43–7.

Greene, W. W. (1966). The psychosocial setting of the development of leukemia and lymphoma. *Annals of the New York Academy of Sciences.* 125, 794–801.

Greer, D. S., Mor, V., & Sherwood, S., et al. (1983). National Hospice Study analysis plan. *Journal of Chronic Diseases,* 36, 737–80.

Hackett, T. P. (1974). Recognizing and treating abnormal grief. *Hospital Physician,* 10, 49–50, 56.

Hamilton, D. L., & Gifford, R. K. (1976). Illusory correlations in interpersonal perception: A cognitive basis of stereotypic judgments. *Journal of Experimental Social Psychology,* 12, 392–407.

Hammen, C. L. & Padesky, C. A. (1977). Sex differences in the expresion of depressive responses on the Beck Depression Inventory. *Journal of Abnormal Psychology,* 86, 609–14.

Hansson, R. O. (1986a). Relational competence, relationships, and adjustment in old age. *Journal of Personality and Social Psychology,* 50, 1,050–8.

Hansson, R. O. (1986b). Shyness and the elderly. In W. H. Jones, J. M. Check, & S. R. Briggs (Eds.), *A Sourcebook on Shyness: Research and Treatment.* New York: Plenum.

Harlow, H. F., & Mears, C. (1979). *The Human Model: Primate Perspectives.* New York: John Wiley.

Harvey, C. D., & Bahr, H. M. (1974). Widowhood, morale and affiliation. *Journal of Marriage and the Family,* 36, 97–106.

Hausmann, C. S. (1981). The expanding role of the funeral director as a counselor. In O. S. Margolis, H. C. Raether, A. H. Kutscher, J. B. Powers,I. B. Seeland, R. DeBellis, & D. J. Cherico (Eds.), *Acute Grief: Counseling the Bereaved.* New York: Columbia University Press.

Helsing, K. J., & Szklo, M. (1981). Mortality after bereavement. *American Journal of Epidemiology,* 114, 41–52.

Helsing, K. J., Szklo, M., & Comstock, G. W. (1981). Factors associated with mortality after widowhood. *American Journal of Public Health,* 71, 802–9.

Henderson, S., Byrne, D. G., & Duncan-Jones, P. (1981). *Neurosis and the Social Environment.* Sydney: Academic Press.

Henry, T. (1964). *Jungle People.* New York: Vintage. (Originally published 1941).

Herd, A. J. (1978). Physiological correlates of coronary-prone behavior. In T. M. Dembrowski, S. M. Weiss, J. L. Shields, S. G. Haynes, & M. Feinleib (Eds.). *Coronary-prone Behavior.* New York: Springer.

Hertz, R. (1907). Contribution à une étude sur la représentation collective de la mort. *Année Sociologique,* 10, 48–137.

Hertz, R. (1960). *Death and the Right Hand.* New York: Free Press.

Heyman, D. K., & Gianturco, D. T. (1973). Long-term adaptation by the elderly to bereavement. *Journal of Gerontology,* 28, 359–62.

Hilgard, J. R. (1953). Anniversary reactions in parents precipitated by children. *Psychiatry,* 16, 73–80.

Hiltz, S. R. (1975). Helping widows: Group discussions as a therapeutic technique. *Family Coordinator,* 24, 331–6.

Hinde, R. A., Spencer-Booth, Y., & Bruce, M. (1966). Effects of 6-day maternal deprivation on rhesus monkey infants. *Nature,* 210, 1,021–33.

Hinkle, L. E. (1974). The effect of exposure to cultural change, social change, and changes in interpersonal relationships on health. In B. S. Dohrenwend & B. P. Dohrenwend (Eds.), *Stressful Life Events: Their Nature and Effects.* New York: Wiley.

Hiroto, D. S. (1974). Locus of control and learned helplessness. *Journal of Experimental Psychology,* 102, 187–93.

Hiroto, D. S., & Seligman, M. E. P. (1975). Generality of learned helplessness in man. *Journal of Personality and Social Psychology,* 32, 311–27.

Hobson, C. (1964). Widows of Blackton. *New Society,* 14, 13.

Hochschild, A. R. (1979). Emotion work, feeling rules, and social structure. *American Journal of Sociology,* 85, 551–75.

Hodgkinson, P. E. (1982). Abnormal grief – the problem of therapy. *British Journal of Medical Psychology,* 55, 29–34.

Hofer, M. A., Wolff, S. B., Friedman, S. B., & Mason, J. W. (1972a). A psychoendocrine study of bereavement. *Psychosomatic Medicine,* 34, 481–91.

Hofer, M. A., Wolff, S. B., Friedman, S. B., & Mason, J. W. (1972b). A psychoendocrine study of bereavement. II. Observations of the process of mourning in relation to adrenocortical function. *Psychosomatic Medicine,* 34, 492–504.

Hollingshead, A. B., & Redlich, F. C. (1958). *Social Class and Mental Illness.* New York: Wiley.

Hollister, L. (1972). Psychotherapeutic drugs in the dying and bereaved. *Journal of Thanatology,* 2, 623–29.

Holmes, T. H., & Rahe, R. H. (1967). The social readjustment rating scale. *Journal of Psychosomatic Research,* 11, 213–18.

Holmes, T. H., & Masuda, M. (1974). Life change and illness susceptibility. In B. S. Dohrenwend & B. P. Dohrenwend (Eds.), *Stressful Life Events.* New York: Wiley.

Horne, R. L., & Picard, R. S. (1979). Psychosocial risk factors for lung cancer. *Psychosomatic Medicine,* 41, 503–14.

Horowitz, M., Wilner, N., & Alvarez, W. (1979). Impact of event scale: A measure of subjective distress. *Psychosomatic Medicine,* 4, 209–18.

Horowitz, M. J., Marmar, C., Weiss, D. S., DeWitt, K. N., & Rosenbaum, R. (1984). Brief psychotherapy of bereavement reactions. The relationship of process to outcome. *Archives of General Psychiatry,* 41,438–48.

Horowitz, M. J., Weiss, D. S., Kaltreider, N., Krupnick, J., Marmar, C., Wilner, N., & DeWitt, K. (1984). Reactions to the death of a parent: Results from patients and field subjects. *Journal of Nervous and Mental Disease,* 172, 383–92.

House, J. S. (1981). *Work Stress and Social Support.* Reading, MA: Addison-Wesley.

House, J. S., Robbins, C., & Metzner, H. L. (1982). The association of social relationships and activities with mortality: Prospective evidence from the Tecumseh Community Health Study. *American Journal of Epidemiology,* 116, 123–40.

Huntington, R., & Metcalfe, P. (1979). *Celebrations of Death: The Anthropology of Mortuary Ritual.* Cambridge: Cambridge University Press.

Huston, P. E. (1971). Neglected approach to cause and treatment of psychotic depression. *Archives of General Psychiatry,* 24, 505–8.

Izard, C. E. (1971). *Patterns of Emotions: A New Analysis of Anxiety and Depression.* New York: Academic Press.

Izard, C. (1977). *Human Emotions.* New York: Plenum.

Jackson, G. G., Dowling, H. F., Anderson, T. O., Riff, L., Saporta, J., & Turck, M. (1960). Susceptibility and immunity to common upper respiratory viral infections – The common cold. *Annals of Internal Medicine,* 53, 719–38.

Jacobs, S., & Ostfeld, A. (1980). The clinical management of grief. *Journal of American Geriatrics Society,* 28, 331–5.

Jacobs, S., Kasl, S., & Ostfeld, A. (1986). The measurement of grief: Bereaved versus non-bereaved. Unpublished manuscript.

Jacobs, S., Kosten, T., Kasl, S., Ostfeld, A., Berkman, L., & Charpentier, M. (1986). Attachment theory and multiple dimensions of grief. Unpublished manuscript.

Jacobs, S., Mason, J., Kosten, T., Kasl, S., Ostfeld, A., Atkins, S., Gardener, C., & Schreiber, S. (1985). Acute bereavement, threatened loss, ego defenses, and adrenocortical function. *Psychotherapy and Psychosomatics,* 44, 151–9.

James, W. (1950). *The Principles of Psychology* (Vol. 2). New York: Dover Publications. (Originally published 1890).

Jemmott, J. B., III, & Locke, S. E. (1984). Psychosocial factors, immunologic mediation, and human susceptibility to infectious diseases: How much do we know? *Psychological Bulletin,* 95, 78–108.

Jenkins, C. D. (1971). Psychological and social precursors of coronary disease. *New England Journal of Medicine,* 284, 244–55, 307–17.

Johnson, J. H., & Sarason, I. G. (1978). Life stress, depression, and anxiety: Internal–external control as a moderator variable. *Psychosomatic Research,* 22, 205–8.

Johnson, S. (1921). *The History of the Yorubas.* Lagos: Christian Missionary Society.

Jones, D. R., Goldblatt, P. O., & Leon, D. A. (1984). Bereavement and cancer: Some data on deaths of spouses from the longitudinal study of Office of Population Censuses and Surveys. *British Medical Journal,* 289, 461–4.

Jones, W. H. (1985). The psychology of loneliness: Some personality issues in the study of social support. In I. G. Sarason & B. R. Sarason (Eds.), *Social Support: Theory, Research, and Applications.* Dordrecht: Martinus Nijhoff.

Junod, H. A. (1927). *The Life of a South African Tribe.* London: Macmillan.

Justice, A. (1985). Review of the effects of stress on cancer in laboratory animals: Importance of time of stress application and type of tumor. *Psychological Bulletin,* 98, 108–38.

Kaprio, J., & Koskenvuo, M. (1983). Mortality after bereavement: A prospective study. Unpublished manuscript, Department of Public Health Science, Unviersity of Helsinki, Finland.

Kaprio, J., Koskenvuo, M., & Rita, H. (1986). Mortality after bereavement: A prospective study of 95,647 widowed persons. Unpublished manuscript.

Kasl, S. V., Evans, A. S., & Neiderman, J. C. (1979). Psychosocial risk factors in the development of infectious mononucleosis. *Psychosomatic Medicine,* 41, 445–6.

Kastenbaum, R. (1969). Death and bereavement in later life. In A. H. Kutscher (Ed.), *Death and Bereavement.* Springfield, IL: C. J. Thomas.

Katcher, A. H., Brightman, V., Luborsky, L., & Ship, I. (1973). Prediction of the incidence of recurrent herpes labiales and systematic illness from psychological measurements. *Journal of Dental Research,* 52, 49–58.

Katz, M. (1982). Background and development of the project. In C. Spielberger, I. Sarason, & N. A. Milgram (Eds.), *Stress and Anxiety,* Volume 8, Part IV, Wartime Bereavement. Washington D.C.: Hemisphere.

Kelley, H. H. (1973). The processes of causal attribution. *American Psychologist,* 28, 107–28.

Kerckhoff, A. C., & Davis, K. E. (1962). Value consensus and need complementarity in mate selection. *American Sociological Review,* 27, 295–303.

Kessler, R. C., Price, R. H., & Wortman, C. B. (1985). Social factors in psychopathology: Stress, social support, and coping processes. In M. R. Rosenzweig & L. W. Porter (Eds.), *Annual Review of Psychology.* Palo Alto, CA: Annual Reviews Inc.

Kitagawa, E., & Hauser, P. (1973). *Differential Mortality in the US: A Study in Socioeconomic Epidemiology.* Cambridge: Harvard University Press.

Klebba, A. J. (1970). *Mortality from Selected Causes by Marital Status: United States, Part A.* U.S. Department of Health Education and Welfare. Public Health Service.

Klein, D. C., Fencil-Morse, E., & Seligman, M. E. P. (1976). Learned helplessness, depression, and the attribution of failure. *Journal of Personality and Social Psychology,* 33, 508–16.

Klein, M. (1934). A contribution to the psychogenesis of manic-depressive states. In E. Jones (Ed.), *Contributions to Psychoanalysis.* London: Hogarth Press.

Klein, M. (1940). Mourning and its relation to manic-depressive states. *International Journal of Psycho-Analysis,* 21, 125–53.

Klerman, G. L. (1978). Affective disorders. In A. M. Nicholi, Jr. (Ed.), *The Harvard Guide to Modern Psychiatry.* Cambridge, MA: Harvard University Press.

Klerman, G. L., & Izen, J. E. (1977). The effects of bereavement and grief on physical health and general well-being. *Advances in Psychosomatic Medicine,* 9, 63–104.

Kobrin, F. E., & Hendershot, G. E. (1977). Do family ties reduce mortality? *Journal of Marriage and the Family,* 39, 737–45.

Koskenvuo, M., Sarna, S., Kaprio, J., & Lönnqvist, J. (1979). Cause-specific mortality by marital status and social class in Finland during 1969–1971. *Social Science and Medicine,* 13, 691–7.

Kramer, M. (1966). *Some Implications of Trends in the Usage of Psychiatric Facilities for Community Mental Health Programs and Related Research* (PHS Pub. No. 1434). Washington D.C.: U.S. Government Printing Office.

Kraus, A. S., & Lilienfeld, A. M. (1959). Some epidemiological aspects of the high mortality rate in the young widowed group. *Journal of Chronic Diseases,* 10, 207–17.

Kruglanski, A. W., & Jaffe, Y. (in press) Lay epistemology: a theory for cognitive therapy. In L. Y. Abramson (Ed.), *An Attributional Perspective in Clinical Psychology.* New York: Guilford.

Krupp, G., & Kligfeld, B. (1962). The bereavement reaction: A cross-cultural evaluation. *Journal of Religion and Health,* 1, 222–46.

Laird, J. D. (1984). The real role of facial response in the experience of emotion: A reply to Tourangeau and Ellsworth, and others. *Journal of Personality and Social Psychology,* 47, 909–17.

Landis, C., & Hunt, W. A. (1932). Adrenaline and avoidance learning. *Psychological Review,* 39, 467–85.

Lange, C. G. (1922). *The Emotions.* Baltimore: Williams & Wilkins. (Originally published in 1885).

Langner, T. S., & Michael, S. T. (1963). *Life Stress and Mental Health: The Midtown Manhattan Study.* New York: Free Press.

Laudenslager, M. L., & Reite, M. L. (1984). Losses and separations: Immunological consequences and health implications. In P. Shaver (Ed.), *Review of Personality and Social Psychology.* Beverly Hills, CA: Sage.

Lazarus, A. A. (1968). Learning theory and the treatment of depression. *Behavioral Research and Therapy,* 6, 83–90.

Lazarus, R. S. (1966). *Psychological Stress and the Coping Process.* New York: McGraw-Hill.

Lazarus, R. S., & Launier, R. (1978). Stress-related transactions between person and environment. In L. A. Pervin & M. Lewis (Eds.), *Perspectives in Interactional Psychology.* New York: Plenum.

Lazarus, R. S., & Folkman, S. (1984). *Stress, Appraisal, and Coping.* New York: Springer Publishing.

Lehmann, H. J. (1971). Epidemiology of depressive disorders. In R. Fieve (Ed.), *Depression in the Seventies: Modern Theory and Research.* Amsterdam, Excerta Medica.

LeShan, L. (1961). A basic psychological orientation apparently associated with malignant disease. *Psychiatric Quarterly,* 35, 314–30.

Levenson, H. (1973). Multidimensional locus of control in psychiatric patients. *Journal of Consulting and Clinical Psychology* 1973, 41, 397–404.

Leventhal, H. (1970). Findings and theory in the study of fear communication. In L. Berkowitz (Ed.), *Advances in Experimental Social Psychology* (Vol. 5). New York: Academic Press.

Leventhal, H. (1984). A perceptual-motor theory of emotion. In L. Berkowitz (Ed.), *Advances in Experimental Social Psychology* (Vol. 17). New York: Academic Press.

Levinger, G., & Breedlove, J. (1966). Interpersonal attraction and agreement: A study of marriage partners. *Journal of Personality and Social Psychology,* 3, 367–72.

Lewinsohn, P. M. (1974). Clinical and theoretical aspects of depression. In K. S. Calhoon, H. E. Adams, & K. M. Mitchell (Eds.), *Innovative Methods in Psychopathology.* New York: Wiley.

Lewinsohn, P. M., Youngren, M. A., & Grosscup, S. J. (1979). Reinforcement and depression. In R. A. Depue (Ed.), *The Psychobiology of Depressive Disorders.* New York: Academic Press.

Lieberman, M. A., & Videka-Sherman, L. (1986). The impact of self-help groups on the mental health of widows and widowers. *American Journal of Orthopsychiatry,* 56, 435–49.

Liem, R., & Liem, J. V. (1978). Social class and mental illness reconsidered: The role of economic stress and social support. *Journal of Health and Social Behavior,* 19, 139–56.

Lindemann, E. (1944). Symptomatology and management of acute grief. *American Journal of Psychiatry,* 101, 141–8.

Lindemann, E. (1950). Modifications in the course of ulcerative colitis in relationship to changes in life situations and reaction patterns. *Life Stress and Bodily Disease,* Association for Research in Nervous and Mental Disorders, 29, 706–23. (Reprinted in Lindemann, E. (1979). *Beyond Grief: Studies in Crisis Intervention.* New York: Aronson).

Lindemann, E. (1979). *Beyond Grief: Studies in Crisis Intervention.* New York: Aronson.

Lloyd, C. (1980). Life events and depressive disorder reviewed. *Archives of General Psychiatry,* 37, Part I: Events as predisposing factors 529–35. Part II: Events as precipitating factors 541–8.

Lopata, H. Z. (1973a). Living through Widowhood. *Psychology Today,* 7, 87–92.

Lopata, H. Z. (1973b). *Widowhood in an American City.* Morristown, N.J.: General Learning Press.

Lopata, H. Z. (1975). On widowhood. Grief work and identity reconstruction. *Journal of Geriatric Psychiatry.* 8, 41–55.

Lopata, H. Z. (1979). *Women as Widows: Support Systems.* New York: Elsevier.

Lowenthal, M. F., & Haven, C. (1968). Interaction and adaptation: Intimacy as a critical variable. *American Sociological Review,* 33, 20–30.

Lubin, B. (1965). Adjective checklists for the measurement of depression. *Archives of General Psychiatry,* 12, 57–62.

Luborsky, L., Mintz, J.,Brightman, V. J., & Katcher, A. H. (1976). Herpes simplex virus and moods: a longitudinal study. *Journal of Psychosomatic Research,* 20, 543–8.

Lund, D. A., Dimond, M., & Juretich, M. (1985). Bereavement support groups for the elderly: Characteristics of potential participants. *Death Studies,* 9, 309–21.

Lund, D., Caserta, M., & Dimond, M. (1986). Testing for gender differences through two years of bereavement among the elderly. *The Gerontologist,* 26, 314–20.

Lund, D., Dimond, M., Caserta, M., Johnson, R., Poulton, J., & Connelly, J. (1986). Identifying elderly with coping difficulties after two years of bereavement. *Omega,* 16, 213–24.

Lundin, T. (1984a). Morbidity following sudden and unexpected bereavement. *British Journal of Psychiatry,* 144, 84–8.

Lundin, T. (1984b). Long-term outcome of bereavement. *British Journal of Psychiatry,* 145, 424–8.

Lynch, J. J. (1977). *The Broken Heart: The Medical Consequences of Loneliness.* New York: Basic Books.

Maas, J. W., Fawcett, J. A., & Dekirmenjian, H. (1968). 3-Methoxy-4-hydroxyphenylglycol (MHPG) excretion in depressive states. *Archives of General Psychiatry,* 19, 129–34.

McCourt, W. F., Barnett, R. D., Brennen, J., & Becker, A. (1976). We help each other: Primary prevention for the widowed. *American Journal of Psychiatry,* 133, 98–100.

McGrath, J. E. (1976). Stress and behavior in organizations. In M. Dunette (Ed.), *Handbook of Industrial and Organizational Psychology.* Chicago: Rand McNally.

McIntosh, J. (1986). Survivors of suicide: A comprehensive bibliography. *Omega,* 16, 355–70.

MacMahon, B., & Pugh, T. F. (1965). Suicide in the widowed. *American Journal of Epidemiology,* 81, 23–31.

McNeill, D. N. (1973). Mortality among the widowed in Connecticut. Unpublished M.P.H. essay, Yale University.

McNeill-Taylor, L. (1983). *Living with Loss: A Book for the Widowed.* Glasgow: Fontana.

Maddison, D. (1968). The relevance of conjugal bereavement for preventive psychiatry. *British Journal of Medicine,* 41, 223–33.

Maddison, D. C., & Viola, A. (1968). The health of widows in the year following bereavement. *Journal of Psychosomatic Research,* 12, 297–306.

Maddison, D. C., & Walker, W. L. (1967). Factors affecting the outcome of conjugal bereavement. *British Journal of Psychiatry,* 113, 1,057–67.

Malinowski, B. (1982). *Magic, Science, and Religion.* London: Souvenir Press. (Originally published 1948).

Mandelbaum, D. G. (1959). Social uses of funeral rites. In H. Feifel (Ed.), *The Meaning of Death.* New York: McGraw-Hill.

Maranon, G. (1924). Contribution à l'étude de l'action émotive de l'adrénaline. *Revue Française d'Endocrinologie,* 2, 301–25.

March, L. (1912). Some researches concerning the factors of mortality. *Journal of the Royal Statistical Society.* 75, 505–38.

Margolis, O., Raether, H., Kutscher, A., Powers, J., Seeland, I., Debellis, R., & Cherico, D. (Eds.) (1981). *Acute Grief: Counseling the Bereaved.* New York: Columbia University Press.

Marris, P. (1958). *Widows and Their Families.* London: Routledge & Kegan Paul.

Maslach, C. (1978). The emotional consequences of arousal without reason. In C. E. Izard (Ed.), *Emotions in Personality and Psychopathology.* New York: Plenum.

Mathison, J. (1970). A cross-cultural view of widowhood. *Omega,* 1, 201–18.

Mawson, D., Marks, I. M., Ramm, L., & Stern, L. S. (1981). Guided mourning for morbid grief: A controlled study. *British Journal of Psychiatry,* 138, 185–93.

Mechanic, D. (1974). Discussion of research programs on relations between stressful life events and episodes of physical illness. In B. S. Dohrenwend & B. P. Dohrenwend (Eds.), *Stressful Life Events.* New York: Wiley.

Mechanic, D. (1978). *Medical Sociology.* New York: Free Press.

Mellström, D., Nilsson, A., Oden, A., Rundgren, A., & Svanborg, A. (1982). Mortality among the widowed in Sweden. *Scandinavian Journal of Social Medicine,* 10, 33–41.

Mendelson, M. (1982). Psychodynamics of depression. In E. S. Paykel (Ed.), *Handbook of Affective Disorders.* London: Churchill Livingstone.

Mielke, R. (1979). *Entwicklung einer deutschen Form des Fragebogens zur Erfassung interner vs. externer Kontrolle von Levenson (IPC).* Bielefelder Arbeiten zur Sozialpsychologie, 46.

Miller, J., & Garrison, H. H. (1982). Sex roles: The division of labor at home and in the workplace. In R. H. Turner & J. F. Short (Eds.), *Annual Review of Sociology.* Palo Alto, CA: Annual Reviews Inc.

Miller, N. E. (1980). A perspective on the effects of stress and coping on disease and health. In S. Levine & H. Ursine (Eds.), *Coping and Health.* New York: Plenum.

Miller, S. I., & Schoenfeld, L. (1973). Grief in the Navajo: psychodynamics and culture. *International Journal of Social Psychiatry,* 19, 187–91.

Miller, W. R., & Seligman, M. E. P. (1973). Depression and the perception of reinforcement. *Journal of Abnormal Psychology,* 82, 62–73.

Miller, W. R., & Seligman, M. E. P. (1975). Depression and learned helplessness in man. *Journal of Abnormal Psychology,* 84, 228–38.

Mineka, S., & Suomi, S. J. (1978). Social separation in monkeys. *Psychological Bulletin,* 85, 1,376–400.

Mitford, J. (1963). *The American Way of Death.* New York: Simon & Schuster.

Monjan, A. (1981). Stress and immunologic competence: Studies in animals. In R. Ader (Ed.), *Psychoneuroimmunology.* New York: Academic Press.

Mor, V., McHorney, C., & Sherwood, S. (1986). Secondary morbidity among the recently bereaved. *American Journal of Psychiatry,* 143, 158–63.

Morgan, L. A. (1976). A re-examination of widowhood and morale. *Journal of Gerontology,* 31, 687–95.

Morgan, L. A. (1981). Economic change at mid-life widowhood: A longitudinal analysis. *Journal of Marriage and the Family,* 43, 899–907.

Morgan, L. A. (1984). Changes in family interaction following widowhood. *Journal of Marriage and the Family,* 46, 323–31.

Murphy, D. L. (1972). Amine precursors, amines, and false neurotransmitters in depressed patients. *American Journal of Psychiatry,* 129, 55–62.

Murphy, G. E. & Robins, E. (1967). Social factors in suicide. *Journal of the American Medical Association,* 199, 81–6.

Murray, C. D. (1930). Psychogenic factors in the etiology of ulcerative colitis and bloody diarrhea. *American Journal of Medical Science, 180,* 239–48.

Myers, J. K., Lindenthal, J. J., & Pepper, M. P. (1974). Social class, life events, and psychiatric symptoms: A longitudinal study. In B. S. Dohrenwend & B. P. Dohrenwend (Eds.), *Stressful Life Events.* New York: Wiley.

Nadler, A., & Fisher, J. D. (1986). The role of threat to self-esteem and perceived control in recipient reaction to help: Theory development and empirical validation. In L. Berkowitz (Ed.), *Advances in Experimental Social Psychology* (Vol. 19). New York: Academic Press.

Nathanson, C. A. (1975). Illness and the feminine role: A theoretical review. *Social Science and Medicine, 11,* 13–25.

National Center for Health Statistics (NCHS) (1970). *Mortality from Selected Causes by Marital Status.* Vital and Health Statistics, Series 20, No. 8.

National Center for Health Statistics (1976a). *Differentials in Health Characteristics by Marital Status: United States 1971–1972.* Vital and Health Statistics, Series 10, No. 104. Washington D.C.: Government Printing Office.

National Center for Health Statistics (1976b). *Selected Symptoms of Psychological Distress.* Vital and Health Statistics, Series 11, No. 37. Washington, D.C.: Government Printing Office.

National Center for Health Statistics (1983). *Sex Differences in Health and Use of Medical Care – United States, 1979:* Vital and Health Statistics, Number 3, Issue 24. Washington D.C., U.S. Government Printing Office.

National Office of Vital Statistics (1956). *Mortality from Selected Cause by Marital Status. United States, 1949–1951, Vital Statistics – Special Reports,* Vol. 39, No. 7, U.S. Public Health Service.

Niemi, T. (1979). The mortality of male old-age pensioners following spouse's death. *Scandinavian Journal of Social Medicine, 7,* 115–17.

Noll, C. T. (1981). Grief and bereavement in the military. In O. S. Margolis, H. C. Raether, A. H. Kutscher, J. B. Powers, I. B. Seeland, R. DeBellis & D. J. Cherico (Eds.), *Acute Grief: Counseling the Bereaved.* New York: Columbia University Press.

Office of Population Censuses and Surveys (1978). *Occupational Mortality. The Registrar General's Decennial Supplement for England and Wales, 1970–1972.* Series DS No. 1. London: Her Majesty's Stationery Office.

Office of Population Censuses and Surveys (1986). *Mortality Statistics: Review of the Registrar General on Deaths in England and Wales, 1974.* Series DHI No. 16. London: Her Majesty's Stationery Office.

Osterweis, M. (1985). Bereavement and the elderly. *Aging, 348,* 5–41.

Osterweis, M., Solomon, T., & Green, M. (1984). *Bereavement: Reactions, Consequences, and Care.* Washington D.C.: National Academy Press.

Overmier, J. B., & Seligman, M. E. P. (1967). Effects of inescapable shock upon subsequent escape and avoidance learning. *Journal of Comparative and Physiological Psychology, 63,* 23–33.

Pare, W. P., Rothfeld, B., Isom, K. E., & Varady, A. (1973). Cholesterol synthesis and metabolism as a function of unpredictable shock stimulation. *Physiology and Behavior, 11,* 107–10.

Parkes, C. M. (1962). Reactions to bereavement. Unpublished M.D. thesis, University of London.

Parkes, C.M. (1964a). Recent bereavement as a cause of mental illness. *British Journal of Psychiatry, 110,* 198–204.

Parkes, C. M. (1964b). The effects of bereavement on physical and mental health: A study of the medical records of widows. *British Medical Journal, 2,* 274–9.

Parkes, C. M. (1965). Bereavement and mental illness. *British Medical Journal,* 38, 1–26.

Parkes, C. M. (1971a). Psychosocial transactions: A field for study. *Social Science and Medicine,* 5, 101–15.

Parkes, C. M. (1971b). Determination of outcome of bereavement. *Proceedings of the Royal Society of Medicine,* 64, 279.

Parkes, C. M. (1975a). Determinants of outcome following bereavement. *Omega,* 6, 303–23.

Parkes, C. M. (1975b). Unexpected and untimely bereavement: A statistical study of young Boston widows and widowers. In B. Schoenberg, I. Gerber, A. Wiener, D. Kutscher, Peretz, D. & Cam, A. (Eds.), *Bereavement: Its Psychological Aspects.* New York: Columbia University Press, 1975.

Parkes, C. M. (1979). Evaluation of a bereavement service. In A. De Vries, & A. Carmi (Eds.), *The Dying Human.* Ramat Gan, Israel: Turtledove, 389–402.

Parkes, C. M. (1980). Bereavement counselling: Does it work? *British Medical Journal,* 281, 3–10.

Parkes, C. M. (1985). Bereavement. *British Journal of Psychiatry,* 146, 11–17.

Parkes, C. M. (1986). *Bereavement: Studies of Grief in Adult Life.* London: Penguin. (Originally published 1972).

Parkes, C. M., & Brown, R. (1972). Health after bereavement: a controlled study of young Boston widows and widowers. *Psychosomatic Medicine,* 34, 449–61.

Parkes, C. M., & Weiss, R. S. (1983). *Recovery from Bereavement.* New York; Basic Books.

Parkes, C. M., Benjamin, B., & Fitzgerald, R. G. (1969). Broken heart: A statistical study of increased mortality among widowers. *British Medical Journal,* 1, 740–3.

Paulay, D. (1977). Slow death: One survivor's experience. *Omega,* 8, 173–9.

Paykel, E. S. (1985). Life stress, social support, and clinical psychiatric disorder. In I. G. Sarason & B. R. Sarason (Eds.), *Social Support: Theory, Research, and Applications.* Dordrecht: Martinus Nijhoff.

Paykel, E. S., Myers, J. K., Dienelt, M. N., Klerman, G. L., Lindenthal, J. J., & Pepper, M. P. (1969). Life events and depression: A controlled study. *Archives of General Psychiatry,* 22, 11–21.

Pedder, J. R. (1982). Failure to mourn, and melancholia. *British Journal of Psychiatry,* 141, 329–37.

Pennebaker, J. W. (1982). *The Psychology of Physical Symptoms.* New York: Springer Verlag.

Pennebaker, J. W., & Beall, S. (1986). Cognitive, emotional, and physiological components of confiding: Behavioral inhibition and disease. Unpublished manuscript.

Pennebaker, J. W., & O'Heeron, R. C. (1984). Confiding in others and illness rate among spouses of suicide and accidental death victims. *Journal of Abnormal Psychology,* 93, 473–6.

Perlin, S., & Schmidt, A. (1975). Psychiatry. In S. Perlin (Ed.), *A Handbook for the Study of Suicide.* New York: Oxford University Press.

Phillips, D. L., & Segal, B. (1969). Sexual status and psychiatric symptoms. *American Sociological Review,* 34, 58–72.

Pihlblad, C. T., & Adams, D. L. (1972). Widowhood, social participation, and life satisfaction. *Aging and Human Development,* 3, 323–30.

Pittmann, N. L. & Pittmann, T. S. (1979). Effects of amount of helplessness training and internal–external locus of control on mood and performance. *Journal of Personality and Social Psychology,* 37, 39–47.

Polak, P. R., Egan, D., Vandebergh, R., & Williams, W. V. (1975). Prevention in mental health: A controlled study. *American Journal of Psychiatry,* 132, 146–9.

Pollock, G. (1972). On mourning and anniversaries: The relationship of culturally constituted defense systems to intra-psychic adaptive processes. *Israel Annals of Psychiatry,* 10, 9–40.

Pouissaint, A. F. (1984). The grief response following a homicide. Paper presented at the 92nd Annual Convention of the American Psychological Association, Toronto, Canada.

Prange, A. J., Wilson, I. C., Knox, A. E., McClane, T. K., Breese, G. R., Martin, B. R., Alltop, L. B., & Lipton, M. A. (1972). Thyroid–imipramine clinical and chemical interaction. Evidence for a receptor deficit in depression. *Journal of Psychiatric Research,* 9, 187–205.

Preston, C. (1980). The clergy as bereavement counselors. In B. M. Schoenberg (Ed.). *Bereavement Counseling: A Multidisciplinary Handbook.* Westport, CT: Greenwood Press.

Purisman, R., & Maoz, B. (1977). Adjustment and war bereavement – some considerations. *British Journal of Medical Psychology,* 50, 1–9.

Rabin, P. L., & Pate, J. K. (1981). Acute grief. *Southern Medical Journal,* 74, 1,468–70.

Rabkin, J. G., & Struening, E. L. (1976). Life events, stress, and illness. *Science,* 194, 1,013–20.

Radcliffe-Brown, A. R. (1964). *The Andaman Islanders.* New York: Free Press. (Originally published, 1922).

Radloff, L. (1975). Sex differences in depression: The effects of occupation and marital status. *Sex Roles,* 1, 249–65.

Rahe, R. H. (1968). Life change measurement as a predictor of illness. *Proceedings of the Royal Society of Medicine,* 61, 1,124–6.

Rahe, R. H. (1979). Life change events and mental illness: An overview. *Journal of Human Stress,* 5, 2–10.

Rahe, R. H., & Arthur, R. J. (1978). Life change and illness studies: Past history and future directions. *Journal of Human Stress,* 4, 3–15.

Rahe, R. H., & Lind, E. (1971). Psychosocial factors and sudden cardiac death. A pilot study. *Journal of Psychosomatic Research,* 15, 19–24.

Rahe, R. H., & Paasikivi, J. (1971). Psychosocial factors and myocardial infarction. II. An outpatient study in Sweden. *Journal of Psychosomatic Research,* 15, 33–9.

Rahe, R. H., Meyer, M., Smith, M., Kjaer, G., & Holmes, T. (1964). Social stress and illness onset. *Journal of Psychosomatic Research,* 8, 35–44.

Rahe, R. H., Rubin, R. T., & Arthur, R. J. (1974). The three investigators' study: Serum uric acid, cholesterol, and cortisol variability during stresses of everyday life. *Psychosomatic Medicine,* 36, 258–68.

Rahe, R. H., Rubin, R. T., Arthur, R. J., & Clark, B. R. (1968). Serum uric acid and cholesterol variability. *Journal of the American Medical Association,* 206, 2,875–80.

Rahe, R. H., Rubin, R. T., Gunderson, E. K. E., & Arthur, R. J. (1971). Psychologic correlates of serum cholesterol in man: A longitudinal study. *Psychosomatic Medicine,* 33, 399–410.

Ramsay, R. W. (1977). Behavioural approaches to bereavement. *Behavioural Research Therapy,* 15, 131–5.

Ramsay, R. W. (1979). Bereavement: A behavioral treatment of pathological grief. In P. O. Sjoden, S. Bates, & W. S. Dorkens III (Eds.), *Trends in Behavior Therapy.* New York: Academic Press.

Rando, T. (1984). *Grief, Dying, and Death.* Champaign IL: Research Press Company.

Raphael, B. (1971). Crisis intervention: Theoretical and methodological considerations. *Australia and New Zealand Journal of Psychiatry,* 5, 183–90.

Raphael, B. (1977). Preventive intervention with the recently bereaved. *Archives of Geriatric Psychiatry,* 34, 1,450–4.

Raphael, B. (1978). Mourning and the prevention of melancholia. *British Journal of Medical Psychology,* 41, 303–10.

Raphael, B. (1980). A psychiatric model for counseling. In B. M. Schoenberg (Ed.), *Bereavement Counseling: A Multidisciplinary Handbook.* Westport: Greenwood Press.

Raphael, B. (1984). *The Anatomy of Bereavement: A Handbook for the Caring Professions.* London: Hutchinson.

Redick, R. W., & Johnson, C. (1974). *Marital Status, Living Arrangements, and Family Characteristics of Admissions to State and County Mental Hospitals and Outpatient Psychiatric Clinics: United States, 1970.* Statistical Note 100, N.I.M.H. Washington D.C.: U.S. Government Printing Office.

Rees, W., & Lutkins, S. (1967). Mortality of bereavement. *British Medical Journal,* 4, 13–16.

Registrar General (1971). *Statistical Review of England and Wales, Part III, 1967.* Office of Population Censuses and Surveys. London.

Reite, M., Short, R., Seiler, C., & Pauley, J. D. (1981). Attachment, loss, and depression. *Journal of Child Psychology and Psychiatry,* 22, 141–69.

Remondet, J. H., Hansson, R. O., Rule, B., & Winfrey, G. (1986). Rehearsal for widowhood. *Journal of Social and Clinical Psychology.*

Richards, J., & McCallum, J. (1979). Bereavement in the elderly. *The New Zealand Medical Journal,* 89, 201–4.

Robertson, J., & Bowlby, J. (1952). Responses of young children to separation from their mothers. *Courrier de la Centre Internationale de l'Enfance,* 2, 131–42.

Robertson, N. C. (1974). The relationship between marital status and risk of psychiatric referral. *British Journal of Psychiatry,* 124, 191–202.

van Rooijen, L. (1979). Widow's bereavement: Stress and depression after 1½ years. In I. G. Sarason & C. D. Spielberger (Eds.), *Stress and Anxiety,* (Vol. 6). Washington: Hemisphere.

Rosenblatt, P. C. (1981). Grief in crosscultural and historical perspective. In P. K. Pegg & E. Metze (Eds.), *Death and Dying.* London: Pitman.

Rosenblatt, P. C., & Burns, L. H. (1986). Long-term effects of perinatal loss. *Journal of Family Issues,* 7, 237–53.

Rosenblatt, P. C., Walsh, R. P., & Jackson, D. A. (1976). *Grief and Mourning in Cross-Cultural Perspective.* New Haven: Yale: HRAF.

Rosenman, L., Shulman, A., & Penman, R. (1981). Support systems of widowed women in Australia. *Australian Journal of Social Issues,* 16, 18–31.

Rubin, R. T., Gunderson, E. K. E., & Arthur, R. J. (1971). Life stress and illness patterns in the U.S. Navy. V. Prior life change and illness onset in a battleship crew. *Journal of Psychosomatic Research,* 15, 89–94.

Rubin, R. T., Miller, R. G., Clark, B. R., Poland, R. E., & Arthur, R. J. (1970). The stress of aircraft carrier landings. II. 3-methoxy-4-hydroxyphenylglycol excretion in naval aviators. *Psychosomatic Medicine,* 32, 589–96.

Rudestam, K. E. (1977). Physical and psychological responses to suicide in the family. *Journal of Consulting and Clinical Psychology,* 45, 162–70.

Rush, B. (1835). *Medical Inquiries and Observations upon the Diseases of the Mind.* Philadelphia: Grigg and Elliot.

Salzberger, R. C. (1975). Death: Beliefs, activities, and reactions of the bereaved – some psychological and anthropological observations. *The Human Context,* 7, 103–16.

Sanders, C. (1980). A comparison of adult bereavement in the death of a spouse, child, and parent. *Omega,* 10, 303–22.

Sanders, C. (1981). Comparison of younger and older spouses in bereavement outcome. *Omega*, 11, 217–32.

Sanders, C. (1983). Effects of sudden versus chronic illness death on bereavement outcome. *Omega*, 13, 227–41.

Sanders, C., Mauger, P. A., & Strong, P. N. (1979). *A Manual for the Grief Experience Inventory*. Loss and Bereavement Resource Center, University of South Florida.

Sarason, I. G., & Sarason, B. R. (Eds.) (1985). *Social Support: Theory, Research, and Applications*. Dordrecht: Martinus Nijhoff.

Sarason, I. G., Levine, H. M., Basham, R. B., & Sarason, B. (1983). Assessing social support: The social support questionnaire. *Journal of Personality and Social Psychology*, 44, 127–39.

Schachter, S. (1959). *The Psychology of Affiliation*. Stanford, CA: Stanford University Press.

Schachter, S. (1964). The interaction of cognitive and physiological determinants of emotional state. In L. Berkowitz (Ed.), *Advances of Experimental Social Psychology* (Vol. 1). New York: Academic Press.

Schachter, S., & Singer, J. E. (1962). Cognitive, social, and physiological determinants of emotional state. *Psychological Review* 69, 379–99.

Schaefer, D., Coyne, J. C., & Lazarus, R. S. (1981). The health-related functions of social support. *Journal of Behavioral Medicine*, 4, 381–406.

Schildkraut, J. J. (1965). The catecholamine hypothesis of affective disorders: A review of supporting evidence. *American Journal of Psychiatry*, 122, 509–22.

Schildkraut, J. J. (1978). Current status of the catecholamine hypothesis of the affective disorders. In M. Lipton, A. Dimascio, & K. Killam (Eds.), *Psychopharmacology: A Generation of Progress*. New York: Raven.

Schleifer, S. J., Keller, S. E., Camerino, M., Thornton, J. C., & Stein, M. (1983). Suppression of lymphocyte stimulation following bereavement. *Journal of the American Medical Association*, 250, 374–7.

Schmale, A. H. J., & Iker, H. P. (1966). The affect of hopelessness and the development of cancer. *Psychosomatic Medicine* 28, 714–21.

Schoenberg, B. M. (Ed.) (1980). *Bereavement Counseling: A Multidisciplinary Handbook*. Westport, CT: Greenwood Press.

Schoenberg, R., Carr, A. C., Kutscher, A. H., Peretz, D., & Goldberg, I. (Eds.), (1974). *Anticipatory Grief*. New York: Columbia University Press.

Schroeder, D. H., & Costa, P. T., Jr. (1984). Influence of life event stress on physical illness: Substantive effects or methodological flaws? *Journal of Personality and Social Psychology*, 46, 853–63.

Seay, B., Hansen, E., & Harlow, H. F. (1962). Mother–infant separation in monkeys. *Journal of Child Psychology and Psychiatry*, 3, 123–32.

Seligman, M. E. P. (1972). Learned helplessness. *Annual Review of Medicine*, 23, 407–12.

Seligman, M. E. P. (1975). *Helplessness*. San Francisco, CA: W. H. Freeman.

Seligman, M. E. P., & Maier, S. F. (1967). Failure to escape traumatic shock. *Journal of Experimental Psychology*, 74, 1–9.

Seligman, M. E. P., Maier, S. F., & Solomon, R. L. (1971). Unpredictable and uncontrollable aversive events. In F. R. Brush (Ed.), *Aversive Conditioning and Learning*. New York: Academic Press.

Selye, H. (1936). A syndrome produced by diverse nocuous agents. *Nature*, 138, 32.

Selye, H. (1976). *The Stress of Life*. New York: McGraw Hill (2nd ed.).

Sen, P. (1980). The role of the nursing profession in loss management. In B. M. Schoenberg (Ed.), *Bereavement Counseling: A Multidisciplinary Handbook*. Westport, CT: Greenwood Press.

Shekelle, R. B., Raynor, Jr., W. J., Ostfeld, A. M., Garron, D. C., Biellauskas, L. A., Liu, S. C., Maliza, C., & Oglesby, P. (1981). Psychological depression and 17-year risk of death from cancer. *Psychosomatic Medicine, 43*, 117–25.

Sheldon, A. R., Cochrane, J., Vachon, M. L. S., Lyall, W., Rogers, J., & Freeman, S. (1981). A psychosocial analysis of risk of psychological impairment following bereavement. *The Journal of Nervous and Mental Disease,* 169, 253–5.

Shepherd, D., & Barraclough, B. M. (1974). The aftermath of suicide. *British Medical Journal,* 2, 600–3.

Sheskin, A., & Wallace, S. E. (1976). Differing bereavements: Suicide, natural, and accidental death. *Omega, 7*, 229–42.

Shneidman, E. S. (1969). Prologue: Fifty-eighth year. In E. S. Shneidman (Ed.), *On the Nature of Suicide.* San Francisco: Jossey-Bass.

Shoham-Salomon, V., Vakstein, H., & Kruglanski, A. (1986). The differential pattern of bereavement of military and civilian widows in Israel. Paper presented at the 21st International Congress of Applied Psychology, Jerusalem, Israel.

Shurtleff, D. (1955). Mortality and marital status. *Public Health Reports, 70*, 248–52.

Shurtleff, D. (1956). Mortality among the married. *Journal of the American Geriatrics Society, 4*, 654–66.

Silver, R. (1986). The presence and nature of ruminations following loss of a loved one. Paper presented at the 21st International Congress of Applied Psychology, Jerusalem, Israel.

Silver, R., & Wortman, C. (1980). Coping with undesirable life events. In J. Garber & M. E. P. Seligman (Eds.), *Human Helplessness: Theory and Applications.* New York: Academic Press.

Silverman, C. (1968). *The Epidemiology of Depression.* Baltimore, MD: Johns Hopkins University Press.

Silverman, P. (1969). The Widow-to-Widow Program: An experiment in preventive intervention. *Mental Hygiene, 53*, 333–7.

Silverman, P. R. (1972). Widowhood and preventive intervention. *Family Coordinator, 21*, 95–102.

Silverman, P. R. (1976). The widow as caregiver in a program of preventive intervention with other widows. In C. G. Killelie (Ed.), *Support Systems and Mutual Help.* New York: Grune & Stratton.

Silverman, P. R., & Cooperband, A. (1975). On widowhood: Mutual help and the elderly widow. *Journal of Geriatric Psychiatry, 8*, 9–27.

Sines, J. O., Cleeland, C., & Adkins, J. (1963). The behavior of normal and stomach lesion susceptible rats in several learning situations. *Journal of Genetic Psychology, 102*, 91–4.

Singh, B., & Raphael, B. (1981). Postdisaster morbidity of the bereaved. *Journal of Nervous and Mental Diseases, 169*, 203–12.

Sklar, L. S., & Anisman, H. (1981). Stress and cancer. *Psychological Bulletin, 369–406.*

Smith, E. E., Johnson, J. H., & Sarason, I. G. (1978). Life change, the sensation-seeking motive, and psychological distress. *Journal of Consulting and Clinical Psychology, 46*, 348–9.

Smith, W. J. (1978). The etiology of depression in a sample of elderly widows: A research report. *Journal of Geriatric Psychiatry, 11*, 81–3.

Solomon, G. F. (1969). Emotions, stress, the CNS, and immunity. *Annals of the New York Academy of Sciences, 164*, 335–43.

Spiegel, Y. (1978). *The Grief Process.* London: SCM Press.

Spiegelman, M. (1960). Factors in human mortality. *Biology of Aging.* Symposium No. 6, American Institute of Biological Sciences, Washington D.C.

Spielberger, C., Sarason, I., & Milgram, N. A. (1982). *Stress and Anxiety* (Vol. 8), Part IV, Wartime Bereavement. Washington D.C.: Hemisphere.

Stack, J. M. (1982). Grief reactions and depression in family practice: Differential diagnosis and treatment. *Journal of Family Practice,* 14, 271–5.

Stafford, R., Backman, E., Dibona, P. J. (1977). The division of labor among cohabiting and married couples. *Journal of Marriage and the Family,* 39, 43–58.

Statistisches Jahrbuch für die Bundesrepublik Deutschland (1978). Stuttgart: Kohlhammer.

Steele, R. L. (1977). Dying, death, and bereavement among the Maya Indians of Meso-america: A study of anthropological psychology. *American Psychologist,* 32, 1,060–8.

Stein, Z., & Susser, M. W. (1969). Widowhood and mental illness. *British Journal of Preventive and Social Medicine,* 23, 106–10.

Steiner, I. D. (1972). *Group Process and Productivity.* New York: Academic Press.

Stern, K., Williams, G. M., & Prados, M. (1951). Grief reactions in later life. *American Journal of Psychiatry,* 108, 289–94.

Strachey, L. (1971) *Queen Victoria.* Harmondsworth: Penguin Books. (Originally published, 1921).

Stroebe, M. S. (1984). It's representative, but is it interesting? *Contemporary Psychology,* 29, 812–13.

Stroebe, M. S., & Stroebe, W. (1983). Who suffers more? Sex differences in health risks of the widowed. *Psychological Bulletin,* 93, 279–301.

Stroebe, M. S. & Stroebe, W. (1985). Social support and the alleviation of loss. In I. G. Sarason & B. R. Sarason (Eds.), *Social Support: Theory, Research, and Applications.* Dordrecht: Martinus Nijhoff.

Stroebe, M. S., Stroebe, W., Gergen, K. J., & Gergen, M. (1981). The broken heart: Reality or myth? *Omega,* 12, 87–105.

Stroebe, W., & Frey, B. S. (1980). In defence of economic man: Towards an integration of economics and psychology. *Schweizer Zeitschrift für Volkswirtschaft und Statistik,* 2, 119–48.

Stroebe, W., & Stroebe, M. S. (1984) When love dies: An integration of attraction and bereavement research. In H. Tajfel (Ed.), *The Social Dimension* (Vol. 1). Cambridge, England: Cambridge University Press.

Stroebe, W., & Stroebe, M. S. (1986). Beyond marriage: The impact of partner loss on health. In R. Gilmour & S. Duck (Eds.), *The Emerging Field of Personal Relationships.* Hillsdale, N.J.: Erlbaum.

Stroebe, W., Eagly, A. H., & Stroebe, M. S. (1977). Friendly or just polite? The effect of self-esteem on attribution. *European Journal of Social Psychology,* 7, 1–10.

Stroebe, W., Stroebe, M. S., & Domittner, G. (1985). The impact of recent bereavement on the mental and physical health of young widows and widowers. Reports from the Psychological Institute of Tübingen University.

Stroebe, W., Insko, C., Thompson, V. D., & Layton, B. (1971). The effects of physical attractiveness, attitude similarity, and sex on various aspects of interpersonal attraction. *Journal of Personality and Social Psychology,* 18, 79–91.

Stroebe, W., Stroebe, M. S., Gergen, K., & Gergen, M. (1980). Der Kummer Effekt: Psychologische Aspekte der Sterblichkeit von Verwitweten. *Psychologische Beiträge,* 22, 1–26.

Stroebe, W., Stroebe, M. S., Gergen, K. J., & Gergen, M. (1982). The effects of bereavement on mortality: A social psychological analysis. In J. R. Eiser (Ed.), *Social Psychology and Behavioral Medicine.* Chichester: Wiley.

Surtees, P. G. (1980). Social support, residual adversity, and depressive outcome. *Social Psychiatry,* 15, 71–80.

Tajfel, H. (1978). Social categorization, social identity, and social comparison. In H. Tajfel (Ed.), *Differentiation between Social Groups*. London: Academic Press.

Taube, C. A. (1970). *Admission Rates by Marital Status: Outpatient Psychiatric Services, 1969*. Statistical Note 35. Washington, D.C.: National Institute of Mental Health.

Taylor, S. E. (1983). Adjustment to threatening events: A theory of cognitive adaptation. *American Psychologist*, 38, 1,161–73.

Tennant, C., Bebbington, P., & Hurry, J. (1980). Parental death in childhood and risk of adult depressive disorders: A review. *Psychological Medicine*, 10, 289–99.

Tessler, R., Mechanic, D., & Dimond, M. (1976). The effect of psychological distress on physician utilization: A prospective study. *Journal of Health and Social Behavior*, 17, 353–64.

Theorell, T., & Rahe, R. H. (1971). Psychosocial factors and myocardial infarction. I. An inpatient study in Sweden. *Journal of Psychosomatic Research*, 15, 25–31.

Theorell, T., Lind, E., & Floderus, B. (1975). The relationship of disturbing life changes and emotions to the early development of myocardial infarction and other serious illnesses. *International Journal of Epidemiology*, 4, 281–93.

Thompson, L. W., Breckenridge, J. N., Gallagher, D., & Peterson, J. (1984). Effects of bereavement on self-perceptions of physical health in elderly widows and widowers. *Journal of Gerontology*, 39, 309–14.

Thornton, J. W., & Jacobs, P. D. (1971). Learned helplessness in human subjects. *Journal of Experimental Psychology*, 87, 351–67.

Tomkins, S. S. (1962). *Affect, Imagery, Consciousness* (Vol. 1). *The Positive Affects*. New York: Springer.

Tomkins, S. S. (1963). *Affect, Imagery, Consciousness* (Vol. 2). *The Negative Affects*. New York: Springer.

Totman, R. G., & Kiff, J. (1979). Life stress and susceptibility to colds. In D. J. Osborne, M. M. Gruneberg, & J. R. Eiser (Eds.), *Research in Psychology and Medicine* (Vol. 1). New York: Academic Press.

Tourangeau, R., & Ellsworth, P. C. (1979). The role of facial response in the experience of emotion. *Journal of Personality and Social Psychology*, 37, 1,519–31.

Troubridge, L. (1979). *A Book of Etiquette*. Kingswood: Cedar Books. (Originally published, 1929).

Turnbull, C. (1972). *The Mountain People*. New York: Simon & Schuster.

Vachon, M. L. S. (1976). Grief and bereavement following the death of a spouse. *Canadian Psychiatric Association Journal*, 21, 35–44.

Vachon, M. L. S. (1979). Identity change over the first two years of bereavement: Social relationships and social support in widowhood. Unpublished doctoral dissertation. University of York (Canada).

Vachon, M. L. S., Lyall, W. A. L., Rogers, J., Freedman-Leftofsky, K., & Freeman, S. J. J. (1980). A controlled study of self-help intervention for widows. *American Journal of Psychiatry*, 137, 1,380–4.

Vachon, M. L. S., Rogers, J., Lyall, W. A., Lancee, W. J., Sheldon, A. R., & Freeman, S. J. (1982). Predictors and correlates of adaptation to conjugal bereavement. *American Journal of Psychiatry*, 139, 998–1,002.

Vachon, M. L. S., Sheldon, A. R., Lancee, W. J., Lyall, W. A. L., Rogers, J., & Freeman, S. J. J. (1982). Correlates of enduring distress patterns following bereavement: Social network, life situation, and personality. *Psychological Medicine*, 12, 783–8.

Valanis, B., & Yeaworth, R. (1982). Ratings of physical and mental health in the older bereaved. *Research in Nursing and Health*, 5, 137–46.

Vargas, L. A., Loya, F., & Vargas, J. (1984). Grief across modes of death in three ethnic groups. Paper presented at the 92nd Annual Convention of the American Psychological Association, Toronto, Canada.

Videka-Sherman, L., & Lieberman, M. (1985). The effects of self-help and psychotherapy intervention on child loss: The limits of recovery. *American Journal of Orthopsychiatry,* 55, 70–82.

Volkan, V. (1970). Typical findings in pathological grief. *Psychiatric Quarterly,* 44, 231–50.

Volkart, E. H., & Michael, S. T. (1957). Bereavement and Mental Health. In A. H. Leighton, J. A. Clausen, & R. N. Wilson (Eds.), *Explorations in Social Psychiatry.* New York: Basic Books.

Wahl, C. W. (1970). The differential diagnosis of normal and neurotic grief following bereavement. *Archives of the Foundation of Thanatology,* 1, 137–41.

Walker, K. N., MacBride, A., & Vachon, M. L. S. (1977). Social support and the crisis of bereavement. *Social Science and Medicine,* 2, 35–41.

Wallace, S. E. (1973). *After Suicide.* New York: Wiley.

Walls, N., & Meyers, A. W. (1985). Outcome in group treatments for bereavement: Experimental results and recommendations for clinical practice. *International Journal of Mental Health,* 13, 126–47.

Ward, A. W. (1976). Mortality of bereavement. *British Medical Journal,* 1, 700–2.

Warner, S. (1985). Grief and bereavement: A review. *Psychiatric Nursing,* 26, 12–14.

Weiner, H., Thaler, M., Reiser, M., & Mirsky, I. A. (1957). Etiology of duodenal ulcer. I. Relation of specific psychological characteristics to rate of gastric secretion (serum pepsinogen). *Psychosomatic Medicine* 19, 1–10.

Weiss, J. M. (1977). Psychological and behavioral influences on gastrointestinal lesions in animal models. In J. D. Maser & M. E. P. Seligman (Eds.), *Psychopathology: Experimental Models.* San Francisco, CA: Freeman.

Weiss, J. M. (1984). Behavioral and psychological influences on gastrointestinal pathology: Experimental techniques and findings. In W. D. Gentry (Ed.), *Handbook of Behavioral Medicine.* New York: Guilford.

Weiss, J. M., Glazer, H. I., Pohorecky, L. A., Bailey, W. H., & Schneider, L. H. (1979). Coping behavior and stress-induced behavioral depression: Studies of the role of brain catecholamines. In R. A. Depue (Ed.), *The Psychobiology of Depression.* New York: Academic Press.

Weissman, M. M., & Klerman, G. L. (1977). Sex differences and the epidemiology of depression. *Archives of General Psychiatry,* 34, 98–111.

Wenz, F. (1977). Marital status, anomie, and forms of social isolation: A case of high suicide rate among the widowed in an urban sub-area. *Diseases of the Nervous System,* 38, 891–5.

Wheaton, B. (1983). Stress, personal coping resources, and psychiatric symptoms: An investigation of interactive models. *Journal of Health and Social Behavior,* 24, 208–29.

Wikan, U. (1986). The role of emotions in Balinese popular health care. Unpublished Manuscript. Ethnographic Museum of the University of Oslo.

Willner, P. (1985). *Depression: A Psychobiological Synthesis.* Chichester: Wiley.

Wingard, D. L. (1984). The sex differential in morbidity, mortality, and lifestyle. In L. Breslow, J. E. Fielding & L. B. Lave (Eds.), *Annual Review of Public Health* (Vol. 5). Palo Alto: Annual Reviews Inc.

Winton, W. M. (1986). The role of facial response in self-reports of emotion: A critique of Laird. *Journal of Personality and Social Psychology,* 50, 808–12.

Worden, J. W. (1982). *Grief Counseling and Grief Therapy: A Handbook for the Mental Health Practitioner.* New York: Springer.

World Health Organization (1968). *Prevention of Suicide* (Public Health Paper No. 35), Geneva.

Wortman, C., & Brehm, J. W. (1976). Responses to uncontrollable outcomes: An integration of reactance theory and the learned helplessness model. In L. Berkowitz (Ed.), *Advances in Experimental Social Psychology* (Vol. 8). New York: Academic Press.

Wortman, C. B., & Lehman, D. R. (1985). Reactions to victims of life crises: Support attempts that fail. In I. Sarason & B. Sarason (Eds.), *Social Support: Theory, Research and Applications*. Dordrecht: Martinus Nijhoff.

Wretmark, G. (1959). A study in grief reactions. *Acta Psychiatrica et Neurologica Scandinavica Supplement, 136,* 292–9.

Yamamoto, J. (1970). Cultural factors in loneliness, death, and separation. *Medical Times, 98,* 177–83.

Yamamoto, J., Okonogi, K., Iwasaki, T., & Yoshimura, S. (1969). Mourning in Japan. *American Journal of Psychiatry, 126,* 74–182.

Young, M., Benjamin, B., & Wallis, C. (1963). Mortality of widowers. *Lancet, 2,* 254–6.

Zisook, S. & Shuchter, S. (1986). The first four years of widowhood. *Psychiatric Annals, 16,* 288–94.

Zisook, S., DeVaul, R. A., & Click, M. A. (1982). Measuring symptoms of grief and bereavement. *American Journal of Psychiatry, 139,* 1,590–3.

Author index

Subject index

accidental death (*see also* causes of death; mortality; risk factors in bereavement outcome)
  bereavement following, 163, 164, 204
  during bereavement, 102
affective disorders in bereavement, *see* depression; mental illness
age, *see* risk factors in bereavement outcome
agitation in grief, 10
aggression in bereavement reactions, 10, 240
alcohol
  alcoholism in bereavement, 102, 103, 141, 142
  consumption in bereavement, 12
ambivalent relationships, *see* conjugal bereavement; risk factors in bereavement outcome
anger in bereavement, 8, 10, 240
anhedonia in bereavement, 10
anniversary reactions in bereavement, 15
anticipatory grief, 214, 215
anxiety in bereavement reactions, 10, 60–4
appetite disturbances during bereavement, 11
appraisal, cognitive, 88, 89
attachment (*see also* theories of grief), 60–4
  animal models, 61, 62
  between marital partners, *see* health consequences of bereavement; risk factors in bereavement outcome

bereavement (*see also* conjugal bereavement; health consequences of bereavement; risk factors in bereavement outcome; type of loss)
  definition of, 7
broken heart, 1, 163–5, 201
buffering hypothesis, 215, 216, 219

cancer, 106–9
  bereavement reactions following death from, 205
  cause of death of bereaved, 163–5
  and hopelessness, 107, 108
cardiovascular diseases
  cause of death of bereaved, 163–5
  coronary heart disease, 109–11, 163–5
causes of death (*see also entries for specific causes;* mortality; risk factors in bereavement outcome), 163–7, 209–15
childhood bereavement and loss in later life, 200–1
chronic illness and bereavement reactions, 204–9, 214, 215
cirrhosis, *see* alcohol
  cause of death of bereaved, 163–5
condolences (*see also* social support), 238, 242, 243
conjugal bereavement, *see* health consequences of bereavement; risk factors in bereavement outcome
control, 69–74
  emotion, 96–9
  locus of (internal, external), 99, 196, 197
  loss of (*see also* theories of grief, cognitive), 69–74
  problem, 96–9
  sense of, and bereavement outcome, 99, 248
coping in bereavement, (*see also* grief work; social support; theories of grief), 88–99, 238–49
  constraints, 90
  distraction, 97
  drug use for, 97, 99
  individual differences in, 246
  mastery, regain of, 99
  repression, 96
  resources, intrapersonal, 90, 94